Corporate Governance and Compliance with IFRSs

Corporate Governance and Compliance with IFRSs: MENA Evidence

By

Marwa Hassaan

CAMBRIDGE
SCHOLARS
PUBLISHING

Corporate Governance and Compliance with IFRSs:
MENA Evidence,
by Marwa Hassaan

This book first published 2013

Cambridge Scholars Publishing

12 Back Chapman Street, Newcastle upon Tyne, NE6 2XX, UK

British Library Cataloguing in Publication Data
A catalogue record for this book is available from the British Library

ISBN (10): 1-4438-4333-4, ISBN (13): 978-1-4438-4333-1

Respectfully dedicated to my Dad
All words seem inadequate to thank you.

CONTENTS

LIST OF ILLUSTRATIONS

LIST OF TABLES

ABSTRACT

This study examines the influence of corporate governance structures on the levels of compliance with IFRSs disclosure requirements by companies listed on the stock exchanges of two leading MENA countries, Egypt and Jordan. A cross-sectional analysis of a sample of non-financial companies listed on the two stock exchanges for the fiscal year 2007 is employed. Using an unweighted disclosure index, the study measures the levels of compliance by companies listed on the two stock exchanges investigated. Univariate and multivariate regression analyses are used to estimate the relationships proposed in the hypotheses. In addition, the study uses semi-structured interviews in order to supplement the interpretation of the findings of the quantitative analyses. An innovative theoretical foundation is deployed, in which compliance is interpretable through three lenses - institutional isomorphism theory, secrecy versus transparency (one of Gray's accounting sub-cultural values), and financial economics theories. The study extends the financial reporting literature, cross-national comparative financial disclosure literature, and the emerging markets disclosure literature by carrying out one of the first comparative studies of the above mentioned stock exchanges. Results provide evidence of a lack of *de facto* compliance (*i.e.,* actual compliance) with IFRSs disclosure requirements in the scrutinised MENA countries. The impact of corporate governance mechanisms for best practice on enhancing the extent of compliance with mandatory IFRSs is absent in the stock exchanges in question. The limited impact of corporate governance best practice is mainly attributed to the novelty of corporate governance in the region, a finding which lends support to the applicability of the proposed theoretical foundation to the MENA context. Finally, the study provides recommendations for improving *de facto* compliance with IFRSs disclosure requirements and corporate governance best practice in the MENA region and suggests areas for future research.

PART I

STUDY BACKGROUND AND LITERATURE REVIEW

CHAPTER ONE

STUDY BACKGROUND, OBJECTIVES AND STRUCTURE

1.1 Introduction

In a global economy, the financial reporting practices by companies around the world are a key issue. Globalisation of the capital markets has increased the need for high-quality, comparable financial information (Levitt, 1998; Joshi et al., 2008), and consequently, pressure has been increasing for the adoption of a single set of accounting standards worldwide. This explains to a great extent, the efforts of the International Accounting Standards Board (IASB) to produce a set of International Accounting Standards (IASs) for use by private sector entities throughout the world (Levitt, 1998; Al-Shammari et al., 2008; Daske et al., 2008).

The adoption of the International Financial Reporting Standards (IFRSs) by listed companies in many countries around the world is seen as one of the most significant regulatory changes in accounting history (Daske et al., 2008). Proponents of IFRSs suggest that IFRSs adoption improves the reliability and comparability of financial statements, enhances corporate transparency, hence increases market efficiency and encourages cross-border investing (Brown, 2011). For the Middle East and North Africa (MENA) capital markets as emerging economies, compliance with IFRSs may be important in order to attract foreign investors (CIPE, 2003).

One of the main reasons for choosing Egypt and Jordan for this study is that they mandated the adoption of IFRSs by companies listed on their stock exchanges in 1997 (Al-Akra et al., 2010a,b; Samaha and Dahawy, 2011). Consequently, they can be considered as early adopters of IFRSs compared to other countries such as the European Union countries that only required companies listed on their stock exchanges to prepare their financial statements in accordance with IFRSs since 2005 (Joshi et al., 2008; Armstrong et al., 2009). This fact raises the need to investigate the extent of compliance with IFRSs, especially after the introduction of corporate governance requirements for best practices in the MENA region which are supposed to enhance the levels of disclosure and transparency and hence compliance with IFRSs by publicly listed companies, by supporting a better monitoring of management behaviour.

Corporate disclosure practices have been a principal research theme in the area of financial accounting research for five decades since Cerf (1961). Beattie (2005) points out that corporate disclosure research accounts for over 25% of all research output published in the field of financial accounting based on a survey of research published over a ten year period. However, the review of prior compliance literature reveals a shortage in the number of financial disclosure studies that have investigated the association between levels of compliance with mandatory disclosures under IFRSs and corporate governance structures, as will be seen in Chapter Two. Consequently, this study will contribute towards filling this gap. Moreover, to the best of the researcher's knowledge, this study is the first to use the institutional isomorphism theory (organisations adopt structures and practices which are considered legitimate and socially acceptable by other organisations in their field irrespective of their actual usefulness) in providing a theoretical foundation for the impact of corporate governance structures on the levels of compliance with IFRSs in the MENA region.

The remaining part of this chapter is organised as follows. Section 1.2 highlights the background and justification for the study, section 1.3 defines the research questions and objectives, section 1.4 describes the research philosophy and methodology, section 1.5 indicates the importance and intended contribution of this study, and finally, section 1.6 presents the structure of the current study.

1.2 Study Background and Justification

The MENA financial reporting environment is seen as a rich area to examine the influence of several corporate governance-related variables on the extent of compliance with IFRSs, for the following reasons.

Firstly, countries in this region have been confronted by a series of changes in their economic environment, followed by extensive efforts to diversify their economies and develop their stock exchanges. For instance, this involved the development of a new legal framework with new financial disclosure requirements being imposed upon companies listed on their stock exchanges such as securities exchange laws and corporate governance codes (CIPE, 2003; Omar, 2007; Dahawy, 2007; Al-Shammari et al., 2008; IFC and Hawkamah, 2008; Al-Akra et al., 2010a,b; Samaha and Dahawy, 2011). Consequently, this stimulates empirical investigation of the outcomes of such reforms given that the reports released by international institutions claim a *de jure* but not a *de facto* compliance with the requirements of newly developed laws and regulations in the region, that cope with international best practices (*e.g.,* CIPE, 2003; ROSC, 2005; UNCTAD, 2007; IFC and Hawkamah, 2008; ROSC, 2009).

Secondly, the cultural context within the region is characterised by preference for secrecy that is encouraged by low non-compliance costs if any (Abd-Elsalam and Weetman, 2003; Al-Htaybat, 2005; Abdel-salam and Weetman, 2007; Dahawy and Conover, 2007; Al-Shammari et al., 2008; Al-Akra et al., 2009; Al-Omari, 2010; Ismail et al., 2010; Samaha and Dahawy, 2011). Consequently, the growing acceptance of IFRSs by the region's capital markets stimulates an empirical investigation of the extent of *de facto* compliance with the requirements of such standards, as it is acknowledged in the international accounting literature that harmonising national accounting standards with IFRSs would not necessarily lead to harmonised accounting practices and comparable financial reports (Saudagaran, 2004; Nobes, 2006; Dahawy and Samaha, 2010). Research on financial disclosure still reveals the existence of important accounting differences among countries (*e.g.,* Choi et al., 2002; Land and Lang, 2002; Nobes and Parker, 2004; Al- Shammari et al., 2008). Likewise, research on compliance with IFRSs on individual country level reports a lack of complete *de facto* compliance (*e.g.,* Abd-Elsalam and Weetman, 2003; Abdelsalam and Weetman, 2007; Dahawy and Conover, 2007; Samaha and Stapleton, 2008, 2009; Al-Akra et al., 2010a; Alanezi and Albuloushi, 2011).

Thirdly, the pressures from international institutions such as the World Bank (WB), the International Monetary Fund (IMF) and other stakeholders on the governments of developing countries including those in the MENA region, led to mandating the adoption of IFRSs by companies listed on the majority of the MENA region stock exchanges without taking into consideration the necessity of spreading sufficient awareness among different parties affecting and being affected by the financial reporting practices, about the importance of, and the advantages to be gained by following the international best practices. Consequently, there is a need for more research in order to identify the barriers that delay the achievement of complete *de facto* compliance with IFRSs by MENA countries. The same can be said for corporate governance notions, as they are newly introduced in the region and as many corporate governance requirements for best practice may contradict with the native cultural values such as secrecy within the MENA society. Consequently, this may limit its influence on compliance with IFRSs.

The two countries that form the focus of this study (Egypt and Jordan) belong both to the Arab world and to the Middle East classification as well as being part of the MENA region. Both countries were under the UK Protectorate. The Egyptian and the Jordanian stock exchanges were the first to be established in the region (1888 and 1978 respectively). Both countries have strong ties and political importance in the region. Moreover, both countries have similar legal, economic and cultural contexts with minor varying capacities to practise and enforce compliance with IFRSs and corporate governance requirements (CIPE, 2003). In terms of the regulatory framework in these two capital markets, securities exchange laws require that audited financial statements be prepared and submitted to a governmental authority (Capital Market Authority (CMA) in Egypt, and Jordan Securities Commission (JSC) in Jordan). Financial statements of listed companies are audited in accordance with the International Standards of Auditing (ISAs). Enforcement bodies (the CMA in Egypt, and the JSC in Jordan) are in place and non-complying companies may be penalised by delisting according to the Capital Market Law (CML) in Egypt and Securities Law (SL) in Jordan. Both Jordan and Egypt have had firms listed on the International Finance Corporation (IFC) index since late 1970s and 1990s respectively (Ellabbar, 2007). Such institutional and cultural similarities, in addition to the novelty of corporate governance reforms in both jurisdictions may reduce disparities in the influence of corporate governance structures on the levels of compliance with IFRSs by companies listed on the stock exchanges of both jurisdictions. The investigation of the association between compliance with IFRSs and corporate governance structures in two countries that are similar in their economic development stage can best answer the question raised by Dahawy and Samaha (2010) with respect to the possibility of generalising the results of one developing country to others.

Particularly, the choice of these countries' capital markets as the focus of this study is justified for the following reasons:

Firstly, they were early adopters of IFRSs on a mandatory basis in the region (1997), however, evidence provided by prior research reveals a gap between *de facto* and *de jure* compliance with IFRSs in both countries (*e.g.,* Abdelsalam and Weetman, 2007; Dahawy, 2007; Omar, 2007; Samaha and Stapleton, 2008, 2009; Al-Akra et al., 2010a) which are considered as sites of potential extension of European business into MENA markets (CIPE, 2003), making compliance with IFRSs not only a concern for domestic investors but also for foreign ones. This raises the need to reinvestigate compliance practices in such countries using more recent data.

Secondly, they are good examples of transitional economies that were early adopters of economic restructuring and privatisation programmes in the MENA region since the 1990s to mimic the Western free market economy pattern (CIPE, 2003; Abdelsalam and Weetman, 2007; Omar, 2007; Al-Akra et al., 2009, 2010a,b; Al-Omari, 2010; Dahawy and Samaha, 2010). Furthermore, unlike MENA oil-exporting countries (which includes the Gulf Co-operation Council (GCC) countries), securities markets in Egypt and Jordan were established and revitalised in order to function as the main vehicle for implementing the privatisation programme and to be a source of medium and long-term finance (CIPE, 2003). Consequently, it seems justified to investigate whether such changes enhanced the extent of compliance with IFRSs in scrutinised countries specifically 2007 witnessed an extraordinary economic performance in both of them. Additionally, 2007 was the first year in which all IFRSs except IAS 17: Accounting for Leases became mandatory in Egypt.

Thirdly, the introduction of corporate governance requirements for best practices that are based on corporate governance principles issued by the Organisation for Economic Co-operation and Development (OECD) in both countries as part of the regulatory reform that carried out in parallel with the privatisation programme since the second half of the 1990s (Al-Akra et al., 2009; Samaha, 2010), intended to gain the trust of foreign investors and develop the national capital markets by following international recommended practices which mainly aim at improving transparency and disclosure, enhancing monitoring of management behaviour and protecting investors' rights (CIPE, 2003; Dahawy, 2009; Al-Akra et al., 2010a; Samaha, 2010). Hence, this raises the need to document the impact of corporate governance mechanisms for best practice on the levels of compliance with IFRSs and explore the applicability of the theoretical foundation proposed in this study to these two emerging capital markets.

The above discussion emphasises the need to conduct this study, being one of the first, to investigate the association between corporate governance best practice as an emerging culture in the MENA region and the levels of compliance with IFRSs in two leading MENA stock exchanges as claimed by international institutions (CIPE, 2003; IFC and Hawkamah, 2008).

1.3 Research Questions and Objectives

The proponents of globalisation of IFRSs among developed and developing countries argue that it will improve the comparability, and hence the usefulness of financial statements for investment decisions (*e.g.*, Daske et al., 2008; Brown, 2011). However, as mentioned already, the introduction of IFRSs in different MENA region countries and the fact that their adoption is mandated is not a guarantee of full compliance with the requirements of such standards. In other words, the mandating of IFRSs adoption in the region does not automatically result in homogeneity between their actual implementation and the standard setters' expectation. This argument implies that *de jure* compliance (*i.e.*, formal compliance) with IFRSs does not necessarily lead to *de facto* compliance and *de facto* compliance may be problematic (Samaha, 2006; Samaha and Stapleton, 2008, 2009). This argument is supported on the grounds that the cultural context in developing countries is unique and the regulatory agencies and professional bodies in those contexts are not as effective as in Western developed countries (Ahmed and Nicholls, 1994; Naser, 1998; Chamisa, 2000; Ball et al., 2003; Ali et al., 2006; Dahawy and Conover, 2007). This raises the need to revisit this issue using recent data in order to assess the progress in the levels of compliance with such imported standards in scrutinised MENA countries. Based on this, the first question and objective of this study are proposed.

Prior research investigating compliance with IFRSs suggests that differences in the levels of compliance among companies reflect their country of origin (Tower et al., 1999; Street and Bryant, 2000; Street and Gray, 2002; Al-Shammari et al., 2008). Although developing countries in general share similar characteristics, they are not homogeneous in terms of their levels of economic, accounting, professional and institutional development (Chamisa, 2000; Chand, 2005; Hassan, 2008; Samaha, 2010). The same argument applies to the selected MENA capital markets. Although, they have similar legal, economic and cultural contexts, they have some differences in terms of each capital market's capacity to practise and enforce compliance with IFRSs and corporate governance principles (CIPE, 2003). Hence, comparing the results between the two exchanges can answer the question whether the results of investigating compliance practices on the level of one developing country can be generalised. On the other hand, although improved disclosure and transparency are the heart of effective governance (Haniffa, 1999; Samaha, 2010; Samaha and Dahawy, 2011), the recognition of corporate governance best practices by the MENA region countries will result in better compliance with IFRSs only if those practices become part of the cultural values within the scrutinised contexts. Egypt and Jordan regulatory reforms following the commencement of the privatisation programmes in both countries since the mid 1990s support better Board of Directors (BOD)' monitoring function and investor protection, hence improved disclosure and transparency. Thus, it is important to explore the current influence of corporate governance structures on the levels of compliance with IFRSs disclosure requirements in both countries as leading MENA stock exchanges (CIPE, 2003; Al-Akra et al., 2010a; Samaha and Dahawy, 2011). Also, given the lack of consensus among researchers regarding the theoretical foundation of financial disclosure practices, and the findings of prior research that investigated Egypt and Jordan which showed that financial disclosure theories fail to explain all financial disclosure practices in such contexts (Abd-Elsalam, 1999; Al-Htaybat, 2005), it is deemed necessary in this study to employ an innovative theoretical framework. This will be a step forward in filling the gap in the theoretical foundation of financial disclosure and corporate governance research particularly on the level of emerging exchanges. Founded on this, the second and third questions and objectives of this study are proposed.

Based on the above, the main research questions are identified as follows:

1. What is the extent of compliance with IFRSs disclosure requirements by companies listed on the two selected stock exchanges?
2. How could differences in the levels of compliance with IFRSs be explained by BOD independence, BOD leadership (*i.e.,* whether the Chief Executive Officer (CEO) and the Chair positions are held by the same person or by two different persons), BOD size and ownership structure?
3. To what extent do institutional isomorphism theory, secrecy versus transparency as one of Gray (1988) accounting sub-cultural values, agency theory and cost-benefit analysis help to explain the levels of compliance with IFRSs disclosure requirements within the MENA context?

Consequently, to answer this study questions and drawing on a comprehensive review of accounting and business environments in the Egyptian and Jordanian contexts, compliance literature and financial disclosure studies that have investigated these two stock exchanges as well as corporate governance literature, the study objectives can be stated as follows:

Objective 1: To investigate the level of compliance with IFRSs disclosure requirements for the fiscal year 2007 by companies listed on the stock exchanges of the selected two countries in order to evaluate the progress in compliance levels compared to prior research as well as to enable objective comparison of compliance behaviour between the two countries.

Objective 2: To examine the relationship between BOD independence, BOD leadership, BOD size and ownership structure, and levels of compliance with IFRSs by companies listed on the stock exchanges of the selected two countries.

Objective 3: To investigate the underlying theoretical rationale of corporate financial disclosure practices within the MENA context.

1.4 Research Philosophy and Methodology

This study is undertaken within the functionalist research paradigm, the research being based on investigating the current status and establishing the factual existence of structures (Burrell and Morgan, 1979; Hopper and Powell, 1985; Al-Htaybat, 2005). Consequently, levels of compliance with IFRSs by companies listed on the selected MENA region capital markets will be measured in order to define and analyse the extent of such compliance. This step will be followed by examining the relationship between the chosen corporate governance variables (BOD independence, BOD leadership, BOD size and ownership structure) and levels of compliance with IFRSs. The researcher investigates a sample of annual reports of non-financial companies listed on the two selected stock exchanges for the fiscal year ending 31, December 2007. The extent of compliance is measured using a disclosure index based on IFRSs disclosure requirements for 2007. The model of hypotheses explaining the extent of compliance is defined as the interplay of contradictory forces: inducements deriving principally from the institutional isomorphism theory and secrecy versus transparency as one of the accounting values identified by Gray (1988)[1]. Furthermore, the notions of two financial

[1] Secrecy versus transparency refers to a preference for confidentiality and a restriction of information about business only to those who are closely involved with its management and financing as opposed to a more transparent open and publicly accountable approach (Gray, 1988).

economics theories; namely, the agency theory [2] and cost-benefit analysis[3] that employed in prior research will be used to some extent, in deriving the research hypotheses. The selected corporate governance variables include proxies for board independence, board leadership, board size, government ownership ratio, management ownership ratio, private ownership ratio, and public ownership ratio. Also, control variables include proxies for company size, profitability, gearing, liquidity, type of business activity, and type of audit firm. Statistical analysis is performed using univariate and multivariate analyses. Furthermore, the study employs semi-structured interviews in order to supplement the interpretations of the findings from the quantitative data analysis and to explore the extent to which the institutional isomorphism, cultural theories, and financial economics theories provide the theoretical foundation of compliance practices within the MENA context. Thus, to accomplish this study's objectives, the researcher employed a sequential explanatory triangulation design, employing both quantitative and qualitative data collection and analysis.

1.5 Study Rationale, Significance and Intended Contribution

This study is motivated by a belief that achieving *de facto* compliance with IFRSs by the MENA region listed companies is not an easy task. It is an on-going process which requires strong support from researchers, capital market authorities, accounting regulators, business firms, accounting practitioners and other stakeholders. Hence, continuous assessment of the levels of compliance with IFRSs is important in order to evaluate the progress in compliance behaviour and diagnose barriers to *de facto* compliance over time. The capital markets investigated in this study have been early mandatory adopters of IFRSs. This implies that companies listed on these capital markets have considerable experience with the use of IFRSs on a mandatory rather than on a voluntary basis. This will add to the compliance literature whereas most prior IFRSs/IASs[4] compliance studies examined developed jurisdictions that apply the IFRSs on a voluntary basis (*e.g.*, Street et al., 1999; Tower et al., 1999; Street and Bryant, 2000; Glaum

[2] Agency theory is a contract under which one or more persons [the principal(s)] delegate another person [the agent] to run the business on their behalf (Jensen and Meckling, 1976).

[3] Cost-benefit analysis is based on the notion that management decision to disclose business information is influenced by the trade-off between the costs and benefits of providing such information (Bhusan and Lessard, 1992; Tricker, 2009).

[4] IASs and IFRSs are used interchangeably in the book.

and Street, 2003). On the other hand, scrutinised countries witnessed a change in the ownership structures of companies listed on their stock exchanges as a result of privatising government owned enterprises. In addition, the Egyptian and the Jordanian governments introduced corporate governance mechanisms that are based on the OECD corporate governance principles as a means to enhance transparency and disclosure, by empowering boards, to enable them to carry out an effective monitoring of management behaviour (Al-Akra et al., 2010a; Samaha, 2010; Samaha and Dahawy, 2010). All of this lends support to carrying out this study in order to investigate the impact of corporate governance mechanisms for best practices on the levels of compliance with IFRSs in scrutinised stock exchanges. At the time of commencing this study, in 2008, it was the first to investigate the association between compliance with IFRSs disclosure requirements and corporate governance structures in the MENA region. However, during the time of this study to the best of the researcher's knowledge there are only two studies investigated this issue in the region; Al-Akra et al. (2010a) and Alanezi and Albuloushi (2011). Al-Akra et al. (2010a) investigate the influence of accounting disclosure regulation, governance reforms and ownership changes, resulting from privatisation, on the levels of compliance with mandatory disclosures under IFRSs in Jordan in 1996 and 2004 respectively. Alanezi and Albuloushi (2011) investigate the impact of the existence of a voluntary audit committee on the level of IFRSs required disclosure practices in Kuwait. This study extends both studies in being comparative as well as being the first to investigate the impact of corporate governance structures on the levels of compliance with IFRSs disclosure requirements in Egypt. On the other hand, although there is a number of prior studies that investigate the levels of compliance with IFRSs in the Egyptian context (Abd-Elsalam, 1999; Abd-Elsalam and Weetman, 2003; Samaha, 2006; Abdelsalam and Weetman, 2007; Dahawy and Conover, 2007; Samaha and Stapleton, 2008, 2009; Dahawy, 2009; Ismail et al., 2010), none of them has investigated such issue using a disclosure index that is based on the mandatory IFRSs disclosure requirements for 2007. The same argument applies to Jordan as IFRSs were amended between 2004 (the recent year for Al-Akra et al. (2010a) study) and 2007 (the year of this study). In addition, compared to Al-Akra et al. (2010a) and Alanezi and Albuloushi (2011) studies, this study is the first to investigate the association between board leadership and management ownership ratio, and the extent of compliance with IFRSs disclosure requirements in the MENA region. Furthermore, this study is one of the first comparative studies to investigate the influence of corporate governance structures on *de facto* compliance with IFRSs between two leading MENA emerging capital markets using a disclosure checklist that is organised by standard. This enables objective comparison between levels of compliance with disclosure requirements in total as well as per standard. Hence, enables identification of the requirements whereas compliance is problematic in each jurisdiction. On the other hand, comparing the results between scrutinised countries will enable getting a conclusion with respect to whether MENA developing countries are homogeneous. Finally, this study provides recent evidence on the theoretical foundation of financial disclosure practices in the MENA region in addition to being the first to employ the notions of the institutional isomorphism theory in explaining the influence of corporate governance structures on the levels of compliance with IFRSs disclosure requirements in the MENA countries being studied. In addition, this study provides an overview regarding the perceptions of different parties involved in the financial reporting process in Egypt and Jordan regarding the barriers to full compliance with IFRSs and the impact of corporate governance structures on compliance behaviour of publicly listed companies.

In broad terms, the findings of this study will be of interest to the national as well as the international community, and particularly stakeholders of the MENA region capital markets who are keen to know the strengths and weaknesses in disclosure practices in the region's capital markets. The findings of this study are not only of importance for current and potential investors but will also provide regulators and policy-makers in Egypt and Jordan with recent comprehensive evidence that is expected to enhance their knowledge of the status of their capital markets. This will help them to develop new approaches to overcome weaknesses and strengthen enforcement mechanisms in order to improve financial disclosure practices within their markets, and meet international best practices. Moreover, this study will stimulate more research regarding the issues under investigation in other countries.

With respect to the IASB, the findings of this study will provide a recent evidence regarding the levels of *de facto* compliance with disclosure requirements of IFRSs by two leading emerging capital markets in the MENA region that adopt IFRSs on mandatory basis. The same argument applies to the OECD as a sponsor of corporate governance reforms in scrutinised countries. The findings of this study will provide recent evidence regarding the extent to which the requirements for corporate governance best practices in Egypt and Jordan that are based on the OECD corporate governance principles enhance compliance with IFRSs disclosure requirements.

1.6 Study Structure

Figure 1.1 indicates the general structure of the chapters in this book.

Chapter One: This chapter presents the study background and justification. It highlights how this study will fill the theoretical and empirical gaps in prior literature. In addition, the chapter identifies the study's objectives and the research questions, and gives an indication of the methodology employed, the rationale for the research, and its perceived importance and contribution.

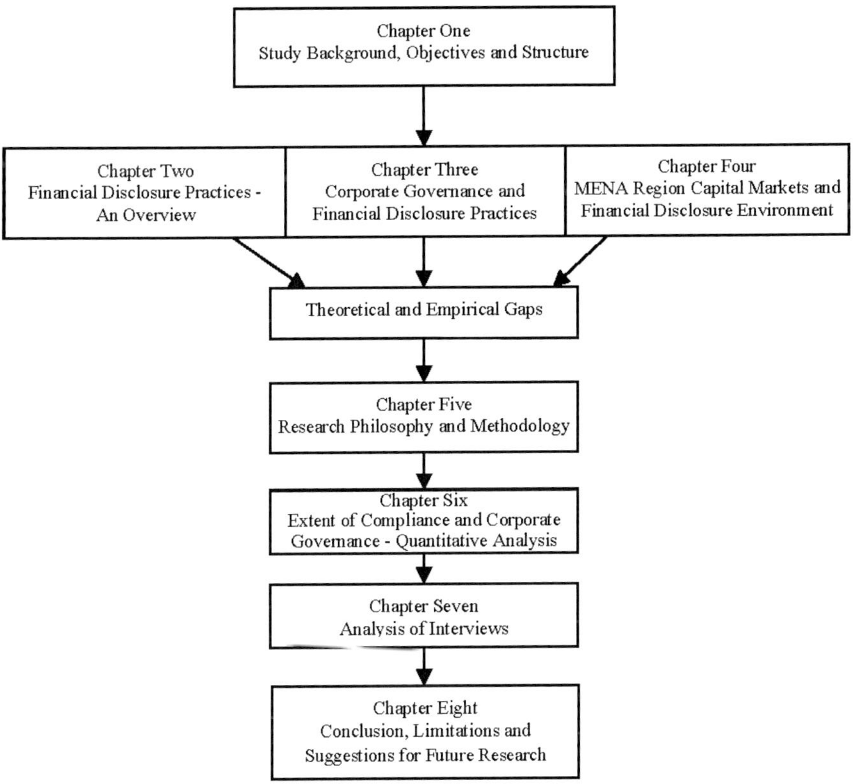

Figure 1.1 Study Structure

Chapter Two: Chapter Two provides an overview of financial disclosure practices, discussing the concept of financial disclosure, disclosure scope, the relationship between mandatory and voluntary disclosure, and how disclosure practices are explained in light of relevant theories. It highlights the issue of compliance with IFRSs, and then provides a review of prior empirical financial disclosure studies that investigated the influence of different corporate attributes on aggregate, mandatory and voluntary disclosure. This review identifies the gaps in prior research that this study intends to fill.

Chapter Three: The third chapter discusses the concept of corporate governance, its importance, and various models associated with it. Additionally, it sheds light on the role of the OECD in raising awareness about the importance of corporate governance and the relevance of the OECD corporate governance principles to the MENA region capital markets. It then addresses the corporate governance variables that are employed as explanatory variables in this study namely, board independence, board leadership, board size and ownership structure.

Chapter Four: Chapter Four provides a general background about the scrutinised MENA region capital markets and their financial disclosure environments indicating capital market development and the financial disclosure regulatory framework in each. In addition, the chapter sheds light on the recent developments in the financial reporting environment which make the selected MENA countries a suitable context for the current study.

Chapter Five: The fifth chapter explains the research philosophy and methodology, how the levels of compliance with IFRSs disclosure requirements are to be assessed, how the disclosure index is constructed, the research samples, research hypotheses and a description of the statistical analyses chosen to analyse the data in the subsequent chapters.

Chapter Six: This chapter presents the descriptive analyses of the levels of compliance with IFRSs by all non-financial companies listed on the selected MENA region stock exchanges. The mean, standard deviation, minimum and maximum values are used to interpret the levels of compliance with IFRSs within each country and between them. Additionally, descriptive statistics of independent variables are presented. The second part in this chapter investigates whether there are significant statistical differences between the Egyptian and the Jordanian contexts. In addition, the variations in the levels of compliance with IFRSs disclosure requirements in 2007 are explained by using corporate governance-related variables through univariate and multivariate statistical analyses.

Chapter Seven: This chapter presents a summary and analysis of the findings of the interview data.

Chapter Eight: This chapter summarises the overall findings, and implications thereof, and concludes the study. The limitations of the study are addressed, and recommendations for future research proposed.

CHAPTER TWO

FINANCIAL DISCLOSURE PRACTICES: AN OVERVIEW

2.1 Introduction

The need for compliance with one set of accounting standards, namely the IFRSs, is increasing day by day as many groups worldwide such as multinational companies, international investors, governments, regulating bodies and capital markets, all recognise that they will benefit from the globalisation of accounting practices (Basoglu and Goma, 2002; Brown, 2011). However, *de jure* compliance is not a guarantee for achieving *de facto* compliance, and a need exists for more research in this area, particularly within the context of emerging capital markets in order to diagnose those factors that influence the levels of *de facto* compliance with IFRSs. This chapter provides a general overview of financial disclosure practices, and is organised as follows. Section 2.2 presents the concept of financial disclosure, disclosure scope and the relationship between mandatory and voluntary disclosure. Section 2.3 discusses the theoretical framework of financial disclosure and how disclosure practices are explained in light of the theoretical foundation employed in this study (the institutional isomorphism theory, secrecy versus transparency as one of Gray (1988) accounting sub-cultural values, and two financial economics theories: the agency theory and cost-benefit analysis). The issue of compliance with IFRSs is highlighted in Section 2.4. Section 2.5 provides a review of prior empirical financial disclosure studies that investigate the influence of corporate attributes on aggregate, mandatory and voluntary disclosure. These studies are classified as developed capital market studies, emerging capital market studies, and cross-national comparative studies. The review of such studies is essential to identify the appearing gaps and the position of the current study among prior ones. Additionally, it provides a background that will help in formulating the research hypotheses in Chapter Five as well as in understanding and explaining the findings of the empirical analysis that appear in Chapter Six. Finally, section 2.6 concludes.

2.2 Corporate Financial Disclosure

Companies' annual reports are considered as the primary regular official medium in which listed companies communicate their audited financial information to the public and other stakeholders specifically in emerging capital markets (Marston and Shrives, 1991; Yeoh, 2005; Naser et al., 2006; Al-Razeen and Karbhari, 2007). Financial disclosure influences the actions of different decision-makers by providing them with the information they need to make rational economic decisions (Solomons, 1986; Haniffa, 1999; Al-Hajraf, 2002; Al-Htaybat, 2005; Atrill and Mclaney, 2008).

Gibbins et al. (1990, p.122) refer to financial disclosure as *"any deliberate release of financial information, whether numerical or qualitative, required or voluntary, or via formal or informal channels".* Also, Hendriksen and Van-Breda (1992, p.851) highlight the importance of financial disclosure by stating that *"disclosure in financial reporting is the presentation of information necessary for the optimum operations of efficient capital market".*

In general, corporate financial disclosure can be referred to as either mandatory (required by laws, regulations and/or formal authorities such as stock exchange regulatory bodies) or voluntary, that is additional (optional) disclosures motivated by management attitude. Akhtaruddin (2005, p.404) refers to mandatory disclosure as *"the presentation of a minimum amount of information required by laws, stock exchanges, and the accounting standards setting body to facilitate evaluation of securities"*, while voluntary disclosure is defined by Meek et al. (1995, p.555) as *"disclosures in excess of requirements, representing free choices on the part of a company's management to provide accounting and other information deemed relevant to the decision needs of users of the annual reports".*

According to proponents of mandatory disclosure, mandating disclosure can be seen as a tool that enforces companies to disclose the information that they otherwise would be reluctant to disclose (Darrough, 1993). This argument applies more to developing capital markets (Al-Htaybat, 2005; Yeoh, 2005), and possibly be due to the cultural values in the majority of developing societies which prefer secrecy and which are not accustomed to voluntary codes (soft laws) (Dahawy, 2007; Al-Omari, 2010).

The regulatory system affects financial disclosure practices through the development of regulations (*e.g.*, CML in Egypt and SL in Jordan), and is expected to result in better investor and creditor protection (Jaggi and

Low, 2000). Regulations help to reduce information asymmetry between informed (*e.g.*, management), and uninformed users such as naive (*i.e.*, non-professional) investors (Healy and Palepu, 2001) as listed companies may prefer to comply with such regulations to avoid paying fines, delisting or even to protect their reputation and gain legitimacy. Thus, regulatory bodies should sort out the disclosure incentives of firms in order to promote efficient disclosure policies (Darrough, 1993). This action is more required in developing countries where there is a possibility of non-compliance with mandatory disclosure requirements due to inadequate regulatory frameworks, weak enforcement mechanisms, ineffectiveness of the capital market, and inefficiency of the accounting profession (Ahmed and Nicholls, 1994; Abd-Elsalam and Weetman, 2003). Furthermore, it is important to spread awareness among different parties that are involved in the financial reporting process concerning the benefits of improving disclosure. This is especially important in developing societies where a transparency culture contradicts with their native culture of secrecy (Gray, 1988). The effective enforcement of mandatory disclosure requirements can also be achieved by independent and expert auditing, and an oversight regulatory system with sufficient power and expertise to achieve effective enforcement (Brown and Tarca, 2005; Owusu-Ansah and Yeoh, 2005).

2.3 Theoretical Framework of Financial Disclosure

Many scholars suggest that disclosure is influenced by the political and socio-economic environment within the country (*e.g.*, Archambault and Archambault, 2003; HassabElnaby et al., 2003; HassabElnaby and Mosebach, 2005; Nobes, 2006; Qu and Leung, 2006; Dahawy, 2007; Ben Othman and Zeghal, 2008, 2010; Mir et al., 2009; Al-Akra et al., 2009, 2010a,b; Al-Omari, 2010; Samaha and Dahawy, 2010). To date there is no single theory that can comprehensively interpret or predict corporate financial disclosure practices (Verrecchia, 2001; Al-Htaybat, 2005), a circumstance which may be attributed to the complexity of this issue (Hope, 2003; Al-Htaybat, 2005). Managers' incentives may differ from one company to another due to the differences in company characteristics as claimed by prior studies (*e.g.*, Haniffa and Cooke, 2002; Abd-Elsalam and Weetman, 2003; Al-Htaybat, 2005; Omar, 2007; Samaha and Stapleton, 2009). Each theory tries to interpret the reasons behind management financial disclosure practices which are influenced to a great extent by the trade-off between the costs and benefits of providing such information (Cooke, 1992; Haniffa and Cooke, 2002; Al-Htaybat, 2005).

Further to the theories that are employed as part of the theoretical foundation in this study, there are many other theories that used to explain financial disclosure practices by prior researchers (*e.g.,* Cooke, 1992; Abayo et al., 1993; Inchausti, 1997; Suwaidan, 1997; Abd-Elsalam, 1999; Haniffa and Cooke, 2002; Abd-Elsalam and Weetman, 2003; Al-Htaybat, 2005; Samaha, 2006; Omar, 2007; Samaha and Stapleton, 2009). The most commonly used are signaling theory, capital need theory, political costs theory, legitimacy theory, resource dependency theory, stewardship theory and stakeholder theory.

Signaling theory has been developed to explain problems of information asymmetry in labour markets and how this can be reduced by the party with more information signaling to others (Morris, 1987; Abd-Elsalam, 1999; Haniffa, 1999). Thus, to reduce signaling costs mangers will disclose all information that is material to investors (Ross, 1979; Haniffa, 1999). Consequently, managers with good news will disclose more to signal company success, thereby increasing the value of the firm's stocks (Verrecchia, 1983; Kasznik and Lev, 1995; Abd-Elsalam, 1999; Haniffa, 1999). On the other hand, mangers with no news will signal this by stressing on the stability of the company performance to avoid being confused with firms with bad news (Ross, 1979; Haniffa, 1999; Vlachos, 2001). Even managers with bad news will effectively signal this to avoid legal disputes (Ross, 1979; Okcabol and Tinker, 1993; Vlachos, 2001). However, signaling theory is criticized on the grounds that it does not explain certain management disclosure practices such as window dressing to opaque bad news (Seligman, 1983; Okcabol and Tinker, 1993; Vlachos, 2001). Furthermore, Okcabol and Tinker (1993) argue that it does not take into consideration that non-disclosure does not necessarily imply bad news or hiding of poor performance as it may be to protect valuable information from competitors.

The capital need theory is based on the assumption that disclosure reduces investor uncertainty and risk, consequently required rates of return will be reduced. This in turn, results in a lower cost of capital. Thus companies can raise capital at the lowest possible cost by making disclosures that will reduce information asymmetry. This will enhance the company's image and reputation in the eyes of potential investors (Mueller et al., 1987; Gray and Roberts, 1998; Diamond and Verrecchia, 1991; Haniffa, 1999; Omar, 2007). However, capital need theory is criticized on the grounds that finding a link between disclosure level and the cost of equity capital is difficult since both variables cannot be observed directly (Hail, 2002).

Political costs theory suggests a further manager incentive to disclose more information. *"This is a first move in recognising that the nexus of contracts of a company is not only between management and shareholders but other stakeholders as well"* (Haniffa, 1999, p.54). Managers will disclose to avoid political costs and counter potential government intrusions (Watts and Zimmerman, 1978; Vlachos, 2001; Al-Htaybat, 2005). Politically visible companies such as large or profitable ones are more in the public eye, thus will disclose more information in order to reduce the likelihood of a political action such as nationalization, expropriation or regulation by the government or a particular pressure group (Watts and Zimmer- man, 1978; Inchausti, 1997). This theory recognises power and conflict in the society and how financial reporting can be used as a tool to mitigate such conflict and influence the distribution of income, power and wealth in the society by affecting the values and attitudes of management (Haniffa, 1999). However, from the researcher's point of view, the notions of this theory are more applicable to developed societies whereas unequal distribution of power is not acceptable, and peoples and governments are aware about the rights and responsibilities of each member in the society in contrast to developing societies whereas power inequality is the norm.

Legitimacy theory highlights how management reacts to community expectations to avoid legitimacy costs and being penalised by the community (Brown and Deegan, 1998; Wilmshurst and Frost, 2000). Hence, this theory emphasises the importance of societal acceptance for company continuity, on the grounds that, company actions affect the environment in which it operates (Ghazali, 2004). *"Legitimacy itself can be considered to be a condition or status. Legitimation, on the other hand, is a process which organisations can undertake (perhaps through particular disclosure strategies) to take them to this state"* (Brown and Deegan, 1998, p.23). This theory is mainly used to explain social and environmental disclosures on the grounds that companies as members in the society are expected to carry out their activities within the boundaries established by the society within which the company operates (Wilmshurst and Frost, 2000; Ghazali, 2004). However, this theory is criticised on the grounds that, it does not take into consideration that legitimacy is interpreted differently from one society to another according to societal values, political system and government ideology (Ghazali, 2004).

Resource dependency theory reflects the strategic view of corporate governance as directors are considered as an essential instrument that links the company with its strategic environment (Haniffa and Cooke, 2002; Tricker, 2009). In other words, this theory *"[s]ees the governing body of a corporate entity as the lynch pin between a company and the resources it needs to achieve its objectives. These resources could include for example, links to relevant markets including potential customers and competitors, access to capital and other sources of finance, provision of know-how and technology, and relationships with business, political and other societal networks and elites"* (Tricker, 2009, p.226). However, directors as a social networking mechanism may sometimes adversely restrict independence and objectivity of governance activities (Tricker, 2009).

Stewardship theory draws on the assumptions of agency theory and transaction cost economics theory (Mallin, 2009). This theory replicates the classical notions of corporate governance as directors' legal responsibility is to shareholders not to themselves, or to other interest group (Tricker, 2009). According to stewardship theory *"[d]irectors are regarded as the stewards of the company assets and will be predisposed to act in the best interest of the shareholders"* (Mallin, 2009, p.14). However, this theory is criticised on the grounds that it is rooted in law, hence it is normative. It is unable to show causal relationship between specific behaviours and company performance (Tricker, 2009, p.225).

Stakeholder theory is concerned with different parties that can affect and be affected by the achievement of an organisation's purposes rather than merely focusing on shareholders (Haniffa, 1999). When a wider stakeholder group such as employees, creditors, customers, suppliers, government and the local community is accounted for by the business firm, the prevailing focus on shareholder value becomes less evident (Mallin, 2009, p.18). However this theory is mainly criticised on the grounds that it does not provide guidelines with respect to how the interests of shareholders and different groups of stakeholders can be balanced given that shareholders and different groups of stakeholders may have contradicting views with respect to firm's corporate governance structures or monitoring mechanisms, hence managers remain unaccountable for their actions due to the absence of well defined measurable objectives (Haniffa, 1999; Mallin, 2009).

It is necessary to enhance the integration between empirical findings and their theoretical foundation and to examine the applicability of different theories within the context of emerging capital markets as such theories do not apply with the same strength as in developed capital markets where most of these theories were initially developed (Abd-Elsalam and Weetman, 2003; Leventis and Weetman, 2004). According to Robbins (1933, quoted by Allen, 1983 as cited in Owusu-Ansah, 1998a, p.90), *"[t]he validity of a particular theory is a matter of its logical derivation from the assumptions which it makes. But its applicability to a given situation depends upon the extent to which its concepts actually reflect the forces operating in that situation".*

This section aims to review the notions of the theoretical standpoints that are relevant to this study: secrecy versus transparency accounting sub-cultural value, agency theory, cost-benefit analysis and the institutional isomorphism theory. This framework is expected to provide additional insights and a comprehensive background that can help in explaining the findings of the empirical analysis that is performed in Chapter Six. The review of such theories is based on an a priori assumption that levels of compliance with IFRSs in any country reflect that country's political and socio-economic environment, and that disclosure is influenced by supply and demand forces of accounting information which is affected to a great extent by the dominant cultural values in a given society.

2.3.1 Secrecy versus Transparency and Corporate Financial Disclosure Practices

Accounting is a socio-technical activity that involves an interaction between both human and non-human resources and cannot be culture free (Violet, 1983; Perera, 1994; HassabElnaby and Mosebach, 2005; Dahawy and Conover, 2007; Dahawy and Samaha, 2010). This viewpoint is confirmed by many researchers who argue that financial disclosure practices are influenced by the cultural values of the preparers of accounting reports (Perera and Mathews, 1990; Fencher and Kilgore, 1994; Dahawy and Conover, 2007).

Ngangan et al. (2005, p.27) see the tension between national cultures of developing countries and cultures of 'exporting' developed countries which originated accounting standards as the main issue that relates to the transfer of accounting technology. This proposition is justified on the grounds that perceptions regarding the significance of financial disclosure by financial statement preparers and users vary among different cultural backgrounds. Within the same context, Saudagaran and Meek (1997, p.129) state that *"[a] nation's accounting standards and practices are the result of a complex interaction of cultural, historical, economic and institutional factors. It is unlikely the mix is alike in any two countries and diversity is to be expected. The factors that influence accounting development at the national level also help explain accounting diversity across nations".*

Culture affects the formulation and enforcement of laws and regulations (Licht, 2001; Al-Omari, 2010). In other words, culture affects the institutional context of the country. Even when the content of accounting standards is the same, monitoring and enforcement remain national (Nobes, 2006). Another important feature of culture is that it allows for some degree of flexibility, as supported by the proposition that cultural values are not fixed and can be modified over time (Pratt and Beaulieu, 1992; Haniffa, 1999). This may partially explain the conclusion that financial disclosure practices in developing countries may improve over time (Al-Htaybat, 2005; Hassan, 2006; Al-Akra et al., 2010a).

To sum up, culture is one of the most influential environmental factors that affect accounting systems and practices (Gray, 1988), consequently its impact cannot be ignored while investigating the gap between *de jure* and *de facto* compliance with IFRSs. Although the work of Hofstede (1980) is criticised on the grounds that the dimensions identified by Hofstede reflect socio-economic make up of the nation rather than culture (Baskerville, 2003) and that its findings were derived from the study of the employees of IBM, hence cannot be generalized (Gernon and Wallace, 1995), the Hofstede/Gray framework is still cited as the basis for most discussions concerning the influence of culture on accounting practices (*e.g.,* Zarzeski, 1996; Abd-Elsalam, 1999; Haniffa, 1999; Haniffa and Cooke, 2002; Archambault and Archambault, 2003; Baskerville, 2003; Qu and Leung, 2006; Abdelsalam and Weetman, 2007; Dahawy and Conover, 2007; Mir et al., 2009). Moreover, Gray (1988) accounting sub-cultural model is the most accepted in international accounting area (Dahawy and Conover, 2007).

The societal values (cultural dimensions) as manifested by Hofstede (1980) are as follows:

1. Large versus small power distance, which refers to the extent to which hierarchy and unequal distribution of power in institutions and organisations are accepted,
2. Individualism versus collectivism, which refers to 'I' versus 'we' - showing a preference for a loosely knit social fabric or independent tightly knit fabric,
3. Masculinity versus femininity, which refers to the extent to which gender roles are differentiated and performance and visible achievement (traditional masculine values) are emphasised over relationships and caring (traditional feminine values), and
4. Strong versus weak uncertainty avoidance, which refers to the degree to which the society feels uncomfortable with ambiguity and uncertain future.

According to Hofstede (1980), societies with high power distance accept inequalities among members where all powers are concentrated in the hands of the superior and centralisation is the norm whereas subordinates expect to receive commands of what they have to do from superiors and recognise that it is not acceptable to question a decision of the superior. Collectivistic societies call for greater emotional dependence of members on their organisations. Such societies reflect dominance of strong relationships where everyone takes responsibility for fellow members of their group like a family, and loyalty and sense of duty influence policies and practices. In cultures which support masculinity, economic growth has a priority over conservation of the environment, and some occupations are considered typically male while others are female. Finally, with respect to uncertainty avoidance, members in high uncertainty avoidance societies avoid ambiguity by developing rigid codes of belief and behaviour. Members in such societies prefer consensus, intolerance of unorthodox behaviour and ideas is the norm, change is resisted and achievement in life is mainly defined in terms of acquired security rather than social recognition. Both Egypt and Jordan score 70 with respect to the level of power distance and 45 with respect to masculinity. Uncertainty avoidance is higher in Egypt than Jordan (80 and 65 respectively). With respect to individualism level, it is relatively higher in Jordan than Egypt (30 and 25 respectively)[1].

Gray (1988) proposes that if the cultural dimensions identified by Hofstede (1980) exist, then accounting values can be linked to societal values and the influence of culture can be assessed. Consequently, Gray (1988) identifies four accounting sub-cultural values which are related to Hofstede's (1980) societal values as follows:

1. Professionalism (versus statutory control), which refers to a preference for the exercise of individual professional judgement and maintaining professional self-regulation in contrast to compliance with prescriptive legal requirements and statutory control,
2. Uniformity (versus flexibility), which refers to a preference for uniformity and consistency over flexibility according to perceived circumstances,
3. Conservatism (versus optimism), which refers to a preference for a cautious approach to measurement so as to handle the uncertainty

[1] The above mentioned scores are reported on Hofstede, G. Website. Available: http://geert-hofstede.com/countries.html. Accessed: 14/2/2012.

of future events as opposed to a more optimistic, laissez-faire, risk taking approach, and

4. Secrecy (versus transparency), which refers to a preference for confidentiality and the restriction of information about business only to those who are closely involved with its management and financing as opposed to a more transparent open and publicly accountable approach.

Among these four values, secrecy versus transparency is more related to financial disclosure practices (Qu and Leung, 2006). Consequently, this accounting sub-cultural value is the one used in interpreting compliance practices in scrutinised stock exchanges which are characterized by preference for secrecy (Dahawy and Conover, 2007; Al-Akra et al., 2009; Al-Omari, 2010). Perera (1989) demonstrates that the level of preference for secrecy in an accounting sub-culture would influence the extent of the information disclosed in accounting reports. Tricker (2009) argues that directors preference for secrecy stems from a belief that secrecy is important to protect strategic plans, guard trade secrets, preserve reputation, and for listed companies, to avoid a leak of stock market price sensitive information.

The importance of the impact of secrecy on financial disclosure practices has been highlighted by many researchers (*e.g.,* Gray and Vint, 1995; Zarzeski, 1996; Abd-Elsalam, 1999; Haniffa, 1999; Haniffa and Cooke, 2002; Abdelsalam and Weetman, 2007; Dahawy and Conover, 2007; Ismail et al., 2010). According to Gray (1988), secretive culture is associated with strong uncertainty avoidance that results from the need to restrict information disclosure to avoid conflict and competition and to preserve security. Secrecy also is associated with large power distance which results in the restriction of information to preserve power inequalities. Furthermore, it is associated with a preference for collectivism as opposed to individualism, having its concern for those closely involved with the company rather than for external parties. Consequently, recognition of the impact of secrecy is expected to help in interpreting the association between levels of compliance with IFRSs and corporate governance-related variables in the empirical part of this study.

2.3.2 Financial Economics Theories Agency Theory

A significant body of work in the area of developing the theoretical foundation of financial disclosure practices and more recently in the development of that of corporate governance has been built on the notions of agency theory. Agency theory has been developed within the discipline of financial economics (Tricker, 2009) and is defined by Jensen and Meckling (1976, p.5) as a *"contract under which one or more persons [the principal(s)] engage another person (the agent) to perform some service on their behalf which involves delegating some decision making authority to the agent"*.

Under agency contracts two potential conflicts of interest may result: the shareholder/ manager conflict which gives rise to the agency cost of equity, and the bondholder/ shareholder management conflict, which gives rise to the agency cost of debt (Abd-Elsalam, 1999).

Agency costs are the sum of monitoring costs, bonding costs, and residual loss (Jensen and Meckling, 1976; Kelly, 1983). Monitoring costs result when the actions of company management are observed and judged by the principal and remuneration is linked with the outcome of monitoring (McColgan, 2004; Omar, 2007). Bonding costs result when the agent endeavours to assure that he/she will not exploit or harm the principal's interests (Denis, 2001; McColgan, 2004; Omar, 2007). Finally, residual loss results when the principal cannot be assured that the agent acts fully in his interest; thus, the principal takes action himself (Omar, 2007).

Owusu-Ansah (1998a) suggests that all agency relationships have two distinguishing characteristics. The first is the degree of decision-making autonomy that the agent exercises which affects the welfare of both the principal and the agent. The second is the differing and varying interests of both parties to the contract. These features create a conflict of interests, whereby the agent acts to maximise his/her utility at the expense of the principal, a phenomenon referred to as opportunism (Mallin, 2009).

In the agency relationship, agents (managers) are considered to have an information advantage over principals (owners). Owners who are not directly involved in running their business believe they are at a disadvantage compared to managers who have access to all information (Cooper and Keim, 1983; Bromwich, 1992; Haniffa, 1999; Fields et al., 2001; Al-Htaybat, 2005; Barako et al., 2006). This problem is referred to as information asymmetry which arises when the principal and the agent have access to different levels of information (Bromwich, 1992; Omar, 2007; Mallin, 2009). Thus, one way of monitoring managers' activities and ensuring that they are not behaving in a manner detrimental to the owners' interest is by demanding access to financial and non-financial information on a regular basis (Haniffa, 1999). Marston and Shrives (1996) and Watson et al. (2002) argue that managers could reduce agency costs and investor uncertainty by disclosing more financial information in annual reports, which would subsequently increase the confidence of shareholders. Mallin (2009) argues that the desire for improved disclosure embodied in corporate governance best practices should help in reducing the information asymmetry problem since shareholders would be better informed about company activities and strategies. Additionally, Healy and Palepu (2001) make the point that the election of a BOD to act on behalf of investors, and the use of intermediaries' information such as that from financial analysts, help to reduce agency costs.

Concerning the interpretative power of agency theory in corporate governance research, Tricker (2009) suggests that this enables researchers to examine the hypothesis that a causal relationship prevails between governance systems established to control the agent and the impact on the interests of the principal. In this regard he states that *"agency theory offers a statistically rigorous insight into corporate governance processes. Because of its simplicity and the availability of both reliable data and statistical tests, agency theory has provided to corporate governance theory building"* (Tricker, 2009, p.220). In a similar vein, Daily et al. (2003) argue that in addition to recognising the self-interested nature of humans, this theory is simple as it reduces large corporations to two participants; managers and shareholders with a clear and consistent identification of the interests of each. Based on this argument, the use of agency theory in prior corporate governance research seems justified (*e.g.,* Haniffa, 1999; Ghazali, 2004; Cheng and Courtenay, 2006; Ghazali and Weetman, 2006; Dey, 2008; Khan, 2010). However, although the agency theory goes some way toward explaining management's motivation to disclose all material information, and whilst it is the most commonly used in corporate governance scholarly research, its opponents argue that it fails to explain non-financial motivations which influence levels of disclosure such as the unwillingness by some companies to avoid the release of material information to their competitors (Okcabol and Tinker, 1993; Vlachos, 2001). Also, it is criticised on the grounds that in corporate governance research, it has a relatively narrow theoretical scope as it interprets corporate governance-related issues in terms of the principal-agent contract, ignoring the fact that board behaviour is influenced by interpersonal communication, group dynamics and political intrigue which cannot be measured (Tricker, 2009). Daily et al. (2003, p.372) state that *"A multitheoretic approach to corporate governance is essential for recognizing the many mechanisms and structures that might reasonably enhance organizational functioning"*. Hence, it can be said that agency theory alone cannot provide a competent theoretical foundation for compliance behaviour, especially within the developing country context where the cultural influence dominates. Consequently, in this study, the employment of other theories in order to enhance the integration between the empirical findings and their theoretical foundation is justified.

Cost-benefit Analysis

Managers' incentives to disclose more information in order to reduce agency costs, to raise capital as cheaply as possible, or to distinguish their companies from other companies, are based on the trade-off between the costs and benefits of providing such information (Bhusan and Lessard, 1992; Al-Htaybat, 2005). In a similar vein, Abd-Elsalam (1999) argues that management decision to comply with mandatory disclosure requirements involves a comparison between compliance and non-compliance costs. This supports the notions of 'Transaction Cost Economics' theory which argues that financial disclosure costs should be incurred to the point at which the increase in costs equals the reduction of the potential loss from non-compliance (Tricker, 2009). This theory is closely related to agency theory with its underlying financial economics basis (Mallin, 2009; Tricker, 2009). In this regard, Stiles and Taylor (2001) argue that both transaction cost economics and agency theories focus on managerial discretion. Additionally, they argue that both theories highlight the important role of BOD in monitoring management behaviour.

As proposed in prior research, there are direct and indirect costs associated with disclosure (Foster, 1986; Haniffa, 1999; Al-Htaybat, 2005). The former include the value of the resources used in gathering, preparing and processing the information, management, supervision, audit and legal fees as well as the dissemination of information (Foster, 1986; Cooke, 1992). Indirect costs include the time spent in deciding what to disclose by corporate managers (Benston, 1976). In most cases, managers must balance the benefits of lower capital cost, extra information and the costs associated with such disclosure like the cost of providing and preparing information. In the meantime, they must consider the effects of such disclosure on their competitive status (Meek et al., 1995; Al-Htaybat, 2005). Within the same context, Vlachos (2001) proposes that in order to assess management's disclosure decision, it is necessary to analyse the different costs of, and benefits from, corporate financial disclosure and to assess which of them are likely to have significant influence on the disclosure decision. However, he argues that although several costs and benefits have frequently been suggested, most cannot be easily measured in monetary terms and, consequently, their empirical testing is difficult.

Many researchers argue that due to transaction costs related to financial disclosure, companies in general are unwilling to incur additional costs through expanded disclosures unless required to do so, or the potential benefits exceed the estimated costs (Gray et al., 1984a; Haniffa, 1999; Suwaidan, 1997). This argument emphasises the importance of accounting regulations and the importance of strict enforcement of such regulations especially within the context of developing countries (Abd-Elsalam, 1999; Fields et al., 2001; Scott, 2003). The same argument applies to the MENA stock exchanges examined in this study as there is a low demand for accounting information by naive investors (Al-Htaybat, 2005; Abdelsalam and Weetman, 2007) and market pressures and regulatory enforcement are not as effective as in developed capital markets - hence, non-compliance costs might be less than compliance costs (Abd-Elsalam, 1999). Consequently, it can be argued that, the stimulation of disclosure practices requires strict enforcement of capital market regulations and awareness raising among producers of accounting information regarding the benefits of improved disclosure to overcome anti-disclosure cultural values such as secrecy, which undoubtedly has a negative impact on management incentives to improve transparency. Developing the moral hazards of management regarding the importance of disclosure and compliance with laws and regulations is expected to change management's way of evaluating the costs and benefits of financial disclosure. Meanwhile, it is important to develop the awareness of naive investors regarding the minimum level of disclosure required of companies to satisfy the enhanced demand for accounting information.

2.3.3 Institutional Isomorphism Theory

Isomorphism is a term that originated in the fields of natural sciences such as mathematics, chemistry and biology (Rodrigues and Craig, 2007). Rodrigues and Craig (2007, p.742) point out that *"[i]somorphism (convergence) describes a process whereby one organization (or set of institutional arrangements, such as IASs) becomes similar to another organization (or set of institutional arrangements) by adopting (or moving closer to) the characteristics of the other organization"*.

Isomorphism is a basic component of the institutional theory which is concerned with the presumed values and beliefs of social and organisational life which influence the way of company operation (Al-Omari, 2010). From this perspective, organisations adopt structures and practices which are considered legitimate and socially acceptable by other organisations in their field irrespective of their actual usefulness (Scott,

1995; Carpenter and Feroz, 2001; Rodrigues and Craig, 2007; Hassan, 2008). This argument is supported by many scholars who demonstrate that for an organisation to gain legitimacy and social acceptability from the external community as well as to develop its image as being modern, rational, responsible and compliant, it must experience institutional isomorphism (Carruthers, 1995; Rodrigues and Craig, 2007). If an organisation fails, it will lose legitimacy (DiMaggio and Powell, 1983; Carruthers, 1995).

There are three forms (mechanisms) of isomorphism as defined by DiMaggio and Powell (1983) as follows:

Firstly, Coercive Isomorphism is indicated by the pressure exerted by government on other organisations through the enactment of legislation (DiMaggio and Powell, 1983).

Secondly, Mimetic Isomorphism is demonstrated by Scott (1995) as the desire to adopt others' practices that are both successful and worthy of adoption. In a similar vein, Rodrigues and Craig (2007) consider it as the ways in which organisations mime the actions of similar but more legitimate or successful organisations in the institutional environment. Furthermore, DiMaggio and Powell (1983) argue that in cases of uncertainty about the proper action, it is appropriate to seek a successful reference group and mimic its approach.

Thirdly, Normative Isomorphism is primarily related to the profession (Hassan, 2008). DiMaggio and Powell (1983) demonstrate how individuals of a similar calling organise in a professional organisation to promote a cognitive base, diffuse shared orientations and organisational practices, and legitimise their activities. Normative isomorphism is derived from two key aspects of such professionalisation: firstly, through formal education and legitimation of the cognitive base by discipline specialists in universities; and secondly, through the expansion of professional networks which span organisations and facilitate the rapid diffusion of new models and practices (DiMaggio and Powell, 1983; Rodrigues and Craig, 2007). Professions exert normative isomorphism through their control of registration and certification procedures, accreditation of University courses, and promulgation of normative, mandatory rules of conduct for use by profession members (Rodrigues and Craig, 2007; Hassan, 2008).

Rodrigues and Craig (2007) recognise that the institutional isomorphism is able to explain the developments in international accounting practices over time. In this regard, they argue the theory to contend *"[t]hat organizations reproduce widely held myths by adopting formal structures and procedures. One widely held myth is that a formally announced practice of an organization (e.g., steadfast total compliance with IFRS) does not differ from its actual, or informal practice (e.g., less than 100% adherence to IFRS). This gap between formal and informal structure or practice is described metaphorically as a decoupling"* (Rodrigues and Craig, 2007, p.743).

Full compliance with IFRSs depends to some extent on the enforcement mechanisms imposed by the organisational actors with responsibility for supporting, imposing or influencing such practice, such as the capital market regulators (*e.g.,* the CMA in Egypt and JSC in Jordan), legal authorities, taxation authorities, and the accountancy profession (DiMaggio and Powell, 1983; Hope, 2003; Hassan, 2006; Rodrigues and Craig, 2007; Hail et al., 2010). However, low investor demand for improved financial disclosure, and low monitoring costs and the weak enforcement of IFRSs in developing capital markets, cause non-compliance costs to be less than compliance costs for listed companies, and direct management incentives towards non-compliance (Abd-Elsalam, 1999; Dahawy and Conover, 2007). Consequently, this bolsters the continuity of decoupling.

For coercive isomorphism, as will be discussed in Chapter Four, although the Egyptian and Jordanian governments developed regulatory frameworks that are consistent with internationally recommended practices by mandating the adoption of IFRSs in 1997 and developing their capital market regulations, the gap reported by prior research between *de facto* and *de jure* compliance (*e.g.,* Abdelsalam and Weetman, 2007; Dahawy, 2007; Omar, 2007; Al-Akra et al., 2010a) indicates that such regulatory requirements seem to be poorly enforced. In respect of mimetic isomorphism, the main reasons for mandating IFRSs were pressure from the international lending institutions particularly the WB and the IMF and the desire to promote a more legitimate or successful image by following globally recommended practices, since they lacked the expertise to develop national standards of the same quality (Dahawy and Conover, 2007; Omar, 2007; Al-Akra et al., 2009). Finally, regarding normative isomorphism, whilst in Egypt and to some extent in Jordan, the last decade witnessed a substantial effort to develop the educational and professional frameworks to promote financial reporting practices (Abd-Elsalam, 1999; Omar, 2007; Al-Omari, 2010), the gap between *de facto* and *de jure* compliance as reported by prior research may signal that this effort is insufficient to improve the quality of accounting profession in these countries due to the unsatisfactory performance of the professional bodies in controlling registration, certification, quality of performance, and ethics associated with accounting and auditing.

In summary, although the first glance shows that countries concerned adopted all forms of institutional isomorphism, the prevailing gap between *de facto* and *de jure* compliance with IFRSs as reported by prior research (*e.g.,* Abd-Elsalam, 1999; Dahawy and Conover, 2007; Omar, 2007; Al-Akra et al., 2010a) shows that the measures taken may be purely window dressing to impress external communities such as the WB and the IMF in order to gain their financial and political support, and legitimacy. It is thus, imperative to consider the influence of the cultural context within these countries as *de facto* compliance should be seen as the outcome of the interaction between cultural context and institutional pressures. With respect to such influence, Rodrigues and Craig (2007) suggest that decoupling may be a result of cultural barriers in understanding the Anglo-American model of accounting, difficulties in translating standards to give the intended meaning of the English text of IFRSs, use of terminology that is incapable of translation into some languages, and the complexity of implementing IFRSs. Consequently, companies may argue that they are applying IFRSs while full compliance with IFRSs is absent.

The review of the forms of institutional isomorphism implies that these forms (mechanisms) should be seen as complementary. Furthermore, from the researcher's viewpoint, to avoid the problem of decoupling, normative isomorphism should come before coercive isomorphism. The adoption of IFRSs in emerging markets requires consideration of the importance of preliminary preparation of national markets, mainly by developing the national cultural values to perceive the importance of compliance with IFRSs in the same way as it is perceived in developed countries where such standards were initially developed. In this regard, Ngangan et al. (2005) recognise that significant differences in the cultural contexts between developing and developed countries affect the cognitive structures and knowledge systems regarding the importance of accounting information disclosure. In secretive cultural contexts such as the Egyptian and the Jordanian stock exchanges (Al-Htaybat, 2005; Dahawy and Conover, 2007; Al-Akra et al., 2009), mandating the adoption of IFRSs is not enough to facilitate comparability of reporting and disclosure practices, because of the lack of convergence of other factors that influence management reporting incentives. This perspective is emphasised by Hail et al. (2010, p.360-361) who state that "*[a]ccounting standards are one of many important institutional elements affecting financial reporting practices in a country . . . it is reasonable to expect that corporate reporting evolves in concert with other institutional factors . . . well-designed set of accounting standards and other elements of the institutional infrastructure should be complementary, i.e., fit and reinforce each other".*

2.4 Compliance with the International Financial Reporting Standards

Accounting standards are defined as "*. . . accounting regulations. At best, they restrict the choice of accounting methods available to management. At worst, they force companies to report financial information in a form which companies would not have chosen voluntarily*" (Sutton, 1984, p.81).

Since the 1970s an extensive effort toward the development of IASs (referred to as the IFRSs since 2002) has been exerted by International Accounting Standards Committee (IASC) (referred to as IASB since 2001). The IASB and its former body the IASC were developed with the purpose to develop in the public interest, a single set of high quality, understandable and enforceable global accounting standards to improve decision making of all user groups; to promote the use of such standards and to achieve convergence of national accounting standards and IFRSs to high quality solutions (IASB, 2008, p.64).

However, opponents of adoption of IFRSs worldwide argue that this one set of accounting standards might not be the best option for both developed and developing countries. For developed countries such as the US and the UK, IFRSs may be seen of lower quality than national standards as well as healthy competition between standard setters is required (Barth et al., 2008; Jamal, 2010). On the other hand, for developing countries it is argued that the IASC/IASB was not initially designed (structurally or operationally) as an effective tool to improve the accounting measurements and practices among developing countries (Kapaya, 2000). Likewise, Chamisa (2000) highlights that the conclusion regarding the relevance of IASs/IFRSs for developing countries should be made with caution due to several limitations associated with developing economies, such as their amorphous and heterogeneous nature. Within the same context some researchers propose that the accounting profession is nationalistic and thus, the development of financial reporting practices must be in light of national socio-political characteristics (Mueller, 1967; Chand and Patel, 2008; Nobes, 1991) as the quality of financial reporting is more attributable to incentives of preparers and the country context (Jamal, 2010). However, the current scene shows that, globalisation and political convenience are forcing an increasing number of countries to adopt IFRSs, resulting in their wide international adoption (Ali et al., 2006; Al-Shammari et al., 2008; Daske et al., 2008; Joshi et al., 2008).

Moreover, many developing capital markets including Egypt and Jordan can be regarded as early adopters of IASs/IFRSs on a mandatory basis as will be discussed in Chapter Four. In contrast with (Nobes, 1991, p.78), who twenty years ago described the IASC's effort toward worldwide standardisation as *"a hopeless and unnecessary target"*, (Rodrigues and Craig, 2007, p.740) argue that *"[t]he push for global adoption of IFRS is part of a general wave of standardization that has taken place in broader, non-accounting contexts over the past 150 years . . . Consequently, in modern society, the global harmonization of accounting standards might be regarded as uncontroversial, unremarkable, and inevitable"*.

On the other hand, proponents of compliance with IASs/IFRSs emphasise that one of the most important merits of compliance with IFRSs is that it enables easy comparison of the results and financial positions of companies across national boundaries, thereby removing barriers to international investment (Emenyonu, 1993; Ali et al., 2006; Samaha and Stapleton, 2009). Furthermore, the adoption of the IFRSs is a prerequisite of listing on foreign stock exchanges (Omar, 2007). Street et al. (1999) argue that the adoption of the IASs/IFRSs can help in lowering the cost of capital and the risk worldwide, reducing the costs of multiple reporting, providing a better understanding of companies' performance across countries by eliminating the confusion arising from different practices and measures of companies' financial positions, promoting international financial investments in the capital markets, and improving the allocation of savings worldwide. In addition, proponents argue that compliance with IFRSs enhances the professional status of the accountancy bodies, and saves costs associated with research and standard-setting efforts (Chandler, 1992; Larson, 1993; Chand, 2005). Peasnell (1993) suggests that for developing countries where there are poor national accounting structures and the accounting profession is not able to effectively regulate accounting and financial reporting, it is preferable to apply the IASs. Furthermore, developing countries fall under pressures from the international lending organisations, which justify such pressures by referral to their lack of resources and infrastructure to enable them to prepare their own standards, as well as their need to manage changes in line with modern and international harmony (Kapaya, 2000; Al-Htaybat, 2005; Ellabbar, 2007). According to Vlachos (2001), compliance helps to secure the minimum amount of information needed for decision-making and ensures that unsophisticated investors are not fooled.

Mandating the adoption of IFRSs worldwide reflects the success of the IASB, as supported by the international institutions such as the WB and IMF in persuading national governments worldwide of the merits of following a single set of accounting standards to connect their national capital markets as part of a global economy. Furthermore, the IASB-FASB project on convergence reflects to a great extent, their support to the adoption of IFRSs worldwide (Joshi et al., 2008)[2]. However, given that IFRSs originated in developed countries, it is necessary to acknowledge that it will take some time before full compliance with IFRSs is achieved in developing contexts, because these are different in their economies, institutional infrastructures, and accounting systems as well as in their ability to swiftly adopt IFRSs (Ali et al., 2006). In this regard other scholars argue that even with *de jure* compliance with IFRSs, important accounting differences still exist in different jurisdictions (Choi et al., 2002; Nobes and Parker, 2004; Saudagaran, 2004; Chand and Patel, 2008; Dahawy and Samaha, 2010). Ball et al. (2003, p.260) state that some countries adopt IFRSs to gain *"instant respectability"* or to serve as a *"politically correct substitute"* for their own accounting standards without developing the appropriate infrastructure that enables compliance with IFRSs. Consequently, given the increasing importance of compliance with IFRSs worldwide, it is important for all countries to take the appropriate steps to narrow the gap between *de facto* and *de jure* compliance, and thus achieve the most from the standards.

2.5 Financial Disclosure - Empirical Studies

Financial disclosure is a rich field of empirical enquiry (Healy and Palepu, 2001). In general, the most important contribution to this research effort during the 1960s was the development of the disclosure index as a research tool to measure the extent of corporate financial disclosure (Cerf, 1961). The next stream of research in the area focused on developing a theoretical framework to provide the basis for interpreting financial disclosure behaviour (*e.g.,* Cooke, 1992; Abayo et al., 1993; Inchausti, 1997). More recently, researchers became concerned with investigating the issue of the worldwide adoption of a unified set of accounting standards. This line of research is concerned with investigating the applicability of full compliance with IFRSs, and the association between levels of compliance with IFRSs and disclosure environment attributes (*e.g.,* Vlachos, 2001; Al-Htaybat, 2005; Samaha, 2006; Dahawy and Conover, 2007; Omar, 2007; Al-Shammari et al., 2008; Samaha and Stapleton, 2008, 2009; Dahawy, 2009; Al-Akra et al., 2010a). Appendix A provides a

[2] For more details about the development of IFRSs see Black (2003) and Laskawy (2009).

summary of many empirical studies on financial disclosure which used disclosure indices as a research instrument.

This section presents an analytical overview of the general themes of prior research that examined different issues relating to financial disclosure practices since the pioneer study of Cerf (1961). Its purpose is twofold: firstly, to critically analyse the different aspects relating to prior financial disclosure studies, focusing on single developing capital market studies and cross-national comparative studies in order to develop the necessary background for establishing the appropriate research methodology for this study, and interpreting the findings of the statistical analysis; secondly, to identify the gap in the literature which this study intends to fill.

To produce a more meaningful overview of prior literature in this field, the remaining parts of this section will discuss previous studies in terms of the structure of the financial disclosure index, the type of financial disclosure practices under scrutiny, financial disclosure theories and explanatory variables employed, sample size, study period, and statistical analysis techniques used. The section will end with a discussion of such studies in respect of the range of countries covered.

2.5.1 Structure of Financial Disclosure Index

The review reveals the existence of great differences among the financial disclosure indices used by previous researchers, quite likely attributable to the absence of a theory providing the basis for determining the number or type of information items to be included in the disclosure index. The number of information items included in the indices ranged from a very limited number such as in Tai et al. (1990) who used only 11 mandatory items, and Barrett (1976) who used a mix of 17 voluntary and mandatory items to a large number of information items such as in Craig and Diga (1998) who used 530 mandatory items, Vlachos (2001) who used 514 and Al-Akra et al. (2010a) who applied the Price Waterhouse Cooper checklist for the fiscal year 2004 that contains 641 items.

Additionally, the majority of researchers applied unweighted disclosure indices. Some researchers, especially early ones, used weighted indices reflecting the views of a specific user group such as financial analysts, regarding the relative importance of various information items (Cerf, 1961; Singhvi, 1968; Singhvi and Desai, 1971; Buzby, 1975; Stanga, 1976; Belkaoui and Kahl, 1978; Firth, 1979, 1980; McNally et al., 1982; Ho and Wong, 2001; Al-Hajraf, 2002; Eng and Mak, 2003; Barako et al., 2006). The last group of researchers apply both weighted and unweighted approaches (Choi, 1973; Chow and Wong-Boren, 1987; Wallace, 1988; Al-Razeen and Karbhari, 2004). However, the use of weighted indices is criticised since weighted indices may reflect the subjectivity of either researchers or users rather than the actual relative importance of items, and thus, unweighted indices are preferred (Cooke, 1989a,b, 1992, 1993). Furthermore, some studies which apply both weighted and unweighted indices report that there are no significant differences between either (Choi, 1973; Chow and Wong-Boren, 1987). Consequently, most researchers use a dichotomous, unweighted disclosure index.

Furthermore, it is noticed that many researchers such as Cerf (1961), Abd-Elsalam (1999) and Al-Htaybat (2005) apply self-constructed disclosure indices, while others such as Hassan (2006), Dahawy and Conover (2007) and Hassan et al. (2009) apply existing ones. A few researchers such as Malone et al. (1993) and Al-Hajraf (2002) have developed a disclosure index for the purpose of measuring disclosure practices by firms of a specific industry type, but in general, researchers construct comprehensive indices with the purpose of examining financial disclosure practices in a wide range of industries.

2.5.2 The Type of Financial Disclosure Practices Scrutinised

The review of previous studies reveals that the type of financial disclosure practice being assessed ranges from only mandatory disclosure, only voluntary disclosure, or an aggregate (overall disclosure). Voluntary disclosure studies include those of Chow and Chow and Wong-Boren (1987), Cooke (1989b), Hossain et al. (1994), Hossain et al. (1995), Meek et al. (1995), Suwaidan (1997), Haniffa (1999), Depoers (2000), Haniffa and Cooke (2002), Eng and Mak (2003), Al-Razeen and Karbhari (2004), Anderson and Daoud (2005), Ghazali and Weetman (2006), Al-Akra et al. (2010b), Elsayed and Hoque (2010), Samaha and Dahawy (2010, 2011). Mandatory financial disclosure studies include those of Tai et al. (1990), Ahmed and Nicholls (1994), Wallace et al. (1994), Owusu-Ansah (1998b), Abd-Elsalam (1999), Naser et al. (2002), Al-Shiab (2003), Abd-Elsalam and Weetman (2003), Glaum and Street (2003), Owusu-Ansah and Yeoh (2005), Dahawy and Conover (2007), Dahawy (2009), Al-Akra et al. (2010a) and Ismail et al. (2010). Studies measuring overall or aggregate disclosure practices using both mandatory and voluntary items whether mixed or separated include those of Cerf (1961), Singhvi and Desai (1971), Buzby (1975),Stanga (1976), Wallace (1988), Cooke (1989a), Cooke (1992), Wallace et al. (1994), Al-Mulhem (1997), Inchausti (1997),

Al-Htaybat (2005), Hassan (2006), Samaha (2006), Omar (2007) and Samaha and Stapleton (2008, 2009).

It is recognised that since Cerf's (1961) pioneering study, the aggregate financial disclosure research has represented a cornerstone for the first stream of financial disclosure empirical work. From the late 1970s voluntary disclosure-based empirical studies occurred, based on the assumption that either there is full compliance with mandatory disclosure requirements or there are no mandatory disclosure requirements and that voluntary practices exist according to several company characteristics (Al-Htaybat, 2005; Hassan, 2006). Most recently, many researchers have recognised the importance of assessing levels of compliance with mandatory disclosure requirements as determined by laws and regulations. The importance of evaluating such levels of compliance is shown by the findings, which report the existence of low compliance with mandatory disclosure requirements, especially in developing countries. The assessment of IASs/IFRSs compliance levels in different developed and developing countries internationally has prompted several studies since the late 1990s (*e.g.*, Abd-Elsalam, 1999; Street and Gray, 2002; Al-Shiab, 2003; Abd-Elsalam and Weetman, 2003; Archambault and Archambault, 2003; Glaum and Street, 2003; Samaha, 2006; Abdel-salam and Weetman, 2007; Dahawy and Conover, 2007; Omar, 2007; Samaha and Stapleton, 2008, 2009; Dahawy, 2009; Al-Akra et al., 2010a; Ismail et al., 2010).

2.5.3 Financial Disclosure Theories and Explanatory Variables

The reliance on financial disclosure theories (*e.g.*, agency theory, signaling theory, capital need theory, political cost theories, and cultural theories) in previous studies accompanied the development of voluntary financial disclosure literature for the purpose of interpreting the determinants of management decisions to provide additional information in annual reports. Subsequently, researchers employed financial disclosure theories in all disclosure studies (regardless of whether they examined voluntary or mandatory disclosure practices) in order to explain variations in levels of financial disclosure among sampled companies (*e.g.*, Cooke, 1992; Abayo et al., 1993; Inchausti, 1997; Suwaidan, 1997; Abd-Elsalam, 1999; Haniffa, 1999; Haniffa and Cooke, 2002; Abd-Elsalam and Weetman, 2003; Al-Htaybat, 2005; Omar, 2007; Samaha and Stapleton, 2008, 2009). Furthermore, corporate attributes and cultural factors have been used as explanatory variables in prior studies to explain the differences in levels of voluntary and/or mandatory disclosure practices among companies, as is discussed in Chapter Five (hypotheses section) (*e.g.*, Firth, 1979; McNally et al., 1982; Chow and Wong-Boren, 1987; Cooke, 1991; Hossain et al., 1994; Raffournier, 1995; Suwaidan, 1997; Abd-Elsalam, 1999; Haniffa, 1999; Depoers, 2000; Haniffa and Cooke, 2002; Street and Gray, 2002; Abd-Elsalam and Weetman, 2003; Al-Htaybat, 2005; Hassan, 2006; Dahawy and Conover, 2007; Omar, 2007; Samaha and Stapleton, 2009; Dahawy, 2009; Al-Akra et al., 2010a,b; Elsayed and Hoque, 2010; Ismail et al., 2010; Samaha and Dahawy, 2010, 2011). The researchers attribute differences in levels of voluntary disclosure and no or low levels of compliance with mandatory disclosure requirements including IASs/IFRSs, to several company characteristics such as company size, gearing, age, liquidity, profitability, listing status, legal form, type of auditor, and type of industry. Additionally, levels of disclosure have been attributed to culture-related factors such as race, education, and familiarity, and most recently to corporate governance structures such as ownership structure, existence of audit committee and board characteristics (*e.g.,* Haniffa and Cooke, 2002; Al-Akra et al., 2010a,b; Samaha, 2010; Samaha and Dahawy, 2010; Alanezi and Albuloushi, 2011; Samaha and Dahawy, 2011). A few researchers do not employ any explanatory variables (*e.g.,* Yeoh, 2005; Dahawy and Conover, 2007). However, generally, the number of such variables ranges from one (*e.g.,* entry into a broadly based capital market as in Choi, 1973; Firm size as in Firth, 1980; and Ownership structure as in Chau and Gray, 2002) to 14 (*e.g.,* Haniffa, 1999; Haniffa and Cooke, 2002).

2.5.4 Sample Size, Study Period, and Statistical Analyses

Previous studies differ in terms of sample size and study period. Sample size ranges from 15 companies (Dahawy and Conover, 2007) to 761 companies (Archambault and Archambault, 2003). The majority of studies use cross-sectional analysis based on the assumption that disclosure practices improve over time (*e.g.,* Cerf, 1961; Cooke, 1989a,b, 1991, 1992, 1993; Malone et al., 1993; Suwaidan, 1997; Depoers, 2000; Chau and Gray, 2002; Abd-Elsalam and Weetman, 2003; Ali et al., 2004; Al-Razeen and Karbhari, 2004; Dahawy and Conover, 2007). Relatively few, such as Inchausti (1997), Hassan (2006) and Hassan et al. (2009), use panel data. The main purpose of studies investigating financial disclosure practices over a period exceeding one year is either to examine whether disclosure levels improve over time or whether the variation in disclosure level can be attributed to a specific company characteristic. The longest study period covered by a previous study is ten years (Barrett, 1976).

In terms of statistical tools suitable for the examination of associations between levels of financial disclosure (dependent variable) and explanatory variables, Cooke (1998) proposes that no one procedure is the best, and that multiple approaches help to ensure robust results. Likewise, Wallace et al. (1994) observe that there is no agreement on the approach to be followed when examining the relationships between the dependent and explanatory variables. Prior studies employ parametric and/or non-parametric statistical tests (*e.g.*, Firth, 1979; Cooke, 1989a; Hossain et al., 1994; Suwaidan, 1997; Craig and Diga, 1998; Abd-Elsalam, 1999; Camfferman and Cooke, 2002; Al-Shiab, 2003; Akhtaruddin, 2005; Al-Htaybat, 2005; Omar, 2007; Samaha and Stapleton, 2008, 2009; Al-Akra et al., 2010a,b; Ismail et al., 2010; Samaha and Dahawy, 2010, 2011). Regression analysis is employed by almost all researchers to examine the relationship between independent variables (*i.e.*, corporate characteristics, corporate governance, and culture-related variables) and the level of financial disclosure.

2.5.5 The Range of Scrutinised Capital Markets

Generally, the majority of financial disclosure literature is concentrated on developed countries, specifically Anglo-saxon countries such as the US and the UK. Before the late 1980s such studies investigating developing countries were rare. As revealed in Appendix A, findings from prior studies tend to confirm that a wide gap exists between financial disclosure practices in developing capital markets compared to their developed counterparts. Research extended to explore financial disclosure practices in emerging capital markets mainly attributes this phenomenon to the influence of secrecy, unfamiliarity, language barriers, the wide spread of unsophisticated investors, and weak enforcement of accounting standards and regulations resulting in compliance costs being greater than non-compliance costs for listed companies (*e.g.*, Abd-Elsalam, 1999; Haniffa, 1999; Haniffa and Cooke, 2002; Al-Htaybat, 2005; Hassan, 2006; Abdelsalam and Weetman, 2007; Dahawy and Conover, 2007; Samaha and Stapleton, 2008, 2009; Al-Akra et al., 2010a,b; Ismail et al., 2010).

Single Developed Capital Market Studies

As previously mentioned, studies in developed countries far outweigh those in developing ones. However, as the purpose of this study is to investigate financial disclosure practices in emerging markets, Appendix A provides a summary of 25 single developed capital market studies published during the last 50 years (Cerf, 1961; Singhvi and Desai, 1971; Buzby, 1975; Stanga, 1976; Belkaoui and Kahl, 1978; Firth, 1979, 1980; McNally et al., 1982; Cooke, 1989a,b, 1991, 1992, 1993; Malone et al., 1993; Wallace et al., 1994; Hossain et al., 1995; Raffournier, 1995; Inchausti, 1997; Depoers, 2000; Street and Gray, 2002; Glaum and Street, 2003; Anderson and Daoud, 2005; Arcay and Vazquez, 2005; Owusu-Ansah and Yeoh, 2005; Yeoh, 2005). These are considered the most influential as they have either introduced new empirical facts or presented rigorous analytical tools that help in supporting the research methods employed in this study. The chosen developed capital market studies use financial disclosure indices in order to assess financial disclosure practices in ten developed countries, namely the US, the UK, Germany, Sweden, New Zealand, Canada, Japan, Spain, Switzerland and France. With the exception of samples used by Cooke (1991, 1992, 1993), the number of sampled companies in developed capital market studies is relatively high compared to that in the developing capital market context, attributable to the challenge of collecting data in such environments due to the lack of databases and the culture of secrecy surrounding the dissemination of information. This problem only arises in the literature related to developing countries (*e.g.,* Abd-Elsalam, 1999; Hassan, 2006; Omar, 2007). The review of developed capital market studies shows that financial disclosure theories succeeded in providing a satisfactory and competent explanation for differences in disclosure levels among companies. This is to be expected since these theories originated in Western environments.

Single Developing Capital Market Studies

Generally, the extent of financial disclosure in developing countries is much lower than that in developed countries (*e.g.,* 50% in Samaha, 2006 and Samaha and Stapleton, 2008, 2009 applied to Egypt compared to 93% in Owusu-Ansah and Yeoh, 2005 applied to Newzealand). It is also noticed that except for the studies of Haniffa (1999); Haniffa and Cooke (2002), Samaha (2006) and Samaha and Stapleton (2008, 2009), which use samples of 167, 167, 281 and 281 companies respectively, the norm in single developing country studies is to adopt a small sample size, usually not exceeding 100 companies, in contrast to the developed country studies. Appendix A provides a summary of 46 single developing capital market studies using a disclosure index covering India (Singhvi, 1968), Bangladesh (Ahmed and Nicholls, 1994; Akhtaruddin, 2005), Malaysia (Hossain et al., 1994; Haniffa, 1999; Haniffa and Cooke, 2002; Ghazali and Weetman, 2006), Zimbabwe (Owusu-Ansah, 1998a,b), Tanzanya

(Abayo et al., 1993), Nigeria (Wallace, 1988); Kenya (Barako et al., 2006), Mexico (Chow and Wong-Boren, 1987), Singapore (Eng and Mak, 2003), Czech Republic (Patton and Zelenka, 1997), Saudi Arabia (Al-Mulhem, 1997; Al-Razeen and Karbhari, 2004), Kuwait (Al-Hajraf, 2002; Alanezi and Albuloushi, 2011), the UAE (Al-Jifri, 2008), Qatar (Naser et al., 2006), Turkey (Aksu and Kosedag, 2006), Egypt (Abd-Elsalam, 1999; Abd-Elsalam and Weetman, 2003; Hassan, 2006; Samaha, 2006; Abdelsalam and Weetman, 2007; Dahawy and Conover, 2007; Samaha and Stapleton, 2008, 2009; Dahawy, 2009; Hassan et al., 2009; Elsayed and Hoque, 2010; Ismail et al., 2010; Samaha and Dahawy, 2010, 2011), and Jordan (Suwaidan, 1997; Naser, 1998; Naser et al., 2002; Al-Shiab, 2003; Al-Htaybat, 2005; Omar, 2007; Al-Akra et al., 2010a,b). The review of single developing capital market studies in Appendix A that investigated MENA countries reveals that these were published during the period from 1997 (Al-Mulhem, 1997; Suwaidan, 1997) to 2011 (Alanezi and Albuloushi, 2011; Samaha and Dahawy, 2011). Compliance with IASs/IFRSs is investigated in Egypt by Abd-Elsalam (1999), Abd-Elsalam and Weetman (2003), Samaha (2006), Abdelsalam and Weetman (2007), Dahawy and Conover (2007), Samaha and Stapleton (2008, 2009), Dahawy (2009) and Ismail et al. (2010). In Jordan, mandatory disclosure practices are investigated by all researchers except Suwaidan (1997). Al-Htaybat (2005) and Omar (2007), investigate aggregate disclosure as further divided into mandatory and voluntary items. The two available studies exploring financial disclosure practices in Kuwait (Al-Hajraf, 2002; Alanezi and Albuloushi, 2011) scrutinise compliance with IAS 30 (Accounting for Banks and Financial Institutions) and compliance with IFRSs disclosure requirements respectively. Naser et al. (2006) investigate voluntary disclosure practices in Qatar while Al-Jifri (2008) investigates compliance with mandatory disclosure requirements in the UAE. The periods covered in those studies range from 1980 (Suwaidan, 1997) to 2007 (Ismail et al., 2010), the research samples range from 15 companies (Dahawy and Conover, 2007) to 281 companies (Samaha, 2006; Samaha and Stapleton, 2008, 2009), and the maximum number of items included in the disclosure index is 641 items (Price Waterhouse Cooper checklist for 2004) in Al-Akra et al. (2010a).

In conclusion, the review of prior research investigated compliance with IAS/IFRSs disclosure requirements in single MENA region countries reveals scarecity in the number of studies that used recent data. Only two studies investigate annual reports for the fiscal year 2007 (Ismail et al., 2010 on Egypt and Alanezi and Albuloushi, 2011 on Kuwait). However, Ismail et al., 2010 unreasonably employed the checklist developed by the

CMA for the year 2000 ignoring the fact that 2007 was the first year in which all IFRSs except IAS 17: Accounting for Leases became mandatory in Egypt according to the Ministerial Decree No. 243 of 2006 (Hassaan, 2007; Elsayed, 2010), hence the year 2000 checklist does not recognise the amendments to disclosure requirements under IFRSs during a seven year period. With respect to Jordan, the most recent data used in investigating compliance with IFRSs relates to 2004 (Al-Akra et al., 2010a). In addition, only two studies (Al-Akra et al., 2010a on Jordan and Alanezi and Albuloushi, 2011 on Kuwait) investigate the association between compliance with IFRSs and corporate governance structures. Furthermore, many studies highlight the reduced applicability of Western financial disclosure theories to developing capital markets (*e.g.,* Abd-Elsalam, 1999; Abd-Elsalam and Weetman, 2003; Al-Htaybat, 2005; Samaha and Stapleton, 2008, 2009; Elsayed and Hoque, 2010). This is confirmed by the findings of Al-Htaybat (2005) which show that financial disclosure theories (agency, capital need, political costs and signaling theories) fail to explain disclosure practices in 1997. Also, Abd-Elsalam (1999) observes that only agency theory and capital need theory apply to the Egyptian context, and the applicability of signaling theory is not clear. It is further noticed that, all studies using panel data analyses show that financial disclosure practices improve over time (*e.g.,* Abd-Elsalam, 1999; Al-Htaybat, 2005; Hassan, 2006; Al-Akra et al., 2010a).

Cross-national Comparative Capital Market Studies

The review of comparative financial disclosure studies reveals a relative shortage of research in the area. Furthermore, the review of the 14 comparative financial disclosure studies listed in Appendix A indicates that the majority of these studies were concerned with developed capital markets (Choi, 1973; Barrett, 1976; Spero, 1979; Meek et al., 1995; Hussain, 1996; Zarzeski, 1996; Camfferman and Cooke, 2002). Beginning in the late 1990s, this line of research extended to developing markets (Craig and Diga, 1998; Tower et al., 1999; Vlachos, 2001; Chau and Gray, 2002; Ali et al., 2004; Al-Shammari et al., 2008). Only one study (Al-Shammari et al., 2008) investigated compliance with IFRSs among GCC member countries (Bahrain, Kuwait, Oman, Qatar, Saudi Arabia, and the UAE) and reported a lack of *de facto* compliance with IFRSs among GCC member countries, and that despite political and cultural ties among such countries, there are significant differences among companies based on size, leverage, industry and internationality.

As revealed in Appendix A, many comparative studies consider disclosure practices among South Asian countries (Craig and Diga, 1998; Tower et al., 1999; Chau and Gray, 2002; Ali et al., 2004). A few made a comparison between developed and developing countries such as Chau and Gray (2002), and Archambault and Archambault (2003), but comparing the quality of financial disclosure in developed and developing contexts which are completely different in terms of their stage of economic development, cultural values and accounting regulation requirements, is seen as unreasonable and questionable. This viewpoint is supported by Vlachos (2001, p.124) who argues that findings are expected to be biased in favour of the country with more disclosure minima. Spero's (1979) study is one of the rigorous earlier comparative efforts exploring developed countries with similar characteristics. By performing several statistical tests, Spero was the first to provide evidence that different weighting schemes are of less importance compared to item selection, as his findings reveal that companies that view disclosure positively, disclose many items and have high scores regardless of item weights (Spero, 1979).

Within the context of emerging capital markets, the study of Craig and Diga (1998) is one of the first rigorous attempts to compare disclosure practices among a number of developing countries. The investigation of mandatory disclosure practices in five emerging Asian markets, as indicated in Appendix A, reveals that unlike pre-expectations, banks and utilities (which have been assumed to have a high political cost exposure in these countries) were the industry groups with the lowest levels of disclosure. This conclusion highlights the importance of examining the applicability of different financial disclosure theories within the context of developing countries.

Since 2000, the number of cross-national comparative disclosure studies has increased (*e.g.,* Chau and Gray, 2002; Vlachos, 2001; Camfferman and Cooke, 2002; Archambault and Archambault, 2003; Ali et al., 2004). The review in Appendix A reveals that several of these studies investigated the association between levels of financial disclosure and many explanatory variables. For example, some researchers explored the relationship between levels of financial disclosure and corporate attributes among different countries such as Vlachos (2001); Chau and Gray (2002), and Ali et al. (2004). Other studies such as Archambault and Archambault (2003) investigated the association between levels of financial disclosure and culture, national politics, economics, corporate finance, and reporting systems among 37 countries worldwide.

Generally, cross-national comparative disclosure studies demonstrate two methodological approaches (Vlachos, 2001), the first based on a comparison of disclosure practices in a sample of companies from a limited number of countries as followed in this study (*e.g.*, Hussain, 1996; Vlachos, 2001; Camfferman and Cooke, 2002; Chau and Gray, 2002; Ali et al., 2004). Usually the purpose of this approach is to assess the quality of disclosure practices and to identify the factors influencing disclosure practices in each country and the strength of each. The second approach is based on a comparison of a sample of companies from multiple countries (*e.g.*, Barrett, 1976; Zarzeski, 1996; Craig and Diga, 1998; Tower et al., 1999; Al-Shammari et al., 2008), usually with the intention to rank companies and countries based on disclosure scores.

Concerning the quality of cross-national comparative studies, Vlachos (2001, p.127) argues that companies and/or countries under scrutiny must be comparable (*i.e.*, similar in terms of their economic, social and political systems).

Finally, the review of these studies indicates that further to the shortage of comparative studies investigating developing markets in general and the MENA markets in particular, no prior comparative study has explored the association between the levels of compliance with IFRSs and corporate governance structures within the MENA context as is intended by this study.

2.5.6 Justification for Current Study

The critical overview of previous studies that investigated financial disclosure practices reveals that even on the level of a single country the results have been mixed and inconsistent. This can be attributed to the same reasons claimed by prior researchers (*e.g.*, Wallace and Naser, 1995; Ahmed and Courtis, 1999; Vlachos, 2001). These reasons include the lack of uniformity in the statistical approaches employed, the differing nature of the explanatory variables examined in these studies and their proxies, the changes in countries' disclosure requirements over time, the type of disclosure investigated, the period of the study and the differences in the disclosure index content.

Given the shortage in comparative financial disclosure studies investigating developing capital markets in general and the MENA capital markets in particular, together with the detailed rationale provided in Chapter One, this study seems to be justified. To the best of the researcher's knowledge, this study is the first comparative study that investigates the association between corporate governance structures and levels of compliance with IFRSs disclosure requirements in the MENA region and the first to investigate such relationship in Egypt. In addition, it is the first to investigate compliance practices in Egypt and Jordan using a checklist that is based on IFRSs disclosure requirements for the year 2007. This study extends the study of Al-Akra et al. (2010a) in Jordan by using more recent data, investigating the impact of board leadership and management ownership ratio on the levels of compliance with IFRSs, in addition of comparing the findings with those of another MENA country in a similar stage of economic development. This will enable getting a conclusion with respect to the possibility of generalising the results of one developing country to others. Finally, to the best of the researcher's knowledge, this study is the first to employ the institutional isomorphism theory to explain the association between compliance with IFRSs and corporate governance structures as well as being one of the first comparative studies that carry out interviews with different parties involved in financial reporting process to support the interpretation of the research findings.

2.6 Summary

This chapter has provided the core theoretical background underpinning the research hypotheses and against which the research findings will be explained. It began with an indication of the concept of financial disclosure, the scope of financial disclosure and the relationship between mandatory and voluntary disclosures. Thereafter, a review of the theoretical framework that is relevant to this study was presented. A discussion of the development, objectives and the issue of compliance with IFRSs was then provided. Finally, the chapter offered a critical discussion of prior empirical studies which investigated the relationship between aggregate, mandatory and voluntary disclosure and corporate attributes. These studies were reviewed and classified as developed capital market studies, emerging capital market studies, and cross-national comparative studies, and their main findings were reported. The chapter concluded by identifying the gap in the financial disclosure literature which this study aims to fill. The next chapter will discuss different aspects of corporate governance as a means of providing the core background required to investigate the association between corporate governance structures and levels of compliance with IFRSs in the selected MENA countries.

CHAPTER THREE

CORPORATE GOVERNANCE AND FINANCIAL DISCLOSURE PRACTICES

3.1 Introduction

Across the globe a series of events over the last two decades placed corporate governance at the top of the agenda for business communities, international financial institutions, governments, and capital market regulators. Specifically, these were the Asian financial crisis and the high-profile corporate scandals such as WorldCom, Enron, Lehman Brothers and Tyco. Furthermore, in academia, the topic continues to attract much attention from researchers (*e.g.*, Beasley, 1996; Shleifer and Vishny, 1997; Haniffa and Cooke, 2002; Ghazali and Weetman, 2006; Brown, 2007; Ezat and El-Masry, 2008; Felo, 2009; Al-Akra et al., 2010a,b; Samaha, 2010; Samaha and Dahawy, 2010, 2011). Corporate governance is concerned with the system of directing and controlling companies, and it is the responsibility of BOD (Cadbury Committee Report, 1992). It is a fundamental element in improving economic efficiency and growth as well as enhancing investor confidence (OECD, 2004). *"Corporate governance involves a set of relationships between a company's management, its board, its shareholders and other stakeholders. Corporate governance also provides the structure through which the objectives of the company are set, and the means of attaining those objectives and monitoring performance are determined"* (OECD, 2004, p.11). The BOD actions are subject to laws, regulations and shareholders in general meeting and the role of shareholders in governance is to appoint the directors and auditors and to make sure that the governance structure is appropriate (Cadbury Committee Report, 1992).

The development of corporate governance is a global phenomenon, influenced by legal, cultural, ownership, and other structural differences (Mallin, 2009), but as yet there is no widely accepted paradigm or theoretical foundation in its respect (Tricker, 2009). As a company grows, the number of its shareholders increases, and its activities become more complex such that owners need to be more vigilant in monitoring and controlling management's activities (CIPE, 2003).

For emerging capital markets, good corporate governance practice may be essential to guarantee the success of their reform programmes and to create a healthy investment climate. However, the corporate governance codes for best practice were initiated in developed countries and only recently introduced in developing ones. Hence, its contribution towards enhancing capital market performance in such countries is subject to the extent to which the conditions for robust governance practice are consistent with the existing values, past experiences and the needs of all parties involved in the financial reporting process. It is expected, therefore, to be some time before the impact of applying corporate governance can be measured in developing contexts as this needs to develop, and favourable attitudes and belief must be formed as well as efforts being made to develop the human resource capabilities to apply corporate governance requirements for best practice.

A number of studies have been conducted in the last decade for the purpose of investigating the relationship between corporate governance and corporate disclosure practices in different countries (*e.g.,* Chen and Jaggi, 2000; Ho and Wong, 2001; Haniffa and Cooke, 2002; Gul and Leung, 2004; Abdelsalam and Street, 2007; Ezat and El-Masry, 2008; Felo, 2009; Al-Akra et al., 2010a,b; Samaha, 2010; Samaha and Dahawy, 2010, 2011; Abed et al., 2011; Alanezi and Albuloushi, 2011). Furthermore, to the best of the researcher's knowledge this study is the first comparative study to examine the influence of corporate governance structures (namely, board independence, board leadership, board size and ownership structure) on the overall compliance with mandatory IFRSs disclosure requirements for 2007 in two MENA region emerging capital markets. As disclosure lies at the core of all corporate governance statutes and codes, investigating the association between corporate governance structures and the levels of compliance with IFRSs disclosure requirements is expected to enrich financial disclosure as well as corporate governance literature.

This chapter aims to provide the core background required to investigate the association between corporate governance structures and levels of compliance with IFRSs in Egypt and Jordan. It begins by presenting the concept of corporate governance in section 3.2. Section 3.3 discusses the importance of corporate governance and highlights the role of the OECD in raising awareness of the importance of corporate governance. Section 3.4 indicates the relevance of the OECD corporate governance principles to the MENA region capital markets, and then corporate governance variables that are employed as test variables in this study, are discussed in sections 3.5 and 3.6. Finally, the chapter concludes with a summary in section 3.7.

3.2 The Concept of Corporate Governance

Whilst there is no generally agreed definition of corporate governance, it is nevertheless clear that a broad spectrum of definitions exist in the literature, ranging from narrow, agency theory-based definitions to broader, stakeholder-based definitions. Within the same context Mavrommati (2008, p.22) argues that *"[d]ifferent authors vary widely in where they draw the boundaries of the subject. In its narrowest sense, the term may describe the formal system of accountability of senior management to the shareholders. At its most expansive, the term is stretched to include the entire network of formal and informal relations involving the corporate sector and their consequences for society in general"*. Historically, the term governance is derived from the Latin word 'gubernare' which means to rule or to steer (Tricker, 1984; Maassen, 2002; Mavrommati, 2008). An example of the first strand of corporate governance definitions is that provided by Koh (1994, p.23) who claims it to be: *"the process and structure used to direct and manage the business and affairs of the corporation with the objective of enhancing long-term value for shareholders and financial viability of the business"*.

Examples of the second strand of corporate governance definitions are those provided by Dahya et al. (1996), and Maier (2005 cited in Khan, 2010, p.88). Dahya et al. (1996, p.71) define it as *"the manner in which companies are controlled and in which those responsible for the direction of companies are accountable to the stakeholders of these companies"*. In a similar vein, Maier (2005, p.5 quoted in Khan, 2010, p.88) argues that *"[c]orporate governance defines a set of relationships between a company's management, its board, its shareholders and its stakeholders. It is the process by which directors and auditors manage their responsibilities towards share-holders and wider company sakeholders. For shareholders it can provide increased confidence of an equitable return on their investment. For company stakeholders it can provide an assurance that the company manages its impact on society and the environment in a responsible manner"*.

There is a significant difference between these two schools of thought; the former seems to support the agency theory as it is based on the idea that companies are mainly accountable for protecting the interests of shareholders. The latter seems to be in favour of the stakeholder theory which requires companies to be accountable to a wider range of interested parties.

Finally, the most comprehensive definition of corporate governance is provided by the WB (1999 as cited in Maassen, 2002, p.13) which claims that *"[c]orporate governance refers to that blend of law, regulation and appropriate voluntary private sector practices which enable the corporation to attract financial and human capital, perform efficiently, and thereby perpetuate itself by generating long-term economic value for its shareholders, while respecting the interests of stakeholders and society as a whole. The principal characteristics of effective corporate governance are: transparency (disclosure of relevant financial and operational information and internal processes of management oversight and control); protection and enforceability of the rights and prerogatives of all shareholders; and, directors capable of independently approving the corporation's strategy and major business plans and decisions, and of independently hiring management, monitoring management's performance and integrity, and replacing management when necessary"*.

The review of previous corporate governance studies and definitions reveals that accountability is an important concept that is highly correlated with corporate governance. Keasey and Wright (1993:291) refer to accountability as involving *"the monitoring, evaluation and control of organisational agents to ensure that they behave in the interests of shareholders and other stakeholders"*. Furthermore, understanding the concept of corporate governance requires complete recognition of the differences between the role of management and that of governance as both may seem at first glance to be homogeneous (Cochran and Wartick, 1988; Haniffa, 1999; Mavrommati, 2008). Management is the process of planning, organising, influencing and controlling the operations of the business. Meanwhile as proposed by Tricker (1984), governance tackles four principal activities: formulating strategic direction for the future of the enterprise in the long run, managing the business and ensuring that appropriate operational planning, controlling, organising and leadership are fulfilled at the heart of the executive management function, monitoring and overseeing management performance and disclosure of information, and finally, responding to those making a legitimate demand for accountability. Based on these aforementioned activities the basic functions of the BOD are defined as strategic, governance and institutional functions (Pearce and Zahra, 1991; Treichler, 1995; Mavrommati, 2008). With respect to corporate governance models, there are two main defined models; one-tier board model and two-tier board model (Haniffa, 1999; Maassen, 2002; Mavrommati, 2008). Maassen (2002) argues that these models are the outcome of the diversity of the role of corporate board in the governance of the corporation, the leadership structure, the organisation structure and the composition of boards. Also, Haniffa (1999) proposes that the model of corporate governance depends on the country's cultural and corporate environments. The US and the UK models are considered as examples of pure one-tier board model while the German model is an example of pure two-tier board model (Haniffa, 1999; Maassen, 2002; Mavrommati, 2008). Under the one-tier board model the power to govern is derived from ownership and the board oversees the running of the firm and reports regularly to members on the stewardship of their investment; and independent auditors report on the fairness of presentation of the company financial statements (Macdonald and Beattie, 1993; Haniffa, 1999). However, under the two-tier board model there are two boards; supervisory and management and there is a clear distinction between governance and management. Under the two-tier board model the supervisory board does not take an active part in management (Haniffa, 1999).

3.3 Importance of Corporate Governance: The OECD Principles

Since the declaration of the G7 Summit Meeting in 1998 regarding the new focus on 'Corporate Behavior and Incentives' and the adoption of a set of principles of corporate governance by the OECD in mid-1999, many countries have developed codes of best practice or have initiated legal, regulatory, and institutional corporate governance reform projects and programmes (CIPE, 2003; Al-Akra et al., 2010a,b; Al-Omari, 2010; Samaha, 2010; Shanikat and Abbadi, 2011). The rising concern with corporate governance is seen as a response to criticisms of the financial reporting function's inability to meet user needs, the widespread of creative accounting and accounting scandals, the limited independence and role of auditors, disagreement between executive compensation and company performance, and the geographic dispersion of shareholders (Macdonald and Beattie, 1993; Haniffa, 1999).

The significance of corporate governance is highlighted by a number of factors: the liberalisation and deregulation of capital markets worldwide, the widespread cross-border transactions, and the increased financial sophistication of capital markets (Mavrommati, 2008; Al-Akra et al., 2010a; Samaha, 2010). In broad terms, good corporate governance practice is beneficial for different parties. For shareholders it is important to protect their rights and limit management's opportunistic behaviour. For business firms, the application of strong corporate governance rules will improve their reputation and enhance their competitive position. For capital markets, sound corporate governance practices and strong rule enforcement will enhance the trust of national and foreign investors, thereby facilitating access to more capital that is necessary to achieve economic development (Jensen and Meckling, 1976; Haniffa, 1999; Oman, 2001; CIPE, 2003; Dey, 2008; Mavrommati, 2008). Moreover, good corporate governance has the potential to lower corporate resources' expropriation by managers, which in turn enables better asset allocation and better performance. Also, the desire for improved transparency raised by good corporate governance and IFRSs disclosure requirements is expected to reduce the problem of information asymmetry (Mallin, 2009).

Discussion about the importance of good corporate governance practices will not be complete without shedding light on the role of the OECD in reviewing and examining corporate governance issues as well as in developing an understanding and raising awareness of the importance of corporate governance for public companies and the economy as a whole. The most important contribution of the OECD is the release of six competent corporate governance principles which are followed or considered as a benchmark by the majority of countries worldwide, including the MENA countries studied in this research[1]. Both Egypt and Jordan corporate governance codes and regulatory frameworks are based on the OECD corporate governance principles and developed under its sponsorship (Al-Akra et al., 2010a; Al-Omari, 2010; Samaha, 2010; Samaha and Dahawy, 2011). Those principles satisfy the quality criterion that for corporations to reap the full benefits of the global capital market where a larger pool of investors is available, corporate governance arrangements must be credible, well understood across borders, and in conformity with internationally accepted principles. The OECD principles can be summarised as follows (OECD, 2004):

3.3.1 Ensuring the Basis for Effective Corporate Governance

"The corporate governance framework should promote transparent and efficient markets, be consistent with the rule of law, and clearly articulate the division of responsibilities among different supervisory, regulatory and enforcement authorities" (OECD, 2004, p.17).

[1] It is interesting to know that Sir Adrian Cadbury the Chairman of the Cadbury Committee (Committee on the Financial Aspects of Corporate Governance) which developed the Cadbury code for corporate governance in 1992 had an appreciated contribution in the development of the OECD principles (OECD, 2004).

3.3.2 The Rights of Shareholders and Key Ownership Functions

"The corporate governance framework should protect and facilitate the exercise of shareholders' rights"(OECD, 2004, p.18). These involve basic rights relating to secure methods of ownership, registration, share transfer, voting in general shareholder meetings, electing and removing members of the board and sharing in the profits of the corporation. Additionally, shareholders have the right to participate in, and to be sufficiently informed on, decisions concerning important corporate changes (OECD, 2004).

3.3.3 The Equitable Treatment of Shareholders

"The corporate governance framework should ensure the equitable treatment of all shareholders, including minority and foreign shareholders. All shareholders should have the opportunity to obtain effective redress for violation of their rights" (OECD, 2004, p.20). All shareholders of the same series of a class should be treated equally; insider trading and abusive self-dealing should be prohibited, and members of the board and key executives should be required to disclose to the board whether they, directly, indirectly or on behalf of third parties, have a material interest in any transaction or matter directly affecting the corporation (OECD, 2004).

3.3.4 The Role of Stakeholders in Corporate Governance

"The corporate governance framework should recognise the rights of stakeholders established by law or through mutual agreements and encourage active cooperation between corporations and stakeholders in creating wealth, jobs, and the sustainability of financially sound enterprises" (OECD, 2004, p.21).

3.3.5 Disclosure and Transparency

"The corporate governance framework to ensure that timely and accurate disclosure is made on all material matters regarding the corporation, including the financial situation, performance, ownership, and governance of the company" (OECD, 2004, p.21). In the researcher's opinion, this is the core OECD principle. Information should be prepared and disclosed in accordance with high quality standards of accounting and financial and non-financial disclosure. Furthermore, an annual audit should be conducted

by an independent, competent and qualified auditor in order to provide an external and objective assurance to the board and shareholders that the financial statements fairly represent the financial position and performance of the company in all material respects. Finally, channels for disseminating information should provide for equal, timely and cost efficient access to relevant information by users and the corporate governance framework should be complemented by an effective approach that addresses and promotes the provision of analysis or advice by analysts, brokers, rating agencies and others, that is relevant to decisions by investors, free from material conflicts of interest that might negatively impact the integrity of their analysis or advice (OECD, 2004).

3.3.6 The Responsibilities of the Board

"The corporate governance framework should ensure the strategic guidance of the company, the effective monitoring of management by the board, and the board's accountability to the company and the shareholders" (OECD, 2004, p.24). Consequently, it is recommended that a sufficient number of board members should be independent of mangament. *"Furthermore, the separation between the CEO and Chair positions is recommended"* (OECD, 2004, p.63).

The review of the OECD corporate governance principles reveals that they depict the framework for good corporate governance practices that mainly aim to protect the interests of minority shareholders. This is highly desired in Egypt and Jordan in order to reap the benefits of the privatization programme that resulted in ownership dispersion (Al-Akra et al., 2010a; Samaha, 2010). Furthermore, these principles emphasise the importance of disclosure and transparency and the important role of the BOD in effectively monitoring management behaviour and overseeing the disclosure practices (Al-Akra et al., 2010a; Samaha, 2010; Samaha and Dahawy, 2011).

3.4 OECD Corporate Governance Principles Implementation in the MENA Region

This section considers the levels of recognition of the OECD corporate governance principles in the MENA region in general and in the scrutinised stock exchanges in particular. As is discussed in more detail in Chapter Four, Egypt developed its code of corporate governance in 2005 as a further step towards globalising its capital market and attracting foreign direct investments. In 2007 Jordan developed a code of corporate governance for its banks, followed by a code of corporate governance for listed shareholding companies in 2008, on a comply or explain basis. However, the requirements for corporate governance best practices under these codes are initially supported by the regulatory framework in Egypt and Jordan (company laws and security exchange laws), that were issued before the codes as part of the regulatory reforms that took place since the mid 1990s.

3.4.1 Ensuring the Basis for Effective Corporate Governance

"The foundation of any corporate governance framework is provided by the basic legal framework, as reflected in the basic company, civil, and securities laws, the regulations of the stock exchange (especially the listing rules), and the basic accounting standards in place. These laws are the basic rules for board and management behavior and in the long term tend to reflect the values of the underlying business culture" (CIPE, 2003, p.22).

This argument highlights the importance of developing a supportive infrastructure for the corporate governance framework. The assessment of such infrastructure in the MENA region generally and in the scrutinised stock exchanges in particular, reveals that company laws and capital market laws (securities laws) are the main sources of corporate governance legal frameworks and practices. Most of the rules and regulations that govern the MENA capital markets including Egypt and Jordan are either recently issued or updated in conjunction with international practices, as are the codes of corporate governance that broadly comply with the OECD principles (CIPE, 2003; Al-Shammari et al., 2008; IFC and Hawkamah, 2008; Al-Akra et al., 2009; Samaha and Dahawy, 2011)[2]. Nevertheless, *de jure* compliance with the international regulatory framework in the MENA region is only one face of the coin, and the other more important face in the researcher's opinion, is compliance in practice.

The majority of the MENA listed companies including those listed on the Egyptian Exchange (EGX) and Amman Stock Exchange (ASE) have a unitary board structure (one-tier board)[3] (CIPE, 2003). In most cases, the controlling shareholders are able to choose all board members and the assigned persons are either inexperienced in the field of activity of the firm or in financial matters, or are closely connected with executive board

---

[2] For details of the regulatory framework for listed companies in different MENA exchanges, see the MENA stock exchanges Websites.

[3] Is also known as the *'arm's length'* system because shareholders maintain their distance and give executives a free hand to manage (Mavrommati, 2008, p.100).

members or the Chairman, and may feel obligated to act in the interest of the controlling shareholders (CIPE, 2003; ROSC, 2009). Furthermore, rules and regulations are not supported by a code of ethics that would help in instituting moral commitment within management. This may be attributed to the lack of efficiency in the MENA capital markets, insufficient development of the judiciary bodies to support strict enforcement of capital market laws and regulations, and an issuer's culture, as issuers are not yet accustomed to transparency and corporate governance sound principles (CIPE, 2003; Asfour, 2004; Sharar, 2007; Al-Shammari et al., 2008). This argument implicitly highlights the importance of appreciating that corporate governance good practice is not only influenced by formal laws, accounting standards, and regulations, but also by their actual enforcement and most importantly, by societal values. Consequently, cultural values operate as a significant antecedent that cannot be ignored when evaluating corporate governance practices.

3.4.2 The Rights of Shareholders and Key Ownership Functions

As reported by CIPE (2003) and IFC and Hawkamah (2008), shareholders' rights are identified under capital market laws and by-laws and company laws in the majority of the MENA capital markets. The regulations indicate shareholders' rights in securing ownership registration, participating and voting in general shareholders' meetings, as well as involvement in decisions concerning fundamental corporate changes (*e.g.,* articles 144, 170, 172, 175 of the Jordanian Companies Law 22 of 1997; articles 59, 66, 72, 157 of the Egyptian Companies Law 159 of 1981). In general terms, shareholders' rights identified by the majority of MENA region countries comply with the OECD principles (CIPE, 2003; ROSC, 2005; IFC and Hawkamah, 2008; ROSC, 2009). However, still directors and managers can influence the extent of compliance with legal requirements in practice (IFC and Hawkamah, 2008). For instance, in Egypt boards do not generally safeguard a formal and transparent director nomination and election process and in practice the general nomination and election processes are controlled by the major owner and far from formal and transparent (ROSC, 2009). Consequently, many boards in Egypt are constituted with family members, government officials, and related parties and are often selected for their loyalty to the major owner regardless of their qualification (ROSC, 2009). CIPE (2003) attributed such situation to the lack of culture, poor awareness among small investors, and the speculative nature of stock trading.

3.4.3 The Equitable Treatment of Shareholders

Regulations in the majority of MENA countries, require shareholders to be treated equally as they have the same voting rights (CIPE, 2003). Furthermore, in the majority of MENA countries, shareholders have the right before others to buy additional shares of the new issue to preserve equity (IFC and Hawkamah, 2008). However, in practice, many directors such as the case of Egypt feel accountable only to the major owner and minority shareholders may find it difficult to get their rights mainly, due to inefficient court system (ROSC, 2009). The situation is not different in Jordan. Although articles of the Companies Law 22 of 1997 (articles 157 and 159) state that the Chairman and the BOD are responsible before shareholders for any violation of law or any negligence in the management of the company, due to the lack of experience in commercial matters by the Jordanian court system it is difficult for minority shareholders to hold directors accountable for their violations (Sharar, 2007).

With respect to insider trading and self-dealing transactions, laws in many MENA capital markets including Egypt and Jordan prohibit this kind of transactions, and unlawful action is penalised by imprisonment and fines (CIPE, 2003). Thus, board members, company officers or other persons having access to information not available to the public and affecting the price of the company's securities are not allowed to trade (*e.g.,* articles 158 and 166 of the Jordanian companies Law 22 of 1997 and article 108 of the Jordanian SL of 2002; article 64 of the Egyptian CML 95 of 1992). However, from the researcher viewpoint, the weak monitoring, lack of strict enforcement of laws, slow court system, and the low consideration for moral hazards, may stand as barriers to compliance with this requirement.

For related party transactions, CIPE (2003) reports that disclosure requirements relating to related party transactions are well articulated in the MENA context (*e.g.,* article 148 of the Jordanian companies Law 22 of 1997; article 4 of the EGX Listing Rules of 2002).

3.4.4 The Role of Stakeholders in Corporate Governance

Stakeholders include investors, creditors, employees and suppliers (Sharar, 2007). *"The role of stakeholders in corporate governance in the MENA is not as developed as in many other countries. It is a question of culture and requires education, increased awareness and in most of the cases, a wider and much more comprehensive coverage in laws, rules and regulations"* (CIPE, 2003). This argument is emphasised by Sharar (2007, p.107) who states that stakeholders are not defined in the Jordanian legislation. However, as a source of capital, banks in the region used to be stakeholders in most of the listed companies. Whether as creditors or shareholders, banks are entitled to demand the observation of standards by the companies they finance, which should improve financial disclosure practices by listed companies, hence improve governance practices (CIPE, 2003).

3.4.5 Disclosure and Transparency

As reported by CIPE (2003) and IFC and Hawkamah (2008), companies listed on all MENA stock exchanges including the EGX and ASE are legally required to disclose their financial, non-financial and operational performance on a continuous and regular basis (*e.g.,* articles 12 to 27 of the EGX Listing Rules of 2002 and articles 64 and 65 of the Egyptian Companies Law 159 of 1981; articles 140 and 141 of the Jordanian Companies Law 22 of 1997 and article 43-a-1 of the Jordanian SL). The majority of MENA countries mandate the adoption of IFRSs[4], and MENA capital markets regulations require financial statements to be audited based on the ISAs (CIPE, 2003; ROSC, 2005, 2009). Consequently, it can be argued that disclosure requirements in the MENA context are in conformity with the OECD principles. Compliance with these requirements is monitored and enforced by the capital market regulatory bodies (*e.g.,* the CMA in Egypt and the JSC in Jordan). Non-compliance is subject to controversial sanctions such as delisting from the stock exchange (*e.g.,* articles 34 and 35 of the EGX Listing Rules of 2002; section 17 of the Jordanian SL).

3.4.6 The Responsibilities of the Board

As indicated in previous sections, the majority of the MENA listed companies including those listed on the EGX and ASE have a unitary board structure. In order for boards to effectively carry out their responsibilities they must be able to exercise objective and independent judgment. In addition, they are supposed to oversee company convergence with laws and regulations (OECD, 2004). However, the review of corporate governance practices within the MENA region including Egypt

[4] Concerning the adoption of IFRSs in the MENA region; Kuwait was the first to mandate IASs/IFRSs (1990) followed by Egypt (1997), Jordan (1998), Bahrain (2001), the UAE (2003), and finally Oman in 2007.

and Jordan promulgates that the role of the BOD in providing strategic guidance and overseeing management behaviour is not sufficiently recognised in practice (ROSC, 2005; IFC and Hawkamah, 2008; ROSC, 2009).

The CIPE (2003) report, and the IFC and Hawkamah (2008) MENA region corporate governance survey, emphasise the weakness of disclosure of corporate governance-related information among companies listed on the MENA region stock exchanges. Furthermore, the review of the extent of implementation of the OECD corporate governance principles in the MENA region capital markets reveals these to be recognised to varying degrees. In broad terms, the IFC and Hawkamah (2008, p.18) corporate governance survey results for both MENA banks and listed companies follow a similar trend, with all respondents scoring relatively high (50% and above) on disclosure and transparency, as well as the control environment, both of which are typically codified in laws and regulations, while respondents failed to break the 50% threshold for the other indicators, namely board practices (47%), shareholder rights (42%), and commitment to good corporate governance (40%) (IFC and Hawkamah, 2008). This result implies that corporate governance is not yet completely accepted as part of the national values in the MENA region. This conclusion is supported by the findings of Boytsun et al. (2011) which show that social norms have a direct significant impact on corporate governance.

3.5 Board Characteristics

"A professional, independent and vigilant board is essential for good corporate governance. Ultimately, the board cannot substitute for talented professional managers. Nor can it change the economic environment in which a company operates. It can, however, influence the company's performance and sustainability through its guidance to, and oversight of management" (IFC and Hawkamah, 2008, p.25). This point of view is supported by Samaha and Dahawy (2011, p.69) who argue that the BOD is the *"central internal control mechanism"* in monitoring management behaviour. Board characteristics in this study cover board independence, board leadership and board size. This section discusses these three variables that will be employed as test variables in this study.

3.5.1 Board Independence

Board independence is an outcome of the number of independent directors in the BOD. *"An independent director is a director who has no material relationship with the company beyond his or her directorship. An independent director should be independent in character and judgment, and there should be no relationships or circumstances which could affect, or might appear to affect, the director's independent judgment"* (IFC and Hawkamah, 2008, p.29). Typically, a board with more independent directors is expected to be more effective in monitoring management and lead to improved financial disclosure (Haniffa and Cooke, 2002; Dey, 2008). It is expected that insiders cannot effectively monitor themselves on behalf of shareholders (Muslu, 2005). Moreover, insiders may impair the otherwise helpful contributions of independent directors (Jensen, 1993; Muslu, 2005). With respect to corporate financial disclosure, board independence is considered as a mechanism that can influence disclosure practices, since a majority of independent directors will maximise the board's ability to force management to meet all the disclosure requirements (Haniffa and Cooke, 2002; Ghazali and Weetman, 2006).

As indicated in section 3.3, the importance of board independence is highlighted by the OECD principles which recommend the existence of a sufficient number of independent directors on boards (OECD, 2004). In addition, Cadbury Committee Report (1992) demonstrates the important role of independent non-executive directors on boards (Haniffa, 1999; Ghosh, 2006; Abdelsalam and El-Masry, 2008).

Alternative board structures do exist. The first is the 'all executive board' which reflects the case of owner-managed entrepreneurial firms where there is no separation between owners and management, and hence, shareholder interests are represented on the board. The remaining structures represent the case where there is separation of ownership and control. The majority executive board is common in large companies in most countries, but this model is criticised because the dominance of executive directors may not enable independent directors to exercise genuine independence. The majority independent structure has the advantage of emphasising checks and balances, in addition to improving and monitoring management performance (Tricker, 1994; Haniffa, 1999).

Proponents of board independence use agency theory and resource dependency theory to explain its importance (Haniffa and Cooke, 2002). According to agency theory, independent directors are needed to monitor and control management actions, to limit opportunistic behaviour, and to reduce management's chance of withholding information, thus helping to reduce agency conflicts between managers and shareholders (Jensen and

Meckling, 1976; Fama and Jensen, 1983; Pettigrew and McNulty, 1995; Abdelsalam and El-Masry, 2008; Kelton and Yang, 2008). They provide supervision of information flows from the firm to outside stakeholders (Biondi et al., 2009), and are also perceived as a check and balance mechanism for enhancing board effectiveness (Mangel and Singh, 1993; Haniffa and Cooke, 2002). Additionally, independent boards are better in representing shareholders' interests in major company decisions such as investments, CEO replacements, and takeovers (Byrd and Hickman, 1992; Cotter et al., 1997; Del Guercio et al., 2003; Muslu, 2005). Independent directors may be considered as decision experts (Fama and Jensen, 1983) and can positively influence directors' decisions (Pearce and Zahra, 1992). Anderson et al. (2006) find that board independence is a better predictor of disclosure informativeness compared to audit committee independence. According to the resource dependency theory, independent directors are also seen as mechanisms linking the company to the external environment (Tricker, 1984; Haniffa and Cooke, 2002).

However, those who oppose the idea of more independent directors on firm boards also depend on agency theory and resource dependency theory to explain their position, arguing that more outsiders on boards may result in excessive monitoring (Baysinger and Butler, 1985), or a lack of genuine independence (Demb and Neubauer, 1992; Tricker, 1994). Also, based on stewardship theory insider-dominated boards are preferred for their depth of knowledge, access to current operating information, technical expertise, and commitment to the firm (Muth and Donaldson, 1998). Bhagat and Black (2000) suggest that a reasonable number of insiders may add value through enhanced strategic decisions and by allowing for better monitoring of future CEO candidates. Additionally, Jensen (1993) argues that most outside directors lack the financial incentives to actively monitor management. Insiders can also enhance operational efficiency (Johnson et al., 1996; Brickley et al., 1997; Muslu, 2005).

In the MENA region, the existence of independent directors on the board is recognised in companies listed on scrutinised MENA stock exchanges (IFC and Hawkamah, 2008). However, the issue is that in most cases independent board members lack material independence or they may lack experience (CIPE, 2003; IFC and Hawkamah, 2008; ROSC, 2009; Al-Akra et al., 2010a). As noted by the CIPE (2003, p.37): *"the assigned persons are either inexperienced in the field of activity of the company or in financial matters, or are in close relation with executive board members or the Chairman, and may feel obligated to act in the interest of the controlling shareholders"*. This aspect raises the need to consider the impact of cultural context and the influence of institutional isomorphism mechanisms when examining the possible impact of board independence on the levels of compliance with IFRSs disclosure requirements in emerging capital markets. Independent directors who do meet the experience criterion may be perceived as a threat, since they may leave the board at any time and take away company secrets. So, according to Gray's (1988) accounting sub-cultural model, the preference for secrecy in developing societies may result in strategic information being hidden from independent directors.

On the other hand, based on the notions of institutional isomorphism, agency theory and cost-benefit analysis, it can be proposed that in the scrutinised countries, independent directors are recognised in boards in order for the companies to gain legitimacy and respect. However, in reality they are only independent in name. This arrangement enables decoupling to continue in such countries, such that whilst independent directors are appointed, in reality they are management puppets. On the other hand, absence of monitoring by independent directors will not improve the board performance with respect to overseeing management compliance with IFRSs. In addition, weak enforcement of IFRSs causes non-compliance costs to be less than compliance costs.

Previous research findings concerning the association between board independence and disclosure levels are mixed, making it difficult to predict the relationship between board independence and levels of compliance with IFRSs in the MENA capital markets. Some researchers report a positive relationship (Adams and Hossain, 1998; Adams et al., 1998; Chen and Jaggi, 2000; Xiao et al., 2004; Arcay and Vazquez, 2005; Anderson et al., 2006; Cheng and Courtenay, 2006; Abdelsalam and Street, 2007; Abdelsalam and El-Masry, 2008; Ezat and El-Masry, 2008; Felo, 2009; Samaha and Dahawy, 2010, 2011), whilst others find a negative one (Eng and Mak, 2003; Gul and Leung, 2004; Muslu, 2005), and yet other researchers found no relationship whatsoever (Haniffa, 1999; Ho and Wong, 2001; Haniffa and Cooke, 2002; Ghazali and Weetman, 2006; Al-Akra et al., 2010a,b).

3.5.2 Board Leadership

Board leadership is a governance issue relating to whether the CEO is also the Chair of the BOD. The CEO is a full-time position that is responsible for the daily management of the company as well as setting and implementing company strategies. However, the position of the Chair is usually part-time and the main responsibility is to ensure the effectiveness of the board (Weir and Laing, 2001; Arcay and Vazquez, 2005). The

OECD principles support the separation between the CEO and the Chair positions as a mechanism that can further strengthen board independence, specifically in one tier boards, by improving the balance of power, board objectivity and accountability (OECD, 2004). This requirement agrees with that of the Cadbury Committee Report (1992) which recommends a separation of the two roles in large companies (Abdelsalam and Street, 2006). Forker (1992) addresses the negative impact of a dominant personality on financial disclosure practices in business firms. Separating the two positions can potentially improve the board's monitoring function and reduce the advantages gained by withholding information, thereby improving the quality of reporting (Forker, 1992; Jensen, 1993; Arcay and Vazquez, 2005; Mavrommati, 2008).

Agency theory argues that the separation of the CEO and Chair positions improves the efficiency of management personnel (Haniffa, 1999; Haniffa and Cooke, 2002). As the CEO may have the right to control board meetings, select board members, and agenda items (Fama and Jensen, 1983; Finkelstein and D'Aveni, 1994; Abdelsalam and El-Masry, 2008; Kelton and Yang, 2008), separating roles provides checks and balances over management's performance (Haniffa and Cooke, 2002). Furthermore, as the Chairman's role is to run board meetings and to oversee the hiring, firing, evaluation and compensation of the CEO, combining both roles reduces the availability of independent evaluation of the CEO's performance as the CEOs themselves will select which information to provide to other directors (Jensen, 1993). Additionally, agency theory argues that role duality creates a strong individual power base that could impair board independence, thus compromising the effectiveness of its governing function (Abdelsalam and El-Masry, 2008). Moreover, Dahya and Travlos (2000) argue that outside Chairmen can provide an external perspective to the company that may be important to the development of organisational goals and objectives, and strengthen the link between the company and its environment. It may also worth noting that role duality may negatively affect the quality of performance, as it may be difficult for one person to find the time and have the effort needed to carry out the responsibilities of both positions effectively and efficiently.

Some researchers, however, argue that the separation of the two positions is not essential for good performance (Dahya et al., 1996; Donaldson and Davis, 1991; Rechner and Dalton, 1991; Gul and Leung, 2004). Eisenhardt (1989) and Stewart (1991) actually argue that role duality improves decision-making by permitting a sharper focus on company objectives and promoting swifter implementation of operational decisions. Furthermore, Rechner and Dalton (1991) suggest that role duality leads to clear unfettered leadership of boards and companies. In this regard Haniffa (1999, p.322) states that *"those who favour role duality argue on the basis of stewardship theory in contrast to agency theory which views executive managers as opportunistic shirkers. Stewardship theory adopts a more positive perspective, viewing directors as guardians of corporate assets and wishing to do their best for the company. As such, there is no problem if the two roles are combined"*.

With respect to the MENA region, role duality in listed companies is recognised as the majority of them are family owned which predisposes an aversion to allowing outsiders to manage the enterprise and its profit (CIPE, 2003; IFC and Hawkamah, 2008). In the scrutinised stock exchanges, role duality is more prevalent in Egypt (see section 6.3) 5.

Institutional isomorphism suggests that board leadership has no influence on independence, as long as there is no awareness regarding the importance of separating the positions of the CEO and the Chair and how each can exercise his/her role to improve the quality of financial reporting within the business firm. Consequently, no significant impact on levels of compliance with IFRSs, is expected either way, and decoupling is thus expected to continue due to the existence of cultural barriers to understanding the logic behind the separation of the two positions as recommended under the Anglo-American model of corporate governance. However, since no impact is felt by the separation of the two roles, companies may fall in line with the separation recommendations purely to gain respect. Also, whilst there is no concern regarding the desirability of separating the two positions to provide effective monitoring of management's performance, Gray's (1988) accounting sub-cultural model, the notions of agency theory and cost benefit-analysis would argue that given the secretive culture accompanied with weak monitoring and lack of strict enforcement of compliance, non-compliance costs will continue to be less than compliance costs. Consequently, the separation between the CEO and Chair positions may not result in better compliance with IFRSs disclosure requirements.

Findings from previous research into the association between board leadership and levels of financial disclosure are mixed. Some studies show that role duality is significantly associated with a lower level of financial disclosure (Forker, 1992; Haniffa, 1999; Haniffa and Cooke, 2002; Gul and Leung, 2004; Abdelsalam and Street, 2007; Abdelsalam and El-Masry, 2008). In contrast, some research demonstrates that there is no association between role duality and financial disclosure (Arcay and Vazquez, 2005; Cheng and Courtenay, 2006; Ghazali and Weetman, 2006;

Ezat and El-Masry, 2008), and two studies (Felo, 2009; Abed et al., 2011) reports a positive relationship between role duality and financial disclosure practices. The contradictory nature of these results makes it difficult to predict the type of the relationship between board leadership and levels of compliance with IFRSs in the scrutinised MENA capital markets.

3.5.3 Board Size

Board size is one of the corporate governance mechanisms that help in aligning management and shareholder interests (Arcay and Vazquez, 2005; Abdelsalam and Street, 2007). Good governance practices recommend limitations to the size of the BOD (Arcay and Vazquez, 2005), but there is no general consensus on the optimum. Cochran and Wartick (1988) argue that this should be between 5 to13 members. A larger board is perceived as detrimental as it may allow members to avoid personal responsibility (Cochran and Wartick, 1988). 5

According to article 3.6 of the Egyptian Code of Corporate Governance (ECCG) issued in 2005, role duality is not preferred but not prohibited. However, under the Jordanian Code of Corporate Governance issued in 2008, article 5 in Chapter Two, states that role duality is not allowed.

Concerning the role of board size in aligning management and shareholder interests, previous research reveals two competing views: proponents of large boards argue that such boards bring more knowledge and contributions which can improve the effectiveness of monitoring and strategic decision-making, alleviate the dominance of the CEO, and increase the pool of expertise due to diversity of board members (Tricker, 1994; Klein, 2002; Singh et al., 2004; Ezat and El-Masry, 2008). Consequently, and considering agency theory, it is suggested that large boards are expected to improve management's level of compliance with IFRSs in order to reduce monitoring costs.

Conversely, opponents of large boards argue that such boards are less effective than small boards because their size may result in poor communication and poorer processing of information, as well as precipitating co-ordination difficulties (Jensen, 1993; Huther, 1997; John and Senbet, 1998). Jensen (1993) emphasises this viewpoint, claiming that large boards may be slower to make urgent decisions than smaller boards. Additionally, he observes that as more directors are added, boards lose their ability to be direct and critical in their operation which may result in dominance by the CEO. Moreover, good governance practice calls for limitations on the size of the BOD (Arcay and Vazquez, 2005). Hence, and also considering agency theory, it is concluded that smaller board size is expected to strengthen the monitoring role of the BOD, thereby leading to greater compliance with IFRSs. However, given the dominance of concentrated ownership pattern in scrutinised stock exchanges and the lack of separation between ownership and control in most cases (CIPE, 2003; UNCTAD, 2007; ROSC, 2009; Al-Akra et al., 2010a), board size is expected to have no influence on improving the monitoring function of the board specifically with the lack of material independence and experience of non-executive board members. On the other hand, the lack of awareness regarding the role of board members in overseeing management behaviour and ensuring compliance with IFRSs suggests that the problem of decoupling will continue. Furthermore, given the secretive nature of scrutinised societies and the lack of separation between ownership and control, boards will not enforce management to disclose any information that may affect the company competitive position as long as non compliance costs are less than compliance costs which is the norm in scrutinised stock exchanges due to the absence of strict enforcement of IFRSs.

Findings from previous research into the association between board size and levels of financial disclosure are mixed. Some researchers report a positive relationship (Barako et al., 2006; Ezat and El-Masry, 2008; Al-Akra et al., 2010a). However, others find no association (Lakhal, 2003; Arcay and Vazquez, 2005; Cheng and Courtenay, 2006; Abed et al., 2011).

3.6 Ownership Structure

Ownership structure is defined by Denis and McConnell (2003, p.3) as *"[t]he identities of a firm's equity holders and the sizes of their positions"*. The importance of a firm's ownership structure stems from the fact that distribution of firm stock among shareholders has a significant influence on corporate actions that are dependent on shareholder voting (Abdelsalam and El-Masry, 2008).

Broadly, ownership structure within a firm is either concentrated or dispersed. Ownership concentration arises when a particular group has the most influence among the equity owners, while ownership dispersion occurs when there is a separation of ownership between managers and equity owners as a group (Haniffa, 1999).

A firm's ownership structure may be a possible determinant of firm disclosure practices (Raffournier, 1995; Eng and Mak, 2003; Arcay and Vazquez, 2005). In this regard, Samaha and Dahawy (2011) argue that ownership structure influences the level of monitoring and hence disclosure levels. High levels of concentration of capital may be accompanied by the owner's considerable involvement in the firm's management, which may lead to unrestricted access to information, thus limiting the demand for and supply of company information (Craswell and Taylor, 1992; McKinnon and Dalimunthe, 1993; Raffournier, 1995; Gelb, 2000; Haniffa and Cooke, 2002; Marston and Polei, 2004; Arcay and Vazquez, 2005; Al-Najjar and Taylor, 2008; Ezat and El-Masry, 2008).

Agency theory holds that separation of ownership and control brings the potential for agency costs because of the potential conflict of interests between contracting parties (Jensen and Meckling, 1976; Chau and Gray, 2002; Mallin, 2009). On the other hand, when share ownership is widely held, the potential for conflicts of interests between the principal and the agent is greater than in closely-held companies. Consequently, disclosure is likely to be greater in widely-held companies to enable the principal to effectively monitor whether his/her economic interests are optimised and whether the agent acts in the best interests of the principal as an owner of the firm (Fama and Jensen, 1983; Dumontier and Raffournier, 1998; Haniffa, 1999; Chau and Gray, 2002). Additionally, from the agency theory perspective corporate governance mechanisms are considered as a basic monitoring tool to solve the principal-agent potential conflict. Furthermore, the call for improved transparency and disclosure highlighted by codes of corporate governance and IFRSs is supposed to reduce the problem of information asymmetry (Mallin, 2009).

In the MENA stock exchanges, the shares of most companies are family owned or government owned (CIPE, 2003; Al-Htaybat, 2005; Naser et al., 2006; ROSC, 2009; Tricker, 2009). The dominance of family ownership is expected to negatively influence the level of financial disclosure for two reasons; firstly, the owners have direct access to company information (Naser et al., 2006), and secondly, the secretive nature of these societies makes family shareholders encourage management to keep disclosure to minimum levels as long as compliance costs exceed non-compliance costs, regardless of the impact on the interests of minority shareholders (ROSC, 2009).

Concerning the impact of dominant government ownership there are two distinct points of view. The first argues that disclosure levels will be low as government can directly request any information from company management (Al-Razeen, 1999; Naser et al., 2006), while the second perceives dominant government ownership as advantageous since agency theory holds that it will improve disclosure practices by encouraging management to use competent disclosure policies (Suwaidan, 1997). Thus, to reduce monitoring costs, management will comply with IFRSs.

As demonstrated by IFC and Hawkamah (2008, p.61): *"[s]hareholder rights are generally provided by law and directors and managers do not have the right to abridge them. However, following laws and regulations by* "the letter or book" *rather than* "in spirit" *are two different matters, and directors and managers can influence whether and how legal requirements are complied with in practice"*. This confirms the researcher's belief in the necessity of considering the cultural context and the institutional isomorphism mechanisms when investigating the relationship between ownership structure and levels of compliance with IFRSs in the MENA region. Based on Gray (1988) accounting sub-cultural model, cost-benefit analysis and the notions of institutional isomorphism, it can be suggested that, the secretive culture and the lack of awareness among management of listed companies in the scrutinised stock exchanges of the importance of compliance with IFRSs, in addition to weak enforcement and low demand for improved disclosures by naive investors, cause non-compliance costs to be less than compliance costs, and hence management chooses non-compliance. This contributes to the decoupling problem whereas, to gain legitimacy, companies state that their financial statements are prepared in accordance with IFRSs when this is not the case.

Previous research findings in this field are mixed. Some show a significant association between ownership structure and financial disclosure (*e.g.,* Hossain et al., 1994; Haniffa, 1999; Gelb, 2000; Jaggi and Low, 2000; Debreceny et al., 2002; Haniffa and Cooke, 2002; Eng and Mak, 2003; Marston and Polei, 2004; Arcay and Vazquez, 2005; Barako et al., 2006; Momany and Al-Shorman, 2006; Naser et al., 2006; Abdel-salam and El-Masry, 2008; Ezat and El-Masry, 2008; Al-Akra et al., 2010b; Samaha and Dahawy, 2010, 2011) while others find no association (*e.g.,* Raffournier, 1995; Suwaidan, 1997; Naser, 1998; Naser et al., 2002; Anderson and Daoud, 2005; Trabelsi and Labelle, 2006; Abdelsalam and Street, 2007; Omar, 2007; Al-Akra et al., 2010a). This inconsistency may be attributed to differences in the jurisdictions explored and period(s) of study, and to the use of different measures of ownership by different researchers such as top ten shareholders, family ownership, company insiders' ownership, institutional ownership, government ownership or foreign ownership (*e.g.,* Malone et al., 1993; Ahmed and Nicholls, 1994; Hossain et al., 1994; Raffournier, 1995; Meek et al., 1995; Wallace and Naser, 1995; Al-Mulhem, 1997; Suwaidan, 1997; Naser, 1998; Al-Razeen, 1999; Depoers, 2000; Gelb, 2000; Chau and Gray, 2002; Haniffa and Cooke, 2002; Naser et al., 2002; Al-Htaybat, 2005; Arcay and Vazquez,

2005; Ghazali and Weetman, 2006; Abdelsalam and El-Masry, 2008; Ezat and El-Masry, 2008; Al-Akra et al., 2010a,b). Furthermore, the review of studies employing ownership structure as an explanatory variable for financial disclosure reveals a lack of consensus among researchers concerning the best measure of ownership structure. Consequently, based on the review of the patterns of ownership structure in the listed MENA companies under scrutiny in this study and the availability of ownership structure-related data for these companies, this study examines the influence of ownership structure on the levels of compliance with IFRSs in the scrutinised MENA capital markets using four distinct measures: government ownership ratio, management ownership ratio, private ownership ratio, and public ownership ratio as is discussed in details in Chapter Five.

3.7 Summary

This chapter has provided an extensive overview of different aspects relating to corporate governance that are expected to provide the necessary background required to investigate the association between corporate governance structures and levels of compliance with IFRSs in the selected MENA countries. Consequently, it aimed to support the formulation of research hypotheses and the explanation of research findings that will be presented in subsequent chapters.

The chapter commenced with an analysis of the concept of corporate governance, and proceeded to discuss the importance of corporate governance and the OECD principles. Thereafter, it provided an overview of the implementation of the OECD corporate governance principles in the MENA capital markets, revealing that these principles are recognised in varying degrees. Then the chapter provided a critical discussion of the corporate governance variables to be used as test variables in this study.

It was indicated that the one-tier corporate governance model dominates in most companies in the MENA region capital markets and that most companies listed in Egypt and Jordan are characterised by weak board independence, although independent directors are recognised on their boards as demonstrated by international reports. Additionally, role duality is recognised particularly in Egypt. Finally, concerning ownership structure most companies are closely held with most company shares being family or government held.

The chapter presented a review of prior research investigating the Relationship between corporate governance variables that are relevant to this study and financial disclosure practices as indicated in Tables 3.1 and 3.2[5].

The review reveals mixed results and a relative shortage in this kind of research in general and in the MENA capital markets in particular. Furthermore, the review of the theoretical foundation of prior research promulgates over-reliance on the financial economics theories, particularly agency theory with very limited reliance, if any, on cultural and institutional isomorphism theories. Consequently, this study is justified.

The next chapter will shed light on the development of scrutinised MENA region capital markets and the regulatory framework that influences financial reporting practices in each capital market. This is expected to provide a reasonable background to rely on in understanding and explaining the findings of the empirical analysis that will be performed in Chapter Six.

---

[5] Studies in Bold investigated the association between mandatory financial disclosures and corporate governance structures.

Table 3.1 Board Characteristics and Financial Disclosure Relationship in Previous Empirical Studies

Board Independence		Board Leadership (Role Duality)		Board Size	
Study	**Relationship**	**Study**	**Relationship**	**Study**	**Relationship**
Adams & Hossain (1998)	+	Felo (2009)	+	Barako et al. (2006)	+
Adams et al. (1998)	+	Abed et al. (2011)	+	Ezat & El-Masry (2008)	+
Chen & Jaggi (2000)	+	Forker (1992)	-	**Al-Akra et al. (2010a)**	+
Xiao et al. (2004)	+	Haniffa (1999)	-	Lakhal (2003)	Insignificant
Arcay & Vazquez (2005)	+	Haniffa & Cooke (2002)	-	Arcay & Vazquez (2005)	Insignificant
Anderson et al. (2006)	+	Gul & Leung (2004)	-	Cheng & Courtenay(2006)	Insignificant
Cheng & Courtenay (2006)	+	Abdelsalam & Street (2007)	-		
Abdelsalam & Street (2007)	+	Abdelsalam & El-Masry (2008)	-		
Abdelsalam & El-Masry (2008)	+	Ho & Wang (2001)	-		
Ezat & El-Masry (2008)	+	Arcay & Vazquez (2005)	Insignificant		
Felo (2009)	+	Cheng & Courtenay (2006)	Insignificant		
Samaha & Dahawy (2010)	+	Ghazali & Weetman (2006)	Insignificant		
Samaha & Dahawy (2011)	+	Ezat & El-Masry (2008)	Insignificant		
Eng & Mak (2003)	-				
Gul & Leung (2004)	-				
Muslu (2005)	-				
Haniffa (1999)	Insignificant				
Ho & Wong (2001)	Insignificant				
Haniffa & Cooke (2002)	Insignificant				
Ghazali & Weetman (2006)	Insignificant				
Al-Akra et al. (2010a)	Insignificant				
Al-Akra et al. (2010b)	Insignificant				

Table 3.2 Ownership Structure and Financial Disclosure Relationship in Previous Empirical Studies

Government Ownership		Management Ownership		Private Ownership		Public Ownership	
Study	**Association**	**Study**	**Association**	**Study**	**Association**	**Study**	**Association**
Eng & Mak (2003)	+	Eng & Mak (2003)	-	Diamond & Verrecchia (1991)	+	Haniffa (1999)	+
Al-Razeen (1999)	-	Arcay & Vazquez (2005)	-	Haniffa & Cooke (2002)	+	Haniffa & Cooke (2002)	+
Naser et al. (2006)	-	Ghazali & Weetman (2006)	-	Naser et al. (2006)	-	Al-Htaybat (2005)	+
Naser (1998)	Insignificant	Abdelsalam & El-Masry (2008)	-	Samaha & Dahawy (2010)	-	Arcay & Vazquez (2005)	+
Naser et al. (2002)	Insignificant	Samaha & Dahawy (2010)	-	Samaha & Dahawy (2011)	-	Ezat & El-Masry (2008)	+
Ghazali & Weetman (2006)	Insignificant	Samaha & Dahawy (2011)	Insignificant	Suwaidan (1997)	Insignificant	Al-Akra et al. (2010b)	+
Al-Akra et al. (2010a)	Insignificant			Depoers (2000)	Insignificant	**Naser et al. (2002)**	Insignificant
Samaha & Dahawy (2010)	Insignificant			Omar (2007)	Insignificant	**Al-Akra et al. (2010a)**	Insignificant
Samaha & Dahawy (2011)	Insignificant			**Al-Akra et al. (2010a)**	Insignificant		
				Al-Akra et al. (2010b)	Insignificant		

CHAPTER FOUR

MENA REGION: CAPITAL MARKETS AND FINANCIAL DISCLOSURE ENVIRONMENT

4.1 MENA Region Context - An Overview

The Arab MENA region capital markets can be categorised into two distinct economic groups. The first is capital importers, among which are Egypt and Jordan which represent an example of lower-middle-income non-oil dependent economies that went through economic restructuring processes referred to as economic reform programmes in the 1990s (Samaha and Stapleton, 2008, 2009; Al-Akra et al., 2009; Hassan et al., 2009; Al-Omari, 2010). Securities markets in these countries were revitalised to be the main vehicle for implementing privatisation programmes and to be a source of medium and long-term finance (CIPE, 2003; Dahawy and Samaha, 2010; Al-Akra et al., 2010a,b; Al-Omari, 2010). The second group is oil-exporting countries, which includes the GCC countries that hold 45% of the world's oil reserves (Al-Shammari et al., 2008). Fueled by petrodollars such countries recently emerged as global economic players (Fofack, 2009), having achieved macroeconomic stability mainly because of the continuous increase in oil prices. They are income surplus countries and capital exporters. The remaining MENA capital markets are weak, either because of political and economic instability of their jurisdictions (the West Bank and Gaza, and Iraq), or because their jurisdictions are in their early stages of economic reform (Lebanon, Syria, Algeria, Sudan, Libya, and Yemen) (CIPE, 2003).

In general, the MENA region capital markets are described as emerging, small and illiquid (Tricker, 2009). This characterisation is emphasised by the CIPE (2003, p.11) which states that *"[t]raditionally, the financial sector in the MENA region countries is a bank based sector and the securities markets are still in an early stage of development, playing a limited role in economic growth"*.

As aforementioned in Chapter One, Jordan's Stock Exchange was established in 1978. Egypt's Stock

Exchange, however, has a long tradition and was the first to be established in the Middle East (Abd-Elsalam, 1999), beginning its activities in the late 1800s. It was ranked as the fifth most active market in the world (ROSC, 2004). However, following the Egyptian revolution in 1952, the activities of the market witnessed a setback for many decades until the development of the Egyptian stock exchange took place in 1995 as part of what is referred to as the Egyptian economic reform programme.

This chapter provides a brief overview of different aspects that influence financial reporting practices in each of the scrutinised MENA capital markets. Hence, it creates the foundation for understanding and explaining the findings of the empirical analysis reported in Chapter Six. Consequently, the rest of this chapter is organised as follows. Section 4.2 provides an overview of the capital market development and financial disclosure regulatory framework in Egypt, Section 4.3 highlights the same aspects in Jordan, and finally, section 4.4 concludes.

4.2 Egypt's Stock Exchange and Financial Reporting Practices

The careful review of the Egyptian modern history demonstrates that the Arab Republic of Egypt has always been the regional leading reformer. The Economic development in this country has gone through four significant phases: Pre-nationalisation (before 1956), Post-nationalisation (1956-1973), Open Door Policy (1974-1990), and the Extensive Economic Restructuring (1991 to date). Each reflects the political strategy adopted by the ruler. Additionally, the performance of the Egyptian Stock Exchange is always heavily influenced by government foreign policies which subsequently affect internal economic performance[1].

The Egyptian economy is unique as Egypt is one of the few developing countries that transformed from a capitalist economy to a planned economy, and then returned to a capitalist one (Hassan, 2008; Desoky,

---

[1] Most recently on the 25th of January, 2011, Egypt witnessed a cold blood revolution. The primary demands from protesters were the end of President Hosni Mubarak's regime after 30 years of ruling, the end of emergency law, better management of country resources, improving minimum wages and controlling corruption. Following this revolution the EGX closed down for several weeks until it recommenced on 28th of March, 2011 and it is expected to recover in the near future. The most important gain from this revolution from the researcher's viewpoint is the change in monitoring culture. This is expected to have a positive impact on *de facto* compliance with IFRSs and corporate governance best practices. For Details of Articles of all laws see: CMA Website,

2009; Dahawy and Samaha, 2010). The move from market imperfections and controls in the 1970s and 1980s to a free market economy in the 1990s is challenging to the government, private sector institutions in general and the accounting profession in particular (Dahawy and Samaha, 2010). In order to reap the benefits from the transition to a market economy and promote confidence of foreign investors, it is necessary to develop the financial reporting system and improve disclosure and transparency to enable investors to better evaluate and compare the financial performance of business firms (HassabElnaby et al., 2003; Aly et al., 2010; Dahawy and Samaha, 2010; Elsayed and Hoque, 2010). In a similar vein, HassabElnaby and Mosebach (2005, p.22) argue that *"[a]s economies develop, the function of accounting becomes more important and the practices become more sophisticated"*.

The harmonisation of the Egyptian Accounting Standards with IASs/IFRSs began with the launch of the government's economic reform and structural adjustment programme in the early 1990s which commenced under pressure from the international institutions specifically the WB and the IMF as a condition of their providing financial support to Egypt (Dahawy and Conover, 2007; Samaha and Stapleton, 2008, 2009; Dahawy and Samaha, 2010). In 1997 the Ministry of Economy and Foreign Trade issued Ministerial decree No. 478 for the year 1997 according to which, a permanent accounting and auditing committee was established with responsibility for setting accounting and auditing standards. Thereafter, Ministerial decision No. 503 was issued in October 1997, which mandated the adoption of twenty two IASs (Samaha, 2006; Samaha and Stapleton, 2008, 2009). In 2002, a new version of harmonised Egyptian Accounting Standards was issued, and the last was in 2006 which includes 35 Egyptian Accounting Standards that are an Arabic translation of the equivalent IFRSs except for IAS 17: Accounting for Leases (Hassaan, 2007; Dahawy and Samaha, 2010; Elsayed, 2010). Mandating IFRSs enabled Egypt to access international exchanges, saved time and effort needed for developing national standards from scratch, improved fairness of financial statements prepared by Egyptian companies (Samaha and Dahawy, 2011).

In summary, the laws regulating the incorporation of companies in Egypt are as follows[2]: Firstly, the Companies Law No. 159 of 1981 regulates joint stock companies, limited liability companies and limited by

---

[2] http://www.cma.gov.eg/cma/content/english/accounting_criteria_en/accounting_criteria_en.htm, Accessed: 20/2/2010.

shares partnership companies. Secondly, the Investment Law No.8 of 1997 regulates investment in specific industrial locations or economic sectors by offering specific income tax exemptions or tax free zones. Thirdly, the Public Business Sector Law No. 203 of 1991 regulates the incorporation of public business sector companies.

The legislation regulating companies listed on the EGX includes: Firstly, the CML No. 95 of 1992 and its Executive Regulations No. 135 of 1993 concerned with regulating the EGX by monitoring the market status in general and maintaining steadiness and growth. Secondly, the Central Depository Law No.93 of 2000 which maintains all registration, clearance and settlement procedures associated with trading transactions, the main purpose being to reduce risks associated with trading physical securities, to enhance market liquidity, and to assure fast securities exchange. Thirdly, Decree No. 30 of 2002 of the CMA's BOD on Securities Listing and De-Listing Rules of the Cairo and Alexandria Stock Exchanges (Dahawy, 2007; ROSC, 2009).

In general, the primary source of Companies Law No.159 of 1981 is the French civil law. However, the Anglo-American common law concepts prevail in the CML No. 95 of 1992, and the Central Depository Law' No. 93 of 2000 (Dahawy, 2007; ROSC, 2009).

According to the CML, listed companies are required to comply with the Egyptian Accounting Standards issued by the Ministry of Foreign Trade that are in conformity with IFRSs (article 12 of Stock Exchange Listing Rules of 2002).

The legal framework contains a number of overlapping, ambiguous provisions, which result in some legal uncertainty. For example, it is not clear whether shareholders are able to hold the board and management accountable for a breach of their duties, and whether the definition of a related party provided in the CML is applicable to other laws (ROSC, 2009). Thus, there are ongoing efforts to issue a unified law that would replace many laws and dispersed provisions. The Unified Companies Law aims to remove conflicts and obstacles to local and foreign investments in Egypt, and to enhance transparency (Dahawy, 2007; Dahawy and Samaha, 2010; Samaha and Dahawy, 2011).

The review of the development of the regulatory framework for business firms in Egypt reveals that issuance of the Public Business Sector Companies Law No. 203 of 1991 was a turning point in the privatisation programme since it permits privatisation of government owned companies, previously prohibited by Law No. 97 of 1983. Consequently, the implementation of this law resulted in the removal of 314 public sector companies, initially established as Affiliated Companies, from the control of their government's ministries to the control of 17 state holding companies as a preliminary step towards full privatisation. Hassan (2006, p.91) reports that between the adoption of the Egyptian privatisation programme in 1994 and the end of June 2002, 60% of the original portfolio was privatised via Initial Public Offerings (IPO), sales to employee, shareholder associations, liquidations, asset sales, and leasing.

The Cairo and Alexandria Stock Exchanges currently referred to as the EGX are among the oldest stock exchanges worldwide, the latter being developed in 1888 and the former in 1903. For almost 40 years they experienced stagnation during the nationalisation regime until they were revitalised in 1992 as one entity with two trading floors (CIPE, 2003; Desoky, 2009).

Since the 1990s, Egypt's has made significant contributions in aligning corporate financial reporting requirements with IFRSs as well as in revitalising the EGX (CIPE, 2003; Hassan, 2006). Significant progress in the Egyptian economy has resulted according to the international reports. The stock market boomed, GDP grew about 5% per year in 2005-06, topping 7.2% in 2007, and GDP per capita was $5,400 (CIA World Factbook Egypt, 2008). Even the IMF (2007) reports that Egypt's economy continues to achieve impressive performance because of high growth levels resulting from the reforms and solid macroeconomic management, and that the ongoing structural reforms continue to promote a dynamic private sector-driven economy.

Certainly, the activities of the EGX increased considerably, market capitalisation growing by an average of 40% per annum over the period 1995-2000 (Ministry of Foreign Trade, 2002; CMA, 2003 cited in Samaha, 2006). Inflation in 2007 was estimated at 8.8% (CIA World Factbook Egypt, 2008). In 2002 there were 1.5 million investors, compared with only 25,000 in the mid-1990s (CASE, 2001 cited in Samaha, 2006, p.118; Samaha and Dahawy, 2011). Furthermore, the international profile of the EGX has been enhanced since 1997 by its inclusion in the emerging market indices of international organisations such as the IFC, Morgan Stanley, and Standard and Poor's (Samaha, 2006). Additionally, ING Barings and EFG Hermes have created country indices for Egypt (MOEFT, 2000; Samaha, 2010; Samaha and Dahawy, 2011). In 2007, the value traded on Egypt's Stock Exchange was estimated at US$49,388.19 million, the volume of shares traded was 683.84 million, the number of transactions was 8,161,607, and market capitalisation was US$134,903.52 million[3]. According to an index developed by the IFC and

[3] For more details see: the Arab Monetary Fund (AMF) Web site,

Hawkamah to measure the strength of good protection for minority shareholders in the MENA region, it was estimated to be 5.3 out of 10 (IFC and Hawkamah, 2008)[4]. The number of listed companies on the EGX in 2007 was 435[5]. This level of progress was considered as a signal that the Egyptian economy is moving towards the globalisation era (Dahawy and Samaha, 2010; Samaha and Dahawy, 2011). However, from the researcher's point of view, such efforts were not enough to close the *de jure* compliance gap in both accounting and auditing practices as will be further discussed in Chapters Six and Seven. This point of view is supported by the argument that such economic growth not necessarily to be accompanied by an improvement in financial reporting practices (Samaha and Dahawy, 2011).

In Egypt, the CMA founded in 1980, is the regulatory agency responsible for ensuring the development of a transparent and secure market for investors. It used to play a major role in creating an environment that enhances public confidence to promote investment in Egyptian companies (Dahawy and Conover, 2007). It is responsible for developing, regulating and enforcing the legal and regulatory framework in the capital market. Furthermore, the CMA enforces the CML, its executive regulations and related decisions through receiving and approving requests to issue new securities, handling licensing of all companies in the securities industry, and ensuring disclosure by capital market participants and adherence to the Egyptian Accounting Standards based upon IFRSs. The EGX is responsible for enforcing the listing rules and the General Authority for Investment and Free Zones (GAFI) is tasked with supervising the implementation of Companies Law.

Most recently (July, 2009), the Egyptian Financial Supervisory Authority replaced the CMA, the Egyptian Insurance Supervisory Authority and Mortgage Finance Authority and became responsible for supervising non-bank financial institutions and markets, including the capital and derivatives markets, as well as activities related to insurance services,

---

http://www.amf.org.ae/sites/default/files/econ/amdb/AMDB\%20Performance/Yearly\%20Performance/en/prv_yearly_summary.htm. Accessed: 22/3/2010.

[4] The scoring method applied by IFC and Hawkamah, 2008 is based on the assumption that good protections for minority shareholders are associated with larger and more active stock markets.

[5] More details about EGX see: the EGX Website, http://directories.globalcustodian.com/directories/organisations/epcDetails.jsf/Stock+Exchanges/Cairo+amp\%3B+Alexandria+Stock+Exchange. Accessed: 22/5/2010.

mortgage finance, financial leasing, factoring, and securitization (ROSC, 2009).

4.2.1 Egypt's Code of Corporate Governance

Corporate governance was introduced in Egypt in consequence of the Economic Reform Programme and the need to gain the trust of the international community to attract foreign investments (Dahawy, 2007; Samaha and Dahawy, 2011). Laws which govern the incorporation of companies in Egypt, and companies listed on the EGX, provide the legal regulatory framework for corporate governance practices in Egypt, in which respect, the Report on the Observance of Standards and Codes (ROSC) (ROSC, 2001) mentions that 62% of the OECD principles were applied by Egyptian companies that were scrutinised. The new listing rules issued by the CMA in 2002 aimed to enhance the implementation of corporate governance best practice by listed companies, and include comprehensive disclosure requirements (Articles 12 to 19), and detailed requirements for financial statements preparation and presentation (Articles 20 to 33). Article 4 requires the presentation of complete information about the company's board members. Additionally, Articles 34 and 35 indicate delisting rules which compel publicly-listed companies to make a commitment to disclosure requirements, or to risk delisting. The application of the aforementioned listing rules resulted in delisting of 99 non-compliant companies in 2003 (ROSC, 2004).

The re-assessment of corporate governance practices in the Egyptian Capital Market by the WB in 2004 revealed that Egypt applied 82% of the OECD principles (ROSC, 2004), indicating improvements over time. The major areas of improvement include: basic shareholders' rights, cost/benefit of voting, and disclosure standards (ROSC, 2004). However, the report reveals that all items of the third principle 'Role of Stakeholders in Corporate Governance' showed no progress compared to the first assessment in 2001, thus signaling an area for improvement.

In 2003, the Egyptian government established the Egyptian Institute of Directors (EIoD), to work jointly with a number of international organisations such as the WB and the United Nations. One of the EIoD's main goals is to spread awareness and improve corporate governance practices in the country. It holds various training and advocacy activities, including the provision of information on corporate governance principles, codes and best practices. Furthermore, the EIoD exerts continuous efforts towards improving good corporate governance practices and strengthening the boards of directors in regional companies by hosting international and national conferences, offering competitions to create awareness, and developing manuals and procedures to help in implementing corporate governance (Dahawy, 2007; Samaha, 2010; Samaha and Dahawy, 2011).

In 2005, the CMA further contributed to corporate governance reforms by restructuring its organisation and initiating a separate sector focused on corporate finance and corporate governance. Now, in addition to other central departments, the CMA includes three major sectors: Corporate Finance and Corporate Governance, Market Regulation, and Market Surveillance and Enforcement (UNCTAD, 2007).

The first ECCG was introduced in 2005 by the Ministry of Investment and the GAFI. This code is based on the OECD corporate governance principles. It was issued with the purpose of improving the quality of financial reporting by listed companies, improving decision making, attracting investors, particularly foreign ones, hence fostering the economic development in Egypt (Samaha and Dahawy, 2011). It was published in Arabic, and it includes guidelines for joint-stock companies listed on the stock exchange, and companies that use the banking systems as a major source of finance. The code indicates that its rules should be considered as an addition to the corporate-related provisions stated under various laws as well as the executive regulations and decrees regarding their implementation. The ECCG rules are neither mandatory nor legally binding; rather, they promote and regulate responsible and transparent behaviour in managing corporations according to international best practice and aim to ensure equilibrium between various party interests (Dahawy, 2007; GAFI, 2007; UNCTAD, 2007; Samaha and Dahawy, 2011).

Finally, in 2006, the Ministry of Investment issued the Code of Corporate Governance for the Public Enterprise Sector based on the OECD working group report on Privatisation and Corporate Governance of State Owned Assets, and the ECCG issued in 2005. The code presents the principles of governing state-owned companies by presenting an organisational and legal framework for such entities. It focuses on the actions of the state as regulator versus its role as owner. It also introduces the principles for equitable treatment of all shareholders including the state as a shareholder and conflict of directors (EIoD, 2006).

Several Egyptian non-profit organisations have also begun to recognise the importance of corporate governance in developing a sound business environment in Egypt. The Egyptian Junior Businessmen Association (EJB) is one such organisation and is concerned with creating an awareness campaign comprised of several events including workshops and roundtables. In 2006 this association issued the Corporate Governance Manual for Family Businesses which is regarded as the first guide in

Egypt and the MENA region for family companies seeking growth, continuity and sustainability for their businesses (Dahawy, 2007; UNCTAD, 2007).

4.3 Jordan's Stock Exchange and Financial Reporting Practices

Unlike the majority of Asian Arab countries, the Hashemite Kingdom of Jordan is considered as a lower-middle-income economy with limited natural resources, and for years its economy was based on financial assistance from the Gulf countries (Al-Htaybat, 2005; Al-Akra et al., 2009)[6].

Similar to Egypt, the Jordanian political system crucially influences the country's economic policies, and hence the performance of the domestic capital market. The country's long ruler was King Hussain who was in power for about 45 years (from 1953 to 1999). He successfully navigated competing pressures from the major powers (US, USSR, and UK), various Arab states, Israel, and a large internal Palestinian population, despite several wars (CIA World Factbook Jordan, 2008).

The early stages in the Jordanian economy's development date back to the early 1950s, attributable to the influx of Palestinian refugees since 1948 due to the Israeli occupation of Palestine. Those refugees supported the Jordanian economy by moving their savings to Jordan and creating new demand in the domestic market for houses, goods and services (Kanaan and Kardoosh, 2002; Al-Htaybat, 2005). During the period from the late 1660s to the late 1980s, Jordan's economic growth was further improved by increases in Arab aid as well as the great support provided by Iraq (Al-Htaybat, 2005). In 1995 the country issued the Investment Promotion Law No.16 of 1995 as a first measure to attract investments in various projects that were expected to bring wealth and prosperity to the country (Haddad, 2005).

In February 1999, King Abdallah II, the eldest son of King Hussain, assumed the throne following his father's death. Since then, he has refocused the government's agenda on economic restructuring by committing his country to the goals of privatisation, liberalisation, and modernisation of the law. Jordan's economy witnessed significant positive changes in the era of King Abdullah II (Al-Htaybat, 2005; Omar, 2007; CIA World Factbook Jordan, 2008; Al-Akra et al., 2009). As a result, the

---

[6] For more details see: The WB Website, http://web.worldbank.org/WBSITE/EXTERNAL/DATASTATISTICS/0,contentMDK:20420458menuPK:64133156pagePK:64133150piPK:64133175theSitePK:239419,00.html, Accessed: 22/3/2010).

Jordanian government signed a free trade agreement with the USA under the umbrella of the World Trade Organisation (WTO) in April 2000. Additionally, in 2000 Jordan became a member in the WTO. It also increased co-operation with the IMF, the WB, the EU, and USAID (Al-Htaybat, 2005; CIA World Factbook Jordan, 2008). In addition, thanks to government support, the role of the industrial sector in fostering the economic development in Jordan was enhanced (Al-Akra et al., 2009).

Like Egypt, the Jordanian government adopted in1993 a new programme known as the Economic Reform Programme to deal with this series of economic developments and to develop balanced relationships with other countries at regional and international levels. The main objectives of that programme are to create new markets, promote privatisation, and to facilitate trade with countries within and outside the Middle East (Al-Htaybat, 2005; Al-Akra et al., 2010a,b; Al-Omari, 2010). The most common forms of privatisation agreements in Jordan are total or partial sale, concessions, lease contracts, management contracts, private infrastructure development, and operations such as Build, Operate and Transfer (BOT) contracts (Omar, 2007).

The package of laws and regulations issued in Jordan to govern the business sector practices as well as the financial reporting practices by companies listed on the ASE includes the following[7]: The Companies Law No. 12 of 1964, amended by the Companies Law No.1 of 1989 which was the first source of regulation of corporate financial reporting in Jordan (Abu-Nassar and Rutherford, 1996; Al-Htaybat, 2005; Haddad, 2005).

Prior to 1997, there was no accounting and auditing standard-setting body in Jordan, and the process of regulating accounting practices in Jordan was purely promulgated by the government (the Ministry of Industry and Trade) with a very minor role for the private sector (Al-Akra et al., 2009). However, after the issuance of the new Companies Law of 1997 as an amendment to the previous Company Act of 1989, and the issuance of the SL of 1997, these two statutes became the main source of accounting practices in Jordan (Al-Htaybat, 2005). Companies Law No. 22 of 1997 was enacted with other regulations such as the Investment Promotion Law of 1995 and the SL No. 23 of 1997 in order to deal with the deficiencies of the previous legislation (Naser et al., 2002; Omar, 2007). According to Article 140 of the Companies Law of 1997[8], the BOD of the public shareholding

[7] For Details of Articles of Jordanian Laws see: ASE Website, http://www.exchange.jo/pages.php?menu_id=119\&local_type=0\&local_id=0\&local_details=0. Accessed: 20/2/2010.

[8] For Details of Articles in this Law see: Ministry of Industry and Trade,

companies shall, within a maximum of three months from the end of the company's fiscal year, prepare the following accounts and statements to be presented to the annual general meeting: the annual balance sheet of the company, its profit and loss account, cash flow statement and notes comparing these with the last year's accounts, all duly certified by the company's auditor, as well as the BOD annual report on the company's activities and performance and forecasts of activities for the following year.

The Articles within the Companies Law of 1997 reveal that disclosure requirements for consolidated financial statements for holding companies (Article 208) and for foreign companies (Article 243) were introduced, thereby making this legislation more competent and comprehensive than the Companies Law of 1989. Financial statements are required to be prepared and audited in accordance with internationally recognised accounting and auditing standards (article, 195)

The disclosure requirements of SL of 2002 which became effective in March, 2004 are similar to those of the SL of 1997 with minor differences such as the requirement of identifying the insiders who have access to the information before others in the company (article 108). In addition, the new Law has extended the tasks and authorities of the Audit Committee (Omar, 2007).

In 2000 the government issued Privatisation Law No. 25 in order to provide the legal and institutional framework for the privatisation programme (Omar, 2007). In the same year the Executive Privatization Commission (EPC) was developed to be responsible for formulating privatisation policy, and identifying candidate enterprises and measures for privatisation (Omar, 2007).

Three years later, Investment Law 2003 was issued, which together with the Investment Promotion Law, supported the work of the Jordanian Investment Board (JIB) that was developed for the purpose of increasing foreign and local investments in Jordan.

The Jordanian Income Tax Law is seen as complementary to the Companies Law No. 22 of 1997 (Al-Shiab, 2003; Omar, 2007) as it provides companies with regulations relating to some matters such as depreciation (Article 3j) which are not covered by the Companies Law of 1997. In 1985 Income Tax Law No. 57 was issued, to be amended by Income Tax Law No. 4 of 1992, Law No. 14 of 1995, and most recently, Law No. 25 of 2001 which became effective on 1st January, 2002[9].

---

http://www.mit.gov.jo/portals/0/tabid/502/Companies\%20Law.aspx. Accessed: 12/10/2010.

[9] For Details of Articles in these Laws see: Income Tax Department,

Finally, a new Accountancy Profession Law No. 73 of 2003 was issued provisionally on 16th June of that year. This was supported by the establishment of the High Council for Accounting and Auditing headed by the Minister of Industries and Trade, and the creation of an improved Jordanian Association of Certified Public Accountants (JACPA). Although the issuance of this Law is a significant step toward regulating the profession, it is criticised on the grounds that, some of its provisions need further clarification and refinement (Omar, 2007).

Omar (2007, p.156) comments on the package of laws that affects disclosure practices in Jordan by arguing that *"the influence of the Income Taxes Law and the Audit Law is limited, while there is some effect of the Companies Act on the financial reporting for Jordanian shareholding companies. However, the most influential regulations which affect the disclosure requirements in Jordan are the Securities Exchange Law (SEL) and IASs"*.

Given the above, it would seem appropriate to issue a unified law to replace the dispersed provisions.

Concerning the adoption of IFRSs in Jordan, this was stimulated by the open trade agreements with foreign partners in the EU and USA as well as pressures from the WB and other international lending institutions which necessitated the development of the Jordanian accounting system to enhance the credibility of financial statements (Al-Shiab, 2003; Haddad, 2005; Omar, 2007; Al-Akra et al., 2009). Jordan is a member of the IASB. Prior to 1998; the date listed companies were forced to apply the IASs issued by the IASC according to the requirements of the SL of 1997 (Naser et al., 2002; Al-Akra et al., 2009; Al-Omari, 2010), the JACPA lacked the power to enforce company compliance with the IASs since there was no legal obligation (Haddad, 2005; Al-Akra et al., 2009). Thus, before 1998 the Amman Financial Market (AFM) which was founded in 1978 was seen as an unregulated financial market as listed companies were not mandated to adopt a specific set of disclosure requirements (Al-Shiab, 2003; Al-Akra et al., 2009). Consequently, one of the main contributions of what is referred to as the Economic Reform Programme is the massive development and restructuring of Jordan's Financial Market in order to globalise its activities. To achieve this objective a number of steps have been taken such as the use of electronic trading since 2000, developing settlement and clearance systems, the elimination of obstacles to investment, and improving transparency (Omar, 2007).

---

http://www.incometax.gov.jo/incometax/en_main\%20menue/en_legislations/En_LawMain.aspx. Accessed: 9/3/2010.

The restructuring of the AFM resulted in the development of three new institutions, namely: the ASE, JSC, and Securities Depository Centre (SDC) (Omar, 2007; Al-Akra et al., 2009; Al-Omari, 2010). The ASE was established in March 1999 as a non-profit, private institution with administrative and financial autonomy, and authority to function as an exchange for the trading of securities. It is governed by a seven-member BOD, and a CEO oversees day-to-day responsibilities and reports to the board. The ASE is working closely with the JSC on surveillance matters and maintaining strong relationships with other exchanges, associations, and international organisations.

The JSC is responsible for supervising the issuance of, and dealing in, information related to all activities and operations of securities, issuers, insider trading and major shareholding. It has a legal personality with financial and administrative autonomy, and is linked directly to the Prime Minister (Omar, 2007). The JSC in Jordan is the equivalent body to the CMA in Egypt.

The SDC was established in 1999 as a non-profit legal entity with financial and administrative autonomy, and managed by the private sector. It is considered one of the most important institutions, as it holds the ownership register of all issued shares. In addition, the SDC has been recognised by Association of National Numbering Agencies (ANNA) and the JSC as the sole numbering agency in Jordan for the assignment of International Security Identification Number (ISIN) (Omar, 2007).

Resulting from the economic restructuring efforts, the performance of the Jordanian economy has shown gradual improvements since 2001. The growth rate of GDP at constant market prices increased from 5.3% in 2001 (Omar, 2007) to reach 5.7% in 2007 (CIA World Factbook Jordan, 2008). Regarding GDP per capita, it was $4,700 in 2007 and the inflation rate was 5.7% (CIA World Factbook Jordan, 2008). Furthermore, in 2007 investment represented 27.8% of GDP (CIA World Factbook Jordan, 2008). In 2007 value traded on the ASE was estimated at US$17,109.39 million, the number of shares traded was 4,387.00 million[10], the number of transactions was 3,384,300 and market capitalisation was US $41,298.47

Overall the proceeds from the adoption of the privatisation programme in Jordan until 2007 amounted $1271 million (Al-Akra et al., 2009). The strength of investor protection according to the index developed by IFC and Hawkamah was estimated to be 4.3 out of 10 and the number of listed companies on the ASE in 2007 was 245 (IFC and Hawkamah, 2008).

---

[10] For more details about trading statistics at the ASE see: the ASE Website, http://www.ase.com.jo/en/key-statistics-ase. Accessed: 29/3/2010.

4.3.1 Jordan's Code of Corporate Governance

In 2005 the Jordanian Corporate Governance Association was established to promote the implementation of effective corporate governance practices throughout Jordan. In addition, in 2005 a draft of a corporate governance code was available but it was not enforced (Shanikat and Abbadi, 2011). However, since 2007 an official code of corporate governance that is based on the OECD principles exists for the banking sector and is enforced by the Central bank in Jordan and in 2008 a mandatory corporate governance code for shareholding companies listed on the ASE was approved which became effective in January, 2009 12. However, before the actual issuance of the Jordanian code of corporate governance took place, the Jordanian government had already built the corporate governance regulatory framework under the sponsorship of the OECD, through the issuance of the Companies Law of 1997 and the SL of 2002 (Al-Akra et al., 2009, 2010a; Shanikat and Abbadi, 2011). In this regard, Shanikat and Abbadi (2011, p.96) argue that Companies Law and SL in Jordan cover the different aspects of corporate governance framework which is made up of the legislative framework and government oversight, the capital market, disclosure and accounting standards, transparency in privatisation, effective supervision of the BOD, preservation of property rights and protection of minority rights. The Companies Law mainly covers some corporate governance rules that relate to the auditor. On the other hand, the SL helps in activating the rules of governance by defining market regulations, the issuance of shares or bonds and trade procedures. It also states the responsibilities of issuers of securities, brokers and auditors, and the requirements for listing in the stock exchange, protection procedures for minority rights and the requirements for disclosing important information. Furthermore to preserve transparency, the law prohibits related party transactions, promoting rumours, misleading investors and disclosing any matters that may adversely affect the capital market (Shanikat and Abbadi, 2011).

The review of the ROSC (2005) concerning the assessment of corporate governance practices in Jordan before the issuance of the code of corporate governance for shareholding listed companies in 2008 indicated the existence of relatively good disclosure practices. However, although the Companies Law and SL provide many of the rules that regulate corporate governance practices of publicly-listed companies, such rules are not as strong as the OECD corporate governance principles (ROSC, 2005). The ROSC (2005) assessment of Jordan's compliance with each of the OECD Principles of Corporate Governance promulgated that, the corporate governance requirement not materially observed by listed companies on the ASE was board independence. In practice, the boards of most companies lack real independence from controlling shareholders and from management (ROSC, 2005). Thus, applying the Jordanian Code of Corporate Governance on comply or explain basis is expected to improve governance practices within the Jordanian context.

The important issue that is expected to have a negative impact on the levels of compliance with IFRSs disclosure requirements, and hence, transparency by companies listed on the ASE, is the non-existence of an accounting and auditing standard setting body in Jordan which may result in the absence of an official translation of the IFRSs. Consequently, this may result in divergent practices as preparers of financial statements and auditors will interpret the standards according to their understanding.

4.4 Summary

This chapter has provided an overview of the economic environment, specifically the business regulatory framework and capital market development within Egypt and Jordan. As indicated, similar to the majority of MENA countries, Egypt and Jordan mandated the adoption of the IFRSs in 1997. Initially, mandating IASs/IFRSs in both countries was a response to international lending institutions' pressure.

On the other hand, as indicated, in order to align with international practices both countries established the regulatory framework for businesses operating within their jurisdictions, and developed their capital markets. In both countries the Company Law and the SL, referred to in Egypt as the CML, represent the core for the regulatory framework for listed companies.

With respect to corporate governance practices, Egypt has been one of the leaders in the region in creating corporate governance frameworks, and developing supporting institutions such as the EIoD to tackle some of the corporate governance challenges faced by the market. With respect to Jordan, since 2007 a code of corporate governance based on the OECD principles exists for the banking sector and in 2008 a code of corporate governance for shareholding companies listed on ASE was approved which became effective in January, 2009. However, the regulatory framework in Jordan initially provides the basis for good corporate governance practices through the requirements of the Companies law of 1997 and the SL of 2002.

Based on the review of the context within Egypt and Jordan, it is appreciated that enormous developments in the regulatory requirements have occurred during the last two decades. However, to get the best from their *de jure* compliance with the international best practices, there must be a *de facto* compliance with these requirements. The awareness in the scrutinised countries about the importance of *de facto* compliance with the international best practices will enhance the globalisation of the performance of their stock exchanges, attract more local and foreign investments, and hence, achieve the proposed financial and economic development objectives.

The next chapter will discuss the methodology employed to accomplish the research objectives.

CHAPTER FIVE

RESEARCH PHILOSOPHY AND METHODOLOGY

5.1 Introduction

The main concern of any researcher is to answer his/her research question(s), which requires him/her to consider the research methodology and the research method(s) that will be employed. Additionally, the researcher must decide within which research paradigm his/her study will be undertaken (Burrell and Morgan, 1979; Crotty, 2007; Baker and Foy, 2008).

Within the setting of the proposed theoretical foundation discussed in Chapter Two, the empirical part of this study assesses the level of compliance with IFRSs by non-financial companies listed on the stock exchanges of Egypt and Jordan, simultaneously seeking to determine whether a relationship exists between levels of compliance and corporate governance structures in the two capital markets. To best meet these objectives the researcher employs the sequential explanatory triangulation design.

In providing a detailed discussion of the methodology and methods used to test the research hypotheses in order to meet the study's objectives, the rest of this chapter is organised as follows. Section 5.2 discusses research philosophy, section 5.3 introduces the research hypotheses, section 5.4 describes the research design and methodology, section 5.5 indicates the research methods, section 5.6 discusses data analysis, and section 5.7 concludes.

5.2 Research Philosophy

There is an intense debate in the social sciences about the most appropriate philosophical position from which methods should be derived (Easterby-Smith et al., 1993). All researchers build their research implicitly or explicitly, on several fundamental theoretical and philosophical assumptions derived from their beliefs about the nature of the society and the social science world, as well as their knowledge and under-standing of the world and research itself (Hopper and Powell, 1985; Al-Htaybat, 2005).

Burrell and Morgan (1979, p.22) propose that social theory is based on four key paradigms emanating from different sets of assumptions about the nature of social science and society, these being: radical humanist, radical structuralist, interpretive, and functionalist. In this regard they argue that *"[t]o be located in a particular paradigm is to view the world in a particular way. The four paradigms thus define four views of the social world based upon different meta-theoretical assumptions with regards to the nature of science and society"* (Burrell and Morgan, 1979). The radical humanist paradigm perceives the world from a subjective viewpoint, striving to alter societal aspects with regard to human constraints; the radical structuralist paradigm equally questions the status quo and strives for fundamental change, but contrary to the radical humanist paradigm it perceives the world from an objective angle, consequently seeking to change the universal structure; the interpretive paradigm reflects the subjective stand where the status quo is investigated taking into consideration human beliefs and perceptions; and the functionalist paradigm aims to provide a rational explanation of existing social affairs and the current status quo, being concerned with understanding society in a way that enables the generation of knowledge. Additionally, this paradigm is concerned with effective regulation and control of social affairs in order to provide practical solutions to practical problems. In summary, the functionalist paradigm is based on investigating the current status and establishing the factual existence of structures.

Burrell and Morgan (1979, p.26) observe the functionalist paradigm to be rooted in the sociological positivist tradition. It seeks to establish a law for the occurrence of phenomena, and predict their occurrence through causal relationships between study variables (Hussey and Hussey, 1997; Al-Htaybat, 2005).

Given the foregoing discussion, this study is mainly undertaken within the functionalist research paradigm. The levels of compliance with IFRSs by companies listed on the selected MENA capital markets are measured. This step is followed by an examination of the potential relationship between test variables (country, board independence, board leadership, board size and ownership structure) and levels of compliance with IFRSs disclosure requirements. Furthermore, interviews (qualitative method) are conducted to support the interpretation of the findings of the quantitative analysis.

Robson (1993, p.4) observes that the purpose of descriptive research is to depict an accurate profile of persons, events or situations. Given this observation, this study can be classified as descriptive research as it employs a disclosure index and semi-structured interviews to portray an accurate profile of compliance practices by companies listed on the EGX and ASE. The study can also be considered as explanatory, since according to Collis and Hussey (2003) the purpose of explanatory research is to understand phenomena by establishing causal relationships, and this study is explanatory in two respects. Firstly, it employs several corporate governance variables to explain compliance practices by companies listed on the EGX and ASE. Secondly, it uses different strands of relevant theories (cultural theories, institutional isomorphism theory, and two financial economics theories) to explain levels of compliance with IFRSs disclosure requirements and the influence of corporate governance structures on compliance practices within the MENA context.

5.3 Research Hypotheses

The review of prior compliance literature as well as the chosen MENA region capital markets financial disclosure environments reveals that further to the secretive nature of MENA societies, enforcement of compliance with IFRSs is relatively weak and market pressures for more disclosure are less robust than in developed capital markets. Hence, non-compliance costs are less than compliance costs for MENA listed companies (Al-Htaybat, 2005; Abdelsalam and Weetman, 2007; Dahawy and Conover, 2007; Samaha and Stapleton, 2008, 2009). On the other hand, as indicated in Chapters Three and Four, corporate governance is newly introduced in the scrutinised countries as part of the regulatory reforms that accompanied the privatisation programmes commenced in the 1990s (Al-Akra et al., 2009, 2010a; Samaha, 2010; Samaha and Dahawy, 2011) and as many of the associated requirements for good practice (*e.g.*, board independence, separation between the CEO and Chair positions; improved disclosure and transparency, investor protection and board responsibility for overseeing management behaviour and financial reporting practices) may contradict with the native cultural values (*e.g.*, secrecy), this is expected to diminish its impact on the levels of compliance with IFRSs. Furthermore, based on the research questions, objectives and the extensive review of disclosure theories employed in prior research in the area of financial disclosure, particularly, agency theory and cost-benefit analysis together with the notions of institutional isomorphism theory and secrecy versus transparency, as one of Gray's (1988) accounting sub-cultural values, this study examines whether differences exist between the levels of compliance with IFRSs disclosure requirements between the selected MENA capital markets. The study then explores whether the levels of compliance are influenced by certain corporate governance variables (board independence, board leadership, board size and ownership structure).

This section illustrates the development of the research hypotheses formulated to examine whether differences between Egypt and Jordan exist and to address the association between the corporate governance structures used in this study as test variables and levels of compliance with IFRSs. Additionally, the section illuminates those variables to be used as control variables (company size, profitability, gearing, liquidity, type of business activity, and type of audit firm) as identified in previous research as being associated with financial disclosure practices and compliance.

5.3.1 Differences in IFRSs Compliance Levels and in the Dominant Corporate Governance Structures

The differences between countries such as the Egyptian and the Jordanian contexts with respect to their capacity to enforce compliance with IFRSs and corporate governance best practices may affect levels of compliance with IFRSs disclosure requirements in each jurisdiction. Believing this possibility, Al-Shammari et al. (2008, p.129) used country as an explanatory variable in their study on GCC countries, arguing that *"[t]he sample countries have many features in common in their regulatory frameworks, in addition to economic and cultural ties. This closeness could suggest that levels of compliance will be similar. However, it has been proposed that the roles of external auditors and independent enforcement bodies are crucial in promoting compliance with accounting standards"*.

In a similar vein, previous research investigating IFRSs adoption reports that differences in compliance levels among companies reflect their country of origin (Tower et al., 1999; Street and Bryant, 2000; Al-Shammari et al., 2008). Hence, it seems interesting to investigate whether similarities between the Egyptian and the Jordanian settings in their legal, economic and cultural contexts reduce the differences in levels of compliance with mandatory IFRSs disclosure requirements between both jurisdictions. Additionally, whether such similarities reduce the differences in company characteristics as well as disparities in the dominant corporate governance structures between the Egyptian and the Jordanian contexts.

According to the institutional isomorphism theory, as both jurisdictions mandated the adoption of IFRSs under pressures from the international lending institutions to gain respect and legitimacy, they did not give sufficient consideration to the importance of preliminary preparation of their markets (*i.e.,* the development of national values accepting the importance of compliance with IFRSs, as prevail in the developed countries where such standards originated) and institutional infrastructure. This largely accounts for the existing gap between *de jure* and *de facto* compliance reported by previous research investigating the EGX and ASE on an individual basis (*e.g.,* Al-Htaybat, 2005; Abdelsalam and Weetman, 2007; Omar, 2007; Samaha and Stapleton, 2008, 2009; Al-Akra et al., 2010a; Ismail et al., 2010). The same argument applies to the introduction of corporate governance requirements for best practices that are based on the OECD principles.

Based on Gray's (1988) accounting sub-culture model, the secretive nature of societies in both jurisdictions is expected to reduce the levels of compliance (Abd-Elsalam, 1999; Al-Htaybat, 2005; Samaha and Stapleton, 2008, 2009; Ismail et al., 2010). Indeed, the importance of the impact of secrecy on financial disclosure practices has been highlighted by many researchers (*e.g.,* Gray and Vint, 1995; Zarzeski, 1996; Abd-Elsalam, 1999; Haniffa, 1999; Haniffa and Cooke, 2002; Abdelsalam and Weetman, 2007; Dahawy and Conover, 2007; Samaha and Stapleton, 2008, 2009; Ismail et al., 2010). Secretive cultures are associated with strong uncertainty avoidance that results from the need to restrict information disclosure so as to avoid conflict and competition and to preserve security. Secrecy is also associated with large power distance resulting in the restriction of information to preserve power inequalities (Gray, 1988).

On the other hand, agency theory supposes that low investor demand for improved disclosure, and hence low monitoring costs, reduces management incentives to comply with IFRSs (Abd-Elsalam, 1999; Omar, 2007). Finally, based on cost-benefit analysis, the weak enforcement of IFRSs and low sanctions if any in both jurisdictions cause non-compliance costs to be less than compliance costs for listed companies, and thus, directs management incentives toward non-compliance (Abd-Elsalam, 1999; Al-Htaybat, 2005).

Based on the above discussion, the first research hypothesis can be stated as follows:

H1 There are no significant statistical differences between the Egyptian and the Jordanian contexts. This hypothesis can be further divided into the following two hypotheses.

H1a There are no significant statistical differences between Egypt and Jordan in their levels of compliance with overall mandatory IFRSs disclosure requirements.

H1b There are no significant statistical differences between Egypt and Jordan in their dominant corporate governance structures and other company characteristics.

5.3.2 Explanatory Corporate Governance Variables

Although improved disclosure and transparency are the heart of effective governance, better compliance with IFRSs in the MENA region jurisdictions, including Egypt and Jordan will only be forthcoming if cultural values change to embrace best corporate governance practice. This assertion is confirmed by the international reports which claim the existence of a gap between *de jure* and *de facto* compliance with corporate governance best practices in the MENA capital markets including Egypt and Jordan (*e.g.,* CIPE, 2003; ROSC, 2005; UNCTAD, 2007; IFC and Hawkamah, 2008; ROSC, 2009), as well as the findings of prior studies carried out within the MENA context that recognise the negative impact of secrecy on compliance practices (*e.g.,* Dahawy and Conover, 2007; Dahawy, 2009; Al-Omari, 2010; Ismail et al., 2010). Thus, it is important to explore the current influence of corporate governance structures on the levels of compliance with IFRSs disclosure requirements within the MENA context. Although the existence of an audit committee is an important mechanism for providing an oversight of the internal audit activities as well as overseeing the overall relationship with the external auditor including the non-audit services that might be provided by the external auditor (OECD, 2004), the non-availability of data relating to this variable for most of the companies listed on the EGX, resulted in excluding this variable from the empirical analysis.

The relationship between the selected corporate governance explanatory variables (test variables) and the extent of compliance with IFRSs disclosure requirements is explored by statistically testing the following hypotheses.

BOD Independence

Board independence is an important governance mechanism that is supported by corporate governance reforms in Egypt and Jordan (Al-Akra et al., 2010a,b; Samaha, 2010; Samaha and Dahawy, 2010, 2011). The detailed discussion of board independence provided in section 3.5.1 confirmed that board independence is recognised in scrutinised countries however in most cases independent directors lack material independence (CIPE, 2003; IFC and Hawkamah, 2008; ROSC, 2009). The lack of material independence will not improve BOD monitoring function, hence compliance with IFRSs disclosure requirements will not improve. Dominance of secretive culture may result in hiding company strategic information from independent directors and hence will not enable them to carry out their responsibilities as expected. Furthermore, based on the notions of the institutional isomorphism and cost-benefit analysis, it can be proposed that, independent directors are recognised in boards in order for the companies just to gain legitimacy and respect regardless of their role in monitoring compliance with IFRSs. Hence, decoupling will continue as companies will state that they comply with IFRSs while full compliance is absent. In addition, weak enforcement of IFRSs by the capital market authorities causes non-compliance costs to be less than compliance costs. Consequently, as a result compliance with IFRSs disclosure requirements will not improve.

The lack of empirical evidence with respect to the association between board independence and levels of compliance with mandatory IFRSs disclosure requirements within the Egyptian context and the availability of only one study that investigates such issue within the Jordanian context using earlier data; 1996 and 2004 respectively (Al-Akra et al., 2010a), support the need for further investigation.

The findings of prior studies that investigate the association between board independence and voluntary disclosures within the Egyptian context report a significant positive relationship (Ezat and El-Masry, 2008; Samaha, 2010; Samaha and Dahawy, 2010, 2011). They attribute this result to the proposition that board independence improves the monitoring function of the board, hence results in better transparency. However, the findings of prior research that investigates the association between board independence and disclosure practices in Jordan (mandatory and voluntary) do not support any significant association between board independence and the extent of disclosure (Al-Akra et al., 2010a,b). Accordingly, the second research hypothesis can be stated as follows:

H2 There is no significant statistical relationship between BOD independence and the extent of compliance with IFRSs disclosure requirements. This hypothesis can be further divided into the following two hypotheses.

H2a There is no significant statistical relationship between BOD independence and the extent of compliance with IFRSs disclosure requirements in the Egyptian context.

H2b There is no significant statistical relationship between BOD independence and the extent of compliance with IFRSs disclosure requirements in the Jordanian context.

Board Leadership

As previously mentioned in section 3.5.2, role duality is recognised in scrutinised stock exchanges, and it is more obvious within the Egyptian context, although according to article 3.6 of the ECCG it is not considered as a best practice.

According to the notions of the institutional isomorphism, separating the CEO and Chair positions has no influence on independence, as long as there is no awareness regarding the importance of separating the positions of the CEO and the Chair in improving the monitoring function and hence the quality of financial reporting within the business firm. Consequently, no significant impact on levels of compliance with IFRSs is expected when the positions are carried out by two different persons, due to the existence of cultural barriers to understanding the logic behind the separation of the two positions as recommended under the Anglo-American model of corporate governance. However, since no impact is felt by the separation of the two roles, companies may fall in line with the separation recommendations purely to gain respect. On the other hand, based on Gray's (1988) accounting sub-cultural model, the notions of agency theory and cost benefit-analysis, the secretive culture accompanied with weak monitoring whether the two positions are separated or held by one person and the lack of strict enforcement of compliance, non-compliance costs will continue to be less than compliance costs. Consequently, the separation between the CEO and Chair positions may not result in better compliance with IFRSs disclosure requirements and decoupling is thus expected to continue (companies state that financial statements are prepared in accordance with IFRSs while full compliance is absent).

As previously indicated in section 3.5.2 the findings from previous research into the association between board leadership and levels of financial disclosure are mixed. On the level of developing countries, some studies show that role duality is significantly associated with a lower level of financial disclosure (Haniffa, 1999 and Haniffa and Cooke, 2002 in Malaysia on the impact of culture and corporate governance on companies' financial disclosure practices). In contrast, others demonstrate that there is no association between role duality and financial disclosure or reporting quality (Ghazali and Weetman, 2006 in Malaysia on the impact of corporate governance structures on voluntary disclosures in annual reports; Ezat and El-Masry, 2008 in Egypt on the impact of corporate governance structures on the timeliness of corporate internet reporting), and one study (Abed et al., 2011 in Jordan on the impact of corporate characterisitics on the inclusion of forecasts in the narrative sections of annual reports) reports a positive relationship between role duality and corporate disclosure practices. The contradictory nature of these results and the non availability of a study that investigates the association between board leadership and levels of compliance with mandatory IFRSs disclosure requirements in both of scrutinised stock exchanges, make it difficult to predict the type of the relationship between board leadership and levels of compliance with IFRSs in the scrutinised MENA jurisdictions. Accordingly, the third research hypothesis can be stated as follows:

H3 There are no statistically significant differences in the levels of compliance with IFRSs disclosure requirements between companies that separate the positions of the CEO and the Chair and those that do not. This hypothesis can be further divided into the following two hypotheses.
H3a There are no statistically significant differences in the levels of compliance with IFRSs disclosure requirements between companies that separate the positions of the CEO and the Chair and those that do not in the Egyptian context.
H3b There are no statistically significant differences in the levels of compliance with IFRSs disclosure requirements between companies that separate the positions of the CEO and the Chair and those that do not in the Jordanian context.

Board Size

As demonstrated in sub-section 3.5.3 board size is one of the corporate governance mechanisms that help in aligning management and shareholder interests (Arcay and Vazquez, 2005; Abdelsalam and Street, 2007).

Given that ownership in scrutinised stock exchanges is still concentrated and that to a great extent there is no separation between ownership and control (CIPE, 2003; UNCTAD, 2007; ROSC, 2009; Al-Akra et al., 2010a), as demonstrated in sub-section 3.5.3, board size is expected to have no impact on improving the monitoring function of the board specifically with the lack of material independence of board members. On the other hand, the lack of experience and awareness regarding the role of board members in overseeing management behaviour and ensuring compliance with IFRSs mean that the problem of decoupling will continue. Furthermore, given the secretive nature of scrutinised societies and the lack of separation between ownership and control, boards will not enforce management to disclose any information that may affect company's competitive position as long as non compliance costs are less than compliance costs which is the norm in scrutinised stock exchanges due to the absence of strict enforcement of IFRSs.

As previously mentioned in section 3.5.3 findings from previous research into the association between board size and levels of financial disclosure are mixed. Some researchers report a positive relationship (Barako et al., 2006; Ezat and El-Masry, 2008; Al-Akra et al., 2010a). However, others find no association (Lakhal, 2003; Arcay and Vazquez, 2005; Cheng and Courtenay, 2006; Abed et al., 2011). The contradictory nature of these results and the non availability of a study that investigates the association between board size and levels of compliance with IFRSs disclosure requirements in the Egyptian context and the availability of only one study that investigates such association in the Jordanian context (Al-Akra et al., 2010a) make it difficult to predict the type of the relationship between board size and levels of compliance with IFRSs in the scrutinised MENA capital markets. Accordingly, the fourth research hypothesis can be stated as follows:

H4 There is no significant statistical relationship between BOD size and the extent of compliance with IFRSs disclosure requirements. This hypothesis can be further divided into the following two hypotheses.
H4a There is no significant statistical relationship between BOD size and the extent of compliance with IFRSs disclosure requirements in the Egyptian context.
H4b There is no significant statistical relationship between BOD size and the extent of compliance with IFRSs disclosure requirements in the Jordanian context.

Ownership Structure

The detailed discussion of ownership structure provided in section 3.6 demonstrated inconsistencies in its impact on financial disclosure practices, and hence a need to revisit this issue. Considering the patterns of ownership structure in the listed MENA region companies examined in this study and the availability of ownership structure-related data for these companies, this study investigates the influence of ownership structure on levels of compliance with IFRSs in Egypt and Jordan, using four distinct measures: government ownership, management ownership, private ownership, and public ownership.

Government Ownership

Two distinct viewpoints emerge regarding the impact of dominant government ownership as indicated in Chapter Three. The first perceives this as advantageous, potentially improving disclosure practices and stimulating management to adopt competent disclosure policies (Suwaidan, 1997; Denis and McConnell, 2003). In this regard, Eng and Mak (2003) suggest government ownership increases moral hazard and the possibility of agency problems due to the conflict between the pure profit goals of a commercial enterprise and goals related to the interests of the nation; thus management is expected to disclose more information to reduce monitoring costs. Also, Cheng and Courtenay (2006) argue that dominant government ownership may result in more disclosure by company management in order to reflect the state's commitment to transparency. This argument is emphasised by Li and Harrison (2008) who state that when the government is a major owner, it is important for the BOD to appear to be legitimate and accountable to the public to support the political goals of bureaucrats. Thus, levels of compliance with IFRSs disclosure requirements are expected to increase to reduce agency costs.

The other viewpoint is that dominant government ownership promotes low disclosure levels as governments can directly request any information required from company management (Al-Razeen, 1999; Naser et al., 2006). Government-controlled enterprises may not need to attract potential investors as they can obtain cheaper funds from local banks. Also, political affiliations may result in less detailed information being disclosed to protect the beneficial owners (Ghazali, 2004). Agency theory argues that this reduces monitoring costs, and hence, management incentives to improve disclosure. Furthermore, dominant government ownership results in the government appointing many of the board members from its officials regardless of their qualification or experience. This creates the problem of 'who watches the watchers' since management in such companies is overwhelmingly chosen from government officials (Tsamenyi et al., 2007; Mensah, 2002).

Simultaneously, Gray's (1988) accounting sub-cultural model, cost-benefit analysis, and institutional isomorphism confirm a management preference for secrecy within MENA societies, to preserve their reputation. In addition, the lack of awareness among listed companies' managements regarding the importance of compliance, the lack of awareness among BOD members regarding the importance of best corporate governance practice in improving disclosure practices, the weak enforcement of laws and regulations, and low demand for improved disclosures due to government's direct access to company information or the lack of qualified government officials to monitor company compliance with IFRSs, all precipitate lower non-compliance than compliance costs. Furthermore, the lack of incentives for members of the public (who implicitly own government shares) to directly monitor the management of government owned firms in the studied stock exchanges causes non-compliance costs to be less than compliance costs, and thus will not stimulate management to improve compliance. These circumstances contribute to the problem of decoupling.

Previous research results concerning the association between government ownership and levels of financial disclosure are mixed. For instance, Eng and Mak (2003) report a positive relationship while Al-Razeen (1999) and Naser et al. (2006) report a negative one and Ghazali and Weetman (2006) find a negative, but insignificant relationship. On the level of scrutinised stock exchanges, the results of all studies that investigate the association between government ownership and the extent of corporate disclosure do not support the existence of any association (Naser, 1998 in Jordan; Naser et al., 2002 in Jordan; Al-Akra et al., 2010a in Jordan; Samaha and Dahawy, 2010, 2011 in Egypt). Accordingly, hypothesis 5a can be stated as follows:

H5a There is no significant statistical relationship between the government ownership ratio and the extent of compliance with IFRSs disclosure requirements. This hypothesis can be further divided into the following two hypotheses.

H5a1 There is no significant statistical relationship between the government ownership ratio and the extent of compliance with IFRSs disclosure requirements in the Egyptian context.

H5a2 There is no significant statistical relationship between the government ownership ratio and the extent of compliance with IFRSs disclosure requirements in the Jordanian context.

Management Ownership

Dominant management ownership is expected to reduce levels of compliance with IFRSs as managerial ownership has the potential to align the interests of shareholders and managers (Kelton and Yang, 2008), and reconcile agency conflicts that may arise between managers and shareholders. Hence, it is likely to reduce the latter's demands for monitoring (Jensen and Meckling, 1976; Eng and Mak, 2003; Abdelsalam and El-Masry, 2008). Having the potential to reduce the asymmetry resulting from the separation of ownership from control, such ownership is expected to precipitate a larger volume of unstructured information for shareholders (Mavrommati, 2008). Furthermore, Gray's (1988) accounting sub-cultural model, institutional isomorphism and cost-benefit analysis, all suggest the following outcomes: a) a secretive culture which causes management to minimise disclosure to safeguard trade secrets, b) a lack of awareness among management and board members of listed companies on the scrutinised stock exchanges regarding the importance of compliance with IFRSs and best corporate governance practices that encourage transparency, c) weak enforcement of laws and regulations by capital market authorities and weak sanctions if any, d) low demand for improved disclosures and insufficient monitoring from small shareholders who cannot put voting pressures on management of listed companies who are in most cases dominant shareholders and members of the BOD. The combination of these outcomes will cause non-compliance costs to be less than compliance costs for company management, and thus, will not stimulate management to improve levels of compliance with IFRSs. Consequently, full compliance will not be in evidence.

The results of most previous research on the association between management ownership and levels of financial disclosure show a negative association (*e.g.,* Eng and Mak, 2003; Arcay and Vazquez, 2005; Ghazali and Weetman, 2006; Abdelsalam and El-Masry, 2008). On the level of scrutinised stock exchanges this association was examined only in Egypt by Samaha and Dahawy (2010, 2011) who investigate the association between management ownership and levels of voluntary disclosures. Although Samaha and Dahawy (2011) do not find any association, Samaha and Dahawy (2010) report a significant negative association. Hence, the effect of managerial ownership on the levels of compliance with IFRSs is expected to be substitutive. Accordingly, research hypothesis 5b can be stated as follows:

H5b There is a significant negative statistical relationship between the management ownership ratio and the extent of compliance with IFRSs disclosure requirements. This hypothesis can be further divided into the following two hypotheses.

H5b1 There is a significant negative statistical relationship between the management ownership ratio and the extent of compliance with IFRSs disclosure requirements in the Egyptian context.

H5b2 There is a significant negative statistical relationship between the management ownership ratio and the extent of compliance with IFRSs disclosure requirements in the Jordanian context.

Private Ownership

As mentioned in Chapter Four, the dominance of private ownership is common among companies listed on both the EGX and ASE. This results in private investors' active involvement in company management either as executives or as directors. In most cases, private ownership in the scrutinised stock exchanges takes the form of private entities which are family owned.

Agency theory suggests that the dominance of private shareholders may reduce the requirement for management monitoring (Eng and Mak, 2003; Abdelsalam and El-Masry, 2008). Hence, when share ownership is less diffused, levels of financial disclosure are negatively affected. Many researchers agree, suggesting that the demand for greater disclosure is decreased as owners have access to all company information (Schadewitz and Blevins, 1998; Archambault and Archambault, 2003; Eng and Mak, 2003). Consequently, in this case the main role of corporate governance would be to align the interests of strong private shareholders and weak minority shareholders rather than to align the interests of managers and owners (Mavrommati, 2008).

Furthermore, Gray's (1988) accounting sub-cultural model, institutional isomorphism, agency theory and cost-benefit analysis suggest the following: a) the secretive culture causes private shareholders to encourage management to minimise disclosure to preserve trade secrets and company strategic plans, b) the lack of awareness among management and BOD members of listed companies regarding the importance of compliance with IFRSs and of following best corporate governance practices to enhance transparency, c) the weak enforcement of laws and regulations, and d) low demand for improved disclosures due to private shareholders' direct access to company information and insignificant voting pressures from small shareholders. These outcomes cause non-compliance costs to be less then compliance costs, and hence management is not encouraged to improve disclosure levels, and the decoupling problem is enhanced, companies claiming they are applying IFRSs whereas full compliance is actually absent.

In contrast, agency theory may also propose that when private ownership is dominant, the owner is able to monitor and influence management performance by personally sitting on the BOD to protect the

economic stakes (Shleifer and Vishny, 1997; Li and Harrison, 2008), thereby improving management compliance with IFRSs.
Similar to government ownership, no consensus exists among researchers regarding the influence of private ownership on compliance levels with financial disclosure requirements. Some researchers report private ownership to be complementary (improving IFRSs compliance levels) as substantial shareholding by block investors (*e.g.,* private shareholders) may result in more disclosure in order to reduce information asymmetry (Diamond and Verrecchia, 1991; Haniffa and Cooke, 2002). On the contrary, Naser et al. (2006) report that concentrated ownership and financial disclosure are substitutes (dominance of private shareholders reduces levels of financial disclosure) while yet other scholars find no association between these two variables (Suwaidan, 1997; Depoers, 2000; Omar, 2007). On the level of scrutinised stock exchanges, this issue has been examined in Egypt by Samaha and Dahawy (2010, 2011) who report a negative association. However in Jordan Suwaidan (1997), Omar (2007) and Al-Akra et al. (2010a,b) do not find any association. Accordingly, research hypothesis 5c can be stated as follows:

H5c There is no significant statistical relationship between the private ownership ratio and the extent of compliance with IFRSs disclosure requirements. This hypothesis can be further divided into the following two hypotheses.
H5c1 There is no significant statistical relationship between the private ownership ratio and the extent of compliance with IFRSs disclosure requirements in the Egyptian context.
H5c2 There is no significant statistical relationship between the private ownership ratio and the extent of compliance with IFRSs disclosure requirements in the Jordanian context.

Public Ownership

Agency theory suggests that the dominance of public ownership effectively separates ownership from the control of corporate decisions (Fama and Jensen, 1983; Li and Harrison, 2008). Public shareholders delegate internal control to the BOD which then delegates decision-making to management (Li and Harrison, 2008).

Researchers argue that the dominance of public ownership improves levels of financial disclosure in order to solve the conflict of interest between managers and shareholders. As public investors lack first-hand access to information, management needs to disclose more information to prove it is acting in the best interests of shareholders (McKinnon and

Dalimunthe, 1993; Gelb, 2000; Arcay and Vazquez, 2005). Consequently, it is expected that levels of compliance will be higher in companies with dominant public ownership. However, Gray's (1988) accounting sub-cultural model, institutional isomorphism and cost-benefit analysis argue the opposite because: a) the secretive culture in the studied stock exchanges causes management to avoid outflow of stock market price-sensitive information, b) secrecy is also associated with large power distance and a preference for collectivism, c) the lack of awareness among management and the BOD of listed companies regarding the importance of compliance and following corporate governance best practices to enhance transparency, d) weak enforcement of laws and regulations, e) low demand for improved disclosures due to the lack of awareness among public investors in developing capital markets including the scrutinised stock exchanges regarding their right to ask for more disclosures, f) the absence of independent board members with the primary responsibility of protecting public shareholders' rights, and g) public shareholders in the MENA region do not exercise their rights. In addition, based on agency theory low monitoring costs will not encourage management to improve compliance with IFRSs. Consequently, all these factors cause non-compliance costs to be less than compliance costs and hence, motivate management to minimise disclosure, whilst simultaneously contributing to the decoupling problem.

The results of most prior studies show a positive association between public ownership and levels of financial disclosure (*e.g.,* Haniffa, 1999; Haniffa and Cooke, 2002; Arcay and Vazquez, 2005). In Egypt this issue was investigated with respect to voluntary disclosures by Ezat and El-Masry (2008) who report a significant positive relationship. However in Jordan although Al-Akra et al. (2010b) results support the existence of a significant negative association and Al-Htaybat (2005) supports the existence of a significant positive relationship, Naser et al. (2002) and Al-Akra et al. (2010a) findings do not support the existence of association between public ownership ratio and the levels of compliance with IFRSs. Accordingly, research hypothesis 5d can be stated as follows:

H5d There is no significant statistical relationship between the public ownership ratio and the extent of compliance with IFRSs disclosure requirements. This hypothesis can be further divided into the following two hypotheses.

H5d1 There is no significant statistical relationship between the public ownership ratio and the extent of compliance with IFRSs disclosure requirements in the Egyptian context.

H5d2 There is no significant statistical relationship between the public ownership ratio and the extent of compliance with IFRSs disclosure requirements in the Jordanian context.

5.3.3 Control Variables

The review of financial disclosure studies (Appendix A) particularly those conducted in Egypt and Jordan (*e.g.,* Naser et al., 2002; Abd-Elsalam and Weetman, 2003; Omar, 2007; Samaha and Stapleton, 2009; Al-Akra et al., 2010a,b; Samaha and Dahawy, 2010, 2011), as well as the availability of data, led to the decision to incorporate the following firm-specific characteristics in the multivariate analysis as control variables: company size, profitability, gearing, liquidity, type of business activity, and type of audit firm.

Company Size

Several studies have used company size as an explanatory variable for financial disclosure on the ground that larger companies are more likely to disclose a greater number of items than smaller ones (*e.g.,* Haniffa and Cooke, 2002; Naser et al., 2002; Eng and Mak, 2003; Ali et al., 2004; Ghazali, 2004; Alsaeed, 2005; Akhtaruddin, 2005; Aksu and Kosedag, 2006; Barako et al., 2006; Omar, 2007; Samaha and Stapleton, 2009). Referring to political cost theory, many researchers argue that large companies are more likely to provide more disclosure and to comply with mandatory disclosure requirements as they may be more subject to public scrutiny or more sensitive to criticism for falling short of disclosure requirements compared to small firms (Singhvi, 1968; Singhvi and Desai, 1971; Buzby, 1975; Firth, 1979; Abd-Elsalam, 1999; Al-Htaybat, 2005).

Referring to agency theory, many researchers propose that large companies are more likely to disclose more information because of large numbers of shareholders and the associated pressures (*e.g.,* Hossain et al., 1995; Meek et al., 1995; Al-Mulhem, 1997; Abd-Elsalam, 1999; Ali et al., 2004; Al-Htaybat, 2005; Omar, 2007).

Also, using capital need theory, many researchers claim that larger companies are more likely to disclose more information in order to raise funds at lower costs (*e.g.,* Cooke, 1991; Meek et al., 1995; Abd-Elsalam, 1999; Ali et al., 2004; Al-Htaybat, 2005; Omar, 2007).

Furthermore, using cost-benefit analysis, many researchers argue that large firms are more likely to disclose more information because for them, the costs of non-compliance are higher than the costs of compliance. Also, large companies are more likely to disclose more information because of lower costs associated with collecting and publishing information and limited impact on the competitive position compared to small companies (*e.g.,* Singhvi, 1968; Singhvi and Desai, 1971; Buzby, 1975; Firth, 1979; Ahmed and Nicholls, 1994; Abd-Elsalam, 1999; Ali et al., 2004; Al-Htaybat, 2005).

Abd-Elsalam (1999, p.43) summarises the possible impacts of company size as a determinant of disclosure levels, claiming it to be *"a comprehensive variable which can proxy a number of corporate attributes such as competitive advantage, information productive costs and political costs. In other words, it is a reflection of agency theory (e.g., large number of shareholders and debt-holders), capital need theory (more likely to collect capital from outsiders) and political costs (in the public eye)"*.

Most previous research investigating the association between company size and levels of financial disclosure, has revealed a positive correlation (*e.g.,* Inchausti, 1997; Depoers, 2000; Haniffa and Cooke, 2002; Eng and Mak, 2003; Akhtaruddin, 2005; Naser et al., 2006). Consequently, company size is adopted in this study as a control variable, being expected to demonstrate a positive relationship with compliance levels.

Company Profitability

Many previous studies have used company profitability as an explanatory variable (*e.g.,* Wallace and Naser, 1995; Meek et al., 1995; Patton and Zelenka, 1997; Inchausti, 1997; Naser, 1998; Naser et al., 2002; Haniffa and Cooke, 2002; Al-Htaybat, 2005; Omar, 2007), on the grounds that agency theory suggests that the separation between ownership and control raises the need for investors to monitor management performance to ensure their interests are protected (Al-Htaybat, 2005). In this regard, Lang and Lundholm (1993) argue that disclosures are likely to relate to a firm's profitability, only if perceived information asymmetry between managers and investors is high.

Based on signaling theory, Wallace and Naser (1995); Abd-Elsalam (1999) and Al-Htaybat (2005) suggest that highly profitable firms are more likely to signal their superior performance to the market by disclosing greater information in their annual reports. This viewpoint is shared by other researchers, such as Singhvi and Desai (1971) who argue that managers are incentivised to disclose more information when a company's profit is higher than the average for the industry, as this will enhance public confidence in its continuity, and thus lead to an increase in management compensation.

Another explanation based on political cost theory is provided by Inchausti (1997) who argues that managements of companies with high profits are motivated to disclose more in order to justify these profits.

Evidence relating to the association between firm profitability and levels of financial disclosure is mixed. Some studies report a positive association between these variables (*e.g.,* Singhvi, 1968; Singhvi and Desai, 1971; Raffournier, 1995; Akhtaruddin, 2005; Aksu and Kosedag, 2006), while others report a significant negative association between them (*e.g.,* Belkaoui and Kahl, 1978; Wallace and Naser, 1995). Consequently, company profitability is employed as a control variable in this study, however the direction of the relationship between the two variables is unpredictable.

Company Liquidity

Liquidity is used as a proxy for the company's ability to meet its short term debts without selling its long term assets. It is used by investors, regulators and creditors to evaluate the ability of the company to continue as a going concern (Omar, 2007). Consequently, management will disclose more information about company ability to meet debts and continue as a going concern to alleviate any doubts in this regard by investors and creditors (Wallace and Naser, 1995; Omar, 2007).

Abd-Elsalam (1999) suggests that according to signaling theory, firms with a high liquidity ratio are expected to disclose more information in order to be differentiated from other companies with a lower liquidity ratio. However, according to agency theory, firms with a low percentage of liquidity tend to disclose more information in order to reduce the conflict between shareholders and creditors (Abd-Elsalam, 1999).

Evidence from prior research on this issue is mixed. Belkaoui and Kahl (1978) report a positive relationship between liquidity and disclosure in Canadian firms, explaining this in terms of signaling theory. In contrast, Wallace et al. (1994) and Naser et al. (2002) find a negative relationship, accounting for this using agency theory. Consequently, liquidity is used in this study as a control variable, recognising that the direction of the relationship between company liquidity and compliance levels is unpredictable.

Company Gearing

Gearing or leverage is one of the company characteristics used in previous empirical financial disclosure studies. Referring to agency theory, Jensen and Meckling (1976) proposed that highly leveraged firms would disclose more information in order to reduce monitoring costs. Malone et al. (1993)

argue that a high leverage ratio may cause managers to disclose more information to meet lenders' requirements; however, when the leverage ratio is low managers are more concerned with disclosing information to meet shareholders' needs. Within the same context, and in line with agency theory, Abd-Elsalam (1999) argues that more disclosure occurs when a company is highly leveraged so as to reduce agency costs. However, Zarzeski (1996) argues that companies with high debt ratios share more private information with their creditors, and thus, the need for detailed disclosure is diminished as creditors already have direct access to information. Also, Eng and Mak (2003) highlight a negative association between leverage and levels of financial disclosure, and that the agency costs of debt are controlled through restrictive debt covenants in debt agreements rather than increased disclosure of information in annual reports.

Evidence regarding the association between gearing and level of financial disclosure is mixed. Some studies report a positive relationship (*e.g.,* Schipper, 1981; Chow and Wong-Boren, 1987; Malone et al., 1993; Wallace et al., 1994; Hossain et al., 1995; Naser, 1998; Naser et al., 2002; Barako et al., 2006), whilst others find a negative relationship (*e.g.,* Zarzeski, 1996; El-Gazzar et al., 1999; Eng and Mak, 2003). Consequently, gearing is employed in this study as a control variable, recognising that the direction of the relationship between the two variables is unpredictable.

Type of Business Activity

The association between industry type and levels of financial disclosure has been empirically examined by several researchers (*e.g.,* Stanga, 1976; Belkaoui and Kahl, 1978; McNally et al., 1982; Wallace, 1987; Cooke, 1989a,b, 1991, 1992; Wallace et al., 1994; Abd-Elsalam, 1999; Haniffa and Cooke, 2002; Al-Htaybat, 2005; Omar, 2007; Al-Akra et al., 2010a,b; Ismail et al., 2010). The use of this variable in such research is based on the assumption that levels of financial disclosure differ among industries. Within the same context, Meek et al. (1995) propose that proprietary costs vary across industries for several reasons such as the differences in the nature of their products, and their research and development. They give an example of chemical companies which are more sensitive about disclosure to competitors and the public than companies in other industries. This viewpoint is supported by Inchausti (1997) who argues that industry type affects the culture of financial reporting within companies, which is why firms belonging to particular industries may disclose more information than required. Abd-Elsalam (1999) also claims that companies prefer to adopt the same disclosure policies adopted by others from the same industry, fearing that anything different might be interpreted as bad news by the market. Furthermore, some businesses such as banks may disclose more information due to political pressures (Craig and Diga, 1998). The domination effect is also used to explain disparities in disclosure practices among companies as the dominant companies are considered as role models by other companies, and are hence expected to influence the disclosure policies by their followers (Cooke, 1989b; Suwaidan, 1997). Additional reasons are differences in accounting policies and systems among different industries and social responsibility (Suwaidan, 1997). Finally, companies with diversified activities are expected to disseminate more information compared to un-diversified ones (Craig and Diga, 1998).

Stanga (1976) was the first to investigate the relationship between type of business activity and levels of financial disclosure (Vlachos, 2001). Based on the evidence provided by prior research that the former influences the latter (*e.g.,* Stanga, 1976; Belkaoui and Kahl, 1978; Cooke, 1989a,b, 1991, 1992; Haniffa and Cooke, 2002), type of business activity is employed in this study as a control variable.

Type of Audit Firm

The type of auditor has previously been used as an explanatory variable for financial disclosure practices (*e.g.,* Singhvi and Desai, 1971; Firth, 1979; Malone et al., 1993; Meek et al., 1995; Inchausti, 1997; Patton and Zelenka, 1997; Dumontier and Raffournier, 1998; Haniffa and Cooke, 2002; Glaum and Street, 2003; Al-Htaybat, 2005; Abdelsalam and Weetman, 2007; Omar, 2007; Samaha and Stapleton, 2009; Ismail et al., 2010) on the grounds that a large, highly reputable audit firm will insist on its clients disclosing more information and complying with financial disclosure regulations (Firth, 1979; Malone et al., 1993; Ahmed and Nicholls, 1994; Inchausti, 1997; Dumontier and Raffournier, 1998; Street and Bryant, 2000; Abdelsalam and Weetman, 2007). Additionally, large audit firms are more likely to associate themselves with clients who disclose more (Ahmed and Nicholls, 1994; Ali et al., 2004), possibly using the amount of disclosure as an indicator of those clients' audit quality (Ahmed and Nicholls, 1994; Abd-Elsalam, 1999; Omar, 2007). Owusu-Ansah (1998b) argues that large audit firms have many clients thus their economic dependence on a certain client is less than in small audit firms, and are thus more likely to report misstatements. Additionally, they act to preserve their reputation since any damage to that will result in a loss to their customers or demands to reduce their fees. Moreover, their exposure to legal liability is greater as investors are more likely to depend on the annual reports audited by large firms.

Wallace et al. (1994) argue that international audit firms have more influence on financial disclosure practices than local audit firms because international audit firms are larger and possess more auditing expertise. Furthermore, international audit firms' staff are usually highly qualified and more familiar with IASs and practices compared to their counterparts in local audit firms. This viewpoint is supported by Dumontier and Raffournier (1998) and Joshi et al. (2008) who argue that large (big 4) audit firms have greater ability than small (non-big 4) ones to apply IASs/IFRSs as they have the required experience and the economic resources.

In line with signaling theory, Hossain et al. (1995) argue that the choice of external auditor can be used as a signal of firm value. Furthermore, in line with agency theory, the use of a large audit firm to monitor disclosure practices helps to reduce agency costs by alleviating the conflict of interest between managers and owners (Hossain et al., 1994; Wallace and Naser, 1995; Naser, 1998; Naser et al., 2002; Ali et al., 2004; Al-Htaybat, 2005; Anderson and Daoud, 2005; Barako et al., 2006; Omar, 2007).

Based on the existing evidence of a relationship between the type of auditor and levels of company disclosure (*e.g.,* Singhvi and Desai, 1971; Ahmed and Nicholls, 1994; Raffournier, 1995; Wallace and Naser, 1995; Inchausti, 1997; Patton and Zelenka, 1997; Suwaidan, 1997; Naser et al., 2002; Al-Shiab, 2003; Glaum and Street, 2003; Samaha and Stapleton, 2009), type of auditor is employed in this study as a control variable, it being expected that auditing by a big 4 audit firm positively impacts on levels of compliance with IFRSs.

5.3.4 Independent Variables and their Operationalisation

The selection of the independent variables to be employed in this study and their proxies is guided by an extensive review of prior research[1]. Additionally, the choice of the independent variables is influenced by the nature of the business environment in Egypt and Jordan as indicated in Chapters Three and Four.

---

[1] For more details see, parts: 2.5.3 Financial Disclosure Theories and Explanatory Variables, 3.5 Board Characteristics, 3.6 Ownership Structure, 5.3 Research Hypotheses and the Summary of empirical financial disclosure studies presented in Appendix A.

Test Variables:

1. Country (1 if Jordan, 0 if Egypt).
2. BOD Independence (Proxied by the proportion of independent directors to total number of directors on the board).
3. Board Leadership (1 if the Chairman is not the CEO, 0 if the Chairman is the CEO).
4. Board size (Proxied by the total number of directors on the board).
5. Government Ownership ratio (Proxied by the percentage of company shares owned by the government).
6. Management Ownership ratio (Proxied by the percentage of company shares owned by company management).
7. Private Ownership (Proxied by the percentage of company shares owned by private shareholders).
8. Public Ownership (Proxied by the percentage of company shares owned by the free float[2]).

Control Variables:

1. Size of the company (Proxied by total assets).
2. Profitability of the company (Proxied by return on assets [ROA]).
3. Gearing (Proxied by debt to equity).
4. Liquidity (Proxied by quick ratio[3]).
5. Type of business (1 if non-manufacturing; 0 if manufacturing).
6. Type of audit firm (1 if not a big 4, 0 if a big 4).

The independent variables include four dummy (categorical) variables (board leadership, type of business activity, type of audit firm, and country name) and the remaining variables are continuous. Furthermore, the majority of independent variables cannot be measured directly, and are thus measured by proxying them (board independence, government ownership, management ownership, private ownership, public ownership, company size, profitability, gearing and liquidity).

[2] Any party owning less than 5% of company shares.
[3] Quick Ratio= current Assets-Inventories/Current Liabilities.

5.4 Research Design and Methodology

Research methodology can broadly be defined as the overall research approach, beginning with the development of the theoretical foundation and ending with the collection and analysis of data (Collis and Hussey, 2003). Baker and Foy (2008) state that in academic disciplines, research worthiness is assessed based on the amount it advances knowledge, clarifies or adds to a theory and stimulates further investigation. Crotty (2007, p.3) defines research methodology as *"the strategy, plan of action, process or design lying behind the choice and the use of particular methods and linking the choice and use of methods to the desired outcomes"*.

Discussion of research methodology is not complete without some consideration of ontology and epistemology which represent essential methodological issues. Epistemology or the theory of knowledge is defined by Crotty (2007, p.3) as *"a way of understanding and explaining how we know what we know"*. He argues that it is embedded in the theoretical perspective and thereby, in the methodology. Baker and Foy (2008, p.41) refer to epistemology as *"what is regarded as acceptable knowledge in a discipline"*. In addition, Gill and Johnson (1997) argue that our epistemological commitment influences the way we ask a particular question, the assessment of the relevance and the value of different research methodologies to investigate research question(s), and how we evaluate research output. On the other hand, ontology represents another important concept that is highly correlated with epistemology. Baker and Foy (2008, p.41) refer to ontology as *"the theory concerning the nature of social entities"*, arguing that different research approaches relate to different philosophical assumptions about ontology and epistemology. Walliman (2006) supports this viewpoint and considers epistemology and ontology as affecting the theoretical basis of how the world is experienced, what constitutes knowledge and what can be done with that knowledge. Consequently, the epistemological and ontological outlook will both influence the interpretation and understanding of research findings.

Figure 5.1 summarises the study's design and methodology, which aims to secure the objectives, and enhance the understanding and interpretations of the empirical findings.

The ten stages in Figure 5.1 are self-explanatory, culminating in the generation of results from which inferences can be made.

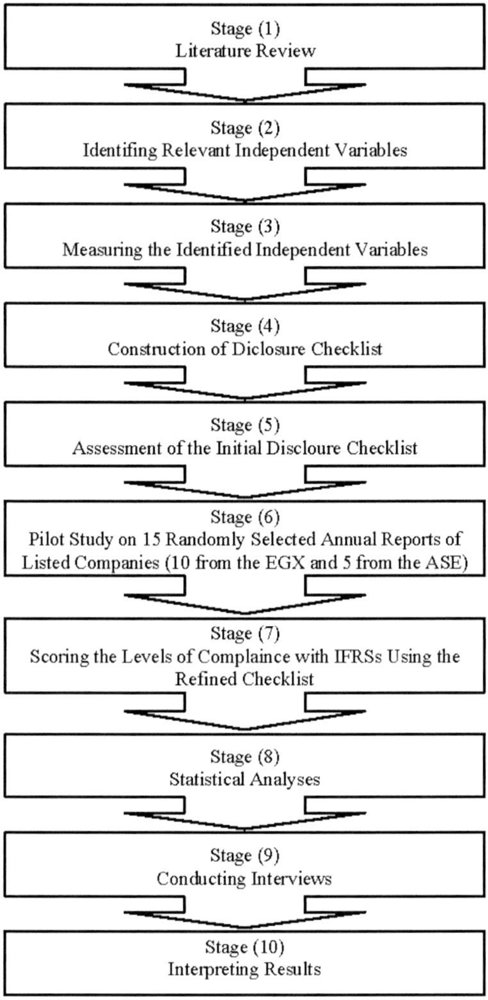

Figure 5.1 Research Design and Methodology

5.5 Research Methods

Crotty (2007, p.30) defines research methods as *"the techniques or procedures used to gather and analyse data related to some research questions or hypotheses"*. They may be quantitative or qualitative, distinguished by the latter collecting data that is mainly in the form of words (opinions, feelings, perceptions, etc) rather than numbers as in quantitative research (Punch, 1998; Walliman, 2006; Neuman, 2006). Quantitative research methods are more unidimensional, less variable and more easily replicable than qualitative research methods (Punch, 1998). The most important advantage of quantitative data is that it enables standardised objective comparisons, whilst the greatest advantage of qualitative methods is flexibility, meaning they are useful in a wider range of research (Punch, 1998). However, both can be complementary (Neuman, 2006). To gain the benefits of each, this study employs both methods, although as the objectives are related to measuring compliance with IFRSs disclosure requirements and its relationship with corporate governance structures, quantitative research methods dominate.

In this study, quantitative research methods are employed through the construction of a disclosure index, scoring compliance levels, developing and testing research hypotheses, and statistically analysing and interpreting the results. On the other hand, in order to improve the interpretation of the empirical findings, semi-structured interviews (qualitative method) are undertaken with parties involved in educating, practising or enforcing the adoption of IFRSs by companies listed on the scrutinised exchanges, and with some individual (naive) investors trading on them. The use of interviews to support the explanation and interpretation of the findings of the primary quantitative method (disclosure index) is classified under sequential explanatory design (Creswell, 2003). This design comprises the collection and analysis of both quantitative and qualitative data, and their final integration in the interpretation of the study findings (Creswell, 2003).

A multi-method strategy (triangulation) combining quantitative (disclosure index) and qualitative (interviews) methods, using primary (interview findings) and secondary (annual reports) data has the advantage of supporting or clarifying results (Saunders et al., 2003; Ghazali, 2004). Moreover, it helps to increase the scope, depth and power of research (Punch, 1998), and to the best of the researcher's knowledge this study is one of the first comparative studies combining both methods to investigate compliance with IFRSs in the MENA region. Hence, it is expected to provide a deeper understanding of this issue in this particular context.

5.5.1 The Disclosure Index

Disclosure refers to any information released by a specific company (Hope, 2003). Wallace (1987) observes that financial disclosure is an abstract concept which cannot be measured directly because it does not possess those characteristics by which one can determine its intensity or quality. In their review of different published approaches to the analysis of narratives in annual reports, Beattie et al. (2004) indicate the disclosure index as among the most commonly used. Hossain et al. (1995) note that a disclosure index can be employed as a proxy for the extent of information disclosed by firms, and Wallace (1988, p.450) defines such an instrument as *"a measure by which the level of financial reporting of one company can be compared with another. It can also be used to measure the degree of disclosure of an item of information by enterprises within a country and is the ratio of actual scores awarded to the company and the scores which that company is expected to earn"*.

Marston and Shrives (1991) note the varying functions of a disclosure index, mentioning its use in determining the extent of disclosure among different companies, measuring the degree of compliance with regulations, and measuring the level of voluntary disclosure.

A disclosure index is used in this study for several reasons. Firstly, it is the most frequently used instrument in financial disclosure research (*e.g.,* Cerf, 1961; Singhvi and Desai, 1971; Buzby, 1974; Stanga, 1976; Firth, 1979; Cooke, 1998; Haniffa and Cooke, 2002; Abdelsalam and Weetman, 2007; Al-Shammari et al., 2008; Samaha and Stapleton, 2008, 2009; Al-Akra et al., 2010a,b). Secondly, it provides a single figure summary indicator of the entire contents of the annual reports of comparable firms, hence it captures differences between financial reporting practices of those firms (Marston and Shrives, 1991; Hossain et al., 1995). Thirdly, it is a tool capable of exploring the nature and the extent of disclosure as well as it facilitates an objective and easy operationalisation of the extent of disclosure (Marston and Shrives, 1991; Omar, 2007).

The extensive review of financial disclosure studies indicates that no one commonly-used set of disclosure indices exists, this being influenced by the research purpose(s), design and context. Hence, the chosen indices depend on the researcher's judgment in the light of the characteristics of the financial market(s) under scrutiny.

Disclosure Items

The choice of the type and number of information items to be included in the disclosure index is an important consideration in its construction. There is no theory governing the choice of items, and hence, these vary in different studies (Wallace, 1988; Wallace and Naser, 1995). Some researchers have constructed disclosure checklists based on the needs of a specific user group such as financial analysts or managers (*e.g.,* Buzby, 1975; Chow and Wong-Boren, 1987; Malone et al., 1993), but the majority have chosen to develop disclosure checklists which are not based on the needs of a specific user group (*e.g.,* Hossain et al., 1994, 1995; Al-Mulhem, 1997; Suwaidan, 1997; Abd-Elsalam, 1999; Haniffa and Cooke, 2002) and this study follows that practice.

To meet this study's objectives, the researcher uses a self-constructed checklist of 275 mandatory disclosure items, based on the IFRSs required to be followed by the IASB in preparing financial statements for the fiscal year beginning January 2007. Although the use of an existing disclosure checklist enables comparability with prior research as indicated by Marston and Shrives (1991), the extensive review of prior research that concerned with Egypt and Jordan (*e.g.,* Abd-Elsalam, 1999; Al-Htaybat, 2005; Dahawy and Conover, 2007; Omar, 2007; Samaha and Stapleton, 2008, 2009; Dahawy, 2009; Al-Akra et al., 2010a; Ismail et al., 2010) promulgates the non-existence of a checklist that is relevant to the IFRSs for the year 2007. Furthermore, objective comparison between the EGX and ASE necessitates the development of an appropriate disclosure checklist that takes into consideration the nature of both contexts.

The initial disclosure index consisted of 539 items of information, which were subsequently refined through the following series of steps:

Firstly, the disclosure index was checked against the dominant laws and regulations in Egypt and Jordan to evaluate its potential applicability to companies operating in manufacturing and non-manufacturing sectors on the scrutinised stock exchanges[4]. A number of IFRSs were then excluded, being inconsistent with the requirements of the national regulations governing their matter in the two countries. Exclusions were: IAS 12:Income Taxes, IAS 17:Leases, IAS 19:Employee Benefits, and IAS 26:Accounting and Reporting by Retirement Benefit Plans. Additionally, IAS 29:Financial Reporting in Hyper Inflationary Economies was excluded due to its irrelevance to the nature of the economies of Egypt and Jordan, and IAS 34:Interim Financial Reporting was excluded as it is beyond the scope of this study. This step resulted in reducing the number of items to 474.

Secondly, To make sure that the checklist items reflect the reporting trend of investigated companies and to enable more objective comparison of compliance behaviour between scrutinised countries and among companies, following the recommendations of prior researchers (*e.g.,*

[4] When a requirement of IFRSs contradicts with the requirements of national laws, companies must follow the requirements of national laws.

Cooke and Wallace, 1989; Marston and Shrives, 1991; Haniffa, 1999; Ghazali, 2004), the disclosure index was checked against a sample of the annual reports of listed companies for the fiscal year ending 31 December, 2007. This enabled the researcher to determine the potential applicability and relevance of the disclosure index items to the accounting practices that are common among listed non-financial companies on the EGX and ASE. Based on this review, some IFRSs which were not observed in the annual reports of the piloted companies were excluded. These IFRSs are IFRS 2:Share Based Payment, IAS 10:Events after the Balance Sheet Date, IAS 20:Accounting for Government Grants and Disclosure of Government Assistance, IAS 32:Financial Instruments Presentation, and IAS 40:Agriculture. The scoring of the remaining annual reports confirmed that the excluded IFRSs do not reflect the reporting trend in investigated stock exchanges as they were not recognised in scrutinised companies.

Thirdly, to avoid the problem of duplication of an information item in the event of it being required by more than one standard, a careful review of the information items was made to ensure that the most comprehensive requirement was the one selected and that no information items were repeated.

Fourthly, a draft of the refined checklist was further reviewed by two Accounting Staff members; one from Egypt and the other from Jordan, the researcher's first supervisor, an auditor in the KPMG auditing firm, and an expert in financial reporting practices in the MENA region to verify its validity and make sure that the checklist items are clear, well presented and accurately reflect the requirements of the IFRSs.

The final disclosure checklist includes 275 items (see Appendix B), being divided into 20 sub-indices. The first sub-index demonstrates IFRS 3:Business Combinations which to the best of the researcher's knowledge is investigated for the first time in the MENA region. The remaining sub-indices demonstrate IAS 1:Presentation of Financial Statements, IAS 2: Inventories, IAS 7:Cash flow Statements, IAS 8:Accounting Policies, Changes in Accounting Estimates and Errors, IAS 11:Construction Contracts, IAS 14:Segment Reporting, IAS 16: Property, Plant and Equipment, IAS 18:Revenue, IAS 21:The Effects of Changes in Foreign Exchange Rates, IAS 23:Borrowing Costs, IAS 24:Related Party Transactions, IAS 27: Consolidated and Separate Financial Statements, IAS 28:Investments in Associates, IAS 31: Investment in Joint Ventures, IAS 33:Earnings per Share, IAS 36:Impairment of Assets, IAS 37:Provisions, Contingent Liabilities and Contingent Assets, IAS 38:Intangible Assets, and IAS 40: Investment Property.

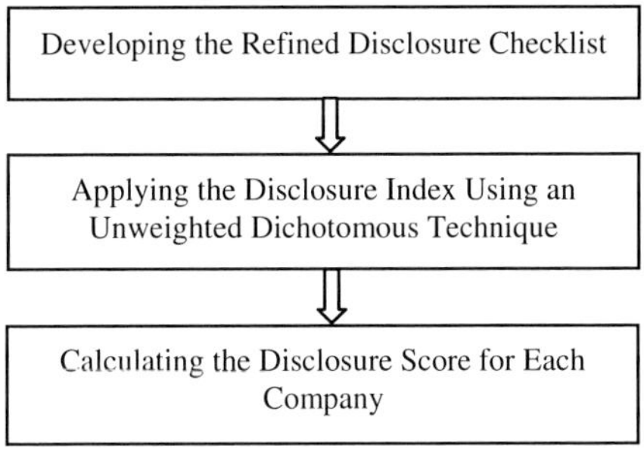

Figure 5.2 Scoring Disclosure Items

The organisation of the disclosure index by standard was driven by study's objectives, and its nature as a comparative study. In addition to enabling measurement of levels of compliance with overall mandatory IFRSs, this structure was expected to enable a clear and accurate measurement of the level of compliance with every single standard, and hence to improve the objectivity of the comparison across both the countries, and companies within the same country. Given that the majority of disclosure checklists used in existing literature are organised by topic, the design of the index in this study goes one step further.

Scoring and Weighting the Disclosure Items

The review of previous studies has revealed that the extent of disclosure can be assessed using either the weighted or unweighted approaches. Figure 5.2 demonstrates the steps followed by the researcher in order to assign scores to the population of non-financial companies listed on the stock exchanges of Egypt and Jordan.

Figure 5.2 shows that in scoring the corporate annual reports, the refined disclosure checklist was employed and then a dichotomous scale was applied (the disclosure item scored 1 if it was disclosed and 0 if it was not disclosed although the company had to disclose it). Finally, disclosure scores were calculated for submission to statistical analyses.

This method of scoring and weighting corporate annual reports is similar to that in previous studies (*e.g.,* Ahmed and Nicholls, 1994; Abd-Elsalam, 1999; Haniffa, 1999; Al-Htaybat, 2005; Omar, 2007), and justified by the nature of this study as it does not spotlight the information needs of any particular user group of such reports. It is assumed that each item is of equal importance, thereby removing the subjectivity involved in assigning weights to different information items when user preferences are known. Furthermore, prior research indicates that there might be no significant difference between the weighted and unweighted disclosure index especially when the index includes a large number of information items (Firth, 1980; Chow and Wong-Boren, 1987; Abraham, 2008). Also, a weighted approach might be misleading because the relative importance of each item may vary from company to company, industry to industry, and from time to time (Abd-Elsalam, 1999). The problem of inapplicable items across sectors has been reduced by excluding banks and financial institutions from the sample.

To avoid the problem of penalising a company for non-disclosure of an inapplicable information item, a careful review of the entire annual report was made before scoring it (Street and Bryant, 2000), thereby ensuring that any missing item was properly accounted for. Thus, if the item was not mentioned in the annual report and the auditor's report was unqualified and did not mention any issues relating to that item, it was assumed that the item was not applicable. Finally, the scores for information items were added to calculate the disclosure score for each company (Haniffa, 1999). Following Wallace (1988) the total disclosure index and sub-disclosure indices (for each standard) were calculated as the ratio of actual scores awarded to a company to the maximum score applicable to that company. This approach ensures that companies are not penalised for non-disclosure of an irrelevant item. The calculation of the disclosure index (dependent variable) for each company under this approach is as follows:

$$DI = ADS/MD$$

Where:
DI refers to the disclosure index ($0 \leq DI \leq 1$)
ADS refers to the actual disclosure score for a particular company
MD refers to the maximum disclosure score possible for that company (≤ 275items)

Reliability and Validity of Disclosure Scores

Wallace (1987) argues that financial disclosure is an abstract concept that cannot be measured directly, and that requires the particular scale adopted to quantify disclosure to specify the scoring procedure to provide evidence that the measures are valid and reliable. Sekaran (1992) refers to reliability and validity as two main criteria for testing the goodness of measures. Reliability refers to the ability of different people to code the same text in the same manner (Weber, 1990), whilst validity refers to the extent to which the variables generated from the classification procedure represent what the researcher intends it to present (Weber, 1990; Marston and Shrives, 1991). In a similar vein, Collis and Hussey, 2003 argue that reliability is concerned with the credibility of research findings which can be proved if those findings can be repeated, while validity is the extent to which the research findings accurately reflect the reality.

In order to improve reliability in this study, the procedures followed are stated in detail (Cooke and Wallace, 1989; Abd-Elsalam and Weetman, 2003). This is expected to facilitate replication of disclosure scores reported in this study by other researchers. All annual reports were read before scoring in order to be familiar with the nature of each company's activities and avoid penalties for inapplicable items. Additionally, following Owusu-Ansah (1998a), the reliability of the scoring instruments employed was further assessed by randomly selecting a sample of annual reports that were already scored by the researcher and asking another investigator (an academic staff member who performs audit work) to score them. Whereas differences in scores were found, they were minor ones, hence no significant differences in scores were evident.

With respect to validity, four types of validity (face validity, content validity, criterion validity and concurrent validity) are applicable to this study (Neuman, 2006).

1. Face validity, is applicable to this study by developing a disclosure index that can measure the extent of compliance with IFRSs disclosure requirements by companies listed on the scrutinised stock exchanges. This is achieved by following the steps discussed in sub-section 5.5.1 in order to refine the disclosure index employed in this study.
2. Content validity is also achieved by developing a disclosure index that can answer the research question that relates to the extent of compliance with IFRSs disclosure requirements by companies listed on the scrutinised stock exchanges. To develop a disclosure index that can capture all the aspects related to the levels of compliance with IFRSs disclosure requirements that are mandatory in Egypt and Jordan in 2007, the information items of the disclosure checklist were taken from the IFRSs issued by the IASB and are mandatory in both countries.
3. With respect to criterion validity which concerns with whether the disclosure index used some standards or criterion to measure the extent of disclosure accurately, the researcher achieved by taking the information items of the disclosure checklist from the IFRSs issued by the IASB, reviewing the disclosure index by academic and professional staff and by

following the principles of scoring that adopted in prior research. Furthermore, the disclosure index employed in this study can be used in future research to investigate the progress in levels of compliance with IFRSs disclosure requirements and whether it is affected by other independent variables after consideration to any changes in the disclosure requirements under each IFRS.

4. With respect to concurrent validity which concerns with whether the indicator (disclosure index) is associated with a preexisting valid indicator, the disclosure index employed in this study is based on IFRSs' disclosure requirements that are developed by the IASB and satisfies face validity as above mentioned.

5.5.2 Data Collection

The data were obtained from company annual reports (a secondary source) and interviews (a primary source). The use of companies' annual reports facilitates the gathering and checking of data by others at any time. There are two major advantages of using annual reports: firstly, the firm can exercise editorial control to prevent any possible journalistic interpretation or distortion of company information, and secondly, the report can be used for the purpose of comparison (Lavers, 1993; Naser et al., 2006). Although companies frequently disclose their information through other channels such as the media, interim financial statements, and preliminary announcements to the stock exchange, annual reports remain the most important mechanism, especially in developing markets (Abd-Elsalam and Weetman, 2003; Naser et al., 2006). Hence, the annual report is widely viewed as a major official and legal document produced by a company on a regular basis, and acts as a significant forum for the presentation of the firm's communication within political, social and economic systems (Gray et al., 1995; Naser et al., 2006). Consequently, the principal sources of data for this study are the annual reports of non-financial companies listed on the EGX and ASE.

After investigating the appropriate sources of data in the scrutinised stock exchanges at the time of commencing this research (2008), it was found that the Zawya database and the Egypt for Information Dissemination Company (EGID) were the best available options to secure the required data as listed companies consider such data as confidential, and refuse to provide any information when they are directly contacted. Consequently, annual reports and all of the information relating to corporate governance variables and other company characteristics were purchased separately from the information companies (Zawya and EGID) after providing an official claim stating that any information acquired would be used solely for research purposes[5]. Another obstacle was that the majority of annual reports were in Arabic, and the Arabic vocabulary used varies between the two countries. To eliminate potential problems arising from this situation, the researcher used her competent knowledge of Arabic language to conduct a very careful reading of the annual reports.

The extensive review of previous research (using panel data) on disclosure in MENA region countries shows that in general, disclosure practices improve over time (*e.g.*, Abd-Elsalam, 1999; Al-Htaybat, 2005; Hassan, 2006; Omar, 2007). This argument is further supported by the findings of a recent study on the Jordanian context, that demonstrate the great progress in compliance with IFRSs in 2004 compared to 1996 (Al-Akra et al., 2010a). In order to keep the investigation manageable, the study analysed the state of compliance in a single year, that being the fiscal year ending 31 December, 2007. This choice was supported for the following reasons. Firstly, this is the first recent year for which the majority of data required to undertake this comparative study is available, and thus the study avoids the problem of a smaller sample size due to the non-availability of data for more than one year. Secondly, as indicated in Chapter Four this year witnessed an extraordinary economic performance in scrutinised countries; that was before the international economic crunch that began in 2008. In addition, it was the first year to mandate the full version of IFRSs (except IAS 17: Accounting for Leases) in Egypt.

Study Population

The annual reports of the entire population of non-financial companies listed on the EGX and ASE (311 companies - 145 from Egypt, and 166 from Jordan) for the fiscal year ending 31 December, 2007, formed the study population. Institutions that provide financial services such as banks and insurance companies were excluded because their reports are not comparable with those of non-financial companies as they are subject to other disclosure requirements[6]. Then the following two criteria were applied:

---

[5] It is worthy to mention that since the second half of 2009, the ASE provides the annual reports for free on its website which signal its efforts to improve disclosures overtime.

[6] Currently the ASE classifies real estate companies under the Financial Sector instead of the Service Sector as it used to, although such companies do not provide financial services. The ASE attributes this change to the vision of the current

1. The firm should have a complete annual report for the year ended 31 December, 2007.
2. There should be information related to corporate governance structures within the company for the year 2007.

After the imposition of these criteria, the final sample contained 75 companies from Egypt and 91 companies from Jordan. Table 5.1 depicts the application of the above mentioned study sample selection criteria.

As indicated in table 5.1, to meet the first criterion 92 companies (17 listed on the EGX and 75 listed on the ASE) were excluded and to meet the second criterion an additional 53 companies listed on the EGX were excluded. To enable objective comparison between scrutinised stock exchanges an equal sample of 75 Jordanian listed companies was randomly selected[7].

Table 5.1 Study Sample

Criterion	Egypt	Jordan	Total
Number of Non-financial Listed Companies	145	166	311
Number of Companies Excluded Under the First Criterion	17	75	92
Number of Companies Excluded Under the Second Criterion	53	None	53
The Remainder	75	91	166
Final Sample	75	75	150

Interview Method

Interviews can be defined as a method of gathering information through verbal questioning (Sarantakos, 2005). Punch (1998) argues that interviews are very effective in exploring people's perceptions, meanings, definitions of situations and constructions of reality. Qualitative data such as interview findings can be employed to supplement, validate, explain or reinterpret quantitative data obtained from the same setting (Ghazali, 2004; Miles and Huberman, 1994).

Interviews are categorised in terms of their structure into three main types - structured, semi-structured, and unstructured. This study carried out face-to-face semi-structured in which questions to be asked and the detailed information to be gathered were all pre-determined, although the

management of the ASE. However, this is not the case for real estate companies that are listed on the EGX.

[7] Appendix C presents a list of the sample companies indicating their stock exchange and sector (manufacturing or non-manufacturing).

question sequence could vary according to the situation (Kvale, 1996). Semi-structured interviews are appropriate in studies investigating the relationships between variables as they allow 'why', 'what' and 'how' questions to be asked, thereby being more revelatory (Saunders et al., 2003; Ghazali, 2004). Such interviews were used in this study to obtain the views of different groups involved in enforcing, teaching, and adopting IFRSs in Egypt and Jordan concerning the different factors influencing *de facto* compliance with IFRSs. It was also believed that they would enable the researcher to estimate the degree of awareness among national investors regarding the level of disclosures that must be provided by companies listed on the stock exchanges of their jurisdictions, and the concept of corporate governance. Interviewees' views were expected to support the interpretation of the findings of the empirical analyses, and to facilitate the assessment of the applicability of the Western theoretical foundations to the MENA region emerging capital markets.

The interviews were conducted following the statistical analysis so that the researcher could build on the analysis and perform more informed and organised interviews. Also, given the secretive nature of the MENA societies and the sensitivity of the issue of this study, it was decided to undertake face-to-face interviews since these would be likely to reduce the reluctance of participants to be truthful. Easterby-Smith et al. (1993) and Ghazali (2004) recommend face-to-face interviews when the subject matter is highly confidential or commercially sensitive, or when the interviewee may be reticent about an issue. Additionally, they provide an opportunity for the interviewer to clarify the study's objectives and importance and to ensure that the interview questions are well understood by all participants.

The Interview Sample

The researcher planned to conduct 40 interviews (20 in Egypt and 20 in Jordan - four persons from each of the following groups in each jurisdiction):

Regulators (Disclosure Monitoring Staff at the CMA in Egypt and the JSC in Jordan) as they are responsible for enforcing and monitoring compliance with disclosure rules and regulations, and presumed to have significant influence on the levels of compliance with IFRSs by listed companies.

Financial Accounting professors at the Egyptian and the Jordanian Universities, as they are responsible for determining and teaching the content of IFRSs modules to undergraduates and postgraduates in accounting departments at their affiliates; and hence, play a vital role in enhancing familiarity with IFRSs requirements and their updates among their graduates.

Accountants at listed companies as they are responsible for preparing their companies' financial statements, and presumed to follow the requirements of IFRSs.

Naive Investors as they are among the primary users of listed companies' annual reports for rational investment decision-making, and should be aware of the minimum level of disclosures that must be made by listed companies in accordance with IFRSs as required by company laws, SL and corporate governance best practices. Furthermore, they should be aware of their rights to monitor and exert pressure on listed companies' BODs and managements to improve their disclosures.

Auditors from the big 4 international audit firms (KPMG, Pricewaterhouse Coopers, Deloitte and Touche, and Ernst and Young), as many of listed companies are audited by these firms and the staff in these firms have good knowledge and experience with IFRSs, and extensive training on any updates of these standards compared to auditors in local audit firms who may have limited experience and knowledge.

Despite the original intention, the researcher could only complete 12 interviews (60%) in Egypt, and 8 interviews (40%) in Jordan because it was difficult to persuade individuals to participate, possibly a reflection of the secretive nature of both societies and political conservatism. It was especially hard to secure participation from those in sensitive positions due to the unwillingness of some organisations to allow contact with their staff. None of the big 4 audit firms granted access, citing company policy which precludes participation in research. However, this did not affect the quality or the interpretive power of the interview data.

Regarding other groups of respondents, through networking and personal contacts, the researcher could persuade participants, especially in Egypt (the researcher's home country) to co-operate. The researcher applied a snowball sampling technique[8] to increase interviewee numbers. For instance, the chief of the

Disclosure Monitoring Department in the CMA facilitated meetings with other members from the CMA. The same happened in Jordan, where an officer at the JSC helped the researcher to contact another member of the JSC staff. Also, an academic staff member helped the researcher to contact two investors at the ASE and an accountant in one of the companies listed on the ASE.

---

[8] This implies that the researcher makes contact with one or two cases and then asks them to identify further cases (Saunders et al., 2003).

Table 5.2 Interviewees in Egypt

Respondent	Years of Experience	Qualification
Regulator (1)	3	Diploma in Financial Analysis
Regulator (2)	6	Bachelor's Degree in Law
Regulator (3)	2	Bachelor's Degree in Accounting
Regulator (4)	15	Bachelor's Degree in Accounting
Academic Staff (1)	10	PhD in Financial Accounting
Academic Staff (2)	22	PhD in Financial Accounting
Academic Staff (3)	15	PhD in Financial Accounting
Academic Staff (4)	20	PhD in Financial Accounting
Accountants (1)	7	Bachelor's Degree in Accounting
Accountants (2)	10	Bachelor's Degree in Accounting
Investor (1)	3	*Bachelor's Degree*
Investor (2)	4	*Bachelor's Degree*

Table 5.3 Interviewees in Jordan

Respondent	Years of Experience	Qualification
Regulator (1)	8	Master's Degree in Finance
Regulator (2)	3	Bachelor's Degree in Business and Banking Administration
Academic Staff (1)	6	PhD in Financial Accounting
Academic Staff (2)	13	PhD in Financial Accounting
Academic Staff (3)	6	PhD in Financial Accounting
Accountant (1)	12	Bachelor's Degree in Accounting
Investor (1)	5	*Bachelor's Degree*
Investor (2)	9	*PhD*

Before conducting any of the interviews, the researcher sent e-mails/letters to the potential interviewees explaining the purpose of the study and to obtain their permission (Appendix D). People who agreed to be interviewed were contacted by telephone to arrange a suitable time and to inform them of the themes to be covered during the interview to allow them to consider the information being requested. This procedure was very effective, for example respondents from the CMA prepared some supporting documentation to show to the researcher during the interview, in addition to providing certain publications that are under preparation as part of the CMA's efforts to improve disclosure practices in Egypt. Interviews were conducted between 21st September and mid-November, 2010. Tables 5.2 and 5.3 indicate the qualification and years of experience for each respondent in Egypt and Jordan respectively.

As indicated in Table 5.2, all interviewees held at least a university degree in a related subject. Of the four regulators, one had a Diploma in Financial Analysis, two had Bachelor's Degrees in Accounting and the fourth, a Bachelor's Degree in Law. It is recognised that some of the members at the CMA with responsibility for monitoring compliance with IFRSs are not qualified to do that task. Years of experience in that position for respondents from that group ranged from 2 to 15 years. All academic staff members were professors of Financial Accounting at the Egyptian universities, held PhD degrees in Financial Accounting, were responsible for preparing and teaching IFRSs courses to undergraduate and postgraduate students, and had long experience in that field ranging from 10 to 22 years. Accountants also had reasonable experience (7, 10 years respectively). Finally, it is recognised that respondents from the investor group had relatively limited experience in trading on the EGX (3, 4 years respectively).

As indicated in Table 5.3, all respondents from Jordan held at least a university degree in a related subject.

Similar to the CMA staff, not all members of the JSC staff with responsibility for monitoring compliance with IFRSs are qualified to do that job. The two respondents from the JSC staff had been in their positions for 8 and 3 years respectively. All academic staff members held a PhD in Financial Accounting at the Jordanian universities and were responsible for preparing and teaching accounting courses which include only an introduction to IFRSs. Their experience ranged from 6 to 13 years. The only accountant who agreed to participate had 12 years experience with IFRSs. Finally, respondents from the investor group had experience of trading on the ASE for 5 and 9 years respectively.

Ethical Considerations

Researchers should acknowledge ethical considerations when conducting social research, especially when using qualitative approaches, as these involve collecting data from people and about people. Issues to be managed relate to harm, consent, deception, privacy, and confidentiality of data (Punch, 1998). Furthermore, the researcher should consider ethical issues during data analysis by disassociating names from responses to protect the secrecy of the interviewees, and once the data is analysed, the researcher should discard it to ensure that it cannot be misused by a third party. Additionally, during interpretation, writing and dissemination of the final research report, the researcher should not use language or words that are biased because of gender, sexual orientation, racial or ethnic group, and findings should not be falsified or invented to meet the researcher's need (Creswell, 2003).

To meet the ethical requirements, the researcher adopted the abovementioned actions, in addition to following Aston University's ethical guidelines, which require researchers to express the title, aims and importance of a study in a language that is understandable to a lay person, and to use an invitational, rather than coercive or overly persuasive tone. Additionally, the researcher must explain how an individual was chosen to participate and how many other people will be asked to take part.

The researcher showed all interviewees a letter declaring her status as a PhD student at Aston Business School and that the interview was part of her research. She emphasised that all information obtained during the interviews would be regarded as confidential, used for research purposes only, and that the interviewee had the right to withdraw from the interview at any time, or to refuse to answer specific interview questions. The researcher respected the interviewees' preference not to be tape-recorded, and asked each interviewee to read the notes taken by the researcher during the interview to confirm they were a correct and full expression of their contribution. To guarantee confidentiality and anonymity the researcher offered to send an electronic copy of this work or any related publication to the interviewees as well as offering acknowledgment of their participation if they wished. All respondents except investors refused to sign the interviewee consent forms (Appendix E) because they did not want to reveal their identities.

5.6 Data Analysis

5.6.1 Quantitative Data Analysis

After calculating the disclosure indices (dependent variable), and summarising the independent variables in matching columns, the next step was to analyse the data. Haniffa (1999, p.319) notes that *"[t]he first step in data analysis is to get a feel of the data so that appropriate statistical methods can be undertaken"*. As indicated in the discussion in sub-section 2.5.4, existing research employs different statistical approaches to examine the relationship between the extent of disclosure and different company characteristics, in which respect Ghazali (2004, p.131) observes that *"[i]n analysing data, a decision has to be made regarding the appropriate statistical techniques"*.

Two types of statistical tests, parametric and non-parametric, exist. Field (2005, p.64) argues that normality of data distribution is the most important assumption to be met when applying parametric tests.

Collis and Hussey (2003) confirm this, highlighting that such tests are more powerful than non-parametric ones. However, Pallant (2001) observes that non-parametric statistical tests (distribution-free tests) can be employed when the data violates the assumptions of parametric analysis, and that they are appropriate when data is measured on nominal and ordinal scales and for small samples (Pallant, 2001).

Normality Test

Normal refers to a symmetrical bell shaped curve (Pallant, 2001). A wide range of approaches can be employed to test the normality of distribution of a given set of data such as plotting histograms, stem and leaf plotting, skewness and kurtosis, Kolmogorov-Smirnov and Shapiro-Wilk tests. In this study the Kolmorgorov-Smirnov (K-S) and Shapiro-Wilk tests were used to check the normality of all variables (dependent and independent).

Descriptive Analysis

One type of data analysis is descriptive analysis obtained by considering the mean, minimum, maximum, and standard deviation for the total disclosure score (the primary dependent variable) as well as for each IFRS/IAS (sub-index). Additionally, the study provides a descriptive analysis for all test and control variables to gain insight into the dominant corporate governance structures and corporate attributes in the Egyptian and Jordanian contexts.

Univariate Analysis

Univariate analysis demonstrates the relationship between the dependent and each of the independent variables. Since the distribution of the total disclosure index (dependent variable) and all of the continuous independent variables is not normal as shown by normality tests performed in Chapter Six, Spearman's rank correlation coefficient was mainly used to assess the association between continuous independent variables and the total disclosure index. Rank correlation is used to examine whether variables move together. In other words, whether high ranks of one variable are associated with high ranks of the other (positive correlation), whether low ranks of one variable are associated with high ranks of the other (negative correlation), or whether the ranks in the two variables are unrelated (not significant) (Abd-Elsalam, 1999).

For the categorical independent variables (board leadership, type of business activity, and type of audit firm), a non-parametric alternative using the Mann-Whitney U test was performed to test for differences in the median disclosure indices between the two groups. Additionally, the Mann-Whitney U test and Chi- square test were employed to test whether there are significant differences between the Egyptian and the Jordanian contexts (H1).

Multivariate Analysis

This study employs multiple regression in order to test mainly how well a set of corporate governance-related variables (board independence, board leadership, board size and ownership structure) is able to explain the dependent variable (total disclosure index) and which variable in the set of independent variables best explains compliance with IFRSs disclosure requirements in the focus contexts. The multiple regression model includes all of the independent variables (*i.e.,* all test and control variables) as is discussed in detail in Chapter Six.

Given that the dependent and independent variables were not normally distributed as is seen later in Chapter Six, the conventional Ordinary Least Square (OLS) method was not preferable. Consequently, non-parametric techniques appeared to be more appropriate for analysing the relationship between the dependent and independent variables. However, as non-parametric tests may fail to detect differences between groups (Pallant, 2001), the researcher used transformed data using normal scores which is an extension of rank regression to make the data distribution appears more normal.

Although the rank method yields distribution-free test statistics and may therefore be useful for data with non-linear relationships between independent and dependent variables, Cooke (1998) observes that it incorporates some weaknesses such as the difficulty of interpreting the regression coeffecients (□j) for most values. Also, the structure of errors cannot be normal and the transformation of individual observations into ranks is, to some extent, arbitrary.

To eliminate some of the weaknesses of rank regression, Cooke (1998) proposes the use of normal scores, in which approach, the transformed data are substituted by scores on normal distribution rather than ranks. Hence, significance levels would be more meaningful and have greater power than when using ranks, and the regression coefficients derived using normal scores would be meaningful.

Previous researchers (*e.g.,* Cooke, 1998; Haniffa and Cooke, 2002; Abd-Elsalam and Weetman, 2003; Ghazali, 2004; Al-Htaybat, 2005) have adopted the normal score transformation method. Following these, it was decided to gain the benefits of that approach. The transformation was made by dividing the normal distribution by the number of observations plus one region, on the basis that each region has equal probability. Then the regression analysis was conducted using the normal scores.

The multiple regression routines were tested using stepwise search on SPSS 16, allowing the researcher to see at what stage independent variables are incorporated into the regression equation, and their importance (Cooke, 1989a; Norusis, 1993).

Before running the multiple regression analysis, the researcher must check for any significant multicollinearity between the independent variables (Haniffa, 1999) as demonstrated in Chapter Six. Multicollinearity refers to the existence of a strong correlation between two or more independent variables in a regression model (Field, 2005). Field (2005) argues that the presence of multicollinearity represents a threat to multiple regressions. For instance, a good independent variable may be found to be statistically insignificant and be rejected from the model (Type II error) because of a collinearity problem (Field, 2005). If the independent variables are highly correlated then it would be difficult to know which variable is more important, as the regression model could include either one (Field, 2005).

Multicollinearity can be checked using two approaches. The first is based on screening the correlation matrix. The most commonly used cut-off point is 0.7 (Tabachnick and Fidell, 2001). This cut-off point is applied by many researchers in financial disclosure studies (*e.g.,* Wallace et al., 1994; Al-Mulhem, 1997; Suwaidan, 1997; Omar, 2007) who consider independent variables as having a problem of multicollinearity when their correlation is above 0.7. As will be seen in Chapter Six, the correlation matrix was conducted using the Spearman rank correlation.

The second way of checking for multicollinearity is by calculating the Variance Inflation Factor (VIF), which indicates whether a high correlation exists between independent variables. For all variables, if the VIF remains below 10 while running the regression models, the absence of a multicollinearity problem is confirmed. Moreover, tolerance, which is the reciprocal (1/VIF), should be above 0.2 (Field, 2005). As Chapter Six confirms, the VIF for all variables remained below 10 and tolerances were found to be above 0.2 while running the regression models; thus, the problem of multicollinearity was not detected.

5.6.2 Qualitative Data Analysis

Unlike quantitative data, qualitative data is rarely subjected to statistical testing, and instead, the analysis process mainly involves making sense out of text (the words of the participants) (Creswell, 2003; Neuman, 2006).

The approaches commonly used in qualitative data analysis (*e.g.,* coding, memoing, content analysis and grounded theory) are more diverse and less standardised compared to those associated with quantitative data analysis.

As the purpose of the interviews in this study is interpretive, the researcher decided to apply coding as this provides clear and simple procedures to manage, analyse and generate the results from qualitative data (Omar, 2007). Coding can be used as an index and as a basis for storing and retrieving qualitative data (Punch, 1998). Rubin and Rubin (1995) state that it is the process of grouping interviewees' responses into categories that bring together similar ideas, concepts or themes.

Coding can be done using software programs such as Nvivo or manually. In this study the researcher decided to use a manual method as the number of interviews and the interview material were manageable. Also, as qualitative data analysis depends mainly on deep understanding of data by the researcher and as software programs do not analyse qualitative data in depth, it was decided that the use of software was inappropriate.

In analysing the interview data, the researcher followed the undermentioned steps suggested by Collis and Hussey (2003), as being necessary for the analysis of qualitative data:

1. All interviews were transcribed into English after ascertaining the validity of the English translation by a linguistic specialist. The researcher then added her thoughts and reflections in a separate field (column) to help with the tentative analysis.
2. The material collected from interviews was properly referenced to indicate who was involved, the date, and the time of the interview.
3. A code was allocated to each identified theme. This helped in storing, retrieving and reorganising the data in a variety of ways.
4. The codes were reviewed and grouped into smaller categories according to emergent patterns or themes.
5. The findings were summarised and recorded, and deficiencies were highlighted and remedied.
6. The researcher used her summaries to construct generalisations with which to confront existing theories and interpret the findings of the quantitative analysis.

Furthermore, in order to give the reader *"some of the flavour of the replies"* (Oppenheim, 1992), most of the responses are reported in full to support the interpretation of the findings of quantitative analyses as will be seen in Chapter Seven.

5.7 Summary

This chapter has indicated the research methodology employed to achieve the study objectives, having considered the usefulness of both quantitative and qualitative research approaches and methods. The method of measurement used in respect of the levels of compliance with IFRSs disclosure requirements by companies listed on the EGX and ASE has been presented, and the method of examination of the causal relationship between corporate governance test variables (board independence, board leadership, board size, government ownership, management ownership, private ownership, and public ownership) and the dependent variable (overall level of compliance with mandatory IFRSs disclosure requirements) has also been shown. In this respect, a discussion of the quantitative research method (disclosure index) as the main research tool, and semi-structured interviews (qualitative research method) to support the interpretation of the findings of the quantitative analysis, was provided.

The chapter identified the research hypotheses and discussed the construction of the unweighted disclosure index used to measure the level of compliance with IFRSs. Having identified the research population and provided details of the eventual sample, the chapter then demonstrated the procedures followed in conducting the empirical analysis, explaining the use of descriptive, univariate and multivariate analyses.

With respect to the qualitative aspect of the study (semi-structured interviews), details of the interview sample, ethical considerations, and the general analytical procedures were presented. The next chapter will report the results of the quantitative data analysis.

PART II

EMPIRICAL ANALYSIS

CHAPTER SIX

QUANTITATIVE ANALYSIS

6.1 Introduction

The main purpose of this chapter is to answer the research questions presented in Chapter One. In respect of the first research question, comprehensive descriptive statistics are obtained which allow for the evaluation of the extent of compliance with IFRSs disclosure requirements by companies listed on the EGX and ASE. To answer the second research question that seeks to identify corporate governance factors significantly associated with compliance levels, the statistical techniques of univariate and multiple regression are used. Initially, the effect of each individual variable on the degree of compliance with IFRSs disclosure requirements is determined (univariate analysis), subsequent to which regression analysis is performed to establish the joint influence of corporate governance structures on the levels of compliance among companies listed on the scrutinised stock exchanges.

Consequently, the remaining part of this chapter is organised as follows. Section 6.2 provides the descriptive analysis of the extent of compliance with IFRSs disclosure requirements by companies listed on the EGX and ASE. Section 6.3 provides the descriptive analysis of test and control variables in the investigated companies. Section 6.4 reports the results of the test for statistical significant differences between the Egyptian and the Jordanian contexts (H1). Section 6.5 presents the results of the univariate analysis investigating the relationship between the overall level of compliance with mandatory IFRSs disclosure requirements and each corporate governance-related variable. Section 6.6 reports the outcome of the multivariate analysis and answers the last research question by analysing and interpreting the statistical output and its theoretical implications. Finally, section 6.7 summarises and concludes the chapter.

6.2 Descriptive Results of Compliance with IFRSs

As indicated in Chapter Five the disclosure index employed in this study is based on mandatory IFRSs disclosure requirements for the fiscal year beginning 1 January, 2007. It includes 275 mandatory disclosure items divided into 20 sub-indices[1].

The disclosure scores were calculated as a ratio by dividing the actual score awarded by the maximum possible score for each company. Table 6.1 presents the descriptive statistics for all disclosure indices.

[1] Details of the disclosure items appear in Appendix B.

Table 6.1 Descriptive Statistics of the Extent of Compliance with IFRSs by Companies Listed on the EGX and ASE (Total Score and Sub-scores)

Country	Minimum %	Maximum %	Mean %	Std. Deviation	Applicability	Number of companies above 50%	Percentage of companies above 50%	Rank
				Total Score				
Egypt	68	91	80	0.04	75	75	100%	NA Jordan
	56	88	76	0.07	75	75	100%	NA **Sub-index 1**
				(IFRS 3: Business Combinations)				
Egypt	43	100	81	0.27	7	4	57%	9
Jordan	0	100	67	0.43	12	9	75%	9
				Sub-index 2 (IAS 1: Presentation of Financial Statements)				
Egypt	75	97	89	0.05	75	75	100%	7
Jordan	66	95	84	0.07	75	75	100%	4
				Sub-index 3 (IAS 2: Inventories)				
Egypt	0	100	95	0.16	67	63	94%	5
Jordan	25	100	80	0.27	51	35	69%	5
				Sub-index 4 (IAS 7: Cash Flow Statements)				
Egypt	33	100	93	0.12	75	71	95%	6
Jordan	44	100	84	0.24	75	72	96%	4
				Sub-index 5 (IAS 8: Accounting Policies, Changes in Accounting Estimates and Errors)				
Egypt	0	100	61	0.29	12	5	42%	14
Jordan	33	100	59	0.24	9	2	22%	11
				Sub-index 6 (IAS 11: Construction Contracts)				
Egypt	17	100	63	0.44	5	2	50%	13
Jordan	33	50	46	0.08	4	0	0%	14
				Sub-index 7 (IAS 14: Segment Reporting)				
Egypt	0	100	61	0.47	7	4	57%	14
Jordan	0	100	55	0.38	19	12	63%	12
				Sub-index 8 (IAS 16: Property, Plant and Equipment)				
Egypt	20	100	80	0.18	75	70	93%	10
Jordan	56	100	91	0.12	75	75	100%	2
				Sub-index 9 (IAS 18: Revenue)				
Egypt	0	100	96	0.18	75	71	95%	4

Country	Minimum %	Maximum %	Mean %	Std. Deviation	Applicability	Number of companies above 50%	Percentage of companies above 50%	Rank
Jordan	0	100	90	0.28	75	65	88%	3
Sub-index 10 (IAS 21: The Effects of Changes in Foreign Exchange Rates)								
Egypt	0	100	97	0.17	68	67	99%	3
Jordan	0	100	19	0.34	60	9	15%	17
Sub-index 11 (IAS 23: Borrowing Costs)								
Egypt	67	100	99	0.06	56	56	100%	2
Jordan	0	100	62	0.40	60	42	70%	10
Sub-index 12 (IAS 24: Related Party Disclosures)								
Egypt	0	100	40	0.24	65	13	20%	17
Jordan	0	100	54	0.30	68	35	51%	13
Sub-index 13 (IAS 27: Consolidated and Separate Financial Statements)								
Egypt	0	100	88	0.33	33	29	88%	8
Jordan	0	100	69	0.46	18	12	67%	8
Sub-index 14 (IAS 28: Investment in Associates)								
Egypt	0	100	43	0.33	40	16	40%	12
Jordan	0	100	76	0.36	25	21	84%	6
Sub-index 15 (IAS 31: Investment in Joint Ventures)								
Egypt	0	100	71	0.41	6	4	67%	12
Jordan	13	83	45	0.25	9	3	33%	15
Sub-index 16 (IAS 33: Earnings per Share)								
Egypt	0	80	31	0.19	75	5	7%	19
Jordan	0	100	37	0.21	75	11	15%	16
Sub-index 17 (IAS 36: Impairment of Assets)								
Egypt	100	100	100	0.00	3	3	100%	1
Jordan	100	100	100	0.00	8	8	100%	1
Sub-index 18 (IAS 37: Provisions, Contingent Liabilities and Contingent Assets)								
Egypt	14	100	72	0.16	75	69	92%	11
Jordan	0	100	62	0.25	74	47	64%	10
Sub-index 19 (IAS 38: Intangible Assets)								
Egypt	0	100	36	0.34	19	8	42%	18
Jordan	0	100	75	0.35	25	17	68%	7
Sub-index 20 (IAS 40: Investment in Property)								
Egypt	0	100	52	0.42	7	4	57%	15
Jordan	0	100	54	0.38	15	7	47%	13

Table 6.2 The Extent of Compliance with IFRSs Disclosure Requirements in Previous Studies Conducted in Egypt

Study	Year	Min. Level of Compliance (%)	Max. Level of Compliance (%)	Mean (%)
Abd-Elsalam (1999); Abd-Elsalam & Weetman (2003)	1995	57	98	83
Samaha (2006); Samaha & Stapleton (2008; 2009)	2000	16	90	50
Dahawy & Conover (2007)	2004	52	76	62
Dahawy (2009)	2002	32	73	55
Ismail et al. (2010)	2007	66	84	77
This study (2011)	2007	68	91	80

6.2.1 Descriptive Statistics for Total IFRSs Disclosure Index (Total Score)

As seen in Table 6.1, the average level of compliance with IFRSs disclosure requirements is 80% in Egypt and 76% in Jordan. In other words, 80% of the 275 items (220 items) of the disclosure checklist were disclosed by companies listed on the EGX, while 76% of the 275 items (209 items) of the disclosure checklist were disclosed by companies listed on the ASE. This implies a relative similarity between the levels of compliance with the overall IFRSs disclosure requirements between the two stock exchanges.

The total disclosure index varied among companies listed on the EGX, ranging from 68% (United Housing and Development Company) to 91% (Egyptian Chemical Industries). The variation in the level of compliance with the total disclosure index was indicated by a standard deviation of 0.04. For companies listed on the ASE the range was from 56% (Palaces Realestate and Development P.L.C) to 88% (Jordan Phosphate Mines). This variation was indicated by a standard deviation of 0.07, indicating the variability in the levels of compliance in Egypt to be less than in Jordan.

It is recognised that the minimum level of compliance with IFRSs disclosure requirements by companies listed on the EGX is higher than that of companies listed on the ASE (68% and 56% respectively), a difference possibly explained by the shortage of qualified accountants in Jordan as was confirmed by interviewees (see Chapter Seven).

There is a number of studies that investigated the levels of compliance with IFRSs disclosure requirements in Egypt. Their findings are compared with those from this study in Table 6.2.

Table 6.2 clearly demonstrates inconsistencies in the results obtained by reported studies. However, none of the reported studies reveals a full compliance with IFRSs. This may imply that the CMA's efforts to force full compliance with IFRSs disclosure requirements from listed companies remain insufficient, and that selective disclosure remains the practice, supported by low non-compliance costs. However, the observed increase in the minimum level of compliance with IFRSs disclosure requirements during the period from 1995 (the year of Abd-Elsalam and Abd-Elsalam and Weetman studies) to 2007 (the year of this study) from 57% to 68% may indicate enhanced awareness among listed companies' managements regarding the importance of improving transparency and the improved experience in applying IFRSs on a mandatory basis. Thus, progress in compliance levels can be observed over time. That said, stringent enforcement and strict punishment would foster full compliance much swifter.

Table 6.3 The Extent of Compliance with IFRSs Disclosure Requirements in Previous Studies Conducted in Jordan

Study	Year	Min. Level of Compliance (%)	Max. Level of Compliance (%)	Mean (%)
Naser et al. (2002)	1998	34	85	64
Al-Shiab (2003)	2000 (most recent)	16	91	56
Omar (2007)	2003	67	93	82
Al-Akra et al. (2010a)	2004 (most recent)	58	90	79
This study (2011)	2007	56	88	76
Naser et al. (2002)	1998	34	85	64

Compared to the findings of a more recent study that was conducted on the best performing 15 companies listed on the EGX for the fiscal year 2004 (Dahawy, 2007), a significant increase is seen in the levels of compliance with IFRSs disclosure requirements. The average level of compliance reported by Dahawy and Conover, 2007 was 62% (compared to 80% in this study) with the minimum compliance level 52% (compared to 68% in this study) and the maximum 76% (compared to 91% in this study). This difference may be attributed to the use of a more comprehensive disclosure index, and a much larger sample in this study and/or the relative improvement in the monitoring and enforcement functions of the CMA in 2007 (the year of this study) compared to 2004 (the year of Dahawy and Conover's study). However, this disparity supports the notion advanced in this study that overall progress in compliance levels in the Egyptian context may be a positive sign that the national norms are moving towards compliance but that more time is needed for certain disclosure requirements to become part of the culture of Egyptian corporate management. Finally, compared to the findings of Ismail et al. (2010) who investigate a sample of 39 financial and non-financial companies listed on the EGX in 2007, there is an approximate similarity with respect to the average level of compliance with IFRSs (77% compared to 80% in this study) and in the minimum level of compliance with IFRSs disclosure requirements (66% compared to 68% in this study). This supports the findings of this study. Yet, the difference in the maximum level of compliance (84% compared to 91% in this study), is most likely attributed to the sample differences as well as the structure of the disclosure index.

With respect to the Jordanian context, table 6.3 compares the results of this study with previous such studies conducted in Jordan.

As seen in Table 6.3, similar to the case of Egypt there is a relative inconsistency in the results obtained by reported studies. In addition, it is clear that there is a great progress in compliance levels by companies listed on the ASE during the period from 1998 (the year of Naser et al. study) to 2007 (the year of this study) as the average level of compliance increased from 64% to 76%. The same conclusion is derived by comparing the findings of this study with those of Al-Shiab's (2003) which showed that in year 2000 the average level of compliance was 56% (compared to 78% in this study) and the minimum compliance level was 16% (compared to 59% in this study). Omar (2007) showed a relatively similar average level of compliance with IFRSs (82%) to this study but a higher maximum level of compliance (93%) and a higher minimum level of compliance (67%) by companies listed on the ASE for the fiscal year 2003. However, comparing the findings of this study with those of the most recent study investigating compliance with IFRSs disclosure requirements within the Jordanian context (Al-Akra et al., 2010a), reveals a relative similarity in the minimum (58% compared to 56% in this study), maximum (90% compared to 88% in this study) and the average levels of compliance with IFRSs disclosure requirements (79% compared to 76% in this study).

In broad terms, the variation in the reported range of disclosure indices among studies can be attributed to the following reasons. Firstly, the differences in study sample. Secondly, variations in the years being studied, and the structure and the degree of comprehensiveness of the checklist used in measuring the extent of compliance. Thirdly, modifications to IFRSs disclosure requirements over time. Lastly, the impact of changing political and institutional preferences and attitudes over time is a common characteristic of developing countries and may directly or indirectly influence the level of enforcement of laws and regulations including disclosure requirements.

On the other hand, the non-increase in the average compliance levels reported in either Al-Akra et al. (2010a) or this study, compared to Omar (2007) can be partially attributed to the researcher's proposition that, similar to the case of Egypt, certain barriers to full compliance still remain in the Jordanian context. Essentially, these relate to the dominance of secretive culture and low demand for improved disclosures. Additionally, some technical barriers prevail relating to the qualification and competency of accounting practitioners in Jordan and the JSC monitoring staff, non existence of an official Arabic translation of IFRSs in Jordan, and to the weak enforcement of IFRSs disclosure requirements by the JSC as demonstrated by interviewee responses that will be reported in Chapter Seven. In a similar vein, Tai et al. (1990) suggest that difficulties in interpreting disclosure requirements and insufficient awareness of general accounting concepts contribute to low levels of compliance with mandatory disclosure requirements. Also, Abd-Elsalam and Weetman (2003) argue that low levels of compliance with mandatory disclosure requirements may result from the lack of familiarity or unavailability of regulations in native language.

6.2.2 Descriptive Statistics for Sub-indices

The findings reported in Table 6.1 show that there is a wide range of variations in the average levels of compliance with disclosure requirements under individual IFRSs (sub-indices). These large variations are recognised on individual country level as well as between the two scrutinised countries. As indicated in Table 6.1 the average levels of compliance with disclosure requirements on the level of individual IFRSs in the Egyptian context ranged from full compliance (100% compliance level) with respect to IAS 36: Impairment of Assets (Sub-index 17) to a low level of compliance (31%) with respect to IAS 33: Earnings per Share (Sub-index 16). Interestingly, in the Jordanian context, the average levels of compliance with both standards relatively were not different (100% and 37% respectively). Yet, a wide gap is found with respect to the average levels of compliance with the requirements under IAS 21: The Effects of Changes in Foreign Exchange Rates (sub-index 10) which achieved the lowest average level of compliance in the Jordanian context (19%) compared to 97% in the Egyptian context. The same applies with respect to IAS 23: Borrowing Costs (sub-index 11) which is ranked the 2nd with respect to the average level of compliance with its requirements in the Egyptian context (99%) and the 10th in the Jordanian context (62%). On the contrary, a gap is witnessed with respect to the average levels of compliance with the requirements of IAS 16: Property, Plant and Equipment (Sub-index 8) which is ranked the 10th with respect to the average level of compliance with its requirements in the Egyptian context (80%) and the 2nd in the Jordanian context (91%). The same applies to

IAS 28: Investment in Associates (Sub-index 14) which is ranked the 12th in the Egyptian context (43%) and the 6th in the Jordanian context (76%) and IAS 38: Intangible Assets (Sub-index 19) which is ranked the 18th in the Egyptian context (36%) and the 7th in the Jordanian context (75%). Differences in the extent of compliance on the level of individual IFRSs between the scrutinised stock exchanges are most likely attributed to differences in the capacity of applying and enforcing the requirements under each standard, given that developing countries are not completely homogeneous.

In terms of the rank of some standards based on the average levels of compliance with their requirements between the two scrutinised contexts, similarity in rank is recognised with IFRS 3: Business Combinations (sub-index 1) which is ranked the 9th in both countries. The same applies to sub-index 3 (IAS 2: Inventories) which is ranked the 5th in both countries and sub-index 13 (IAS 27: Consolidated and Separate Financial Statements) which is ranked the 8th in both countries. This implies that there is a relative similarity in compliance behaviour between both countries on the level of some individual IFRSs.

The reported low levels of compliance with some IFRSs disclosure requirements either on individual country level or on the level of both scrutinised countries may be attributed to the preference for secrecy, fear of competition, low non-compliance costs, and weak monitoring. Lack of awareness of the importance of compliance and improved transparency among management of the majority of listed companies are also potential reasons for lack of full compliance with the requirements of some standards such as the case of IAS 16: Property, Plant and Equipment within the Egyptian context. Also, in Jordan, the shortage of qualified accountants and non-availability of an official Arabic translation of IFRSs may be a major obstacle to achieving full compliance with IFRSs, such as the case of IAS 21: The Effects of Changes in Foreign Exchange Rates.

Moreover, it was recognised that for some IFRSs which were applicable to a few companies, technical difficulties (such as the case of IAS 11: Construction Contracts) or the novelty of some kinds of transactions (such as the case of IAS 14: Segment Reporting, IAS 31: Investment in Joint Ventures and IAS 40: Investment Property) may justify low levels of compliance to some extent as lack of experience may result in misunderstanding and interpretation difficulties. Thus, this may signal the need for training accountants in companies in which these standards are applicable on their appropriate application. Meanwhile, the full compliance with the requirements of IAS 36: Impairment of Assets, although it only applies to 3 companies in Egypt and 8 in Jordan implies that, IFRSs that do not contradict with the secretive culture of MENA societies, that are understood and can be properly applied without interpretation difficulties, and strictly monitored by security exchange regulatory bodies, are more likely to be fully complied with by companies listed on the two stock exchanges. Consequently, if this stage is reached with respect to all IFRSs, this can solve the problem of decoupling (companies report that the financial statements are prepared in accordance with IFRSs while full compliance is absent).

The above discussion supports the notions of the institutional isomorphism theory, Gray's (1988) secrecy versus transparency accounting sub-cultural value, agency theory and cost-benefit analysis that were comprehensively discussed in Chapter Two. Furthermore, the interpretation of the determinants of compliance levels are supported by interviewee responses as revealed in Chapter Seven.

6.2.3 Fully Disclosed and Rarely Disclosed Information Items

This section reports those information items that were fully disclosed (100% compliance) and those that were rarely disclosed (less than 50% compliance) within each disclosure sub-index. The extent of compliance with each disclosure item is calculated by dividing the number of companies disclosing an item bythe number of companies to which that item was applicable. This is expected to provide insight regarding the disclosure behaviour by companies listed on scrutinised stock exchanges. Additionally, it can help in diagnosing barriers to full compliance with IFRSs disclosure requirements. Table 6.4 demonstrates the fully disclosed, and the rarely disclosed items by companies listed on the EGX and ASE.

The information in Table 6.4 reveals that some similarities exist between management behaviour in Egypt and Jordan with respect to compliance and non-compliance with different disclosure requirements under each IFRS. However, there are also differences in compliance behaviour with respect to certain disclosure items under each IFRS which may be attributed to the differences in each country capacity to enforce and apply all IFRSs disclosure requirements.

The shortage of qualified accountants in Jordan and the non-existence of an official Arabic translation of IFRSs, negatively affect compliance levels with some individual disclosure items because there are insufficient number of accountants who are capable of understanding and applying many of the IFRSs requirements. This obstacle does not, however, commonly feature in respect of companies listed on the EGX.

Table 6.4 Items Fully Disclosed and Rarely Disclosed Under Each IFRS

Sub-index	Egypt		Jordan	
	Fully Disclosed Items (100% Compliance)	Rarely Disclosed Items (<50% Compliance)	Fully Disclosed Items (100% Compliance)	Rarely Disclosed Items (<50% Compliance)
Sub-index 1 (IFRS 3)	1;4;8;11	6;7	1;2;3;4;5;6;7;8;9	
Sub-index 2 (IAS 1)	12;13;14;15;16;18;19;20;22;23;24;25;26;27;28;31;34;35;37;38;39;40;42;43;44;58;60;62;74;75;77;78;81;89;90;91;92;93;99;112;113;114;115;116;117	66;67;96;98	12;13;14;15;16;17;18;19;20;21;22;23;24;25;26;27;31;33;34;35;36;37;38;39;40;41;47;48;49;50;51;52;54;55;56;57;58;59;60;71;72;73;74;75;77;78;81;84;89;91;92;93;102;112;113;114	67;96;97;106
Sub-index 3 (IAS 2)			119;120;121;122;123	
Sub-index 4 (IAS 7)	124;128;129;130	126	124;127;128;129;134	126
Sub-index 5 (IAS 8)	135;136;137;141;142;143;144;145	138;139;146;147	135;136;137;144;145;146;147	138;139;140;141;142;143
Sub-index 6 (IAS 11)	152		148;150;151	149;152;153
Sub-index 7 (IAS 14)		161;164,168	157;162;163;164;165,168	155;161
Sub-index 8 (IAS 16)	174;175;178;180;181;183	176;177;182;189;190	174;175;178;179;180;181;183;185;187;188;189;190	172;173;176;177;182
Sub-index 9 (IAS 18)	193;194;195		192;193;194;195	
Sub-index 10 (IAS 21)				196;197;198
Sub-index 11 (IAS 23)	200	199	200	
Sub-index 12 (IAS 24)		203;204;205;209;210;211;212		209;210;211;212
Sub-index 13 (IAS 27)			214	
Sub-index 14 (IAS 28)		218;219;220;223;224;225;226		220;226
Sub-index 15 (IAS 31)		228;229	227;228;233;234	229;230;231;232
Sub-index 16 (IAS 33)		236;237;238;240;242,243		236;240;242;243
Sub-index 17 (IAS 36)	244;245		244;245	
Sub-index 18 (IAS 37)	255;256	252;253	257	250;252;253
Sub-index 19 (IAS 38)		260;264;265;266;267;268	264;265;266;268	
Sub-index 20 (IAS 40)	272	269;270;271;275	269;270;272;273;274	271;275

In both jurisdictions, as indicated by interviewees, the main reasons for low or non-compliance with particular disclosure requirements may be the preference for secrecy, and lack of awareness regarding the importance of compliance with all IFRSs disclosure requirements. Managements fail to disclose on the grounds that the information required is too detailed or may be misused by competitors. However, in broad terms there is progress in the compliance levels in respect of IFRSs individual disclosure requirements compared with previous studies investigating these stock exchanges at the individual country level (*e.g.,* Abd-Elsalam and Weetman, 2003; Omar, 2007). This may be attributed to the improved awareness among managements of listed companies regarding the importance of compliance with these items (*i.e.,* compliance with these items has become embedded within the disclosure sub-cultural values), the enhanced familiarity with respect to their proper application, and the improved monitoring of these items by the regulatory bodies in the two stock exchanges. For instance, disclosing the capitalisation rate used to determine the amount of borrowing costs eligible for capitalisation (item 201) achieved 98% and 83% compliance by companies listed on the EGX and ASE respectively compared to 79% in Abd-Elsalam (1999) and 33% in Omar (2007).

In contrast, compliance levels with some disclosure requirements, such as disclosing the rights, preferences and restrictions attaching to each class of shares (item 67) remain low. The same can be said for most of the disclosure requirements under IAS 33: Earnings per Share. This may be explained by the secretive culture, and the lack of awareness regarding the importance of transparency. Overall, this reflects the existence of decoupling since listed companies state that they prepare their financial statements in accordance with IFRSs, but the reality is different. The issue of low monitoring costs is of relevance here. Also, this position raises doubt about the reliability of audit reports, which in most cases particularly in Egypt, are prepared by big 4 affiliates.

6.3 Descriptive Statistics for Independent Variables

As indicated in Chapter Five, independent variables include seven corporate governance-related test variables and six control variables[1]. Ten are continuous variables, these being: board independence ratio, board size, government ownership ratio, management ownership ratio, private ownership ratio, public ownership ratio, company size, profitability,

[1] Independent variables were defined in sub-section 5.3.4.

gearing and liquidity; the remainder are categorical variables: board leadership, auditor type and industry type. Table 6.5 displays the descriptive statistics for the independent variables.

Table 6.5 shows that the ratio of independent non-executive directors on the BOD of Egyptian companies ranges from 0% to 100%, meaning that the BOD of some companies listed on the EGX may consist entirely of executive directors or vice versa. However, on average more than 50% of the BOD members are independent which agrees with the recommendation of the OECD principles and that of the ECCG. In Jordan board independence ranges from 0% to 86% with an average of 40%. This implies that board independence is more recognised in Egypt than Jordan. However, this is only one face of the coin, the most important is the impact of this recommended mechanism on disclosure practices by listed companies in scrutinised stock exchanges as will be further investigated in the following parts of this chapter.

In respect of board leadership, the CEO and the Chair positions are held by two different persons in 51% of the companies listed on the EGX compared to 81% in the companies listed on the ASE which implies that companies listed on the ASE complies better with the OECD requirements for best practices which recommend the separation of the CEO and Chair positions. For board size, it ranges from 3 to 9 members in Egypt and 3 to 13 in Jordan, with an average board size of 5 members in Egypt compared to 7 members in Jordan. Thus board sizes in both countries are not as large as those in developed countries.

With respect to government ownership ratio, this ranges from 0% to 98% in companies listed on the EGX with an average of 19%. For companies listed on the ASE, the government ownership ratio ranges from 0% to 69% with an average of 7%. This implies that government ownership is more dominant in Egypt compared to Jordan, which may reflect the greater progress in privatisation programme in Jordan compared to Egypt.

Table 6.5 Summary of Descriptive Statistics for Independent Variables

Independent Variable	Egypt (N=75)				Jordan (N=75)			
	Min.	Max.	Mean	Standard Deviation	Min.	Max.	Mean	Standard Deviation
Test Variables								
Board Independence Ratio	0.00	1.00	0.5052	0.1928	0.00	0.86	0.3978	0.2531
Board Leadership	0.00	1.00	0.51	0.503	0.00	1.00	0.81	0.392
Board Size	3.00	9.00	5.17	1.855	3.00	13.00	7.01	2.299
Government Ownership Ratio	0.00	0.98	0.1919	0.2964	0.00	0.69	0.0747	0.1321
Management Ownership Ratio	0.00	1.00	0.1121	0.2361	0.00	0.98	0.1481	0.1998
Private Ownership Ratio	0.00	1.00	0.2353	0.3231	0.00	0.91	0.3421	0.2526
Public Ownership Ratio	0.00	0.86	0.1504	0.2429	0.00	0.94	0.2352	0.2225
Control Variables								
Company Size (In million USD)	624.0000	11388000	522139.500	1533462.4	1705	937650	65951.750	136487.150
Profitability	-0.30	0.31	0.1343	0.0838	-0.18	0.54	0.0670	0.0934
Gearing	0.01	2.22	0.6798	0.3995	0.00	9.57	2.1410	2.4873
Liquidity	0.33	8.58	2.5580	1.5314	0.11	9.52	2.1993	1.9045
Industry	0.00	1.00	0.35	0.479	0.00	1.00	0.52	0.503
Type of Auditor	0.00	1.00	0.31	0.464	0.00	1.00	0.57	0.498

In terms of the management ownership ratio, this ranges from 0% to 100% in companies listed on the EGX with an average 11%. For companies listed on the ASE, the management ownership ratio is relatively higher. It ranges from 0% to 98% with an average of 15%.

The private ownership ratio is seen to range from 0% to 100% in companies listed on the EGX with an average of 24%. However, for companies listed on the ASE the private ownership ratio ranges from 0% to 91% with an average of 34%. This implies that private ownership is more dominant in the Jordanian context.

Finally, with respect to public ownership, the ratio ranges from 0% to 86% in companies listed on the EGX with an average of 15%. For companies listed on the ASE this ratio ranges from 0% to 94% with an average of 24%. This reveals that public ownership is more dominant in Jordan compared to Egypt.

The descriptive statistics of the control variables as in Table 6.5, show that the average firm size in Egypt measured in terms of total assets (USD 522139.5 million) is higher than in Jordan (USD 65951.75 million). This indicates that the Egyptian companies are larger in size compared to their Jordanian counterparts.

Additionally, it can be argued that with more effort by regulators in both stock exchanges, the Egyptian and the Jordanian stock exchanges can attract more direct foreign investments and hence foster the economic transition in their jurisdictions. Profitability measured in terms of return on assets, indicates that in general companies listed on the EGX achieve more profits compared to their counterparts that are listed on the ASE. The average profitability in companies listed on the EGX is 13% compared to 7% in Jordan. The gearing measured in terms of debt to equity, averages 0.68 in companies listed on the EGX compared to 2.14 in Jordan, which implies that companies listed on the ASE are quite highly geared compared to their counterparts in Egypt. This also implies that companies listed on the ASE are heavily depending on debts as a major source of finance. The average liquidity is very high (2.56 by companies listed on the EGX and 2.20 by companies listed on the ASE). This implies the high ability of companies listed on the EGX and ASE to meet their short term obligations, which reflects the large margin of safety in companies listed on scrutinised stock exchanges and their ability to continue as going concerns. This in turn has the potential to attract more direct foreign investments. Finally, the descriptive statistics of the categorical control variables as indicated in Table 6.5 show that 35% of the sample companies that are listed on the EGX are non- manufacturing companies compared to 52% of the sample companies that are listed on the ASE. Also, it is recognised that 31% of the companies listed on the EGX are audited by non-big 4 audit firms compared to 57% of those listed on the ASE. This implies that the majority of companies listed on the EGX (69%) are audited by big 4 affiliates which may be a reason for higher levels of compliance with IFRSs disclosure requirements in the Egyptian context compared to the Jordanian one.

To sum up, the above discussion of the descriptive statistics of test and control variables, indicates the existence of differences between the two scrutinised stock exchanges. This conclusion, in addition to the findings of the assessment of the extent of compliance with IFRSs disclosure requirements in the two stock exchanges discussed in section 6.2, raises the need to investigate whether there are significant statistical differences between the Egyptian and the Jordanian Contexts (H1). This hypothesis is investigated in the next section.

6.4 Differences between the Egyptian and the Jordanian Contexts

After calculating the disclosure indices (dependent variable), summarising the independent variables in matching columns, and conducting a descriptive analysis of the dependent and independent variables, an exploration of any potential significant statistical differences between the Egyptian and the Jordanian contexts (H1) is warranted before investigating the relationship between the extent of compliance with IFRSs disclosure requirements and corporate governance structures of companies listed on the scrutinised stock exchanges. To determine whether to apply parametric or non-parametric tests in the statistical analysis to be conducted in this chapter, it was necessary to check the normality of distribution of the dependent and independent variables as is now indicated.

6.4.1 Normality Test

As indicated in section 5.6, both the K-S Lilliefors test and Shapiro-Wilk test were employed to assess the normality of data distribution. The results of these tests are reported in the following two sub-sections.

Table 6.6 demonstrates the results of the test for normality of the distribution of the dependent variable (total disclosure index) using the K-S and Shapiro-Wilk tests. Both tests were performed on the 150 companies listed on the EGX and ASE. The table indicates the test statistics, the degrees of freedom (df) and significance.

Table 6.6 Tests of Normality of the Dependent Variable

	K-S Test			Shapiro-Wilk Test		
Disclosure Index (N=150)	**Statistic**	**df**	**Sig.**	**Statistic**	**df**	**Sig.**
Total Score	.109	150	.000	.942	150	.000

Table 6.7 Tests of Normality of the Independent Variables

	K-S Test			Shapiro-Wilk Test		
Independent Variable (N=150)	**Statistic**	**df**	**Sig.**	**Statistic**	**df**	**Sig.**
Test (Explanatory) Variables						
Board Independence	.111	150	.000	.969	150	.002
Board Size	.126	150	.000	.929	150	.000
Board Leadership	.423	150	.000	.598	150	.000
Government Ownership	.286	150	.000	.633	150	.000
Management Ownership	.276	150	.000	.662	150	.000
Private Ownership	.163	150	.000	.870	150	.000
Public Ownership	.207	150	.000	.807	150	.000
Control Variables						
Total Assets	.396	150	.000	.246	150	.000
Return on Assets	.083	150	.000	.939	150	.000
Debt to Equity	.328	150	.000	.637	150	.000
Quick Ratio	.167	150	.000	.866	150	.000
Type of Business	.375	150	.000	.630	150	.000
Type of Auditor	.372	150	.000	.631	150	.000

As indicated in Table 6.6, significance is less than 0.05 for total disclosure index (dependent variable), meaning that it is not normally distributed. Furthermore, the results of the test of normality on individual country level that is reported in Appendix F generally confirm this result. Consequently, this supports the use of non-parametric tests for the univariate analysis and transformed data (normal scores) to run the regression analysis.

Normality of Independent Variables

Table 6.7 presents the results of testing the normality of distribution of the independent variables under the K-S and Shapiro-Wilk tests.

As seen in Table 6.7, significance is less than 0.05 for all independent variables (test and control). This implies that they are not normally distributed. This result is further confirmed by normality tests on individual country level reported in Appendix F and hence, supports the use of non-parametric tests.

Table 6.8 Mann-Whitney U Test Results for Total Disclosure Index (Dependent Variable)

Disclosure Index (N=150)	Mann - Whitney U	Wilcoxon W	Z	Asymp. Sig. (2-tailed)
Total Score	1922.000	4772.000	-3.349	.001

In order to investigate whether significant statistical differences exist between the Egyptian and the Jordanian contexts (H1), the researcher employed the Mann-Whitney U test and Chi-square test (non-parametric tests), which are expected to give more accurate results than parametric tests when the variables are not normally distributed.

The Mann-Whitney U test was used to examine whether significant statistical differences exist between the Egyptian and the Jordanian contexts with respect to the overall compliance with mandatory IFRSs disclosure requirements (total disclosure index), and continuous independent variables (board independence, board size, ownership structure, company size, profitability, gearing and liquidity). Meanwhile, the Chi-square test was used to examine such issue with respect to the categorical independent variables (board leadership, type of business activity, and type of audit firm). Accordingly this hypothesis has been further divided into the following two sub-hypotheses.

H1a There are no significant statistical differences between Egypt and Jordan in their levels of compliance with IFRSs disclosure requirements.
H1b There are no significant statistical differences between Egypt and Jordan in their dominant corporate governance structures and other company characteristics.

The acceptance or rejection of the null hypothesis is based on whether there are significant statistical differences ($P <= 05$).

Significant Differences between Egypt and Jordan in terms of Levels of Compliance with IFRSs Disclosure Requirements

Table 6.8 demonstrates the results of the Mann-Whitney U test for the total disclosure index (dependent variable).

The results show that there are statistically significant differences ($P < .05$) between the two groups of companies: those listed on the EGX and those listed on the ASE with respect to the overall level of compliance with mandatory IFRSs disclosure requirements (total disclosure index). Consequently, H1a will be rejected. This result confirms the findings of the descriptive statistical analysis presented in sub-section 6.2.1 which demonstrates that the overall level of compliance with mandatory IFRSs disclosure requirements is higher in Egypt than in Jordan. As previously indicated, this difference may be mainly attributed to the existence of technical difficulties due to the lack of adequately qualified accountants in Jordan and the unavailability of official Arabic translation of the IFRSs in Jordan.

Significant Differences between Egypt and Jordan in terms of the Independent Variables

Table 6.9 shows the results of the Mann-Whitney U test for continuous independent variables.

Table 6.9 Mann-Whitney U Test Results for Continuous Independent Variables

Disclosure Index (N=150)	Mann-Whitney U	Wilcoxon W	Z	Asymp. Sig. (2-tailed)
		Test Variables		
Board Independence	2023.000	4873.000	-2.971	.003
Board Size	1525.000	4375.000	-4.903	.000
Government Ownership	2647.500	5497.500	-.665	.506
Mnagement Ownership	1974.000	4824.000	-3.411	.001
Private Ownership	1850.000	4700.000	-3.641	.000
Public Ownership	1921.000	4771.000	-3.419	.001
		Control Variables		
Company size	1438.000	4288.000	-5.166	.000
Profitability	1230.000	4080.000	-5.948	.000
Gearing	1876.000	4726.000	-3.522	.000
Liquidity	2230.000	5080.000	-2.191	.028

The results show that there are statistically significant differences ($P < .05$) between companies listed on the EGX and those listed on the ASE with respect to all continuous test and control variables except government ownership ratio ($P > .05$).

Table 6.10 Chi-square Test Results for Categorical Independent Variables

Variable	Egypt (N=75)	Jordan (N=75)	Pearson Chi - square	Asymp. Sig. (2-sided)
		Board Leadership		
Separate Role (Cat. 1)	38 (51%)	61 (81%)	14.379	.000
Dual Role (Cat. 0)	37 (49%)	19 (7%)		
		Type of Business Activity		
Non-manufacturing (Cat. 1)	26 (35%)	39 (52%)	3.910	.048
Manufacturing (Cat. 0)	49 (65%)	36 (48%)		
		Type of Auditor		
Non Big 4 (Cat. 1)	23 (31%)	43 (57%)	9.767	.002
Big 4 (Cat. 0)	52 (69%)	32 (43%)		

With respect to the categorical independent variables, Table 6.10 demonstrates the results of the Chi-square test for the differences between the Egyptian and the Jordanian contexts.

As indicated in Table 6.10 there are significant differences (Sig. < .05) between the Egyptian and the Jordanian contexts with respect to the categorical variables. With respect to board leadership, results show that the proportion of companies listed on the ASE that separate the CEO and Chair positions is higher than that for those listed on the EGX. In other words, separation of the two positions is highly recognised in companies listed on the ASE (81% of the companies) and less so (52%) for those listed on the EGX. This indicates that the OECD recommendation for corporate governance best practices is more recognised in Jordan than in Egypt. Hence, this raises the need to investigate the impact of this mechanism on the levels of compliance with IFRSs in each of the scrutinised stock exchanges. Also, the results show that there are significant differences between the proportion of companies that are audited by big 4 affiliates (69% in Egypt compared to 43% in Jordan) as well as with respect to the type of business activity (65% of the companies listed on the EGX are manufacturing companies compared to 48% of those listed on the ASE). Consequently, hypothesis H1b will be rejected.

The results from the Mann-Whitney U test and the Chi-square test reveals the existence of significant differences between the scrutinised contexts and hence the first research hypothesis will be rejected. These findings support those of the descriptive statistical analysis presented in sections 6.2 and 6.3. Additionally, they imply that although Egypt and Jordan have similarities in their legal, economic and cultural contexts, they are not homogeneous. This lends support to the inapplicability of generalizing the results of one developing country to others. In addition, this raises the need to examine the impact of corporate governance best practices on the levels of compliance with IFRSs in each of the scrutinised stock exchanges.

6.5 Univariate Analysis

Given that the dependent and independent variables are not normally distributed as concluded in sub-section 6.4.1, it was decided to use non-parametric tests. Furthermore, as the investigation of the significant statistical differences between Egypt and Jordan presented in sub-section 6.4.2 indicated that there are significant statistical differences between the two groups of companies (those listed on the EGX and those listed on the ASE), the following analyses are conducted on individual country level.

The researcher employed Spearman's rank correlation coefficient to assess the association between the continuous independent variables (board independence, board size, government ownership, management ownership, private ownership, public ownership, firm size, profitability, gearing and liquidity) and the total disclosure index. For the categorical independent variables (board leadership, type of business activity, and type of audit firm), the non-parametric Mann-Whitney U test was performed to test the impact of each of these on the disclosure level. The remaining part of this section discusses the results of both tests[1].

6.5.1 Univariate Analysis - Egypt

Univariate Analysis - Total Disclosure Index and the Continuous Independent Variables- Egypt

Table 6.11 presents the correlation between the overall level of compliance with IFRSs disclosure requirements (total disclosure index) and continuous independent variables within the Egyptian context. Given that the results of the test of normality for the total disclosure index reported in Appendix F show that P = .2(P > .05), it was decided to double-check the results of the Spearman Rank Correlation (non-parametric test) using the Pearson Product-moment Correlation (parametric test).

As seen in Table 6.11, the results of both the Spearman Rank Correlation and the Pearson Product-moment Correlation support the non existence of any significant correlation between the overall level of

[1] A detailed explanation of these variables, reasons for selection and method of operationalisation of their proxies was presented in Chapter Five.

compliance with mandatory IFRSs disclosure requirements and continuous corporate governance test variables (P > .05).

These findings support the second research hypothesis (H2a: there is no significant statistical relationship between board independence and the extent of compliance with IFRSs disclosure requirements in the Egyptian context). This agrees with the findings of Haniffa (1999), Ho and Wong (2001), Haniffa and Cooke (2002), Ghazali and Weetman (2006) and Al-Akra et al. (2010a,b). Compared with the findings of prior studies that investigated the association between corporate governance attributes and disclosure practices within the Egyptian context, these findings do not support those of Samaha and Dahawy (2010, 2011) which report a significant positive relationship between voluntary disclosure levels and board independence. With respect to the association between board size and compliance with mandatory IFRSs disclosure requirements, these findings support the fourth research hypothesis (H4a: there is no significant statistical relationship between board size and the extent of compliance with IFRSs disclosure requirements in the Egyptian context). This agrees with the findings of Lakhal (2003), Arcay and Vazquez (2005) and Cheng and Courtenay (2006). Compared with the findings of prior studies that investigated the association between board size and disclosure practices within the Egyptian context, these findings do not support those of Ezat and El-Masry (2008) which report a significant positive relationship between voluntary internet disclosure and board size.

Table 6.11 Correlation between Total Disclosure Index and Continuous Independent Variables-Egypt (N=75)

Variable	Total Disclosure IndexVariable			
	Spearman Rank Correlation		Pearson Product-moment Correlation	
	Correlation Coefficient (r)	Significance (two-tailed)	Correlation Coefficient (r)	Significance (two-tailed)
BOD Independence	.072	.538	.008	.945
BOD Size	.052	.657	.066	.574
Government Ownership	.127	.277	.139	.235
Management Ownership	.031	.790	.019	.872
Private Ownership	-.013	.910	-.019	.871
Public Ownership	-.080	.493	-.152	.193
~~Company Size~~	~~.171~~	~~.143~~	~~.051~~	~~.666~~
Profitability	-.022	.850	-.087	.456
Gearing	-.122	.297	-.055	.642
Liquidity	-.003	.978	.042	.722

The lack of correlation between levels of compliance with mandatory IFRSs disclosure requirements and either of board independence or board size within the Egyptian context, supports the proposition that the majority of board members in companies listed on the EGX do not carry out their responsibilities with respect to monitoring management behaviour properly, even when outside directors are recognised on the boards in the Egyptian listed companies, they lack material independence as generally, they are appointed to the board because of their close relationship with executive board members, the Chair or controlling shareholders. They may also lack experience or may have insufficient financial incentive to actively monitor management and protect the interests of minority shareholders. This lends weight to the notions of the institutional isomorphism theory (board members in the Egyptian listed companies, do not contribute to improving the BOD's monitoring function even when they meet the independence criterion, being appointed simply to signal that such companies follow corporate governance best practices, and hence, gain respect, consequently the problem of decoupling will continue as companies will state that financial statements are prepared according to IFRSs while full compliance is absent). Furthermore, the predictions of financial economics theories relevant to this study (weak monitoring reduces monitoring costs and weak enforcement of IFRSs reduces non-compliance costs) and Gray's (1988) accounting sub-cultural model (acceptance of secrecy, absence of awareness regarding the importance of transparency and the lack of material independence by board members may support management's selective disclosure to avoid competition and protect company reputation, even though the lack of disclosure is in breach of the mandatory requirements). Moreover, the interviewees' responses discussed in Chapter Seven also support this proposition.

With respect to the association between government ownership ratio and the levels of compliance with IFRSs disclosure requirements, the findings reported in Table 6.11 support hypothesis H5a1 (there is no significant statistical relationship between the government ownership ratio and the extent of compliance with IFRSs disclosure requirements in the Egyptian context). This result supports the findings of Naser et al. (2002), Ghazali and Weetman (2006), Al-Akra et al. (2010a). In addition, it supports that of Samaha and Dahawy (2010, 2011) in the Egyptian context. This may be explained by the government's ability to access all company information. Agency theory suggests that, this reduces the monitoring costs, and hence reduces management incentives to improve disclosure. Simultaneously, Gray's (1988) accounting sub-cultural model, cost-benefit analysis, and institutional isomorphism all suggest that given the preference to secrecy the government may not encourage full transparency. This may be due to government's intention to sell its shares in the company at a good price as part of the privatisation programme. Additionally, the lack of awareness and the absence of incentives for members of the public who are implicit owners of government shares discourage direct monitoring of the management (generally government officials) of government owned enterprises. This contributes to the decoupling problem as companies declare their compliance with IFRSs, simply to gain respect and legitimacy, when in reality they are not complying. Further support for this result is evident in the interviewees' responses presented in Chapter Seven.

With respect to the association between management ownership ratio and levels of compliance with the overall IFRSs disclosure requirements, the findings reported in Table 6.11 do not support H5b1 (there is a significant negative statistical relationship between the management ownership ratio and the extent of compliance with IFRSs disclosure requirements in the Egyptian context). Although, this result does not agree with the findings of the majority of prior studies investigating the association between management ownership and levels of disclosure, which support a negative relationship (*e.g.,* Eng and Mak, 2003; Arcay and Vazquez, 2005; Ghazali and Weetman, 2006; Abdelsalam and El-Masry, 2008), and with that of Samaha and Dahawy (2010) in the Egyptian context, it supports that of Samaha and Dahawy (2011). This may be explained by reduced agency costs, and predictions based on Gray's (1988) accounting sub-cultural model, cost-benefit analysis, and institutional isomorphism that the secretive culture, lack of management awareness concerning the importance of transparency and compliance, absence of monitoring by board members or stock exchange regulators, and the absence of pressure from minority shareholders, encourage management to keep disclosure levels at a minimum as long as non compliance costs are less than compliance costs. This in turn contributes to the problem of decoupling. Further support for this result is evident in the interviewees' responses presented in Chapter Seven.

With respect to the association between private ownership and levels of compliance with IFRSs disclosure requirements, the findings reported in Table 6.11 support H5c1 (there is no significant statistical relationship between the private ownership ratio and the extent of compliance with IFRSs disclosure requirements in the Egyptian context). This result supports the findings of Suwaidan (1997), Depoers (2000), Omar (2007) and Al-Akra et al. (2010a,b); however, it does not support that of Samaha and Dahawy (2010, 2011) with respect to voluntary disclosure practices in Egypt. This is probably attributable to ease of access to all company information by private investors who are in most cases actively involved in company management either as executives or as directors. Furthermore, based on Gray's (1988) accounting sub-cultural model, cost-benefit analysis, and institutional isomorphism, it can be stated that the secretive culture, and lack of private investor awareness of the importance of transparency will not increase pressures by private investors on management to improve compliance with IFRSs. Furthermore, absence of monitoring from board members or stock exchange regulators, and the absence of pressure from minority shareholders will reduce non compliance costs; hence will not improve compliance levels with mandatory IFRSs. Consequently, this contributes to the problem of decoupling. Further support for this result is evident in the interviewees' responses presented in Chapter Seven.

Finally, with respect to the association between public ownership ratio and levels of compliance with overall IFRSs disclosure requirements, the findings reported in Table 6.11 support H5d1 (there is no significant statistical relationship between the public ownership ratio and the extent of compliance with IFRSs disclosure requirements in the Egyptian context). This result supports that of Al-Akra et al. (2010a). However, it does not support the results of the majority of prior studies which support the existence of a positive association between public ownership and disclosure level (*e.g.,* Haniffa, 1999; Haniffa and Cooke, 2002; Al-Htaybat, 2005; Arcay and Vazquez, 2005). In addition, it does not support the finding of Ezat and El-Masry (2008) in the Egyptian context. This result may be attributed to the reduced agency costs due to the lack of demand for more disclosure by naive public investors in the Egyptian context. Furthermore, Gray's (1988) accounting sub-cultural model, cost-benefit analysis, and institutional isomorphism propose that the secretive culture causes management to avoid the outflow of stock market price-sensitive information. In addition, secrecy is also associated with large power distance and the tendency to collectivism (Gray, 1988). Furthermore, the lack of listed companies' management and BOD awareness regarding the importance of compliance with IFRSs and of following corporate governance best practices to enhance transparency, the weak enforcement of laws and regulations, and the absence of materially independent board members with primary responsibility for protecting public shareholders interests, cause non-compliance costs to be less than compliance costs. The fact that public shareholders in developing stock exchanges do not exercise their rights, adds to this situation, thereby management is not stimulated to improve compliance with IFRSs, and the problem of decoupling escalates. In this respect, Abdelsalam and Weetman (2007) argue that many public shareholders in Egypt are small investors who cannot form pressure groups like those in developed markets. Further support for this result is evident in the interviewees' responses presented in Chapter Seven.

Regarding the association between company size and compliance with the overall IFRSs disclosure requirements, the results reported in Table 6.11 do not support a significant association. This supports the findings of Ahmed and Nicholls (1994), Street and Gray (2002) and Al-Jifri (2008). In addition, this supports the findings of Samaha and Dahawy (2010, 2011) in the Egyptian context. This may be attributed to the similarity in compliance behaviour with mandatory IFRSs disclosure requirements among all companies listed on the EGX. Table 6.11 reveals that no association exists between firm profitability and its level of compliance with IFRS disclosure requirements in the Egyptian context, thereby supporting the findings of some previous studies (*e.g.,* Malone et al., 1993; Al-Mulhem, 1997; Inchausti, 1997; Tower et al., 1999; Ho and Wong, 2001; Eng and Mak, 2003; Barako et al., 2006). In addition, it supports those of Abd-Elsalam (1999), Ezat and El-Masry (2008) and Samaha and Dahawy (2010, 2011) in the Egyptian context. This may be explained by the similarity in compliance behaviour among all companies listed on the EGX. With respect to the association between firm gearing and its level of compliance with IFRSs disclosure requirements, Table 6.11 reveals that no association exists, thereby supporting research outcomes of some prior research (*e.g.,* Hossain et al., 1994; Raffournier, 1995; Wallace and Naser, 1995; Inchausti, 1997; Patton and Zelenka, 1997; Craig and Diga, 1998; Dumontier and Raffournier, 1998; Tower et al., 1999; Ho and Wong, 2001; Haniffa and Cooke, 2002; Aksu and Kosedag, 2006). In addition, it supports those of Abd-Elsalam (1999), Ezat and El-Masry (2008) and Samaha and Dahawy (2010, 2011) in the Egyptian context. This may be explained by the similarities in compliance attitude among all companies listed on the EGX. Finally, Table 6.11 indicates that no association exists between firm liquidity and its level of compliance with IFRS disclosure requirements in the Egyptian context, thereby supporting the findings of Alsaeed (2005), Barako et al. (2006) and Al-Akra et al. (2010a). In addition, it supports that of Abd-Elsalam (1999) and Samaha and Dahawy (2011) in the Egyptian context. This may be due to the similarity among all companies listed on the EGX in their compliance attitude with mandatory IFRSs disclosure requirements.

Univariate Analysis - Total Disclosure Index and the Categorical Independent Variables- Egypt

The Mann-Whitney U test was used to determine whether there are significant statistical differences between the two groups of companies that: separate the CEO and Chair positions and those that do not; carry out manufacturing activities and those that carry out non-manufacturing activities; audited by big 4 affiliates and those audited by non big 4 ones. Table 6.12 presents the results of the Mann-Whitney U test.

With respect to the impact of board leadership, the Mann-Whitney U test results demonstrated in Table 6.12 show that, no statistically significant differences exist between the two groups of companies (*i.e.,* in which the CEO and Chair positions are held by different persons, and those that do not) in the extent of compliance with the overall IFRSs disclosure requirements as the probability value calculated is greater than .05(P = .574). Consequently, H3a: there are no statistically significant differences in the levels of compliance with IFRSs disclosure requirements between companies that separate the positions of the CEO and Chair and those that do not in the Egyptian context, is accepted. This supports the findings of Arcay and Vazquez (2005), Cheng and Courtenay (2006), Ghazali and Weetman (2006). In addition, it supports those of Ezat and El-Masry (2008) that carried out in the Egyptian context. This can be mainly explained by the lack of material independence of the Chair in the Egyptian listed companies when the CEO and Chair positions are separated. This in turn lends support to the institutional isomorphism which suggests that, separating the CEO and Chair positions has no influence on board leadership independence, as long as there is no awareness regarding the importance of separating the positions of the CEO and Chair in improving the monitoring of management behaviour and hence the quality of financial reporting within the business firm. Consequently, no significant impact on levels of compliance with IFRSs, is expected when the two positions are separated, and decoupling is thus expected to continue due to the existence of cultural barriers to understanding the logic behind the separation of the two positions as recommended under the Anglo-American model of corporate governance. In addition, companies may fall in line with the separation recommendations purely to gain respect and legitimacy. Also, Gray's (1988) accounting sub-cultural model, the notions of agency theory and cost benefit-analysis would argue that given the secretive culture accompanied with lack of material independence of the Chair, weak monitoring and lack of strict enforcement of compliance, non-compliance costs will continue to be less than compliance costs. Consequently, the separation between the CEO and Chair positions will not result in better compliance with IFRSs disclosure requirements. Further support for this result is evident in the interviewees' responses presented in Chapter Seven.

With respect to the impact of the type of business activity (manufacturing/ non manufacturing) on the levels of compliance with the overall IFRSs disclosure requirements, the Mann-Whitney U test results demonstrated in Table 6.12 show that, no statistically significant differences exist between the two groups of companies in the extent of compliance with the overall mandatory disclosure requirements as the probability value calculated is greater than .05(P = .978). This supports the findings of some prior research (*e.g.,* Inchausti, 1997; Naser, 1998; Naser et al., 2002; Street and Gray, 2002). In addition, it supports those of Ismail et al. (2010) and Samaha and Dahawy (2011) in the Egyptian context. This may be attributed to the fact that companies listed on the EGX are the largest companies in their sectors and the most important vehicles in the development of the Egyptian economy, hence there are no differences in their attitude with respect to compliance with mandatory IFRSs disclosure requirements.

Table 6.12 Mann-Whitney U Test Results for Categorical Independent Variables Egypt

Disclosure Index	Mann - Whitney U	Wilcoxon W	Z	Asymp. Sig. (2-tailed)
	Board Leadership			
Total Disclosure Index (Total Score)	650.000	1353.000	-.562	.574
	Type of Business Activity			
Total Disclosure Index (Total Score)	634.500	985.500	-.028	.978
	Type of Auditor			
Total Disclosure Index (Total Score)	570.000	846.000	-.322	.748

Finally, with respect to the impact of the type of auditor (big 4/non big 4) on the levels of compliance with the overall IFRSs disclosure requirements, the Mann-Whitney U test results demonstrated in Table 6.12 show that, no statistically significant differences exist between the two groups of companies in the extent of compliance with the overall mandatory disclosure requirements as the probability value calculated is greater than .05(P = .748).

This supports the findings of some prior research (*e.g.,* Naser, 1998; Naser et al., 2002; Street and Gray, 2002). In addition, this supports the findings of Samaha and Dahawy (2010, 2011) in the Egyptian context. Given that none of the companies that are listed on the EGX achieved full compliance with the overall level of compliance with mandatory IFRSs disclosure requirements, this implies that there is no difference between the quality of work performed by big 4 affiliates compared to non big 4 ones. Hence, this raises doubts concerning the quality of audit work performed by big 4 affiliates that operate in Egypt. Some of these audit firms may not be strict as they may consider the companies to be operating in a developing market, and to require more time to adapt to the compliance culture in respect of IFRSs. Additionally, they may fear the prospect of losing the client should they issue qualified reports; and another possibility is that they may perceive their clients as the best of the worst and believe that issuing them with qualified reports will give an advantage to those companies with lower compliance levels but audited by non-big 4 audit firms.

This supports the continuity of decoupling problem in the Egyptian context in two ways. Firstly, listed companies will continue claiming that their financial statements are prepared in accordance with IFRSs while full compliance is absent. Secondly, it seems that in most cases, listed companies engage with big 4 audit firms, paying expensive audit fees merely as window dressing to attract more investors or to avoid extensive monitoring by the disclosure monitoring staff of the CMA.

The above discussion of the findings from the univariate analysis promulgates that none of the corporate governance variables has a significant association with the overall level of compliance with mandatory IFRSs disclosure requirements. This implies that the impact of corporate governance mechanisms that are recommended by the OECD principles and the ECCG is absent in the Egyptian context. For further confirmation a regression analysis was carried out using normal scores to investigate the joint effect of independent variables, however, none of the independent variables appeared to be with significant power to explain variation in the levels of compliance with mandatory IFRSs disclosure requirements within the Egyptian context as will be reported in sub-section 6.6.3.

Table 6.13 Correlation between Total Disclosure Index and Continuous Independent Variables-Jordan (N=75)

Variable	Total Disclosure Index	
	Spearman Rank Correlation Coefficient (r)	Significance (two-tailed)
BOD Independence	.176	.132
BOD Size	.122	.298
Government Ownership	.118	.314
Management Ownership	-.012	.922
Private Ownership	-.166	.154
Public Ownership	-.336[1]	.003
Company Size	.098	.404
Profitability	.179	.124
Gearing	-.070	.551
Liquidity	-.018	.878

Correlation is Significant at the 0.01 Level

6.5.2 Univariate Analysis - Jordan

Univariate Analysis - Total Disclosure Index and the Continuous Independent Variables- Jordan

Table 6.13 presents the correlation between the overall level of compliance with IFRSs disclosure requirements (total disclosure index) and continuous independent variables within the Jordanian context. Given that the results of the test of normality for the total disclosure index (dependent variable) and all of the independent variables as reported in Appendix F shows that all variables are not normally distributed (P < .05), it was decided to use the Spearman Rank Correlation (non-parametric test).

Table 6.13 indicates the existence of a significant negative relationship between public ownership ratio and the extent of compliance with total IFRSs disclosure requirements in the Jordanian context at the 1% significance level (r = -.336 and P = .003 < .05). Hence, H5d2 (there is no significant statistical relationship between the public ownership ratio and the extent of compliance with IFRSs disclosure requirements in the Jordanian context), is rejected. This result supports that of Hossain et al. (1994). In addition, it supports that of Naser et al. (2002)[2] and Al-Akra et al. (2010b) in the Jordanian context. However, it does not support the results of the majority of prior studies which support the existence of a positive association between public ownership and disclosure level (*e.g.,* Haniffa, 1999; Haniffa and Cooke, 2002; Arcay and Vazquez, 2005; Ezat and El-Masry, 2008), and those of Al-Htaybat (2005) in the Jordanian context. This result may be attributed to the lack of demand for more disclosure by public investors in the Jordanian context similar to their counterparts in the Egyptian context. This can be explained by the fact that, the majority of individual investors in Jordan are small unsophisticated investors, and their investment decisions in most of the cases are speculative and uninformed (Naser et al., 2002; Al-Akra et al., 2010a). Reduced agency costs due to the lack of demand for more disclosure by public investors, accounts for this. Furthermore, Gray's (1988) accounting sub-cultural model, cost-benefit analysis, and institutional isomorphism propose that, the secretive culture in Jordan causes management to avoid the outflow of stock market price-sensitive information. In addition, secrecy is also associated with large power

[2] Naser et al. (2002) report a negative but insignificant association between compliance with IASs disclosure requirements and public ownership.

distance and the tendency to collectivism (Gray, 1988). Furthermore, the lack of listed companies' management and BOD awareness regarding the importance of compliance with IFRSs and of following corporate governance best practices to enhance transparency, the weak enforcement of laws and regulations, and the absence of materially independent board members with primary responsibility for protecting public shareholders' interests, cause non-compliance costs to be less than compliance costs. The fact that public shareholders in scrutinised stock exchanges do not exercise their rights, adds to this situation, thereby management is not stimulated to improve compliance with IFRSs, and the problem of decoupling escalates. Further support for this result is evident in the interviewees' responses presented in Chapter Seven.

With respect to the association between board independence and levels of compliance with IFRSs disclosure requirements, as seen in Table 6.13, the results of the Spearman Rank Correlation support the non-existence of a statistically significant relationship between board independence and the overall level of compliance with mandatory IFRSs disclosure requirements ($P > .05$). These findings support the second research hypothesis (H2b: there is no significant statistical relationship between board independence and the extent of compliance with IFRSs disclosure requirements in the Jordanian context). This agrees with the findings of Haniffa (1999), Ho and Wong (2001), Haniffa and Cooke (2002), Ghazali and Weetman (2006). In addition, this result supports those of Al-Akra et al. (2010a,b) in the Jordanian context. On the other hand, the results demonstrated in Table 6.13 with respect to the association between board size and compliance with overall IFRSs disclosure requirements, support the fourth research hypothesis (H4b: there is no significant statistical relationship between board size and the extent of compliance with IFRSs disclosure requirements in the Jordanian context). This agrees with the findings on the level of the Egyptian context. This also agrees with the findings of Lakhal (2003), Arcay and Vazquez (2005), and Cheng and Courtenay (2006). However, this result does not support that of Al-Akra et al. (2010a) who investigated this issue in the Jordanian context and reported a significant positive relationship.

The lack of correlation between levels of compliance with mandatory IFRSs disclosure requirements and either of board independence or board size in the Jordanian context similar to the Egyptian one, supports the proposition that, board members are not aware about their roles, hence they do not carry out their responsibilities properly. Additionally, most outside directors in the Jordanian listed companies similar to their Egyptian counterparts, lack material independence as generally, they are appointed to the board because of their close relationship with executive board members, the Chair or controlling shareholders. They may also lack experience or may have insufficient financial incentive to actively monitor management and protect the interests of minority shareholders. This lends weight to the notions of the institutional isomorphism theory (board members in the Jordanian listed companies, do not contribute to improving the BOD's monitoring function even when they meet the independence criterion, being appointed simply to signal that such companies follow corporate governance best practices, and hence, gain respect). Furthermore, the predictions of financial economics theories relevant to this study (weak monitoring reduces monitoring costs, hence will not stimulate management to improve compliance as well as the weak enforcement of compliance with IFRSs results in low non-compliance costs) and Gray's (1988) accounting sub-cultural model (acceptance of secrecy, absence of awareness regarding the importance of transparency and the lack of material independence by board members support management's selective disclosure to avoid competition and protect company reputation, even though the lack of disclosure is in breach of the mandatory requirements). Moreover, the interviewees' responses reported in Chapter Seven also support this proposition.

With respect to the association between government ownership ratio and the levels of compliance with IFRSs disclosure requirements, the findings reported in Table 6.13 support those on the level of the Egyptian context. Hence, hypothesis H5a2 (there is no significant statistical relationship between the government ownership ratio and the extent of compliance with IFRSs disclosure requirements in the Jordanian context), is accepted. This result supports the findings of Ghazali and Weetman (2006) and Samaha and Dahawy (2010, 2011). In addition, it supports that of Naser et al. (2002) and Al-Akra et al. (2010a) in the Jordanian context. This may be explained by the government's ability to access all company information. Agency theory suggests that, this reduces the monitoring costs, and hence reduces management incentives to improve disclosure. Simultaneously, Gray's (1988) accounting sub-cultural model, cost-benefit analysis, and institutional isomorphism all suggest that given the preference to secrecy, the government may not encourage full transparency. This may be due to government's intention to sell its shares in the company at a good price as part of the privatisation programme. Additionally, the lack of awareness and the absence of incentives for members of the public who are implicit owners of government shares discourage direct monitoring of the management (generally government officials) in companies with dominant government ownership. This contributes to the decoupling problem as companies declare their compliance with IFRSs simply to gain respect and legitimacy, when in reality they are not fully complying. Further support for this result is evident in the interviewees' responses presented in Chapter Seven.

With respect to the association between management ownership ratio and levels of compliance with the overall IFRSs disclosure requirements, the findings reported in Table 6.13 do not support H5b2 (there is a significant negative statistical relationship between the management ownership ratio and the extent of compliance with IFRSs disclosure requirements in the Jordanian context). Although, this result does not agree with the findings of the majority of prior studies investigating the association between management ownership and levels of disclosure which support a negative relationship (*e.g.,* Eng and Mak, 2003; Arcay and Vazquez, 2005; Ghazali and Weetman, 2006; Abdelsalam and El-Masry, 2008; Samaha and Dahawy, 2010), it supports that of this study on the level of the Egyptian context and of Samaha and Dahawy (2011). To the best of the researcher's knowledge this study is the first to investigate the association between management ownership and levels of compliance with IFRSs in the Jordanian context. However, this finding may be explained by the lack of separation between management and control, reduced agency costs, and predictions based on Gray's (1988) accounting sub-cultural model, cost-benefit analysis, and institutional isomorphism that the secretive culture, lack of management awareness concerning the importance of transparency and compliance, absence of monitoring by board members or stock exchange regulators, and the absence of pressure from minority shareholders, encourage management to keep disclosure levels at a minimum as long as non-compliance costs are less than compliance costs. This in turn contributes to the problem of decoupling. Further support for this result is evident in the interviewees' responses presented in Chapter Seven.

With respect to the association between private ownership and levels of compliance with IFRSs disclosure requirements, the findings reported in Table 6.13 support H5c2 (There is no significant statistical relationship between the private ownership ratio and the extent of compliance with IFRSs disclosure requirements in the Jordanian context). This result supports the findings of this study on the level of the Egyptian context. In addition, it supports that of Depoers (2000); and those of Suwaidan (1997), Omar (2007) and Al-Akra et al. (2010a,b) on the Jordanian context. Similar to the case of Egypt, this may be attributable to ease of access to all company information by private investors who are in most cases actively involved in company management either as executives or as directors. Furthermore, based on Gray's (1988) accounting sub-cultural model, cost-benefit analysis, and institutional isomorphism, it can be stated that the secretive culture, and lack of private investor awareness of the importance of transparency will not increase pressures by private investors on management to improve compliance with IFRSs. Furthermore, absence of monitoring from board members or stock exchange regulators, and the absence of pressure from minority shareholders will reduce non compliance costs; hence will not improve compliance levels with mandatory IFRSs. Consequently, this contributes to the problem of decoupling. Further support for this result is evident in the interviewees' responses presented in Chapter Seven.

Regarding the association between company size and compliance with the overall IFRSs disclosure requirements, the results reported in Table 6.13 do not support a significant association. This supports the findings of this study on the level of the Egyptian context. It also supports that of Ahmed and Nicholls (1994), Street and Gray (2002), Al-Jifri (2008) and Samaha and Dahawy (2010, 2011). In addition, this supports the findings of Al-Akra et al. (2010a) in the Jordanian context. However, it does not agree with the findings of the majority of researchers such as Suwaidan (1997), Naser (1998), Naser et al. (2002), Omar (2007) and Al-Akra et al. (2010b) who report a significant association between company size and disclosure levels mainly due to the low costs of disclosing information in large companies compared to small ones. Hence, this association needs to be further investigated using multivariate analysis. Table 6.13 reveals that no association exists between firm profitability and its level of compliance with IFRS disclosure requirements in the Jordanian context similar to the Egyptian context, thereby supporting the findings of some previous studies (*e.g.,* Malone et al., 1993; Al-Mulhem, 1997; Inchausti, 1997; Abd-Elsalam, 1999; Tower et al., 1999; Ho and Wong, 2001; Eng and Mak, 2003; Barako et al., 2006; Ezat and El-Masry, 2008; Samaha and Dahawy, 2010, 2011). In addition, it supports those of Al-Akra et al. (2010a,b) in the Jordanian context. This implies similarity in compliance behaviour with mandatory IFRSs disclosure requirements among companies listed on the ASE. With respect to the association between firm gearing and its level of compliance with IFRSs disclosure requirements, Table 6.13 reveals that no association exists, thereby supporting this research outcomes on the level of the Egyptian context as well as those of some prior research (*e.g.,* Hossain et al., 1994; Raffournier, 1995; Wallace and Naser, 1995; Inchausti, 1997; Patton and Zelenka, 1997; Craig and Diga, 1998; Dumontier and Raffournier, 1998; Abd-Elsalam, 1999; Tower et al., 1999; Ho and Wong, 2001; Haniffa and Cooke, 2002; Aksu and Kosedag, 2006;

Ezat and El-Masry, 2008; Samaha and Dahawy, 2010, 2011). In addition, it supports those of Al-Htaybat (2005) and Al-Akra et al. (2010b) in the Jordanian context. This may be explained by the similarities in compliance attitude with respect to mandatory IFRSs disclosure requirements by companies listed on the ASE. Finally, Table 6.13 indicates that no significant association exists between firm liquidity and its level of compliance with IFRS disclosure requirements in the Jordanian context, thereby supporting the findings of this study and of Abd-Elsalam (1999) on the level of the Egyptian context and those of Alsaeed (2005), and Barako et al. (2006). It also supports that of Al-Htaybat (2005) in the Jordanian context, however, it does not support that of Naser et al. (2002) and Al-Akra et al. (2010b) in the Jordanian context. This may be attributed to the similarity in compliance behaviour with mandatory IFRSs disclosure requirements by companies listed on the ASE in 2007 regardless of the level of liquidity. However, this issue will be further investigated in the multivariate analysis.

Table 6.14 Mann-Whitney U Test Results for Categorical Independent Variables Jordan

Disclosure Index	Mann - Whitney U	Wilcoxon W	Z	Asymp. Sig. (2-tailed)
	Board Leadership			
Total Disclosure Index (Total Score)	377.000	2268.000	-.680	.497
	Type of Business Activity			
Total Disclosure Index (Total Score)	530.000	1196.000	-1.824	.068
	Type of Auditor			
Total Disclosure Index (Total Score)	332.000	1278.000	-3.814	.000

Univariate Analysis - Total Disclosure Index and the Categorical Independent Variables- Jordan

The Mann-Whitney U test was used to determine whether there are significant statistical differences between the two groups of companies that: separate the CEO and the Chair positions and those that do not; carry out manufacturing activities and those that carry out non-manufacturing activities; audited by big 4 affiliates and those audited by non big 4 ones. Table 6.14 presents the results of the Mann-Whitney U test.

The results presented in Table 6.14 indicate that significant statistical differences exist between companies that are audited by big 4 audit firms and those that are not audited by big 4 audit firms in the Jordanian context in terms of the extent of compliance with mandatory IFRSs disclosure requirements as the probability value calculated is less than .05(P = .000). Furthermore, the Mann-Whitney U test results concerning the indices for companies audited by big 4 audit firms and those that are not, indicate that the compliance level with the total IFRSs disclosure requirements is higher in companies audited by big 4 audit firms than those that are not (the mean rank in the 32 companies audited by big 4 affiliates = 49.12 compared to 29.72 in the 43 companies audited by non-big 4 ones). This result seems reasonable as big 4 audit firm staff are usually highly qualified and more familiar with IASs and practices than their counterparts in local audit firms. This result supports the findings of some earlier studies (*e.g.,* Abd-Elsalam, 1999; Glaum and Street, 2003). In addition, it supports those of Suwaidan (1997), Naser et al. (2002), Al-Shiab (2003), Omar (2007) and Al-Akra et al. (2010a) in the Jordanian context.

With respect to the impact of board leadership, the Mann-Whitney U test results demonstrated in Table 6.14 show that, similar to the case of Egypt, no statistically significant differences exist between the two groups of companies (*i.e.,* in which the CEO and Chair positions are held by different persons, and those that do not) in terms of the extent of compliance with the overall mandatory disclosure requirements as the probability value calculated is greater than .05(P = .497). Consequently, H3b: there are no statistically significant differences in the levels of compliance with IFRSs disclosure requirements between companies that separate the positions of the CEO and Chair and those that do not in the Jordanian context, is accepted. This supports the findings of Arcay and Vazquez (2005), Cheng and Courtenay (2006), Ghazali and Weetman (2006) and Ezat and El-Masry (2008). As previously mentioned, the impact of board leadership to the best of the researcher's knowledge has been investigated in the Jordanian context by Abed et al. (2011) study which reports a significant positive relationship between role duality and level of voluntary disclosures in Jordan. Consequently, the finding of the current study may be attributed to the lack of material independence of the Chair in the Jordanian listed companies when the CEO and the Chair positions are separated. This in turn lends support to the institutional isomorphism which suggests that, separating the CEO and the Chair positions has no influence on board leadership independence, as long as there is no awareness regarding the importance of separating the positions in improving the monitoring of management behaviour and hence the quality of financial reporting within the business firm. Consequently, no significant impact on levels of compliance with IFRSs, is expected when the two positions are separated, and decoupling is thus expected to continue due to the existence of cultural barriers to understanding the logic behind the separation of the two positions as recommended under the Anglo-American model of corporate governance. In addition, companies may fall in line with the separation recommendations purely to gain respect and legitimacy. Also, Gray's (1988) accounting sub-cultural model, the notions of agency theory and cost benefit-analysis would argue that given the secretive culture accompanied with lack of material independence, weak monitoring and lack of strict enforcement of compliance, non-compliance costs will continue to be less than compliance costs. Consequently, the separation between the CEO and Chair positions may not result in better compliance with IFRSs disclosure requirements.

Finally, with respect to the impact of the type of business activity (manufacturing/ non manufacturing) on the levels of compliance with the overall IFRSs disclosure requirements, the Mann-Whitney U test results demonstrated in Table 6.14 show that, similar to the case of Egypt, no statistically significant differences exist between the two groups of companies in the extent of compliance with the overall mandatory disclosure requirements as the probability value calculated is greater than .05(P = .068). This supports the findings of some prior research (*e.g.*, Inchausti, 1997; Street and Gray, 2002; Ismail et al., 2010; Samaha and Dahawy, 2011). In addition, it supports those of Naser (1998) and Naser et al. (2002) in the Jordanian context. This may be attributed to the fact that companies listed on the ASE are the largest companies in their sectors and the most important contributors in the development of the Jordanian economy and that such companies are relatively similar in their behaviour with respect to compliance with mandatory IFRSs disclosure requirements.

Based on the findings of the univariate analysis, it appears that public ownership ratio is the most important test variable in explaining the levels of compliance with IFRSs disclosure requirements by non-financial companies listed on the ASE.

The findings from the univariate analysis on the level of the Jordanian context justify carrying out a multivariate analysis for further investigation of those results taking into consideration the interaction between independent variables. The results of the multivariate analysis and their theoretical implications are reported in the next section.

6.6 Multivariate Analysis

As indicated in sub-section 5.6.1, multiple regression analysis was undertaken to shed light on the joint effects of the independent variables on the dependent variable (Total disclosure index). A multiple regression model can also identify variables which, when combined in one regression equation, are the best statistical predictors of the dependent variable (Ghazali, 2004). Multiple regression is based on correlation but it enables a more sophisticated exploration of the inter-relationship among a set of variables (Pallant, 2001).

6.6.1 The Regression Model

The full regression model is constructed as follows:

Yj = β0 + β1 board independencej + β2 board leadershipj + β3 board sizej+
β4 government ownership ratioj + β5 management ownership ratioj+
β6 private ownership ratioj + β7 public ownership ratioj+
β8 total assetsj + β9 return on Assetsj + β10 debt to equityj+
β11 quick ratioj + β12 type of business activityj+
β13 type of audit firmj + εj

Where:
Yj = Total disclosure index for companies (*j = 1, . . . , 75*)
β0 = The intercept
εj= Error term

The dependent variable is the total disclosure index (denotes the overall level of compliance with mandatory IFRSs disclosure requirements), computed for each of the sample companies. The intercept captures the average effects on compliance with IFRSs disclosure requirements of those variables excluded from the model and is assumed to be constant across all the sample companies. The independent variables consist of seven test (explanatory) variables (board independence, board leadership, board size, government ownership ratio, management ownership ratio, private ownership ratio, and public ownership ratio) and six control variables (firm size [proxied by total assets], profitability [proxied by return on assets], gearing [proxied by debt to equity], liquidity [proxied by quick ratio], type of business activity, and type of audit firm) that are employed in the multiple regression analysis and εj represents error term.

Due to the non-normality of distribution of dependent and independent variables, it was decided to use non-parametric tests and to run the regression analysis using normal scores as transforming data is a recommended approach in order to modify their distribution to look more normal (Pallant, 2001; Field, 2005) as explained in detail in Chapter Five. Before conducting the regression analysis it was essential to check for multicollinearity to avoid the potential for misleading results, as indicated in Chapter Five. The following section indicates the results of multicollinearity test.

6.6.2 Multicollinearity

The inclusion of variables that are highly correlated in one equation can result in one of the variables reporting non-significance even though its significance has been widely documented in prior research (Ghazali, 2004). As indicated in Chapter Five, the problem of multicollinearity will be considered when the correlation coefficient (r) exceeds .7 (Pallant, 2001).

Screening the correlation matrix using the Spearman rank correlation revealed the non-existence of the problem of multicollinearity in both of scrutinised stock exchanges as demonstrated below in tables 6.15 and 6.16.

Additionally, VIF and tolerance were inspected for all models using normal scores to ensure that the problem of multicollinearity did not exist. The VIF was lower than 10 and all values of tolerance in the regression models were above 0.2. Therefore, the problem of multicollinearity was not recognised while running the regression analysis. The following section reports the results of regression analysis on individual country level.

6.6.3 Regression Results

The Regression Results-Egypt

Stepwise regression on SPSS was performed, thus enabling the researcher to determine the individual contribution of each predictor in case the regression results proved that independent variables are related to the dependent variable (Landau and Everitt, 2004; Field, 2005). In a Stepwise regression, variables are entered one at a time, if they meet the entry criterion and removed one at a time if they do not meet the retention criterion. In other words, the researcher provides the SPSS with a list of independent variables, then the program selects which variables to enter and the order of their entrance into the regression equation based on a set of statistical criteria (Pallant, 2001). This study uses the defaults of the SPSS Stepwise regression, which are .05 probability for entry and .10 probability for removal. As demonstrated the regression model employed in this study failed to explain compliance behaviour with mandatory

IFRSs disclosure requirements in the Egyptian context[3]. This result confirms and refines the results of the univariate analysis with respect to the non existence of association between the overall level of compliance with mandatory IFRSs disclosure requirements and any of the test or control variables in the Egyptian context. This implies that the compliance behaviour with mandatory IFRSs disclosure requirements by companies listed on the EGX does not follow any pattern in relation to neither corporate governance related variables nor other company attributes under study in this research. From the researcher's point of view, the non-existence of a significant association between levels of compliance with mandatory IFRSs requirements and any of the company attributes that are employed as control variables is a positive sign that generally all companies listed on the EGX have similar attitude with respect to compliance with mandatory requirements (*i.e.,* compliance with the majority of the requirements is now part of their culture). However, the lack of significant association between compliance levels and any of the corporate governance related variables implies that, the influence of corporate governance best practice on the levels of compliance with mandatory IFRSs in the Egyptian context is absent. This may be attributed to its novelty and the lack of awareness of the advantages of material compliance with its requirements in Egypt, meaning that as yet it is not part of the cultural values in the Egyptian context. Building on this, it can be argued that there are other factors mainly related to the secretive culture that is dominant in MENA society that possibly influence the levels of compliance with most of IFRSs disclosure requirements in the Egyptian stock exchange. This suggests that with time, as national cultural values develop to perceive the importance of compliance with IFRSs as it is perceived in developed countries where such standards were initially developed, and as the qualification of the CMA monitoring staff improves, enforcement of mandatory IFRSs becomes more strict, so too are the levels of compliance with IFRSs disclosure requirements.

The outcome of the regression analysis supports the second research hypothesis (H2a: there is no significant statistical relationship between board independence and the extent of compliance with IFRSs disclosure requirements in the Egyptian context). This agrees with the findings of Haniffa (1999), Ho and Wong (2001), Haniffa and Cooke (2002), Ghazali and Weetman (2006) and Al-Akra et al. (2010a,b). However, these findings do not support those of Samaha and Dahawy (2010, 2011) who

[3] Appendix G demonstrates Pearson Correlation coefficients and significance (1-tailed) reported with regression analysis results for Egypt.

report a significant positive relationship between voluntary disclosure levels and board independence. To the best of the researcher's knowledge there is no evidence available from prior research with respect to the association between corporate governance structures and the extent of compliance with mandatory disclosure requirements in the Egyptian context. However, the results support the proposition that, the majority of board members in companies listed on the EGX do not carry out their responsibilities with respect to monitoring management behaviour properly, even when outside directors are recognised on the boards in the Egyptian listed companies, they lack material independence as generally, they are appointed to the board because of their close relationship with executive board members, the Chair or controlling shareholders. They may also lack experience or may have insufficient financial incentive to actively monitor management and protect the interests of minority shareholders. This lends weight to the notions of the institutional isomorphism theory (board members in the Egyptian listed companies, do not contribute to improving the BOD's monitoring function even when they meet the independence criterion, being appointed simply to signal that such companies follow corporate governance best practices, and hence, gain respect, consequently the problem of decoupling will continue as companies will state that financial statements are prepared according to IFRSs while full compliance is absent). Furthermore, the predictions of financial economics theories relevant to this study (weak monitoring reduces monitoring costs and weak enforcement of IFRSs reduces non-compliance costs) and Gray's (1988) accounting sub-cultural model (acceptance of secrecy, absence of awareness regarding the importance of transparency and the lack of material independence by board members may support management's selective disclosure to avoid competition and protect company reputation, even though the lack of disclosure is in breach of the mandatory requirements). Moreover, the interviewees' responses reported in Chapter Seven also support this proposition.

With respect to the impact of board leadership, H3a: there are no statistically significant differences in the levels of compliance with IFRSs disclosure requirements between companies that separate the positions of the CEO and the Chair and those that do not in the Egyptian context, is accepted. This supports the findings of Arcay and Vazquez (2005), Cheng and Courtenay (2006), Ghazali and Weetman (2006). In addition, it supports those of Ezat and El-Masry (2008) in the Egyptian context. This can be mainly explained by the lack of material independence of the Chair in the Egyptian listed companies when the CEO and the Chair positions are separated. This in turn lends support to the institutional isomorphism theory which suggests that, separating the CEO and Chair positions has no influence on board leadership independence, as long as there is no awareness regarding the importance of separating the positions of the CEO and Chair in improving the monitoring of management behaviour and hence the quality of financial reporting within the business firm. Consequently, no significant impact on levels of compliance with IFRSs, is expected when the two positions are separated, and decoupling is thus expected to continue due to the existence of cultural barriers to understanding the logic behind the separation of the two positions as recommended under the Anglo-American model of corporate governance. In addition, companies may fall in line with the separation recommendations purely to gain respect and legitimacy. Also, Gray's (1988) accounting sub-cultural model, the notions of agency theory and cost benefit-analysis would argue that given the secretive culture accompanied with lack of material independence of the Chair, weak monitoring and lack of strict enforcement of compliance, non-compliance costs will continue to be less than compliance costs. Consequently, the separation between the CEO and Chair positions will not result in better compliance with IFRSs disclosure requirements. Further support for this result is evident in the interviewees' responses presented in Chapter Seven.

With respect to the association between board size and compliance with mandatory IFRSs disclosure requirements, these findings support the fourth research hypothesis (H4a: there is no significant statistical relationship between board size and the extent of compliance with IFRSs disclosure requirements in the Egyptian context). This supports the findings of Lakhal (2003), Arcay and Vazquez (2005) and Cheng and Courtenay (2006). However, it does not support the findings of Ezat and El-Masry (2008) who report a significant positive relationship between voluntary internet disclosure and board size in the Egyptian context. This is mainly attributed to the lack of independence and/or experience of board members and the lack of awareness among them with respect to their role in monitoring management behaviour and protecting the interests of shareholders. This supports the notions of institutional isomorphism theory (board members in the Egyptian listed companies, do not contribute to improving the BOD's monitoring function even when they meet the independence criterion, being appointed simply to signal that such companies follow corporate governance best practices, and hence, gain respect). Furthermore, weak enforcement of full compliance with IFRSs disclosure requirements by the CMA staff, weak monitoring and lack of understanding by board members regarding the benefits of transparency, hence, low non compliance costs and reduced agency costs, and dominance of secretive culture will not stimulate management to improve levels of compliance with IFRS.

With respect to the association between government ownership ratio and levels of compliance with IFRSs disclosure requirements, the findings support hypothesis H5a1 (there is no significant statistical relationship between the government ownership ratio and the extent of compliance with IFRSs disclosure requirements in the Egyptian context). This result supports the findings of Naser et al. (2002), Ghazali and Weetman (2006), Al-Akra et al. (2010a). In addition, it supports that of Samaha and Dahawy (2010, 2011) in the Egyptian context. This may be explained by the government's ability to access all company information. Agency theory suggests that, this reduces the monitoring costs, and hence reduces management incentives to improve disclosure. Simultaneously, Gray's (1988) accounting sub-cultural model, cost-benefit analysis, and institutional isomorphism all suggest that given the preference to secrecy the government may not encourage full transparency. This may be due to government's intention to sell its shares in the company at a good price as part of the privatisation programme. Additionally, the lack of awareness and the absence of incentives for members of the public who are implicit owners of government shares discourage direct monitoring of the management (generally government officials) of government owned enterprises. This contributes to the decoupling problem as companies declare their compliance with IFRSs, simply to gain respect and legitimacy, when in reality they are not fully complying. Further support for this result is evident in the interviewees' responses presented in Chapter Seven. With respect to the association between management ownership ratio and levels of compliance with the overall IFRSs disclosure requirements, the findings do not support H5b1 (there is a significant negative statistical relationship between the management ownership ratio and the extent of compliance with IFRSs disclosure requirements in the Egyptian context). Although, this result does not agree with the findings of the majority of prior studies investigating the association between management ownership and levels of disclosure, which support a negative relationship (e.g., Eng and Mak, 2003; Arcay and Vazquez, 2005; Ghazali and Weetman, 2006; Abdelsalam and El-Masry, 2008), and with that of Samaha and Dahawy (2010) in the Egyptian context, it supports that of Samaha and Dahawy (2011).

Table 6.15 Correlation Coefficients for Independent Variables-Egypt

Variable	BOD Ind.	BOD Size	Gov.	Mngt.	Priv.	Public	Size	Prof.	Gearing	Liquid.
BOD Ind.	1									
BOD Size	-.068	1								
Gov.	.183	-.080	1							
Mngt.	-.024	-.082	-.188	1						
Priv.	-.115	.035	-.416[1]	615[1]	1					
Public	.065	.003	.035	-.053	-.080	1				
Size	-.064	-.049	.183	.127	-.155	.112	1			
Prof.	.185	-.189	.195	-.293[2]	-.185	-.112	-.017	1		
Gearing	-.180	-.055	-.390[1]	.098	.247[2]	-.048	-.249[2]	.044	1	
Liquid.	.113	.026	.184	-.267[2]	-.101	-.023	-.182	.325[1]	.001	1

Correlation is Significant at the 0.01 Level
Correlation is Significant at the 0.05 Level

Table 6.16 Correlation Coefficients for Independent Variables- Jordan

Variable	BOD Ind.	BOD Size	Gov.	Mngt.	Priv.	Public	Size	Prof.	Gearing	Liquid.
BOD Ind.	1									
BOD Size	-.205	1								
Gov.	.073	.324[1]	1							
Mngt.	-.264[2]	.285[2]	-.131	1						
Priv.	-.283[2]	.103	-.295[2]	.186	1					
Public	-.381[1]	.067	.004	.148	.023	1				
Size	-.310[1]	.091	.057	.044	-.117	.011	1			
Prof.	.103	.057	.275[2]	-.058	-.179	-.087	.245[2]	1		
Gearing	-.344[1]	.377[1]	-.069	.249[2]	.375[1]	.127	.214	.029	1	
Liquid.	.064	-.119	.051	-.177	-.138	-.175	.015	.369[1]	-.247[2]	1

Correlation is Significant at the 0.01 Level
Correlation is Significant at the 0.05 Level

This may be explained by reduced agency costs, and predictions based on Gray's (1988) accounting sub-cultural model, cost-benefit analysis, and institutional isomorphism that the secretive culture, lack of management awareness concerning the importance of transparency and compliance, absence of monitoring by board members or stock exchange regulators, and the absence of pressure from minority shareholders, encourage management to keep disclosure levels at a minimum as long as non compliance costs are less than compliance costs. This in turn contributes to the problem of decoupling. Further support for this result is evident in the interviewees' responses presented in Chapter Seven.

With respect to the association between private ownership and levels of compliance with IFRSs disclosure requirements, the findings support H5c1 (there is no significant statistical relationship between the private ownership ratio and the extent of compliance with IFRSs disclosure requirements in the Egyptian context). This result supports the findings of Suwaidan (1997), Depoers (2000), Omar (2007) and Al-Akra et al. (2010a,b); however, it does not support that of Samaha and Dahawy (2010); Samaha (2010) with respect to voluntary disclosure practices in Egypt. This is probably attributable to ease of access to all company information by private investors who are in most cases actively involved in company management either as executives or as directors. Furthermore, based on Gray's (1988) accounting sub-cultural model, cost-benefit analysis, and institutional isomorphism, it can be stated that the secretive culture, and lack of private investor awareness of the importance of transparency, will not increase pressures by private investors on management to improve compliance with IFRSs. Furthermore, absence of monitoring from board members or stock exchange regulators, and the absence of pressure from minority shareholders will reduce non compliance costs; hence will not improve compliance levels with mandatory IFRSs. Consequently, this contributes to the problem of decoupling. Further support for this result is evident in the interviewees' responses presented in Chapter Seven.

Finally, with respect to the association between public ownership ratio and levels of compliance with overall IFRSs disclosure requirements, the findings support H5d1 (there is no significant statistical relationship between the public ownership ratio and the extent of compliance with IFRSs disclosure requirements in the Egyptian context). This result supports that of Al-Akra et al. (2010a). However, it does not support the results of the majority of prior studies which report the existence of a positive association between public ownership and disclosure level (*e.g.*, Haniffa, 1999; Haniffa and Cooke, 2002; Al-Htaybat, 2005; Arcay and

Vazquez, 2005). In addition, it does not support the finding of Ezat and El-Masry (2008) in the Egyptian context. This result may be attributed to the reduced agency costs due to the lack of demand for more disclosure by naive public investors in the Egyptian context. Furthermore, Gray's (1988) accounting sub-cultural model, cost-benefit analysis, and institutional isomorphism propose that the secretive culture causes management to avoid the outflow of stock market price-sensitive information. In addition, secrecy is also associated with large power distance and the tendency to collectivism (Gray, 1988). Furthermore, the lack of listed companies' management and BOD awareness regarding the importance of compliance with IFRSs and of following corporate governance best practices to enhance transparency, the weak enforcement of laws and regulations, and the absence of materially independent board members with primary responsibility for protecting public shareholders' interests, cause non-compliance costs to be less than compliance costs. The fact that public shareholders in developing stock exchanges do not exercise their rights, adds to this situation, thereby management is not stimulated to improve compliance with IFRSs, and the problem of decoupling escalates. This supports the argument of Abdelsalam and Weetman (2007) that many public shareholders in Egypt are small investors who cannot form pressure groups like those in developed markets. Further support for this result is evident in the interviewees' responses presented in Chapter Seven.

Regarding the association between company size and compliance with the overall IFRSs disclosure requirements, the findings do not support a significant association. This supports the findings of Ahmed and Nicholls (1994), Street and Gray (2002) and Al-Jifri (2008). In addition, this supports the findings of Samaha and Dahawy (2010, 2011) in the Egyptian context. This may be attributed to the similarity in compliance behaviour with mandatory IFRSs disclosure requirements among all companies listed on the EGX. Findings also reveal that no association exists between firm profitability and its level of compliance with IFRS disclosure requirements in the Egyptian context, thereby supporting the findings of some previous studies (*e.g.,* Malone et al., 1993; Al-Mulhem, 1997; Inchausti, 1997; Tower et al., 1999; Ho and Wong, 2001; Eng and Mak, 2003; Barako et al., 2006). Additionally, findings support those of Abd-Elsalam (1999), Ezat and El-Masry (2008) and Samaha and Dahawy (2010, 2011) in the Egyptian context. This may be explained by the similarity in compliance behaviour among all companies listed on the EGX regardless of their size. With respect to the association between firm gearing and its level of compliance with IFRSs disclosure requirements, results reveal that no association exists, thereby supporting research outcomes of some prior research (*e.g.,* Hossain et al., 1994; Raffournier, 1995; Wallace and Naser, 1995; Inchausti, 1997; Patton and Zelenka, 1997; Craig and Diga, 1998; Dumontier and Raffournier, 1998; Tower et al., 1999; Ho and Wong, 2001; Haniffa and Cooke, 2002; Aksu and Kosedag, 2006). In addition, results support those of Abd-Elsalam (1999), Ezat and El-Masry (2008) and Samaha and Dahawy (2010, 2011) in the Egyptian context. This also may be explained by the similarities in compliance attitude among all companies listed on the EGX. With respect to firm liquidity, findings indicate that no association exists between firm liquidity and its level of compliance with IFRS disclosure requirements in the Egyptian context, thereby supporting the findings of Alsaeed (2005), Barako et al. (2006) and Al-Akra et al. (2010a). In addition, findings support those of Abd-Elsalam (1999) and Samaha and Dahawy (2011) in the Egyptian context. This may be due to the similarity among all companies listed on the EGX in their compliance attitude with mandatory IFRSs disclosure requirements. With respect to the impact of the type of business activity (manufacturing/ non manufacturing) on the levels of compliance, findings show that, type of business activity has no influence on the levels of compliance with mandatory IFRSs disclosure requirements in the Egyptian context. This supports the findings of some prior research (*e.g.,* Inchausti, 1997; Naser, 1998; Naser et al., 2002; Street and Gray, 2002). In addition, it supports those of Ismail et al. (2010) and Samaha and Dahawy (2011) in the Egyptian context. This may be attributed to the fact that companies listed on the EGX are the largest companies in their sectors and the most important vehicles in the development of the Egyptian economy, hence, there are no differences in their attitude with respect to compliance with mandatory IFRSs disclosure requirements. Finally, with respect to the impact of the type of auditor (big 4/non big 4) on the levels of compliance, findings show that, compliance with IFRSs in the Egyptian context is not associated with the type of auditor. This supports the findings of some prior research (*e.g.,* Naser, 1998; Naser et al., 2002; Street and Gray, 2002). Additionally, this supports the findings of Samaha and Dahawy (2010, 2011) in the Egyptian context. Given that none of the companies that are listed on the EGX achieved full compliance with the overall level of compliance with mandatory IFRSs disclosure requirements, this raises doubts concerning the quality of audit work performed by big 4 affiliates that operate in Egypt. As previously stated in sub-section 6.5.1, some of these audit firms may not be strict as they may consider the companies to be operating in a developing market, and to require more time to adapt to the compliance culture in respect of IFRSs. Additionally, they may fear the prospect of losing the client should they issue qualified reports; and another possibility is that they may perceive their clients as the best of the worst and believe that issuing them with qualified reports will give an advantage to those companies with lower compliance levels but audited by non-big 4 audit firms. This supports the continuity of decoupling problem in the Egyptian context in two ways. Firstly, listed companies will continue claiming that their financial statements are prepared in accordance with IFRSs while full compliance is absent. Secondly, it seems that in most cases, listed companies engage with big 4 audit firms, paying expensive audit fees merely as window dressing to attract more investors or to avoid extensive monitoring by the disclosure monitoring staff of the CMA.

The above discussion of the findings from the regression analysis on the level of the Egyptian context promulgates that none of the corporate governance variables has an association with the overall level of compliance with mandatory IFRSs disclosure requirements. This implies that the impact of corporate governance mechanisms that are recommended by the OECD principles and the ECCG is absent in the Egyptian context. The next section reports regression results for the Jordanian context.

The Regression Results-Jordan

This section reports the regression results of the total disclosure index in the Jordanian context using Stepwise regression as demonstrated in Table 6.17[1].

Table 6.17 shows the adjusted R2 = .245, implying that 24.5% of the variation in the total disclosure index (overall compliance with mandatory IFRSs disclosure requirements) in the Jordanian context is explained by the type of auditor, public ownership ratio and firm size. This result confirms and refines the results of the univariate analysis with respect to the existence of a significant relationship between the extent of compliance with IFRSs disclosure requirements, and auditor type and public ownership ratio. Additionally, the model reaches statistical significance with F = 8.988 and the significance = .000(< .01).

The explanatory power of the total disclosure index model reported in this study exceeds that of Al-Akra et al. (2010a), who investigated the same issue in the Jordanian context in 1996 and 2004 respectively. The explanatory power of Al-Akra et al. (2010a) full model for 1996 was very low (6.3%), however, it reached 14.7% in 2004.

---

[1] Coefficient estimates and significance level for independent variables that are excluded from the regression model are presented in Appendix H.

The results reveal that, the influence of corporate governance best practice as recommended by the OECD corporate governance principles which are supported by the regulatory framework in Jordan on the levels of compliance with IFRSs is absent, possibly because of its novelty and the lack of awareness of the advantages of material compliance with its requirements in Jordan similar to the case of Egypt, meaning that as yet it is not part of the cultural values within the Jordanian context. Building on this, it can be argued that there are other factors mainly related to the secretive culture that is dominant in scrutinised MENA societies that possibly influence the levels of compliance with some IFRSs disclosure requirements in the Jordanian context.

Table 6.17 indicates that, type of auditor with the highest Beta coefficient (-.405) is the best predictor in terms of the extent of compliance with the overall mandatory IFRSs disclosure requirements ($t = -3.779$, $P = .000$) followed by public ownership ratio ($t = -2.194$, $P = .032$) and firm size ($t = 2.188$, $P = .032$). From the information in Table 6.17 the total disclosure index model in the Jordanian context can be stated as:

Total Disclosure Index = .451 - .778 Auditor - .240 Public Ownership Ratio +.226 Firm Size

Table 6.17 Regression Results-Jordan (N=75)

Model summary

R	R2	Adjusted R2	Std. Error	F	Sig.
0.525	0.275	0.245	0.832	8.988	.000 [1]

Coefficients						Collinearity Statistics	
Predictor Variable	Unstandardised Coefficients B	Unstandardised Coefficients Std. Error	Standardised Coefficients Beta	t	Sig.	Tolerance	VIF
(Constant)	0.451	0.152		2.967	.004 [1]		
Auditor Type	-0.788	0.206	-0.405	-3.779	.000 [1]	0.889	1.125
Public Ownership	-0.24	0.109	-0.23	-2.194	.032 [2]	0.93	1.075
Firm Size	0.226	0.103	0.226	2.188	.032 [2]	0.954	1.048

Significant at the 0.01 Levels
Significant at the 0.05 Levels

In summary, the regression analysis reveals the type of auditor, public ownership ratio and firm size as the best predictors of the overall level of compliance with mandatory IFRSs disclosure requirements in the Jordanian context; at least among the variables included in the study. Companies listed on the ASE which are audited by big 4 audit firms comply better with the overall IFRSs mandatory disclosure requirements (the coefficient estimate is significant at .01). This result as previously indicated in sub-section 6.5.2 is reasonable as big 4 audit firms' staff are highly qualified and have better experience with IFRSs, and extensive training on any updates of these standards compared to auditors in local audit firms who may have limited experience and knowledge. This result supports the findings of many earlier studies (*e.g.,* Singhvi and Desai, 1971; Ahmed and Nicholls, 1994; Raffournier, 1995; Wallace and Naser, 1995; Inchausti, 1997; Patton and Zelenka, 1997; Abd-Elsalam, 1999; Glaum and Street, 2003; Samaha and Stapleton, 2009). In addition, it supports those of Suwaidan (1997), Naser et al. (2002), Al-Shiab (2003), Omar (2007) and Al-Akra et al. (2010a) in the Jordanian context. However, given that none of the companies listed on the ASE which are audited by big 4 audit firms achieved full compliance with IFRSs disclosure requirements, although unqualified audit reports are issued, raises doubts regarding the quality of audit work performed by big 4 affiliates operating in Jordan. Such behaviour supports the continuity of the decoupling problem in Jordan as the case in Egypt (companies claim that financial statements are prepared in accordance with IFRSs while full compliance is absent). As previously stated, such audit firms may not be strict as they may consider the companies to be operating in a developing market, and to require more time to adapt to the compliance culture in respect of IFRSs. Additionally, they may fear the prospect of losing the client should they issue qualified reports; and another possibility is that they may perceive their clients as the best of the worst and believe that issuing them with qualified reports will give an advantage to those companies with lower compliance levels but audited by non-big 4 audit firms.

On the other hand the regression analysis reveals that public ownership ratio is the only corporate governance related variable that explains variations in the levels of compliance with mandatory IFRSs disclosure requirements in the Jordanian context. However there is a significant negative relationship between public ownership ratio and total disclosure index at the .05 level. In other words, companies with dominant public ownership complied less with the overall mandatory IFRSs disclosure requirements (*i.e.,* they had the lowest total disclosure scores).

Consequently, hypothesis H5d2 (there is no significant statistical relationship between public ownership ratio and the extent of compliance with IFRSs disclosure requirements in the Jordanian context), is rejected. This result supports that of Hossain et al. (1994). In addition as previously mentioned in sub-section 6.5.2, it supports that of Naser et al. (2002) and Al-Akra et al. (2010b) in the Jordanian context. However, it does not support the results of the majority of prior studies which support the existence of a positive association between public ownership and disclosure level (*e.g.,* Haniffa, 1999; Haniffa and Cooke, 2002; Arcay and Vazquez, 2005; Ezat and El-Masry, 2008); and those of Al-Htaybat (2005) in the Jordanian context. This result may be attributed to the lack of demand for more disclosure by public investors in the Jordanian context similar to their counterparts in the Egyptian context. This confirms the proposition that, the majority of individual investors in Jordan are small unsophisticated investors, and their investment decisions in most of the cases are speculative and uninformed (Naser et al., 2002; Al-Akra et al., 2010a,b). As indicated in sub-section 6.5.2 reduced agency costs due to the lack of demand for more disclosure by public investors, accounts for this. Furthermore, Gray's (1988) accounting sub-cultural model, cost-benefit analysis, and institutional isomorphism propose that, the secretive culture in the Jordanian context causes management to avoid the outflow of stock market price-sensitive information. In addition, secrecy is also associated with large power distance and the tendency to collectivism (Gray, 1988). Furthermore, the lack of listed companies' management and BOD awareness regarding the importance of compliance with IFRSs and of following corporate governance best practices to enhance transparency, the weak enforcement of laws and regulations, and the absence of materially independent board members with primary responsibility for protecting public shareholders' interests, cause non-compliance costs to be less than compliance costs. The fact that public shareholders in Jordan similar to Egypt do not exercise their rights, adds to this situation, thereby management is not stimulated to improve compliance with IFRSs, and the problem of decoupling escalates. Hence dominance of public ownership in the Jordanian context results in lower monitoring capacity (Naser et al., 2002; Al-Akra et al., 2010a). Further support for this result is evident in the interviewees' responses presented in Chapter Seven.

In addition, regression results indicate that large companies comply better with IFRSs disclosure requirements (the coefficient estimate is significant at .05). This confirms the findings of the majority of prior researchers (*e.g.,* Inchausti, 1997; Depoers, 2000; Haniffa and Cooke, 2002; Eng and Mak, 2003; Akhtaruddin, 2005; Naser et al., 2006). It also supports the findings of Suwaidan (1997), Naser (1998), Naser et al. (2002), Omar (2007) and Al-Akra et al. (2010b) in the Jordanian context. This may be attributed to low costs of disclosing information in large companies. In addition, as large companies in most of the cases engage with big 4 audit firms, this will improve their compliance with mandatory disclosure requirements compared to small listed companies which engage with non-big 4 audit firms due to the high fees associated with engagement with big 4 ones. In addition, as they are the largest contributors in the Jordanian economy, they are keen about attracting foreign investors by achieving the highest levels of compliance with IFRSs disclosure requirements.

With respect to the association between board independence and levels of compliance with IFRSs disclosure requirements, as seen in Table 6.17, regression results support those of the univariate analysis with respect to the non-existence of a statistically significant relationship between board independence and the overall level of compliance with mandatory IFRSs disclosure requirements. Hence, these findings support the second research hypothesis (H2b: there is no significant statistical relationship between board independence and the extent of compliance with IFRSs disclosure requirements in the Jordanian context). This agrees with the findings of Haniffa (1999), Ho and Wong (2001), Haniffa and Cooke (2002), Ghazali and Weetman (2006). In addition, this result supports those of Al-Akra et al. (2010a,b) on the Jordanian context. As previously stated in sub-section 6.5.2, this finding supports the proposition that, most outside directors in the Jordanian listed companies similar to their Egyptian counterparts, lack material independence as generally, they are appointed to the board because of their close relationship with executive board members, the Chair or controlling shareholders. They may also lack experience or may have insufficient financial incentive to actively monitor management and protect the interests of minority shareholders. This lends weight to the notions of institutional isomorphism theory (board members in the Jordanian listed companies, do not contribute to improving the BOD's monitoring function even when they meet the independence criterion, being appointed simply to signal that such companies follow corporate governance best practices, and hence, gain legitimacy and respect). Furthermore, the predictions of financial economics theories relevant to this study (weak monitoring reduces monitoring costs, hence will not stimulate management to improve compliance as well as the weak enforcement of compliance with IFRSs results in low non-compliance costs) and Gray's (1988) accounting sub-cultural model (acceptance of secrecy as a dominant culture in the Jordanian context similar to the

Egyptian context, absence of awareness regarding the importance of transparency and the lack of material independence by board members support management's selective disclosure to avoid competition and protect company reputation, even though the lack of disclosure is in breach of the mandatory requirements). Moreover, the interviewees' responses discussed in Chapter Seven also support this proposition.

With respect to the impact of board leadership, regression analysis supports the Mann-Whitney U test results demonstrated in Table 6.14 that, similar to the case of Egypt, holding the CEO and Chair positions by two different persons does not improve the monitoring function. Consequently, H3b: there are no statistically significant differences in the levels of compliance with IFRSs disclosure requirements between companies that separate the positions of the CEO and Chair and those that do not in the Jordanian context, is accepted. As previously indicated, this supports the findings of Arcay and Vazquez (2005), Cheng and Courtenay (2006), Ghazali and Weetman (2006) and Ezat and El-Masry (2008). This finding may be attributed to the lack of material independence of the Chair in the Jordanian listed companies when the CEO and the Chair positions are separated. This in turn lends support to the institutional isomorphism which suggests that, separating the CEO and the Chair positions has no influence on board leadership independence, as long as there is no awareness regarding the importance of separating the positions in improving the monitoring of management behaviour and hence the quality of financial reporting within the business firm.

Consequently, no significant impact on levels of compliance with IFRSs, is expected when the two positions are separated, and decoupling is thus expected to continue due to the existence of cultural barriers to understanding the logic behind the separation of the two positions as recommended under the Anglo-American model of corporate governance. In addition, companies may fall in line with the separation recommendations purely to gain respect and legitimacy. Also, Gray's (1988) accounting sub-cultural model, the notions of agency theory and cost benefit-analysis would argue that given the dominant secretive culture accompanied with lack of material independence, weak monitoring and lack of strict enforcement of compliance, non-compliance costs will continue to be less than compliance costs. Consequently, the separation between the CEO and Chair positions may not result in better compliance with IFRSs disclosure requirements. This viewpoint is confirmed by the interviewees' responses reported in Chapter Seven. On the other hand, regression results support those of the univariate analysis with respect to the non-existence of association between board size and compliance with overall IFRSs disclosure requirements. Hence, H4b (there is no significant statistical relationship between board size and the extent of compliance with IFRSs disclosure requirements in the Jordanian context), is accepted. This finding agrees with the findings on the level of the Egyptian context. This also agrees with the findings of Lakhal (2003), Arcay and Vazquez (2005) and Cheng and Courtenay (2006). However, this result does not support that of Al-Akra et al. (2010a) who investigated this issue in the Jordanian context and reported a significant positive relationship. This is mainly attributed to the lack of independence of board members and the lack of awareness among them with respect to their role in monitoring management behaviour and protecting the interests of shareholders. This supports the notions of institutional isomorphism theory (board members in the Jordanian listed companies, do not contribute to improving the BOD's monitoring function even when they meet the independence criterion, being appointed simply to signal that such companies follow corporate governance best practices, and hence, gain respect). Furthermore, weak enforcement and monitoring by the JSC staff and lack of understanding by board members regarding the benefits of transparency, reduced agency costs, dominance of secretive culture will not stimulate management to improve levels of compliance with IFRS.

With respect to the association between government ownership ratio and the levels of compliance with IFRSs disclosure requirements, the regression results support the findings of the univariate analysis. Hence, hypothesis H5a2 (there is no significant statistical relationship between the government ownership ratio and the extent of compliance with IFRSs disclosure requirements in the Jordanian context), is accepted. This result supports the findings of Ghazali and Weetman (2006) as well as the findings of this study, Samaha and Dahawy (2010, 2011) on the level of the Egyptian context. In addition, it supports that of Naser et al. (2002), Al-Akra et al. (2010a) on the Jordanian context. This may be explained by the government's ability to access all company information. Agency theory suggests this reduces the monitoring costs, and hence reduces management incentives to improve disclosure. Simultaneously, the notions of Gray's (1988) accounting sub-cultural model, cost-benefit analysis, and institutional isomorphism are supported. Given the preference to secrecy the government may not encourage full transparency. This may be due to government's intention to sell its shares in the company at a good price as part of the privatisation programme. Additionally, the lack of awareness and the absence of incentives for members of the public who are implicit owners of government shares discourage direct monitoring of the management (generally government officials) in companies with dominant government ownership. This contributes to the decoupling problem as companies declare their compliance with IFRSs when in reality they are not complying, simply to gain respect and legitimacy. Further support for this result is evident in the interviewees' responses presented in Chapter Seven. With respect to the association between management ownership ratio and levels of compliance with the overall IFRSs disclosure requirements, regression results support the findings of the univariate analysis. Hence, H5b2 (there is a significant negative statistical relationship between the management ownership ratio and the extent of compliance with IFRSs disclosure requirements in the Jordanian context), is rejected. Although, this result does not agree with the findings of the majority of prior studies investigating the association between management ownership and levels of disclosure which support a negative relationship (*e.g.,* Eng and Mak, 2003; Arcay and Vazquez, 2005; Ghazali and Weetman, 2006; Abdelsalam and El-Masry, 2008; Samaha and Dahawy, 2010), it supports that of Samaha and Dahawy (2011) as well as the findings of this study on the level of the Egyptian context. As previously stated to the best of the researcher knowledge this study is the first to investigate the association between management ownership and levels of compliance with IFRSs in the Jordanian context. However, this finding may be explained by the lack of separation between management and control, reduced agency costs, and predictions based on Gray's (1988) accounting sub-cultural model, cost-benefit analysis, and institutional isomorphism that the secretive culture, lack of management awareness concerning the importance of transparency and compliance, absence of monitoring by non-executive board members or stock exchange regulators, and the absence of pressure from minority shareholders, encourage management to keep disclosure levels at a minimum as long as non-compliance costs are less than compliance costs. This in turn contributes to the problem of decoupling. Further support for this result is evident in the interviewees' responses presented in Chapter Seven.

With respect to the association between private ownership ratio and levels of compliance with IFRSs disclosure requirements, regression results support those of the univariate analysis. Hence, H5c2 (there is no significant statistical relationship between the private ownership ratio and the extent of compliance with IFRSs disclosure requirements in the Jordanian context), is accepted. As previously stated in sub-section 5.5.2, this result supports the findings of this study on the level of the Egyptian context. In addition, it supports that of Depoers (2000); and those of Suwaidan (1997), Omar (2007) and Al-Akra et al. (2010a,b) in the Jordanian context. Similar to the case of Egypt, this can be explained by ease of access to all company information by private investors who are in most cases actively involved in company management either as executives or as directors. Moreover, based on Gray's (1988) accounting sub-cultural model, cost-benefit analysis, and institutional isomorphism, it can be stated that the secretive culture, and lack of private investor awareness of the importance of transparency will not increase pressures by private investors on management to improve compliance with IFRSs. Additionally, absence of monitoring from board members or stock exchange regulators, and the absence of pressure from minority shareholders will reduce non compliance costs; hence will not improve compliance levels with mandatory IFRSs. Consequently, this contributes to the problem of decoupling. Further support for this result is evident in the interviewees' responses presented in Chapter Seven.

Finally, with respect to control variables other than firm size and type of auditor, regression results confirm the findings of the univariate analysis that, none of the other control variables influences the levels of compliance with mandatory IFRSs disclosure requirements in the Jordanian context. Regression analysis reveals that no association exists between firm profitability and its level of compliance with IFRS disclosure requirements in the Jordanian context similar to the Egyptian context, thereby supporting the findings of some previous studies (*e.g.,* Malone et al., 1993; Al-Mulhem, 1997; Inchausti, 1997; Abd-Elsalam, 1999; Tower et al., 1999; Ho and Wong, 2001; Eng and Mak, 2003; Barako et al., 2006; Ezat and El-Masry, 2008; Samaha and Dahawy, 2010, 2011). In addition, it supports those of Al-Akra et al. (2010a,b) in the Jordanian context. Regression results also confirm the results of the univariate analysis with respect to the non-existence of an association between firm gearing and its level of compliance with IFRSs disclosure requirements, thereby supporting this research outcomes on the level of the Egyptian context as well as those of some prior research (*e.g.,* Hossain et al., 1994; Raffournier, 1995; Wallace and Naser, 1995; Inchausti, 1997; Patton and Zelenka, 1997; Craig and Diga, 1998; Dumontier and Raffournier, 1998; Abd-Elsalam, 1999; Tower et al., 1999; Ho and Wong, 2001; Haniffa and Cooke, 2002; Aksu and Kosedag, 2006; Ezat and El-Masry, 2008; Samaha and Dahawy, 2010, 2011). In addition, they support those of Al-Htaybat (2005) and Al-Akra et al. (2010b) in the Jordanian context. Similar to the results of the univariate analysis regression analysis indicates the non-existence of association between firm liquidity and its level of compliance with IFRS disclosure requirements in the Jordanian context, thereby supporting the findings of this study and of Abd-Elsalam (1999) on the level of the Egyptian context and those of Alsaeed (2005), and Barako et al. (2006). It also supports that of Al-Htaybat (2005) in the Jordanian context. Hence, compliance behaviour with mandatory IFRSs disclosure requirements by companies listed on the ASE is not influenced by company liquidity. Finally, the results of the regression analysis confirm those of the univariate analysis that, the type of firm industry does not affect its level of compliance with mandatory IFRSs disclosure requirements in the Jordanian context. This supports the findings of some prior studies (*e.g.,* Inchausti, 1997; Street and Gray, 2002; Ismail et al., 2010; Samaha and Dahawy, 2011). In addition, it supports the findings of this study on the level of the Egyptian context, and those of Naser (1998) and Naser et al. (2002) in the Jordanian context. As indicated in sub-section 5.5.2, the lack of significant association between level of compliance with mandatory IFRSs disclosure requirements in the Jordanian context and the majority of control variables indicates that the compliance behaviour with mandatory IFRSs disclosure requirements by companies listed on the ASE do not follow any pattern in relation to such variables. Hence, this may signal the relative similarity in compliance behaviour with mandatory requirements in the Jordanian context.

The above discussion promulgates that, the contribution towards enhancing the ASE performance similar to the case of the EGX is subject to the extent to which the conditions for robust governance practice are consistent with the existing values and the needs of all parties involved in the financial reporting process. It is expected, therefore, to be some time before the impact of applying corporate governance can be measured in developing contexts as this needs to develop, and favourable attitude and belief must be formed as well as efforts being made to develop the human resource capabilities that believe in and able to apply corporate governance requirements for best practice.

Significant Differences in the Influence of Corporate governance Attributes between Scrutinised Contexts

This section mainly aims to further investigate whether there are significant differences in the influence of corporate governance related variables on the extent of compliance with mandatory IFRSs disclosure requirements between Egypt and Jordan. In order to investigate this issue, country dummy will be introduced and interacted with all test and control variables as follows:

Compliancej = a0 + a1 board independencej + a2 board leadershipj + a3 board sizej + a4 government ownership ratioj + a5 management ownership ratioj + a6 private ownership ratioj + a7 public ownership ratioj + a8 sizej + a9 profitabilityj + a10 gearingj + a11 liquidityj + a12

*type of business activityj + a13 type of audit firmj + a14 country+a15 country*board independencej + a16 Country*board leadershipj + a17 Country*board sizej + a18country*government ownership ratioj + a19 country*management ownership ratioj + a20 country*private ownership ratioj + a21 country*public ownership ratioj + a22 country*sizej + a23 country*profitabilityj + a24 country*gearingj + a25 country*liquidityj + a26 country*type of business activityj + a27 country*type of audit firmj + εj*

Where:
Compliancej = Total disclosure index (*j = 1, . . . , 150*)
a0 = The intercept
a1 to *a7* = Test variables
a8 to *a13* = Control variables
a14 = Country dummy
a15 to *a21* = Country*Test variables
a22 to *a27* = Country*Control variables
εj = Error term

Table 6.18 demonstrates the Stepwise regression results for total disclosure index[1].

As demonstrated in Table 6.18 and Appendix I the VIF and Tolerance values indicate the non-existence of the problem of multicollinearity (*i.e.,* all VIF values are less than 10 and all Tolerance values are above .2). The adjusted R2 = .191, implying that 19.1% of the variation in the total disclosure index (overall compliance with mandatory IFRSs disclosure requirements) for the entire sample of companies listed on scrutinised MENA stock exchanges, is explained by the regression model. Findings indicate a significantly higher influence of auditing by big 4 audit firms on the levels of compliance with mandatory IFRSs disclosure requirements for companies listed on the ASE than for those listed on the EGX. The interactive variable Country*Type of auditor shows a significant coefficient at .01 level. This result is reasonable as big 4 audit firms' staff are more qualified and have better experience with IFRSs, and extensive training on any updates of these standards than auditors in local audit firms who may have limited experience and knowledge particularly in a country like Jordan that is suffering from a shortage of qualified accountants and auditors. Additionally, big 4 audit firms exert more pressure on their clients to improve compliance with IFRSs. This result

---

[1] Coefficient estimates and significance level for independent variables that are excluded from the regression model are presented in Appendix I.

supports the findings of many earlier studies (*e.g.,* Singhvi and Desai, 1971; Ahmed and Nicholls, 1994; Raffournier, 1995; Wallace and Naser, 1995; Inchausti, 1997; Patton and Zelenka, 1997; Abd-Elsalam, 1999; Glaum and Street, 2003; Samaha and Stapleton, 2009). In addition, it supports those of Suwaidan (1997), Naser et al. (2002), Omar (2007) and Al-Akra et al. (2010a) in the Jordanian context. The coefficient firm size is positive and significant at .05 level for the entire sample. This implies that large companies comply better with IFRSs disclosure requirements (the coefficient estimate is significant at .05). This confirms the findings of the majority of prior researchers (*e.g.,* Inchausti, 1997; Depoers, 2000; Haniffa and Cooke, 2002; Eng and Mak, 2003; Akhtaruddin, 2005; Naser et al., 2006). It also supports the findings of Suwaidan (1997), Naser (1998), Abd-Elsalam (1999), Naser et al. (2002), Omar (2007), Samaha and Stapleton (2009) and Al-Akra et al. (2010b) in the scrutinised contexts. Referring to political cost theory, many researchers argue that large companies are more likely to provide more disclosures and to comply with mandatory disclosure requirements as they may be more subject to public scrutiny or more sensitive to criticism for falling short of disclosure requirements compared to small firms (*e.g.,* Singhvi, 1968; Singhvi and Desai, 1971; Buzby, 1975; Firth, 1979; Abd-Elsalam, 1999; Al-Htaybat, 2005). Referring to agency theory, many researchers propose that large companies are more likely to disclose more information because of large numbers of shareholders and the associated pressures (*e.g.,* Hossain et al., 1995; Meek et al., 1995; Al-Mulhem, 1997; Abd-Elsalam, 1999; Ali et al., 2004; Al-Htaybat, 2005; Omar, 2007). Also, using capital need theory, many researchers claim that larger companies are more likely to disclose more information in order to raise funds at lower costs (*e.g.,* Cooke, 1991; Meek et al., 1995; Abd-Elsalam, 1999; Ali et al., 2004; Al-Htaybat, 2005; Omar, 2007). Furthermore, using cost-benefit analysis, many researchers argue that large firms are more likely to disclose more information because for them, the costs of non-compliance are higher than the costs of compliance. Also, large companies are more likely to disclose more information because of lower costs associated with collecting and publishing information and limited impact on the competitive position compared to small companies (*e.g.,* Singhvi, 1968; Singhvi and Desai, 1971; Buzby, 1975; Firth, 1979; Ahmed and Nicholls, 1994; Abd-Elsalam, 1999; Ali et al., 2004; Al-Htaybat, 2005). Additionally, based on the notions of the institutional isomorphism theory, large companies are more likely to comply with IFRSs to gain legitimacy and respect, hence attract foreign investors.

Table 6.18 Significant Differences between Scrutinised Contexts in the Influence of Independent Variables on the Levels of Compliance with IFRSs Disclosure Requirements

Model summary					
R	R2	Adjusted R2	Std. Error	F	Sig.
0.449	0.202	0.191	0.877	18.565	0.000 [1]

Coefficients						Collinearity Statistics	
Predictor Variable	Unstandardised Coefficients B	Unstandardised Coefficients Std. Error	Standardised Coefficients Beta	t	Sig.	Tolerance	VIF
(Constant)	0.242	0.085		2.842	0.005 [1]		
Country*Auditor	-0.844	0.161	-0.393	-5.252	0.000 [1]	0.970	1.031
Firm Size	0.160	0.075	0.160	2.139	0.034 [2]	0.970	1.031

Significant at the 0.01 Levels
Significant at the 0.05 Levels

With respect to the association between board independence and levels of compliance with IFRSs disclosure requirements, regression results support the non-existence of a statistically significant relationship between board independence and the overall level of compliance with mandatory IFRSs disclosure requirements for the entire sample. Hence, these findings support the second research hypothesis (H2: there is no significant statistical relationship between board independence and the extent of compliance with IFRSs disclosure requirements). This agrees with the findings of Haniffa (1999), Ho and Wong (2001), Haniffa and Cooke (2002), Ghazali and Weetman (2006). In addition, this result supports those of Al-Akra et al. (2010a,b) in the Jordanian context, however, it does not support those of Samaha and Dahawy (2010, 2011) which report a significant positive relationship between voluntary disclosure levels and board independence in the Egyptian context. This supports the proposition that, most outside directors in the scrutinised listed companies, lack material independence as generally, they are appointed to the board because of their close relationship with executive board members, the Chair or controlling shareholders. They may also lack experience or may have insufficient financial incentive to actively monitor management and protect the interests of minority shareholders. This lends weight to the notions of institutional isomorphism theory (board members in the scrutinised listed companies, do not contribute to improving the BOD's monitoring function even when they meet the independence criterion, being appointed simply to signal that such companies follow corporate governance best practices, and hence, gain legitimacy and respect). Furthermore, the predictions of financial economics theories relevant to this study (weak monitoring reduces monitoring costs, hence will not stimulate management to improve compliance, as well as the weak enforcement of compliance with IFRSs results in low non-compliance costs) and Gray's (1988) accounting sub-cultural model (acceptance of secrecy as a dominant culture in the scrutinised contexts and absence of awareness regarding the importance of transparency support management's selective disclosure to avoid competition and protect company reputation, even though the lack of disclosure is in breach of the mandatory requirements). Moreover, the interviewees' responses discussed in Chapter Seven also support this proposition.

With respect to the impact of board leadership, regression analysis reveals that holding the CEO and Chair positions by two different persons does not improve the monitoring function. Consequently, H3: there are no statistically significant differences in the levels of compliance with IFRSs disclosure requirements between companies that separate the positions of the CEO and Chair and those that do not, is accepted. This supports the findings of Arcay and Vazquez (2005), Cheng and Courtenay (2006), Ghazali and Weetman (2006) and Ezat and El-Masry (2008). This finding may be attributed to the lack of material independence of the Chair in the scrutinised listed companies when the CEO and the Chair positions are separated. This in turn lends support to the institutional isomorphism which suggests that, separating the CEO and Chair positions has no influence on board leadership independence, as long as there is no awareness regarding the importance of separating the positions in improving the monitoring of management behaviour and hence the quality of financial reporting within the business firm. Consequently, no significant impact on levels of compliance with IFRSs, is expected when the two positions are separated, and decoupling is thus expected to continue due to the existence of cultural barriers to understanding the logic behind the separation of the two positions as recommended under the Anglo-American model of corporate governance. In addition, companies may fall in line with the separation recommendations purely to gain respect and legitimacy. Also, Gray's (1988) accounting sub-cultural model, the notions of agency theory and cost benefit-analysis would argue that given the dominant secretive culture accompanied with lack of material independence, weak monitoring and lack of strict enforcement of compliance, non-compliance costs will continue to be less than compliance costs. Consequently, the separation between the CEO and Chair positions may not result in better compliance with IFRSs disclosure requirements. This viewpoint is confirmed by the interviewees' responses reported in Chapter Seven. On the other hand, regression results reveal the non-existence of association between board size and compliance with overall IFRSs disclosure requirements for the entire sample. Hence, H4: there is no significant statistical relationship between board size and the extent of compliance with IFRSs disclosure requirements, is accepted. This agrees with the findings of Lakhal (2003), Arcay and Vazquez (2005) and Cheng and Courtenay (2006). However, this result does not support that of Al-Akra et al. (2010a) who investigated this issue in the Jordanian context and reported a significant positive relationship. This finding can mainly be explained by the lack of independence of board members and the lack of awareness among them with respect to their role in monitoring management behaviour and protecting the interests of shareholders. This supports the notions of institutional isomorphism theory (board members in the scrutinised contexts, do not contribute to improving the BOD's monitoring function even when they meet the independence criterion, being appointed simply to signal that companies follow corporate governance best practices, and hence, gain respect). Furthermore, weak enforcement and monitoring by the regulatory bodies, reduced agency costs, dominance of secretive culture and lack of understanding by board members regarding the benefits of transparency, will not stimulate management to improve levels of compliance with IFRS.

With respect to the association between government ownership ratio and levels of compliance with IFRSs disclosure requirements, the regression results reveal the non existence of association. Hence, hypothesis H5a (there is no significant statistical relationship between the government ownership ratio and the extent of compliance with IFRSs disclosure requirements), is accepted. This result supports the findings of Ghazali and Weetman (2006) as well as the findings of Samaha and Dahawy (2010, 2011) on the level of the Egyptian context. In addition, it supports that of Naser et al. (2002), Al-Akra et al. (2010a) in the Jordanian context. This may be explained by the government's ability to access all company information. Agency theory suggests this reduces the monitoring costs, and hence reduces management incentives to improve disclosure. Simultaneously, the notions of Gray's (1988) accounting sub-cultural model, cost-benefit analysis, and institutional isomorphism are supported. Given the preference to secrecy the government may not encourage full transparency. This may be due to government's intention to sell its shares in the company at a good price as part of the privatisation programme. Additionally, the lack of awareness and the absence of incentives for members of the public who are implicit owners of government shares discourage direct monitoring of the management (generally government officials) in companies with dominant government ownership. This contributes to the decoupling problem as companies declare their compliance with IFRSs when in reality they are not complying, simply to gain respect and legitimacy. Further support for this result is evident in the interviewees' responses presented in Chapter Seven. With respect to the association between management ownership ratio and levels of compliance with the overall IFRSs disclosure requirements, regression results do not support H5b (there is a significant negative statistical relationship between the management ownership ratio and the extent of compliance with IFRSs disclosure requirements). Although, this result does not agree with the findings of the majority of prior studies investigating the association between management ownership and levels of disclosure which support a negative relationship (*e.g.,* Eng and Mak, 2003; Arcay and Vazquez, 2005; Ghazali and Weetman, 2006; Abdelsalam and El-Masry, 2008; Samaha, 2010), it supports that of Samaha and Dahawy (2011) in the Egyptian context. This may be explained by the lack of separation between ownership and control, reduced agency costs, and predictions based on Gray's (1988) accounting sub-cultural model, cost-benefit analysis, and institutional isomorphism that the secretive culture, lack of management awareness concerning the importance of transparency and compliance, absence of monitoring by non-executive board members or stock exchange regulators, and the absence of pressure from minority shareholders, encourage management to keep disclosure levels at a minimum as long as non-compliance costs are less than compliance costs. This in turn contributes to the problem of decoupling. Further support for this result is evident in the interviewees' responses presented in Chapter Seven.

With respect to the association between private ownership ratio and levels of compliance with IFRSs disclosure requirements, regression results support H5c (there is no significant statistical relationship between the private ownership ratio and the extent of compliance with IFRSs disclosure requirements). This supports the findings of Depoers (2000); and those of Suwaidan (1997), Omar (2007) and Al-Akra et al. (2010a,b) in the Jordanian context, however, it does not support those of Samaha and Dahawy (2010, 2011) with respect to voluntary disclosure practices in Egypt. This can be explained by ease of access to all company information by private investors who are in most cases actively involved in company management either as executives or as directors. Moreover, based on Gray's (1988) accounting sub-cultural model, cost-benefit analysis, and institutional isomorphism, it can be stated that the secretive culture, and lack of private investor awareness of the importance of transparency will not increase pressures by private investors on management to improve compliance with IFRSs. Additionally, absence of monitoring from board members or stock exchange regulators, and the absence of pressure from minority shareholders will reduce noncompliance costs; hence will not improve compliance levels with mandatory IFRSs. Consequently, this contributes to the problem of decoupling. Further support for this result is evident in the interviewees' responses presented in Chapter Seven.

With respect to the association between public ownership ratio and levels of compliance with IFRSs disclosure requirements, regression results support hypothesis H5d (there is no significant statistical relationship between public ownership ratio and the extent of compliance with IFRSs disclosure requirements). This result supports that of Hossain et al. (1994). Furthermore, it supports that of Naser et al. (2002) and Al-Akra et al. (2010b) in the Jordanian context. However, it does not support the results of the majority of prior studies which report the existence of a positive association between public ownership and disclosure level (*e.g.*,

Haniffa, 1999; Haniffa and Cooke, 2002; Arcay and Vazquez, 2005). In addition, it does not support the findings of Ezat and El-Masry (2008) in the Egyptian context and those of Al-Htaybat (2005) in the Jordanian context. This result may be attributed to the lack of demand for more disclosure by public investors in the scrutinised contexts. In this regard, Naser et al. (2002) and Al-Akra et al. (2010a) argue that, dominance of public ownership in the Jordanian context results in lower monitoring capacity as the majority of individual investors in Jordan are small unsophisticated investors, and their investment decisions in most of the cases are speculative and uninformed (Naser et al., 2002; Al-Akra et al., 2010a,b). In a similar vein, Abdelsalam and Weetman (2007) describe public shareholders in Egypt as small investors who cannot form pressure groups like those in developed markets. Reduced agency costs due to the lack of demand for more disclosure by public investors, accounts for this. Furthermore, the lack of listed companies' management and BOD awareness regarding the importance of compliance with IFRSs and of following corporate governance best practices to enhance transparency, the weak enforcement of laws and regulations, and the absence of materially independent board members with primary responsibility for protecting public shareholders' interests, cause non-compliance costs to be less than compliance costs. The fact that public shareholders in scrutinised stock exchanges do not exercise their rights, adds to this situation, thereby management is not stimulated to improve compliance with IFRSs, and the problem of decoupling escalates. Further support for this result is evident in the interviewees' responses presented in Chapter Seven.

With respect to control variables, regression results for the entire sample reveal that, no association exists between firm profitability and its level of compliance with IFRS disclosure requirements in scrutinised contexts, thereby supporting the findings of some previous studies (*e.g.,* Malone et al., 1993; Al-Mulhem, 1997; Inchausti, 1997; Tower et al., 1999; Ho and Wong, 2001; Eng and Mak, 2003; Barako et al., 2006). Additionally, this supports the findings of Abd-Elsalam (1999), Ezat and El-Masry (2008), Al-Akra et al. (2010a,b) and Samaha and Dahawy (2010, 2011) in scrutinised contexts. Regression results also confirm the non-existence of association between firm gearing and its level of compliance with IFRSs disclosure requirements, thereby supporting the outcomes of some prior research (*e.g.,* Hossain et al., 1994; Raffournier, 1995; Wallace and Naser, 1995; Inchausti, 1997; Patton and Zelenka, 1997; Craig and Diga, 1998; Dumontier and Raffournier, 1998; Tower et al., 1999; Ho and Wong, 2001; Haniffa and Cooke, 2002; Aksu and Kosedag, 2006). In addition, they support those of Abd-Elsalam (1999),

Al-Htaybat (2005), Ezat and El-Masry (2008), Al-Akra et al. (2010b) and Samaha and Dahawy (2010, 2011) in the scrutinised contexts. Similarly, regression results reveal the non-existence of association between company liquidity and its level of compliance with IFRS disclosure requirements in scrutinised contexts. This supports the findings of Al-saeed (2005), and Barako et al. (2006). Additionally, it supports the findings of Abd-Elsalam (1999) in the the Egyptian context. It also supports those of Al-Htaybat (2005) in the Jordanian context. Hence, compliance behaviour with mandatory IFRSs disclosure requirements by companies listed on the scrutinised stock exchanges is not influenced by company liquidity. Additionally, the regression results show that, the type of business activity does not affect the level of compliance with mandatory IFRSs disclosure requirements in the scrutinised contexts. This finding supports those of some prior studies (*e.g.,* Inchausti, 1997; Street and Gray, 2002). In addition, it supports the findings of Ismail et al. (2010) and Samaha and Dahawy (2011) in the Egyptian context, and those of Naser (1998) and Naser et al. (2002) in the Jordanian context. The lack of significant association between level of compliance with mandatory IFRSs disclosure requirements in the scrutinised contexts and the majority of control variables indicates that the compliance behaviour with mandatory IFRSs disclosure requirements by companies listed on scrutinised stock exchanges do not follow any pattern in relation to such variables. This may be considered as a good sign that many of the mandatory disclosure requirements are now part of the financial reporting culture within companies listed on scrutinised MENA stock exchanges which are supposed to be the main vehicle for economic transition in their jurisdictions. Finally, the regression results promulgate that none of the interactive variables; Country*board size, Country*board independence, Country*board leadership, Country*government ownership, Country*management ownership, Country*private ownership and Country*Public ownership, Country*firm size, Country*profitability, Country*gearing, Country*liquidity and Country*type of business activity reports a statistically significant coefficient, suggesting that there are no substantial differences in the impact of board size, board independence, board leadership, government ownership, management ownership, private ownership, public ownership, firm size, profitability, gearing, liquidity and type of business activity on the levels of compliance with mandatory IFRSs disclosure requirements between Egypt and Jordan.

The above discussion infers that, the contribution towards enhancing the performance of scrutinised MENA stock exchanges is subject to the extent to which the conditions for robust governance practice are consistent with the existing values and the needs of all parties involved in the financial reporting process. It is expected, therefore, to be some time before the impact of applying corporate governance requirements for best practice can be measured in such developing contexts as this needs to develop, and favourable attitude and belief must be formed as well as efforts being made to develop the human resource capabilities that believe in and able to apply corporate governance requirements for best practice.

6.6.4 Theoretical Implications

Having tested the overall level of compliance with mandatory IFRSs disclosure requirements of the 2007 annual reports of an equal sample of 75 non-financial companies listed on the EGX and ASE respectively (two leading MENA region emerging stock exchanges) for any association with corporate governance structures, it is possible to advance a theoretical explanation of the results.

Firstly, although the examination of the first research hypothesis with respect to the existence of significant statistical differences between the Egyptian and the Jordanian contexts with respect to the levels of compliance with IFRSs disclosure requirements, and corporate governance and other company attributes, revealed the existence of significant differences, the results of the univariate and multivariate analysis revealed that the impact of corporate governance best practice mechanisms on the levels of compliance with IFRSs disclosure requirements in both of the scrutinised MENA stock exchanges is absent. This finding is consistent with the institutional isomorphism theory as Egypt and Jordan mandated the adoption of IFRSs under pressure from the international lending institutions to gain respect, legitimacy and of course, to obtain loans from such institutions. The same argument applies with respect to governance reforms carried out in both jurisdictions. Regulators did not give enough consideration to the importance of preparing their markets and neglected to develop national cultural values which predispose positive attitudes towards compliance with internationally recommended practices. This contributes to the problem of decoupling since companies listed on both of scrutinised stock exchanges state that their financial statements are prepared in accordance with IFRSs while in reality, a gap exists between *de jure* and *de facto* compliance. The same applies to the corporate governance recommended practices, although they are present, their positive impact on improving disclosure and transparency practices is absent. In the meantime, the existence of some differences between both jurisdictions in the levels of compliance with the requirements of some standards reflects the impact of the unique national context which also has its influence on some disclosure practices. For instance, the qualifications and ability of accounting practitioners in each jurisdiction, and/or the attitude of the political leadership, may facilitate or hinder the understanding, interpretation and proper application of the requirements of IFRSs. Findings also lend support to Gray's (1988) accounting sub-cultural model (the preference for secrecy in MENA societies provides resistance to full compliance with IFRSs disclosure requirements). Furthermore, based on agency theory, companies will better comply with IFRSs disclosure requirements for which there is a demand for improved disclosure, to reduce the monitoring costs. Although in general terms, both societies are very similar, they are however, not identical. Minor differences between both contexts may affect agency costs, consequently affecting compliance levels. Finally, based on a cost-benefit analysis, for disclosure requirements which are strictly enforced by the stock exchange monitoring bodies, compliance will be better as non-compliance costs with such requirements will exceed compliance costs and vice versa.

Secondly, the significant negative impact of public ownership on the levels of compliance with IFRSs in the Jordanian context (companies with a higher proportion of public ownership, comply less with IFRSs disclosure requirements). This result is consistent with institutional isomorphism theory (*i.e.,* as long as all parties involved in the financial reporting process are ignorant of the importance of transparency and *de facto* compliance with corporate governance and accounting international best practices, and as public investors are not aware of which disclosures are mandatory, they do not pressure the BOD or management to improve compliance with IFRSs. Hence, it is difficult to close the gap between *de facto* and *de jure* compliance with IFRSs disclosure requirements in the scrutinised context and the problem of decoupling will continue). This is also consistent with Gray's (1988) accounting sub-cultural model (secretive culture of MENA societies is associated with strong uncertainty avoidance resulting from the need to restrict information disclosure to avoid conflict and competition and to preserve security. Secrecy is also associated with large power distance, causing the restriction of information to preserve power inequalities. Simultaneously, this lends support to agency theory (as public investors do not demand greater compliance with IFRSs disclosure requirements and do not pressure the BOD or management to improve compliance, monitoring costs are low, thereby reducing management incentives to increase compliance). Additionally, this result is consistent with the notions of cost-benefit analysis (the weak enforcement of IFRSs disclosure requirements and low punishment costs, if any, cause non-compliance costs to be less than compliance costs for companies listed on the scrutinised contexts, thus directing management incentives toward non-compliance).

The findings of this chapter are further confirmed by the interviewees' responses presented in the next chapter. Furthermore, these findings have policy implications and related recommendations which will be discussed in Chapter Eight.

6.7 Summary

This chapter has presented statistics obtained from the various tests undertaken to establish the extent of compliance with IFRSs disclosure requirements by scrutinised companies. The results indicated that the average level of compliance with total IFRSs disclosure requirements was 80% by companies listed on the EGX and 76% by companies listed on the ASE.

The test of differences between the Egyptian and the Jordanian contexts with respect to the levels of compliance with overall mandatory IFRSs disclosure requirements, corporate governance structures and other company attributes, revealed the existence of significant statistical differences between both jurisdictions. Hence, univariate and multivariate analysis were conducted on individual country level.

The findings of the univariate and multivariate analysis on the level of the Egyptian context revealed that compliance behaviour with the overall mandatory IFRSs disclosure requirements by companies listed on the EGX do not follow any pattern in relation to any of the independent variables employed in this study. This may be due to the novelty of corporate governance and the lack of awareness about the importance and the advantages of full *de facto* compliance with IFRSs disclosure requirements and corporate governance best practices in the Egyptian context. Additionally, the existence of other factors mainly related to the secretive culture that is dominant in the Egyptian society.

On the level of the Jordanian context, the univariate analysis revealed that public ownership has a significant negative relationship with the level of compliance with overall mandatory IFRSs disclosure requirements. Also, univariate analysis revealed that companies audited by big 4 audit firms comply better with IFRSs disclosure requirements than those audited by non-big 4 audit firms. These findings were confirmed by multivariate analysis which also revealed that company size has a significant positive association with compliance with mandatory IFRSs disclosure requirements in the Jordanian context.

Overall the findings of the univariate and multivariate analysis in both of scrutinised stock exchanges revealed that the impact of corporate governance best practice mechanisms is absent in both of scrutinised stock exchanges. This was explained by the novelty of corporate governance and the lack of awareness about the importance and the advantages of *de facto* compliance with IFRSs disclosure requirements and corporate governance best practices. Hence, it is expected that as national cultural values are developed to recognise the importance of compliance with IFRSs as is the case in developed countries where such standards originated, and as the qualification levels of the monitoring staff of the CMA and JSC and of accounting practitioners particularly in the Jordanian context improve, so too will the levels of compliance with IFRSs disclosure requirements.

Finally, the findings were consistent with the notions of institutional isomorphism theory, Gray's (1988) accounting sub-cultural model, and financial economics theories. Such consistency adds to the theoretical contribution of this study which can be considered as one of the first studies that employ the institutional isomorphism theory in explaining the impact of corporate governance mechanisms on the levels of compliance with mandatory IFRSs in the MENA region.

The next chapter provides a summary of the general findings constructed through the analysis of the interview data.

CHAPTER SEVEN

ANALYSIS OF INTERVIEWS

7.1 Introduction

As indicated in section 5.5 semi-structured interviews were undertaken to assist in the interpretation of the findings of the quantitative data analyses. Two interview questionnaires were designed to best meet the occupation of different respondent groups. This chapter presents a summary of the general findings constructed through the analysis of the interview data. Hence, the remaining part is organised as follows. Section 7.2 discusses the design of the interview questions. Section 7.3 reviews the specific features of all respondents. Section 7.4 provides a summary of generalisations and themes derived from the interview analysis. Section 7.5 links interview results with research objectives and finally section 7.6 provides a summary of the procedures and the findings of the interview data analysis.

7.2 The Interview Questions

As mentioned in Chapter Five, the interviews were conducted after the quantitative data analysis in order to supplement the interpretation of the findings of that analysis.

The interview questions were open-ended to encourage free expression of participants' views, ideas, and perceptions. Two interview questionnaires were designed - the first for the first four groups of respondents (regulators, academic staff, accountants and auditors) and the second for the fifth group (individual investors)[1].

The first questionnaire consisted of two parts, the first covering the first and the last research questions as presented in section 1.3, the main theme being the barriers to full compliance with IFRSs disclosure requirements in Egypt and Jordan. The second part contained six questions relating to the influence of corporate governance structures on the levels of compliance (the second and last research questions). Responses to these questions were expected to provide a more comprehensive picture of the

[1] The Interview Questionnaires are presented as Appendices J and K.

influence of cultural and other factors such as monitoring and enforcement on compliance levels in the scrutinised jurisdictions and how corporate governance requirements for best practice are perceived in MENA societies.

The second questionnaire also had two parts. The first contained three questions relating to the first and the last research questions as presented in section 1.3, the main theme being investor perceptions regarding the importance of compliance with IFRSs disclosure requirements. The second part contained seven questions relating to the second and last research questions the main theme being investor awareness of corporate governance as a concept and investor perceptions of the impact of board composition and ownership structure on the disclosure behaviour of listed companies. The semi-structured interviews with individual investors who rely on annual reports when making their investment decisions were also expected to help in the researcher's exploration of the ideas and beliefs of investors in Egypt and Jordan.

In constructing the interview questions the researcher followed the recommendations of Collis and Hussey (2003) to keep questions simple, avoid using unnecessary jargon or specialist language, phrase questions to keep the meaning clear, avoid asking negative questions because they are easy to misinterpret, ask one question at a time, include questions that serve as cross checks on the answers to other questions, and avoid leading or value-laden questions. The questions were translated into Arabic, as this was the language used. Notes were taken during the interviews, as the interviewees were not prepared to be tape-recorded. Interviewees were encouraged to speak freely, and for verification purposes, they were asked to read the notes taken by the researcher during the interview to ensure their views were accurately reported. The researcher then translated the transcripts from Arabic to English, and to further guarantee the validity of the texts, the researcher asked a linguistic specialist to review her translation.

7.3 Interviewees' Information

As mentioned in Chapter Five, the researcher conducted 12 interviews in Egypt and 8 interviews in Jordan with respondents from four different groups (Regulators, Accountants, Academic Staff, and Individual Investors). Each interview lasted between 30 to 60 minutes and was undertaken between 21st September and mid-November, 2010. For reporting purposes, participants were classified according to their occupation and jurisdiction into Regulators (R), Academic Staff (S),

Accountants (A) and Investors (I). Each individual interviewee is identified by his/her group code, followed by the first letter of his/her jurisdiction (e for Egypt and j for Jordan) and a digit representing his/her serial number within that group. For example, Re1 stands for the first interviewee from the Regulator group in Egypt, and Ij2 stands for the second interviewee from the investor group in Jordan. The precise details of interviewees demonstrated in sub-Section 5.5.2.

7.4 Interview Results and Generalisations

As indicated, the interviews covered two main themes which had emerged from the quantitative analysis, these being: barriers to full compliance with IFRSs disclosure requirements, and the relationship between levels of compliance with IFRSs and corporate governance structures. The following sub-sections indicate how many interviewees talked about a certain theme.

7.4.1 Barriers to Full Compliance with IFRSs Disclosure Requirements

Interviewees identified several factors preventing full compliance with IFRSs disclosure requirements, which after analysis, could be grouped into five main barriers as follows:

1. Non-compliance costs are less than compliance costs for listed companies.
2. Inadequate qualification of accounting practitioners.
3. Low demand for more disclosure by investors.
4. Management resistance.
5. Degree of relevance of each IFRS to the economic development stage of the jurisdiction.

Tables 7.1 and 7.2 indicate the number of interviewees from each group raising each barrier.

Table 7.1 Number of Interviewees Raising Each Barrier to Full Compliance with IFRSs Disclosure Requirements in Egypt

Barrier	Regulators	Accountants	Academic Staff Members	Naïve Investors
Non-compliance costs are less than compliance costs	3 (75%)	1 (50%)	4 (100%)	0 (0%)
Inadequate qualification of accounting practitioners	1 (25%)	0 (0%)	3 (75%)	0 (0%)
Low demand for more disclosure by investors	3 (75%)	1 (100%)	4 (100%)	2 (100%)
Management resistance	3 (75%)	1 (100%)	3 (75%)	0 (0%)
Degree of relevance of each IFRS to the economic development stage of the jurisdiction	4 (100%)	2 (50%)	4 (100%)	0 (0%)

Table 7.2 Number of Interviewees Raising Each Barrier to Full Compliance with IFRSs Disclosure Requirements in Jordan

Barrier	Regulators	Accountants	Academic Staff Members	Naïve Investors
Non-compliance costs are less than compliance costs	0 (0%)	1 (100%)	3 (100%)	0 (0%)
Inadequate qualification of accounting practitioners	2 (100%)	1 (100%)	2 (67%)	0 (0%)
Low demand for more disclosure by investors	2 (100%)	0 (0%)	3 (100%)	2 (100%)
Management resistance	1 (50%)	0 (0%)	3 (100%)	0 (0%)
Degree of relevance of each IFRS to the economic development stage of the jurisdiction	2 (100%)	1 (50%)	3 (100%)	0 (0%)

Low Non-compliance Costs

Table 7.1 shows that three of the four CMA regulators referred to low non-compliance costs as one of the major barriers to full compliance. They attributed this to the stage of market development which makes it difficult to be overly strict with companies since this would result in delisting most of the companies and distorting the image of listed companies, which in turn can negatively affect the international reputation of the national capital market. The regulators believe that negotiations with companies are more effective in improving their awareness of the importance of compliance, and refer to the continuous improvement in the disclosure levels by companies listed on the EGX as justification for this approach. Also, they argue that the number of companies monitored is above the capacity of the CMA staff and that no strict sanctions are imposed by the Egyptian legislation.

"At the moment non-compliance costs are low. As the market is emerging the CMA is afraid to be very strict with companies as that means delisting most of the companies and then the market will close down so we try to improve compliance of companies over time. This works as compliance levels in 2010 are better than in 2007 and so on. It can be said that compliance levels improve with time. Also, although we have competent monitors in the central monitoring authority of the CMA, they serve more companies than their capacity. This may negatively affect the quality of their monitoring but this also will diminish with time as we intend to employ more disclosure monitors." Re1

"Non-compliance costs are less than compliance costs due to non-existence of strict compulsory sanctions in the legislation as well as the whole market culture which require more time to be mature and understand the importance of disclosure and transparency." Re2

"Some companies misuse non-strict enforcement of IFRSs by the CMA due to the lack of cultural awareness. They cannot understand yet that we do not want to distort the reputation of the national market to attract foreign investment. However, we try to develop communication channels with those companies to encourage them to improve compliance and sometimes when we inform a company several times to comply with disclosure requirements and the company insists on ignoring our requirements we impose sanctions on it." Re4

Accountants argue that the lack of accountability, weak enforcement of IFRSs by the CMA as long as the auditor report is unqualified, and the too detailed requirements of some standards which may harm the company's competitive position cause non-compliance costs to be less than compliance costs. However, one of the accountants raises the problem of inequality of treatment of non-compliants which contributes to encouraging companies with major government ownership to ignore full-compliance with IFRSs disclosure requirements.

"Although we do not follow all IFRSs disclosure requirements the CMA does not send us any notes in this regard. For sure we do not do that to mislead investors or anybody else but our management sees some requirements as very detailed, and that these details are useless to investors but if disclosed they may be misused by our competitors. To sum up, the general rule is that as the auditor report is unqualified and no complaints are submitted from investors regarding the quality of our

financial reporting we will not be on the spot. Once you are hired in the company your manager tells you that you have to forget anything you learned at Business School and do the work in that way. So given the lack of accountability any junior employee has to follow the instructions of his manager." Ae2

"There is a major drawback in the capital market reaction toward non-complying companies. They are very strict with small companies but the opposite is true for big ones and those privatised with major ownership held by the government. This is not fair. Also, the general rule from my experience is that as long as there are no complaints regarding the performance of a specific company nobody cares to direct it to improve its compliance and its report is accepted regardless of its shortfalls. Also, companies say that if non-compliance is detected and they are asked to modify there is room for discussion and if the CMA insists they will apply their requirements." Ae2

Academic staff members also highlight the negative impact of low non-compliance costs, attributing this to ineffective control mechanisms, low sanctions if any, lack of accountability, political considerations by the CMA, and cultural influences, such as the preference for secrecy.

"Low non-compliance cost is an important point to mention when talking about barriers to full compliance with IFRSs in a developing country like Egypt. The lack of a code of ethics for the accounting and auditing profession contributes to this problem. This code has been under construction since 1997. Hence, in the light of ineffective control mechanisms and no sanctions of any type on accountants and auditors who fail to comply with accounting and auditing standards, non-compliance will continue. Another thing is the lack of actual independence of auditors. In practice neither the shareholders nor the BOD makes the decision to assign the external auditor and determine the fees. Thus, auditors comply with top management wishes in order to gain higher fees and be reassigned." Se1

"For political reasons the CMA does not exercise its authority to enforce listed companies to comply with IFRSs and corporate governance best practice especially those relating to transparency and disclosure. Consequently, as there are no or low sanctions imposed in case of non-compliance, companies prefer not to comply as in this case non-compliance costs are lower than compliance costs." Se2

"This is normal as the Egyptian market is emerging and thus it is expected to take time until things are done correctly. The company decision to comply with IFRSs is strongly influenced by the business and socio-economic culture particularly, secrecy and window dressing. Adding to this, there is no lobby from naive investors to protect their rights. Thus non-compliance costs are low in our society." Se3

"As long as there is weak monitoring of management compliance with IFRSs, monitoring costs will be low so managers do not need to improve compliance levels and the situation of lack of full compliance will continue." Se4

With respect to Jordan, as indicated in Table 7.2, four respondents talked about low non-compliance costs as a barrier to full compliance with IFRSs disclosure requirements in Jordan. The accountant perceived non-compliance costs as low for those companies with CEOs or major owners in powerful positions.

"Governors are not strict with companies when the CEO or major owners are well known names or in powerful positions. Those persons can change the decisions of political authority. Consequently, for these companies when they hide information nobody will follow them up; thus for them non-compliance costs are very low if any." Aj1

The three academics also highlighted low non-compliance costs as a barrier to achieving full compliance with IFRSs, attributing this problem to the low value of sanctions, weak enforcement and monitoring by the JSC which company managements may abuse, and the lack of individual investor awareness regarding their rights to pressure the BOD and management of listed companies to improve their compliance. They also believed the attitude of JSC staff, who consider compliance with IFRSs as the responsibility of auditors, to be a contributory factor, since companies in Jordan generally depend on auditors to prepare their financial statements due to the shortage in qualified accountants. Furthermore, they raised the problem of the shortage in the number of qualified staff in the JSC to monitor compliance with IFRSs by listed companies. This implies that as long as the auditor report is unqualified, JSC staff will not make a detailed monitoring of the reported accounts to ensure that all IFRSs disclosure requirements are followed properly in producing the company financial statements.

"For companies non-compliance costs are less than compliance costs due to the minor impact and value of the fine in case of punishment. Also, lack of awareness among investors regarding their rights to put pressure on the BOD and management of listed companies to comply with IFRSs disclosure requirements is an important factor." Sj1

"The majority of companies listed on the ASE are audited by big 4 audit firms, even the financial statements are prepared by auditors; thus the JSC considers that, as the auditor report is unqualified this means that companies complied with the requirements of IFRSs or at least the spirit of IFRSs. Also, the shortage in the number of qualified members in the JSC makes it difficult to properly monitor companies to stimulate them to reach 100% compliance with IFRSs. All of this, given the cultural values in our societies may result in low non-compliance costs." Sj2

"Low non-compliance costs is a major barrier to full compliance with IFRSs disclosure requirements due to the probable misuse of implicit flexibility given by the JSC concerning some IFRSs disclosure requirements which may be seen as very detailed or need more competent accounting practitioners." Sj3

The above discussion supports the notions of institutional isomorphism theory that the country mandated the IFRSs simply to acquire legitimacy without building the infrastructure required to guarantee *de facto* compliance with those standards. For instance, in Jordan most respondents pointed to the shortage in the number of qualified accountants in listed companies as well as the shortage of qualified staff members in the JSC to monitor compliance with IFRSs. Additionally, the discussion supports the notions of agency theory as low monitoring costs will not stimulate management to improve compliance, and cost-benefit analysis and the cultural theories, as management's preference for secrecy, and low sanctions if any, promote lower costs for non-compliance than for compliance.

Inadequate Qualification of Accounting Practitioners

Table 7.1 shows that one of the regulators in Egypt talked about the inadequate qualification of some accounting practitioners in some listed companies, especially those with dominant government ownership. He attributed this to the existence of senior accountants with many years of experience but who are not familiar with IFRSs, and to the lack of continuous professional training on the requirements of IFRSs which may result in misunderstandings concerning the requirements of some standards.

"Unfortunately senior accountants in some of the listed companies especially those with major government ownership, graduated a long time ago so they did not study IFRSs. In addition, to save training costs, management of such companies do not encourage their staff to engage in training programmes. This affects the quality of compliance with IFRSs requirements." Re3

However, the fact that only one interviewee mentioned this problem, indicates that inadequate qualification of accounting practitioners is not highly recognised in Egypt.

Conversely, as indicated in Table 7.2, all non-investor participants in Jordan raised the issue of inadequately qualified accountants as a major barrier toward full compliance with IFRSs.

Regulators attributed the lack of full compliance with IFRSs disclosure requirements to the lack of awareness among practitioners, listed companies' management, academic staff members and Jordanian universities, regarding the importance of the proper application of IFRSs and the need for continuous training on their updates.

"Actually, there is still a lack of understanding among different parties particularly our universities, management of listed companies and national accountants of the severe negative impact of inadequate qualification on achieving high levels of compliance with IFRSs. I think we are achieving success in raising the awareness of listed companies of the importance of compliance with IFRSs and they are struggling to do that within the limit of the capabilities of their accountants as we have a shortage in qualified accountants." Rj1

"Inappropriate qualification of accounting practitioners is a major factor which negatively affects their level of competency. The accounting curricula are very weak even the majority of accounting teaching staff in Jordanian universities are not aware of the importance of IFRSs modules and not interested in the implications of IFRSs adoption in Jordan as a developing market." Rj2

Surprisingly, the accountant mentioned this problem, which he attributed to the weak curriculum delivered in Jordanian universities and the poor quality of training courses attended by accountants who are trying to become knowledgeable about IFRSs updates.

"Most accounting practitioners in Jordan are not properly qualified which is why most of the companies depend on the auditing offices to prepare their annual reports. This is not our mistake; even when we are sent to a training course on IFRSs by our company we go to five star hotels where everything is superorganised except the course material and the trainer!" Aj1

Two of the academic staff members also mentioned this problem, believing it to be a part of the current stage of development of Accounting Departments in Jordanian universities, the shortage of academic staff members who are specialised in financial accounting, and the lack of co-ordination between the Jordanian universities and regulators in the ASE to ensure the improvement of accounting practitioners' qualifications.

"The lack of competent practitioners is the major barrier to reaching full compliance with IFRSs disclosure requirements in Jordan as most accounting departments in the Jordanian universities are newly established and do not have adequate numbers of staff members who are specialised in Financial Accounting.". Sj1

"In Jordan we suffer from the problem of a shortage of qualified accounting staff members which severely affects levels of compliance with IFRSs. However, I think now after opening Accounting Departments in the Jordanian universities, the lack of co-ordination between our universities and the ASE regulators will be the major factor that contributes to this problem." Sj3

The above discussion supports the notions of institutional isomorphism particularly in Jordan, whereas IFRSs were mandated by government in order to gain legitimacy, but where the required infrastructure (particularly qualified accountants) to guarantee *de facto* compliance with those standards was not provided.

Low Demand for More Disclosure by Investors

Table 7.1 shows that many respondents in Egypt talked about the issue of low demand for more disclosure by investors.

All interviewees except the investor group blamed this on the lack of awareness among individual investors regarding their rights to pressure the BOD and management of companies in which they are shareholders in order to improve compliance. They believe that given the secretive nature of Egyptian society it is difficult for companies to improve their compliance without pressures.

"Low or non-demand for more disclosure by investors is a major characteristic of the Egyptian investor. This can be attributed to the lack of awareness among individual investors regarding their rights." Re1

"We are doing our best to stimulate listed companies to improve their levels of compliance with IFRSs and we succeeded in that as the levels of compliance improve over time. However, without the support of investors by putting pressure on companies to improve their disclosures it will take a long time to reach the stage of full compliance with IFRSs by listed companies." Re2

"Lack of investor awareness regarding disclosures that must be made by listed companies is a barrier toward full compliance with IFRSs. To date the whole work is done by the CMA without any co-operation from the side of companies or investors." Re3

One of the accountants stated that widespread concentrated ownership in the Egyptian capital market and lack of awareness among naive investors form additional barriers to full compliance with IFRSs disclosure requirements.

"As the majority of listed companies have concentrated ownership, owners have access to all the information they need. In the meantime, naive investors are not aware about their right to ask for company information so our level of compliance is not developed as nobody asks for more disclosures. Also, some disclosure requirements are too detailed which may threaten our competitive position so we prefer not to disclose as long as nobody asks about it." Ae1

All participants from the academic staff group mentioned the ignorance among naive investors regarding their entitlement to demand more disclosure.

"Small investors are not aware of their rights to ask for more disclosures; thus this has a negative impact on reaching the full compliance with IFRSs disclosure requirements." Se1

"Lack of naive investor awareness regarding the minimum level of disclosures to be provided by listed companies makes it difficult to reach full compliance with IFRSs." Se2

"Small investors make their investment decisions based on rumours and they do not know and do not wish to know what disclosures must be made by listed companies, and this of course, has a negative impact on improving the levels of compliance with IFRSs." Se3

"The Egyptian investor is not aware about disclosures that must be made by listed companies; thus, companies will not improve their levels of compliance voluntarily." Se4

This viewpoint is confirmed by the responses of the interviewees from the investor group who had no idea about IFRSs or disclosures that listed companies are obligated to make. They argued that disclosures made by companies are of no importance when making their investment decisions, believing that it does not matter whether listed companies are fully-compliant or otherwise with mandated disclosure requirements. They also stated that they do not trust the accuracy of information disclosed, nor how to use such information. Basically, they accept the situation, seemingly not motivated to agitate for more disclosure by listed companies.

"I have no idea about IFRSs . . . I am not interested to know about mandatory disclosures as I do not trust the accuracy of disclosed information . . . that is why I focus on the trend of the company's stock price when making investment decisions." Ie1

"I do not know what IFRSs are. I do not know how to read and extract important information from the annual reports, and reports are not available for free. We hear about disclosure problems and fraud in developed markets so do you expect excellence in an emerging market!! I ask the brokers about the best investments as they have more experience. I sign buying and selling orders to give my broker the opportunity to do the best for me without even asking me as I have no experience at all in this regard. However, as the stock exchange is a place to raise funds quickly I am interested in investing my savings in it." Ie2

In Jordan, as indicated in Table 7.2, regulators argue that low demand for greater disclosure is a major reason for lack of full compliance with IFRSs. They attributed this to low investor awareness regarding IFRSs disclosure requirements.

"The low demand for more disclosures by national investors is one of the barriers to full compliance with IFRSs disclosure requirements in Jordan. This can be attributed to low awareness among national investors about their rights to ask for more information." Rj1

"The naive national investors do not ask for more disclosure. This is reasonable as in an emerging market which already has a shortage of qualified practitioners it is not strange to have investors who are not aware about their rights to monitor company disclosures. I think all of this is a matter of time." Rj2

Academic staff members also mentioned the negative impact of this issue on improving compliance levels within companies listed on the ASE.

"One of the important barriers to full compliance with IFRSs disclosure requirements is low demand for more disclosure by small national investors." Sj1

"The national culture does not encourage investors to ask for more disclosure. Thus, low levels of demand are expected to continue as a barrier to full compliance with IFRSs disclosure requirements." Sj2

"Given the secretive culture of our societies and the lack of awareness among investors regarding their right to ask listed companies to make full compliance with IFRSs disclosure requirements, it is difficult to stimulate companies to improve their levels of disclosure." Sj3

This point is also concluded through the interviews with investors who indicated that they may be familiar with the name but not with the detailed requirements of IFRSs and that company disclosures are not considered in making their investment decisions. One investor believed that all companies listed on the ASE makes all required disclosures, whilst the other believed otherwise.

"These standards are applicable in Jordan and they determine the rules the company should follow in preparing its financial statements . . . .

Because we are an emerging market and still have a shortage of well developed competent accountants, it is not expected that companies will disclose all required information . . . . I make my investment decision based on the information I hear from the media and my financial broker regarding company prospects as well as the names of the members of the BOD in this company and the names of its major investor(s)." Ij1

"Just the name but I do not know about their requirements . . . . I think in most cases companies disclose the required information . . . . I make investment decisions based on the recommendations of my friends who are major traders in the ASE as well as from information about the historical trend of a company's stock price." Ij2

The above discussion supports the notions of institutional isomorphism (normative isomorphism) as investors are not aware of the importance of compliance with IFRSs disclosure requirements or even of what those requirements are. Additionally, it supports the notions of agency theory as low monitoring costs will not stimulate management to improve compliance. Furthermore, it supports the cultural theories as lack of full compliance may be associated with large power distance which results in the restriction of information to preserve power inequalities. This also supports the notions of cost-benefit analysis as low demand for disclosure may make non-compliance costs less than compliance costs. However, it is concluded that investors in Jordan are relatively more aware about the IFRSs compared to those in Egypt and that they have more trust in the information disclosed by companies listed on the ASE.

Management Resistance

Table 7.1 shows that three regulators identified management resistance as a barrier to full compliance in Egypt, which they believe results from the dominant secretive culture that will take time to change.

"Management resistance is one of the barriers to reaching full compliance with IFRSs. Our market is emerging and being very strict with companies will have a negative impact on the continuity of the market and will market the idea that all listed companies are performing fraudulent actions. We believe that our regulatory framework is efficient but in the meantime with Egyptian culture that believes in rumours and with investors' preference to save their money at banks our market will close down. So our strategy is based on stopping non-compliance that really reflects fraudulent behaviour to protect investors. But in the meantime we try to develop a compliance culture among listed companies by providing training courses, asking companies to develop audit committees and hiring qualified non-executives on these committees." Re1

"The compliance level in listed companies is also negatively affected by management resistance to transparency. This is a cultural issue. For years managers used to keep books for investors and others for the tax authority in order to hide information from their competitors so it is expected to take some time to change that behaviour." Re2

"Management still lack awareness regarding the importance of being transparent so this currently threatens the achievement of full compliance with IFRSs disclosure requirements, but I am sure that will disappear in the future." Re4

The accountant also mentioned this issue as a problem, but insisted that in most cases this is to protect the company image and avoid misuse of important information by competitors.

"Management of the company affects the level of compliance with IFRSs disclosure requirements as some requirements may be too detailed and not supposed to be important for investors but if disclosed they might be used by our competitors so management ask us to ignore disclosing such information." Ae2

All academic staff members highlighted management resistance as a major negative influence, and attributed it to the secretive nature of Egyptian society and the lack of accountability.

"Management of listed companies used for years to control the type and quantity of company information that is disseminated to the public. As IFRSs disclosure requirements encourage transparency and detailed disclosures management will not co-operate until they feel that non-compliance with any of the requirements will put them under investigation." Se1

"Management resists transparency due to the absence of strict compulsory sanctions in the legislation as well as the absence of a market culture which understands the benefits of transparency." Se2

"In light of the current situation of ineffective control mechanisms and no sanctions of any type on accountants and auditors who fail to comply with accounting and auditing standards, management is the main determinant of the levels of compliance with IFESs. Due to the opportunistic behaviour of some managers or to protect their image and

competitive position of their companies they control company disclosures; thus it is difficult to achieve full compliance with the IFRSs." Se3

"Management is the main determinant of levels of compliance with IFRSs. Management's decision to comply with IFRSs is strongly influenced by business and socio-economic culture, particularly secrecy and window dressing. Adding to this there is no lobby from naïve investors to protect their rights." Se4

In Jordan, as indicated in Table 7.2, one of the regulators and two of the academic staff members mentioned management resistance as a barrier to full compliance with IFRSs disclosure requirements. They all attributed that mainly to management ignorance regarding the importance of improved transparency and the lack of independence of auditors, weak sanctions and lack of investor awareness.

"Sometimes management of some companies may not be aware about the importance of detailed compliance with IFRSs disclosure requirements for the company and this has a negative impact on levels of compliance. However this behaviour is less common among modern managers, which gives us ambitions that such behavior will disappear in the near future." Rj2

"Due to the secretive nature of our society, management may resist improving disclosure levels. If we improved investor awareness regarding the disclosures that must be made and imposed more strict sanctions management will change that behaviour." Sj1

"Full compliance with IFRSs disclosure requirements is not a common practice in Jordan and I am sure this is the case in all developing markets. Management is the main determinant of the level of compliance with IFRSs. In Jordan the majority of listed companies ask auditors to prepare their financial statements so for sure this affects auditor independence as, if they ignore management's instructions to keep some information undisclosed to protect the company's competitive position, they will not be engaged in the future." Sj3

The above discussion supports the notions of institutional isomorphism theory (particularly normative isomorphism) as managements of listed companies are not yet aware of the importance of compliance with IFRSs disclosure requirements. Also, it supports the notions of agency theory, as low monitoring costs due to low demand for greater disclosure will not provoke management into improving compliance. Also, cultural theory provides an explanation of company management's secretive and selective behaviour, and the subsequent ignorance among national investors regarding their rights to demand more transparency. Additionally, the ideas expressed in cost-benefit analysis are confirmed, as weak enforcement of IFRSs and low sanctions if any, may make non-compliance costs less than compliance costs for management of listed companies.

Relevance of IFRSs

As indicated in Table 7.1 two of the regulators identified the relevance of IFRSs disclosure requirements to the Egyptian context, attributing this to the problem of familiarity with some requirements and dominant cultural values such as secrecy.

"Not all the requirements of IFRSs are relevant to the Egyptian context. It is better to develop national standards that are suitable to the characteristics and the stage of development of our capital market. The current standards are a typical translation of IFRSs which include many parts that are not clear to some accountants as they may not be common practices in the Egyptian companies." Re3

"The relevance of IFRSs disclosure requirements to the Egyptian business environment affects the levels of compliance with IFRSs. For example, the treatment for accounting errors is done based on the personal experience of the senior accountant, not in accordance with standards. Another example is risk management as company management prefers to keep such information secret because this may affect the company image before creditors or investors, or may be misused by competitors. For R&D costs it is considered as useless so the majority of companies do not have this item as part of their expenses." Re4

The accountant argued that some requirements are very detailed and irrelevant to users within the national market, nor are they disclosed by other listed companies.

"Not all IFRSs requirements are relevant as some are very detailed and there is no need to provide these details as it may harm the company's competitive position. Furthermore, some are not disclosed by other listed companies and nobody asks about them." Ae2

Two of the academic staff members talked about the issue of relevance of IFRSs to the Egyptian context and its impact on levels of compliance with IFRSs disclosure requirements. They attributed this to unfamiliarity with some requirements as companies listed on the EGX are not as developed as those listed on developed capital markets where such standards originated.

"Although no one can deny that IFRSs are the best developed standards worldwide as they guarantee disclosure of the minimum level of information necessary for informed decisions, some of these requirements are not yet suitable to the level of development of our companies and the volume of their transactions. Consequently, some may have unclear translation which makes it difficult to follow or to be monitored by CMA staff. Thus, there is a need to review the translation of the current standards and listed companies must carry out gradual training courses for their accountants and internal auditors to make sure they know and apply accounting standards efficiently." Se1

"The Egyptian government mandated the adoption of IFRSs under pressures from the international lending institutions without developing the capital market to be ready to adopt such requirements in an appropriate manner. So it is expected to take some time until such standards be relevant to our capital market or we have to review such standards and choose only the requirements that are relevant to us to make sure we will have 100% compliance with them." Se3

In Jordan, as indicated in Table 7.2, many respondents argued that IFRSs are not relevant to the Jordanian context mainly because they were developed to meet the requirements of developed capital markets, and because of the lack of qualified accounting practitioners in Jordan and the non-existence of an official translation.

"I think as long as our market is not well infrastructured with qualified competent regulators and accounting practitioners, and as we have a shortage in funds to attract qualified persons to develop accounting standards that fit to our context, we will not have full compliance with IFRSs disclosure requirements. We are all aware that it is inappropriate to apply accounting standards that are developed to meet the needs of developed markets. So this is the challenge of our leadership to build a strong infrastructure soon to make sure that there will be an effective implementation of IFRSs." Rj1

"IFRSs are not completely relevant to Jordan because of lack of sufficiently qualified accounting practitioners and inadequate training, as well as the market system needs more time to mature." Sj1

"We applied IFRSs to attract foreign investment and to globalise our economy although they may not be relevant to Jordan. For IFRSs to be relevant to our environment there must be sufficient and continuous training for accounting practitioners to ensure they are aware of the latest IFRSs and how to apply them. Also, there must be an official translation of IFRSs into Arabic." Sj2

"It is better to have national accounting standards that are more suitable to the characteristics of our market as a developing one. IFRSs are more suitable for developed markets and we only applied them because we are not qualified to develop our own set of standards." Sj3

The above discussion supports the notions of institutional isomorphism, as similar to the Egyptian government, the Jordanian government mandated the adoption of IFRSs mainly to gain legitimacy within the international community. However, it seems that the problem in Jordan is more complicated as there are insufficient qualified regulators and practitioners to efficiently apply IFRSs or to develop a set of accounting standards that best fit their context.

7.4.2 The Relationship between Levels of Compliance with IFRSs and Corporate Governance Variables

In order to support the interpretation of the findings of the quantitative analyses investigating the association between corporate governance structures and levels of compliance with IFRSs disclosure requirements, this section discusses the interviewee responses for the second part of the first and the second questionnaires as indicated in section 7.2.

The Relationship between Board Independence and Levels of Compliance with IFRSs

Perceptions of different interviewees in both countries regarding the influence of board independence on the levels of compliance with IFRSs disclosure requirements are presented in Table 7.3.

Table 7.3 shows that in Egypt, all regulators and two of the academic staff members support a positive association between board independence and levels of compliance with IFRSs disclosure requirements on the grounds that board independence improves the monitoring of management and that management in turn, will disclose more information to reduce the monitoring costs.

Table 7.3 Perceptions of the Influence of Board Independence on Levels of Compliance with IFRSs

Interviewee	No Effect	Positive	Negative
Re1		√	
Re2		√	
Re3		√	
Re4		√	
Ae1	√		
Ae2	√		
Se1	√		
Se2		√	
Se3		√	
Se4	√		
Ie1	√		
Ie2	√		
Ri1	√		
Ri2		√	
Ai1	√		
Si1	√		
Si2	√		
Si3		√	
Ii1	√		
Ij2	√		

The remaining respondents (Ae1, Ae2, Se1, Se4, Ie1 and Ie2) argue, however, that board independence has no effect on the levels of compliance with IFRSs disclosure requirements because of the lack of *de facto* independence and the lack of awareness regarding the role of independent directors in monitoring company compliance with disclosure requirements.

"In most cases if not in all, this 'independence' is not practised in the real world; independent members consider themselves and are also considered by executive members as guests." Ae1

"Independence is just on paper - it has no impact on improving compliance" Ae2 .

"Theoretically, a BOD with more independent directors should be more effective in monitoring management to ensure compliance with IFRSs. However, the novelty of the concept of corporate governance causes companies to adopt the requirements just to gain legitimacy but in the reality they do not understand why this is important. Thus, given the

secretive nature of our society even where there is board independence it has no effect on compliance levels." Se1

"Management is the main determinant of everything within the company including the disclosure policy so it does not matter whether there are independent directors on the board or not." Se4

"No, I do not think so because always the loyalty of the majority of the board members will be to major owners who are also in most cases, the managers of the company." Ie1

"No, as independent directors are chosen by the executive members." Ie2

In Jordan, the majority of respondents (Rj1, Aj1, Sj1, Sj2, Ij1 and Ij2) argue that no association exists between board independence and the levels of compliance with IFRSs disclosure requirements and only two respondents (Rj2 and Sj3) support a positive association on the grounds that it will improve the BOD's monitoring function.

Those who oppose the notion that an association exists argue that the unique nature of the Jordanian culture makes it impossible to achieve real independence. Consequently, board independence will not affect management disclosure behaviour.

"Due to the nature of our society, it is difficult to achieve the advantage of board independence without developing awareness regarding its importance." Rj1

"In our company the majority of board members are independent; however, they are very weak and have no influence at all. Management is the one who decides everything according to its vision." Aj1

"In reality Jordan is a small country and we all have strong blood ties. Unfortunately, these interrelations stand as a barrier toward achieving real independence. I think it is impossible to reach real board independence in Arab countries in general and in Jordan in particular because of our culture." Sj1

"I think in Jordan as a developing market, the independent persons appointed to the BOD of listed companies are chosen for two reasons. The first is to gain respect as the company is applying good governance

practices and the second is to support the executive board members' chosen policies. Consequently, given the secretive nature of our society, weak enforcement and monitoring and lack of understanding by management and those described as independent directors regarding the benefits of transparency, board independence will not make a difference in compliance levels." Sj2

"I think there is no association between board independence and company disclosures." Ij1

"In my opinion according to my experience in the market there is no association." Ij2

Table 7.4 Perceptions of the Influence of Role Duality on Levels of Compliance with IFRSs

Interviewee	No Effect	Positive	Negative
Re1	√		
Re2			√
Re3			√
Re4			√
Ae1	√		
Ae2	√		
Se1	√		
Se2			√
Se3			√
Se4	√		
Ie1	√		
Ie2			√
Ri1			√
Ri2			√
Ai1	√		
Si1	√		
Si2	√		
Si3			√
Ij1			√
Ij2	√		

The above discussion indicates that in Jordan, similar to Egypt, board independence is not an effective mechanism with respect to improving the levels of compliance with IFRSs. This supports the notions of institutional isomorphism that even when companies adopt board independence as proof of their modernity and the introduction of international best practices, this has no impact on its levels of compliance. So the problem of decoupling will continue. Also, as independent directors do not use their authority in monitoring company compliance with IFRSs, management will not improve disclosures so this supports the notions of agency theory, cultural theory, and cost benefit analysis.

The Relationship between Board Leadership and Levels of Compliance with IFRSs

Perceptions of different interviewees in Egypt and Jordan regarding the influence of board leadership on the levels of compliance with IFRSs disclosure requirements are presented in Table 7.4.

Table 7.4 shows that in Egypt six interviewees (Re2, Re3, Re4, Se2, Se3 and Ie2) believe that role duality has a negative impact on compliance levels because this reduces the potential for independent evaluation. The CEO who controls the management of the company will also choose what information to provide to other directors.

However, the remaining interviewees argue that no association exists between board leadership and compliance levels, since in all cases the CEO is the actual operator of the business firm and the board whether there is separation between the two positions or not, and that the CEO is therefore the figure with the power. Additionally, they cited lack of awareness among different parties regarding the purpose of separation between the two roles and/or the benefits of increasing transparency and compliance with IFRSs, contributed towards this situation.

"The ownership in the majority of companies listed on the EGX is concentrated and even when there is a separation between the CEO and the Chair positions, the separation does not help in improving transparency and monitoring of company compliance with IFRSs. This is because in most cases the Chair is chosen because of his close relationship with major shareholders so in such cases I expect that separation of the roles will not affect management disclosure policy, hence levels of compliance with IFRSs will not be enhanced." Re1

"In all cases, the CEO controls everything and the Chair has no role, so I think whether roles are separated or held by the same person that will not affect compliance levels." Ae1

"In our company there is separation between the two positions but they are relatives and the Chair role is just to sign any papers or decisions presented to him by the CEO. Thus, I believe this issue will make no difference." Ae2

"In some companies the Chair is appointed in order to benefit from his political or powerful position to settle any difficulties with the regulatory or monitoring authorities, he knows that so he does not exercise his role. Thus the CEO is still the person who controls everything including the

Chair. Consequently, as long as the CEO does not believe in the importance of compliance, compliance will not be improved." Se2

"The main problem is in our cultural context which prefers secrecy, in addition to absence of accountability and weak monitoring, if any. When the company separates the roles of the CEO and the Chair this is just to say it follows the international best practice but in reality, the CEO and the Chair do not believe in the benefits of doing this so this practice will not enhance transparency or compliance." Se4

"I do not think there is an association between board leadership and level of disclosure because I know that the top manger is always the main controller in any business organisation." Ie1

In Jordan, as indicated in Table 7.4, four respondents (Rj1, Rj2, Sj3 and Ij1) supported a negative association between role duality and compliance levels with IFRSs disclosure requirements on the grounds that it has a negative impact on the monitoring function of the board, and hence, on compliance levels.

The remaining respondents (Aj1, Sj1, Sj2, and Ij2) argued differently, believing that whether the two roles were held by the same person or otherwise, levels of compliance would not be influenced, as no awareness exists regarding the benefits of separating roles. Consequently, disclosure is a feature of management vision.

"I think in Jordan there is no association between board leadership and the levels of compliance with IFRSs as managements are always responsible for determining the extent of company disclosure and the Chair in most cases delegates everything to management." Aj1

"Some companies listed on the ASE have the CEO and Chair positions held by the same person. However, even when the two positions are separated this does not affect the existing compliance levels as in all cases the CEO determines the extent of disclosure. As we are suffering from a weak monitoring system by the governmental authorities and weak small shareholders who are unaware of their rights, there is no pressure to stimulate management whether from inside or outside the firm to improve its compliance." Sj1

"I think it is not clear in our society the importance of separating the positions of the CEO and the Chair in achieving better monitoring of the

company disclosure. Thus, even when the two roles are separated the Chair will not monitor the CEO's performance to make sure that he complies with disclosure requirements." Sj2

"Jordan is a small country and we are all closely related so I do not believe that when the role is separated the Chair will monitor the CEO to make sure that he follows disclosure requirements. The compliance will happen if the CEO has self-accountability and understands the benefits of transparency." Ij2

The above discussion supports the notions of institutional isomorphism since even when the roles are separated, this can be seen merely as window dressing, and in practice there is no difference in the attitude towards compliance, which in turn contributes to the problem of decoupling. Also as the Chair does not use his authority in monitoring company compliance with IFRSs, and given weak monitoring by regulatory bodies and weak small investors, management will determine the extent of disclosure according to its vision. This supports the notions of agency theory, cultural theory, and cost benefit analysis.

A wide range of opinion regarding the impact of ownership structure on compliance levels in Egypt and Jordan is evident from Table 7.5.

As seen in Table 7.5, in Egypt, five respondents (Re2, Re4, Ae1, Se3 and Se4) supported a negative relationship between dominant government ownership and compliance levels on the grounds that management and board members in such companies are government officials with work relationships. Also, the government has access to all the information it needs, and for political reasons, the CMA as a governmental body, may not be strict with government owned companies. All of these factors are expected to negatively influence compliance levels. Only one respondent (Se2) believed a positive relationship exists between dominant government ownership and levels of compliance with IFRSs, arguing that the government is accountable before the people and is responsible for protecting their wealth; hence, it is expected to pressure companies in which it has major ownership to improve their disclosure and hence, improve its public image. Additionally, the financial statements of such companies are further audited by the Central Auditing Organisation (CAO)[2].

---

[2] The Central Auditing Organization Law 144/1988 governs the auditing of government departments and agencies, public sector enterprises, and companies in which ownership interest of public investment is not less than 25 percent (ROSC, 2002, p.4).

Table 7.5 Perceptions of the Influence of Ownership Structure on Levels of Compliance with IFRSs

Interviewee	Government	Management	Private	Public
Re1	No Association	No Association	No Association	No Association
Re2	Negative	Negative	No Association	No Association
Re3	No Association	No Association	No Association	No Association
Re4	Negative	Negative	Negative	Negative
Ae1	Negative	Negative	Negative	Negative
Ae2	No Association	No Association	No Association	No Association
Se1	No Association	No Association	No Association	No Association
Se2	Positive	Negative	Negative	No Association
Se3	Negative	Negative	Negative	No Association
Se4	Negative	Negative	Negative	No Association
Ie1	No Association	No Association	No Association	No Association
Ie2	No Association	No Association	No Association	No Association
Rj1	Negative	Negative	Negative	Positive
Rj2	Positive	No Association	Negative	No Association
Aj1	Negative	Negative	Negative	No Association
Sj1	No Association	Negative	Negative	No Association
Sj2	No Association	Negative	Negative	Positive
Sj3	No Association	Negative	Negative	No Association
Ij1	No Association	No Association	No Association	No Association
Ij2	No Association	No Association	No Association	Positive

The Relationship between Ownership Structure and Levels of Compliance with IFRSs

The other six respondents (Re1, Re3, Ae2, Se1, Ie1 and Ie2) considered that no relationship exists between dominant government ownership and levels of compliance with IFRSs. They gave various reasons for this perspective: a) disclosure requirements are required by laws and regulations so company management should comply with them to avoid being penalised, b) the disclosure behaviour depends on management awareness regarding the importance of compliance and improved transparency, c) given the secretive culture of the Egyptian society and weak monitoring and enforcement of regulations by the CMA and low demand for improved disclosure by naive investors, management determine the extent of disclosure according to their vision.

"I think there is no association between dominant government ownership and the levels of compliance with IFRSs disclosure requirements, as disclosure is regulated by company law and the CML and in case of non-compliance with any of the mandatory requirements the company will be penalised and may be delisted." Re1

"Companies' disclosure policy is bounded by laws and regulations so management in all cases must comply with those requirements regardless of company ownership structure." Re3

"The extent of disclosure mainly depends on management policy so I do not think that ownership structure has any effect." Ae2

"The secretive nature of our society, poor performance of management in companies with dominant government ownership, low demand for more disclosures by government as it has direct access to any information, and lack of awareness among small investors regarding the disclosures that must be made by companies, weak enforcement and sanctions imposed by CMA will all encourage management to disclose according to its vision." Se1

"I do not think so. I think management chooses the level of disclosure according to its agenda regardless of laws or the type of major shareholders." Ie1

"I think such association may exist in developed countries but in Egypt I do not think so because nobody cares about improving disclosure." Ie2

In Jordan two respondents (Rj1 and Aj1) supported a negative association between dominant government ownership and compliance levels on the grounds that the government has access to all company information it wants. Only Rj2 supported a positive relationship, believing that when the government is the major shareholder, it is important for the BOD to comply with disclosure requirements to gain the political support of the public. All the remaining five respondents (Sj1, Sj2, Sj3, Ij1 and Ij2) argued that no association exists between dominant government ownership and levels of compliance with IFRSs disclosure requirements, suggesting that the level of awareness regarding the benefits of improving compliance represents the main determinant of company disclosure level. Additionally, they see the secretive nature of their society and weak enforcement of disclosure requirements as the main antecedent of compliance, rather than dominance of government ownership. Also, they argue that the shortage in competent accounting practitioners negatively affects progress in compliance levels.

"The level of compliance with IFRSs disclosure requirements is mainly a function of management awareness regarding the importance and advantages of disclosure and transparency. Thus, I think it needs more time to understand this culture." Sj1

"The secretive nature of developing societies such as Jordan and weak monitoring of management disclosure policy reduce any possible impact of such variable on the extent of disclosure. Thus, I expect no association between dominance of government ownership and the levels of compliance with IFRSs disclosure requirements." Sj2

"As we are suffering a shortage of competent accountants so I think non-compliance can be attributed to unfamiliarity or poor qualification of accountants and the monitoring body so it is not affected by the ownership structure." Sj3

"I do not think that when the government is a major shareholder this will result in better disclosures as disclosure policy is determined by management according to its vision and the government already can obtain any information about the company at any time." Ij1

"As I understand, disclosures are required by laws but as long as the monitoring body does not follow up non-compliant companies as is the case in all Arab markets, management will disclose only the information they need to disseminate." Ij2

The above discussion indicates that in both Egypt and Jordan the majority of interviewees believed the ideas espoused in Gray's (1988) accounting sub-cultural model, cost-benefit analysis, agency theory, and institutional isomorphism accounted for the prevailing situation. The preference for secrecy by company management, the lack of awareness among management of listed companies regarding the importance of compliance with IFRSs, the weak enforcement of laws and regulations, and low demand for improved disclosures due to the government's direct access to company information or lack of qualification of government officials who monitor company compliance with IFRSs, all cause non-compliance costs to be less than compliance costs and hence, management is not prompted to improve compliance. Additionally, this contributes to the problem of decoupling as companies to gain respect and legitimacy argue that they are complying with the disclosure regulations when they are not.

Concerning the influence of dominant management ownership on compliance levels, as indicated in Table 7.5, in Egypt six respondents (Re2, Re4, Ae1, Se2, Se3 and Se4) argued there is a negative relationship between these two variables on the grounds that the dominance of management ownership will reduce the monitoring costs, and hence result in low levels of compliance. Also, due to the preference for secrecy by management of listed companies, and weak monitoring by the CMA and individual small investors, the dominance of management ownership is expected to have a negative impact on compliance levels.

"In my opinion the dominance of management ownership results in lower levels of compliance with IFRSs disclosure requirements due to management preference for secrecy to protect important information from being available to competitors, and as the majority of board members are from management members or have been chosen by management which is the major owner of company shares, this will reduce monitoring costs so may result in lower levels of compliance with IFRSs disclosure requirements." Re2

"Unfortunately, due to the dominance of the secretive culture, management will not disclose important information and as the majority of company shares are also owned by management this is expected to have a negative impact on the levels of compliance." Re4

"As management is the producer and the main user of company information this will reduce the monitoring costs, and hence will have a negative effect on the levels of compliance." Ae1

"The secretive culture, weak enforcement of regulations and low demand for improved disclosure by small individual investors is expected to increase the possibility of a negative association between the dominance of management ownership and the levels of compliance with IFRSs disclosure requirements." Se2

"As long as there is no effective monitoring of companies' levels of compliance with IFRSs, dominance of management ownership is supposed to have a negative impact on the levels of compliance with IFRSs." Se3

"Low monitoring costs are expected to result in a negative relationship between dominance of management ownership and the levels of compliance with IFRSs." Se4

However, the remaining respondents (Re1, Re3, Ae2, Se1, Ie1 and Ie2) argued that there is no association between levels of compliance with IFRSs and the dominance of management ownership, believing that disclosure is regulated by mandatory disclosure requirements determined by legislation, or due to the lack of awareness of the importance of improving transparency and disclosure levels by company management, irrespective of whether management is the major shareholder or otherwise.

"I think there is no association between dominant management ownership and levels of compliance with IFRSs disclosure requirements, as disclosure is covered by regulations." Re1

"Companies' disclosure policy is bounded by laws and regulations so management in all cases must comply with those requirements regardless of company ownership structure." Re3

"The extent of disclosure mainly depends on management policy so I do not think that ownership structure has any effect." Ae2

"The secretive nature of our society, low demand for more disclosures by small investors, weak enforcement and sanctions imposed by the CMA will encourage management to disclose according to its vision." Se1

"I do not think so. I think management chooses the level of disclosure according to its agenda regardless of laws or the type of major shareholders." Ie1

"I think in Egypt there is an absence of accountability so management determines what to disclose according to its interests." Ie2

In Jordan, as indicated in Table 7.5, the majority of respondents (Rj1, Aj1, Sj1, Sj2 and Sj3) supported a negative association between management ownership and levels of compliance with IFRSs disclosure requirements. They justified their opinions by reference to management's preference for secrecy and fear of competitors.

"When the majority of company shares are owned by management this is expected to increase management preference for secrecy. Thus, I expect that dominance of management ownership results in lower levels of compliance with IFRSs disclosure requirements." Rj1

"Negative - as management may prefer to hide some information from their competitors." Aj1

"The culture of secrecy will cause management to hide important information to avoid competition so I expect dominance of management ownership to result in low levels of compliance with IFRSs." Sj1

"Preference for secrecy encouraged by lack of effective monitoring is expected to result in a negative association between dominance of management ownership and the levels of compliance with IFRSs." Sj2

"The dominance of management ownership supports management's cultural value of secrecy as in this case monitoring costs will be very low." Sj3

Conversely, the remaining respondents (Rj2, Ij1and Ij2) argued that no association exists between dominance of management ownership and compliance levels, suggesting compliance to be influenced by the strictness of enforcement by the regulatory bodies, which is weak, thereby prompting management to disclose according to its vision, regardless of the company's ownership structure. Others argued that compliance is determined by the level of management awareness regarding the importance and benefits of improving transparency.

"I think management policy toward the level of compliance with IFRSs is the same regardless of the dominant type of ownership within the company as this behaviour is influenced by management awareness regarding the benefits of improving compliance with IFRSs disclosure requirements." Rj2

"I think company disclosure policy is the main determinant of the level of disclosure so in my opinion there is no association between the level of compliance with IFRSs and the dominance of management ownership." Ie1

"In my opinion disclosures are required by laws so as long as the monitoring body does not follow up non-compliant companies and impose strict sanctions on them as is the case in all Arab markets, management disclosure will be selective regardless of whether it has a dominant ownership in the company or not." Ij2

The above discussion indicates that the perceptions of the interviewees in Egypt and Jordan regarding the relationship between the dominance of management ownership and the levels of compliance with IFRSs disclosure requirements support the notions of agency theory due to low monitoring costs. Furthermore, they support the ideas proposed in Gray's (1988) accounting sub-cultural model, cost-benefit analysis, and institutional isomorphism as the secretive culture in both countries causes management to keep disclosure levels at a minimum to protect company information from being misused by competitors. Also the lack of management and board members' awareness regarding the importance of compliance with IFRSs and corporate governance best practice that encourage transparency, the weak enforcement of laws and regulations by regulatory bodies, the weak sanctions (if any), the low demand for improved disclosures, and insufficient monitoring from small shareholders who cannot put voting pressures on management who are simultaneously the dominant shareholders and board members, all combine to promote lower non-compliance costs than compliance costs. Hence, management is not encouraged to enhance compliance levels. Consequently, dominance of management ownership is believed to have no impact on the levels of compliance with IFRSs disclosure requirements rather than a negative impact as in all cases management disclosure policy is mainly based on attitudes toward transparency.

Concerning the influence of dominant private ownership on the compliance levels, Table 7.5 shows that in Egypt five respondents (Re4, Ae1, Se2, Se3 and Se4) believed a negative relationship exists between these two variables, due to owners' access to company information, low monitoring costs, and the secretive nature of society.

"The majority of shares in listed companies on EGX are held by families who also hold managerial positions and also members of the BOD of listed companies so they already have access to company information. In addition due to competition they may prefer to hide some information to protect company reputation so this is expected to result in low compliance with IFRSs disclosure requirements." Re4

"When there is a dominance of private ownership, management compliance with IFRSs disclosure requirements will decrease as such shareholders can acquire any information they need and of course small investors do not ask for anything and do not put any pressure on the company's BOD to monitor compliance so levels of compliance are expected to decrease." Ae1

"Private ownership results in low monitoring costs; thus it is expected to have a negative impact on compliance." Se2

"When there is a dominance of private ownership such owners can easily get access to all company information so there is no pressure on the BOD or management to improve compliance so it is expected to have a negative impact on the levels of compliance with IFRSs." Se3

"Due to the secretive nature of our society dominance of private ownership is expected to have a negative impact on the levels of compliance as owners are expected to ask management to hide important information to avoid competition." Se4

Conversely, seven respondents (Re1, Re2, Re3, Ae2, Se1, Ie1 and Ie2) argued that no such relationship exists between dominance of private ownership and compliance levels, on the grounds that disclosure is regulated by mandatory disclosure requirements determined by laws, or determined by the lack of awareness regarding the importance of improving transparency and disclosure levels by company management and board members. For the sake of brevity and to avoid repetition, a selection only of interviewee responses follows:

"I also think there is no association between dominance of private ownership and levels of compliance with IFRSs disclosure requirements for the same aforementioned reasons." Re1

"The dominance of private ownership is expected to have no relationship with the levels of compliance with IFRSs disclosure requirements as compliance with IFRSs is influenced mainly by management attitude." Re2

"Companies' disclosure policy is bounded by laws and regulations so management in all cases must comply with those requirements regardless of company ownership structure." Re3

In Jordan, as indicated in Table 7.5, the majority of respondents (Rj1, Rj2, Aj1, Sj1, Sj2 and Sj3) supported a negative association between private ownership and levels of compliance with IFRSs disclosure requirements. They justified their opinions referring to the fact that private owners have direct access to company information, and by management's and owners' preference for secrecy to counter competition.

"The dominance of private ownership will have a negative impact on compliance with IFRSs if they interfere in company disclosure policy and ask management to hide information from competitors." Rj1

"As dominant ownership by private investors is expected to give them access to company information the secretive nature of our society may result in lower levels of compliance with IFRSs disclosure requirements." Rj2

"I think dominance of private ownership has a negative impact on the levels of compliance with IFRSs as investors in this case already have access to any information they need so it is better to hide information to reduce the threat from competitors." Aj1

"There is a negative association between private ownership and the levels of compliance with IFRSs as private owners have access to information and they do not like company information to be available to the public to avoid competition." Sj1

"I expect dominance of private ownership to lead to lower levels of compliance with IFRSs disclosure requirements as owners in this case have access to company information, they interfere in setting company policies including disclosures and they do not like company information to be available to the public to avoid competition." Sj2

"Dominance of private ownership negatively affects the extent of disclosure in developing countries as investors may ask management to hide important information that may threaten the company reputation or competitive position." Sj3

Only Ij1 and Ij2 argued that no association exists between dominance of private ownership and levels of company disclosure on the grounds that in all cases the company is supposed to disclose the information required by law and in all Jordanian companies, management is the main determinant of the disclosures to be made and nobody asks for better compliance.

"Disclosure is made according to the Jordanian laws and in reality management choose the information to be disclosed regardless of the dominance of any group." Ij1

"As private owners already get all the information they need and also management determines the disclosure policy of the company and nobody whether from inside or outside the company asks for better disclosure, so the situation will continue and management will control the extent of information to be disseminated." Ij2

The above discussion supports the propositions of agency theory, cultural theory, cost-benefit analysis, and institutional isomorphism, in both Egypt and Jordan. Based on agency theory and cost-benefit analysis, direct access to company information by this group of shareholders and lack of demand for improving disclosure by small investors and regulatory bodies, results in low monitoring costs. Also, the preference for secrecy and the lack of awareness by management and possibly by private investors who are generally the managers and members of the BOD, regarding the benefits of compliance with IFRSs disclosure requirements may not encourage management to improve compliance levels. This also contributes to the problem of decoupling as companies will argue that they are applying IFRSs when actually, full compliance is absent. Consequently, the dominance of private ownership is expected to have no impact on the levels of compliance with IFRSs disclosure requirements, if not a negative impact. In Jordan the majority of interviewees strongly supported the claim of a negative association between dominance of private ownership and compliance levels compared to the interviewees in Egypt.

Finally, with respect to the possible impact of dominance of public ownership on the levels of compliance with IFRSs disclosure requirements, as indicated in Table 7.5, in Egypt the majority of respondents (Re1, Re2, Re3, Ae2, Se1, Se2, Se3, Se4, Ie1, Ie2) argued that no association is evident between these two variables, due to the lack of awareness and accountability among management of listed companies regarding the necessity to follow disclosure requirements, and the benefits of protecting the rights of individual investors in attracting foreign investors and improving the reputation of the national stock exchange. Also, some respondents argued that the laws and regulations that govern the disclosure practices by listed companies must be followed. For the sake of brevity and to avoid repetition, a selection only of interviewee responses follows:

"I also think there is no association between dominance of public ownership and the levels of compliance with IFRSs disclosure requirements, as disclosure is regulated by company law and the CML

and in case of non-compliance with any of the mandatory requirements the company will be penalised and may be delisted." Re1

"The dominance of public ownership is expected to have no relationship with the levels of compliance with IFRSs disclosure requirements as compliance with IFRSs is influenced mainly by management and unfortunately public investors have no awareness about their rights and even if they have they do not practise such rights." Re2

"The secretive nature of our society, low demand for more disclosures by the public investors, weak enforcement and sanctions imposed by CMA will encourage management to disclose according to its vision." Se1

"The lack of accountability and lack of management belief in the benefits of improving compliance with IFRSs disclosure requirements in order to attract foreign investment is expected to reduce the expected positive impact of dominance of public ownership on the levels of compliance in a country like Egypt." Se3

"I do not think so. I think management chooses the level of disclosure according to its agenda regardless of laws or the type of major shareholders." Ie1

Only Re4 and Ae1 supported a positive relationship between dominance of public ownership and the levels of compliance with IFRSs on the grounds that dominance of public shareholders is expected to improve the monitoring of the BOD and management of publicly listed companies.

"When the majority of company shares are owned by public investors, this is expected to improve the monitoring of the BOD and management to protect the public shareholders' right to get at least the minimum information required by company law and CML." Re4

"I think when there is a dominance of public ownership, levels of compliance with IFRSs disclosure requirements will improve because public investors will monitor management compliance." Ae1

In Jordan, as indicated in Table 7.5, three respondents (Rj1, Sj2 and Ij2) believed a positive relationship exists between dominant public ownership and compliance levels, in order to reduce monitoring costs.

"Dominance of public ownership is expected to result in better levels of compliance with IFRSs by listed companies in order to reduce monitoring costs and bad reputation in case of being penalised for non-compliance." Rj1

"According to agency theory dominance of public ownership should result in higher levels of compliance with IFRSs disclosure requirements in order to lower the monitoring costs. I think this also applies to Jordan." Sj2

"When the majority of company shares is publicly held, public investors can form a lobby that is able to monitor management disclosure practices and report any misuse to the BOD and the JSC." Ij2

However, the remaining respondents (Rj2, Aj1, Sj1, Sj3 and Ij1) argued that there is no association between dominance of public ownership and levels of compliance with IFRSs disclosure requirements. This was similar to Egyptian interviewees' beliefs. They argued that the preference for secrecy and the lack of awareness and accountability among management of listed companies regarding the necessity to follow disclosure requirements and the benefits of protecting the rights of individual investors in attracting foreign investors and improving the reputation of the national stock exchange, would precipitate such outcomes. Additionally, lack of awareness among public investors about their rights and the flexibility given by the JSC to avoid delisting the majority of non-compliant companies, together with the negative consequences resulting from damage to the international reputation of the ASE, do not stimulate management to improve compliance. Also, some of the respondents argued that no association exists between the dominance of public ownership and compliance levels as there are laws and regulations governing disclosure practices by listed companies and such laws must be followed.

"To be honest we are trying to encourage companies listed on ASE to comply with IFRSs, however due to cultural barriers, mainly secrecy and the lack of awareness among the public regarding their right to put pressure on the BOD and management of listed companies to improve disclosure, levels of compliance with IFRSs disclosure requirements do not improve as expected when there is a dominance of public shareholders." Rj2

"I think dominance of public ownership has no impact on improving the levels of compliance with IFRSs as such investors lack awareness about their rights." Aj1

"The dominance of secretive culture, weak enforcement of laws by JSC and lack of awareness among management, BOD and investors regarding the importance of compliance with IFRSs disclosure requirements, dominance of public shareholders is not expected to result in better compliance levels as argued by different financial disclosure theories that developed in the west." Sj1

"In Jordan the culture and weak enforcement are the main barriers to the existence of a positive association between the dominance of public ownership and the levels of compliance with IFRSs disclosure requirements as proposed by the majority of researchers in the field who investigated this issue in more developed countries." Sj3

"Disclosure is made according to the Jordanian laws and in reality management choose the information to be disclosed regardless of the dominance of ownership of any investor group." Ij1

The above discussion indicates that in Egypt and Jordan there are two viewpoints regarding the influence of dominance of public ownership upon compliance levels with IFRSs. The first argues that dominance of public ownership results in better compliance as a means of reducing monitoring costs and avoiding penalties by the regulatory bodies. This mainly supports the ideas expressed in agency theory, cost-benefit analysis, and institutional isomorphism. The second perspective argues that no association exists between these two variables, which agrees with the notions of agency theory in respect of low monitoring costs. It also supports Gray's (1988) accounting sub-cultural model, cost-benefit analysis, and institutional isomorphism. It can be proposed that the secretive culture in Egypt and Jordan causes management to avoid the outflow of company-sensitive information. Additionally, secrecy is associated with large power distance and a preference for collectivism (Gray, 1988). Furthermore, the lack of awareness among management and BODs of listed companies regarding the importance of compliance with IFRSs and the importance of following corporate governance best practice to enhance transparency, the weak enforcement of laws and regulations, and low demand for improved disclosures due to the lack of awareness among public investors in the two capital markets regarding their right to ask for more disclosures, will cause non-compliance costs to be less than compliance costs. Hence, management will not be stimulated to improve compliance levels. Moreover, this then contributes to the problem of decoupling.

7.5 Linking the Interview Results with the Research Objectives

A clear link can be identified between the interview results and study objectives. It can be seen in two ways.

Firstly, the findings from the quantitative analysis are directly related to the study objectives, and secondly, the interview protocol was built on these findings. This link is further explained as follows:

The first objective was to evaluate the extent of compliance with IFRSs disclosure requirements by companies listed on the EGX and ASE as leading MENA stock exchanges. The first subject in the interview framework was the perceptions regarding barriers to full compliance with these requirements in the interviewee's jurisdiction (Egypt/Jordan). This exploration resulted in an enhanced understanding of the relevance of IFRSs to MENA countries and of the obstacles to full compliance with these standards in Egypt and Jordan. Accordingly, levels of compliance with IFRSs could be explained by reference to the interview results.

The second, third, and fourth objectives of the study were to explore the relationship between different corporate governance variables (BOD independence, board leadership, and ownership structure) and levels of compliance with IFRSs by companies listed on the EGX and ASE. The second subject in the interview framework focused on this relationship. The interview results emphasised that corporate governance variables are not the main determinants of the extent of compliance with IFRSs disclosure requirements in Egypt and Jordan.

The fifth objective of the study was to explore the underlying theoretical rationale of corporate financial disclosure practices within the MENA context. This objective was indirectly met through the analysis of the interview data which emphasised that the study's findings regarding the extent of compliance with IFRSs disclosure requirements and its relationship with corporate governance structures of companies listed on the EGX and ASE are consistent with the suggestions of cultural, institutional isomorphism, and financial economics theories, which based on the discussions in Chapter Two, were found to be relevant to financial disclosure practices in the MENA context.

7.6 Summary

This chapter has presented a summary of generalisations and themes derived from the interview analysis, and linked the interview results with the study objectives.

In total, 20 interviews were conducted (12 in Egypt and 8 in Jordan) with individuals representing regulators, accountants, academicians, and individual investors. The questions posed to the interviewees were the same for the first three groups, but contained some differences for the investor group. They were, however, all generated as a result of the findings from the quantitative analysis, and hence used to gain more detail about certain issues.

The generalisations which could be concluded from the interview data are summarised as follows:

1. The major barriers to full compliance with IFRSs disclosure requirements in the EGX and ASE are: low non-compliance costs, inadequate qualification of accounting practitioners, low demand for more disclosure by investors, management resistance, the degree of relevance of the requirements under each IFRS to the economic development stage of the scrutinised jurisdictions.
2. In Egypt and Jordan board independence is not an effective mechanism for improving compliance levels. This supports the ideas advanced by institutional isomorphism that even when companies adopt board independence as evidence of their modernity and commitment to international best practices, this has no impact on levels of compliance. Hence, the decoupling problem prevails. Also, as independent directors do not exercise their authority in monitoring company compliance with IFRSs, management has no pressure to increase disclosure levels, thereby the proposed theoretical foundation for the analysis is justified.
3. In Egypt and Jordan the separation between the positions of the CEO and the Chair does not necessarily lead to enhancing the level of compliance with IFRSs. This supports the notions of institutional isomorphism that even when roles are separated this is effected merely as window dressing, to gain respect and legitimacy, but in practice the separation does not increase compliance levels, and the problem of decoupling is magnified. Also as the Chair does not use his authority in monitoring management attitude toward compliance with IFRSs, and given the weak monitoring by the CMA in Egypt, the JSC in Jordan and the weak naive investors in

both countries, managements determine the extent of disclosure according to their vision. The proposed theoretical foundation is thus, supported.

4. In Egypt and Jordan the perceptions of the majority of the interviewees support a limited impact of government ownership (if any) on compliance levels, thereby confirming the proposed theoretical foundation. The management preference for secrecy, the lack of management awareness of the importance of compliance with IFRSs, the lack of awareness among BOD members regarding the importance of corporate governance best practice in improving disclosure practices, the weak enforcement of laws and regulations by regulatory bodies, the failure to impose sanctions, the low demand for improved disclosure due to the government's direct access to company information, the lack of qualification of government officials who monitor company compliance with IFRSs, and the resultant low monitoring costs all combine to sustain the status quo, being that management continue with their current levels of compliance. Again, these conditions contribute to the problem of decoupling as companies to gain respect and legitimacy will argue that they are applying IFRSs whereas full compliance with IFRSs disclosure requirements is absent.
5. In Egypt and Jordan the perceptions of the majority of the interviewees is that dominance of management ownership has a limited impact on the levels of compliance with IFRSs disclosure requirements. This supports the notions of the proposed theoretical foundation as the secretive culture in both countries causes management to keep disclosure levels at minimum levels to protect company information from being misused by competitors. Also the lack of awareness by management and board members regarding the importance of compliance with IFRSs and corporate governance best practices that encourage enhanced transparency, the weak enforcement of laws and regulations by regulatory bodies and weak sanctions if any, and the low demand for improved disclosures and insufficient monitoring from small shareholders who cannot put voting pressures on company managements (who are simultaneously dominant shareholders and BOD members), cause non-compliance costs to be less than compliance costs, and thus managements are not stimulated to improve compliance levels. Consequently, dominance of management ownership probably has no impact (although possibly a negative one) on the levels of compliance with IFRSs disclosure requirements because in all

cases, regardless of the ownership structure, compliance is a management affair.

6. In Egypt and Jordan the perceptions of the majority of the interviewees are that a limited impact of dominance of private ownership occurs on compliance levels. Based on agency theory and cost-benefit analysis, direct access to company information by this group of shareholders and lack of demand for improved disclosure by small investors and regulatory bodies, result in low monitoring costs and low sanctions, if any. Also, the preference for secrecy and the lack of awareness by management and possibly private investors (who are generally also the managers and BOD members) regarding the benefits of compliance may not encourage management to improve levels of compliance with IFRSs. This also contributes to the problem of decoupling as companies will argue that they are applying IFRSs whereas full compliance with IFRSs is absent. Consequently, the dominance of private ownership most likely has no impact (but possibly a negative impact) on compliance levels. In Jordan it is recognised that the majority of interviewees provide much stronger support than the interviewees in Egypt, for the contention that a negative association between dominance of private ownership and compliance levels exists.
7. In Egypt and Jordan two distinct viewpoints exist regarding the influence of dominant public ownership upon compliance levels. The first argues that dominance of public ownership will result in better compliance in an effort to reduce monitoring costs and escape penalties by the regulatory bodies. This in turn mainly supports the notions of agency theory and cost-benefit analysis. The other perspective suggests that there is no association between the dominance of public ownership and compliance levels, thereby being in line with agency theory that argues for low monitoring costs. This also supports Gray's (1988) accounting sub-cultural model, cost-benefit analysis, and institutional isomorphism. It can be proposed that the secretive culture in the two countries causes management to avoid any outflow of company-sensitive information. Moreover, secrecy is associated with large power distance and a preference for collectivism. In addition, the lack of awareness among the managements and BODs of listed companies regarding the importance of compliance with IFRSs and the importance of following corporate governance best practice to enhance transparency does not stimulate management to increase disclosure. This absence of stimulation is magnified by the weak

enforcement of laws and regulations, and the low demand for improved disclosures due to the lack of awareness among public investors regarding their right to demand more disclosure. Together these result in non-compliance costs being less than compliance costs. Management's aversion to enhancing disclosure subsequently contributes to the problem of decoupling.

The next chapter brings the study to a conclusion and in so doing highlights its limitations, offering suggestions for future research.

CHAPTER EIGHT

CONCLUSIONS, LIMITATIONS AND SUGGESTIONS FOR FUTURE RESEARCH

8.1 Introduction

This chapter summarises the main results and conclusions of this study and provides suggestions for future research. Hence, the remaining part of this chapter is organised as follows. Section 8.2 provides a summary of the main research findings. Section 8.3 demonstrates the contributions of the study, and section 8.4 considers the implications of the research findings. Section 8.5 discusses the limitations of the study, and finally, section 8.6 suggests areas for future research.

8.2 Research Results and Conclusion

The study has examined the influence of corporate governance structures (board characteristics and ownership structure), on the levels of compliance with mandatory IFRSs disclosure requirements by companies listed on two leading MENA stock exchanges; the EGX and the ASE. The study has employed a cross-sectional analysis of an equal sample of 75 non-financial companies listed on each of the scrutinised stock exchanges for the fiscal year ending 31 December, 2007. Using an unweighted disclosure index of 275 items derived from mandatory IFRSs disclosure requirements for the fiscal year beginning in January 2007 (see Appendix B), this study firstly has measured the levels of compliance by the sample companies listed on the focus stock exchanges. The index encompasses twenty sub-indices in order to facilitate the measurement of levels of compliance with the disclosure requirements under each individual standard (see sub-section 5.5.1). The extent of disclosure in annual reports was derived by computing the ratio of actual scores awarded to the maximum possible score attainable for items appropriate to that company (see sub-section 5.5.1).

Following this step, univariate and multivariate regression analyses were used to examine the association between corporate governance related variables (board independence, board leadership, board size, government ownership ratio, management ownership ratio, private ownership ratio and public ownership ratio) and the extent of compliance with IFRSs disclosure requirements. Then, semi-structured interviews (12 conducted in Egypt and 8 in Jordan) were carried out in order to supplement the interpretation of the findings of the empirical analyses as discussed in Chapter Seven.

An innovative theoretical foundation is deployed, in which compliance is interpretable mainly through the inducements of the institutional isomorphism theory and secrecy versus transparency as one of the accounting sub-cultural values identified by Gray (1988). Furthermore, the notions of the agency theory and Cost-benefit analysis employed in prior research have been used to some extent in deriving the research hypotheses and interpreting the research findings. Hence, the last research question (Q3) was answered by relating the empirical findings to the notions of the proposed theoretical framework. In addition, the analysis of interview data as indicated in Chapter Seven helped in exploring the underlying theoretical rationale for corporate financial disclosure practices in scrutinised MENA countries.

The examination of annual reports for sample companies listed on the two stock exchanges revealed the following:

1. None of the listed companies in either stock exchange achieved 100% compliance level with the overall mandatory IFRSs disclosure requirements. Full compliance was, however, achieved by some companies at the level of individual IFRSs.
2. The average level of compliance with the overall mandatory IFRSs disclosure requirements (total disclosure index) was relatively higher in Egypt than Jordan (80% and 76% respectively) and the maximum level of compliance with IFRSs disclosure requirements was 91% in Egypt and 88% in Jordan. In addition, the minimum level of compliance by companies listed on the EGX was much higher than that of companies listed on the ASE (68% and 56% respectively), the difference mainly attributed to the shortage of qualified accountants in Jordan.
3. On the level of sub-disclosure indices (section 6.2), sub-index 17 (IAS 36: Impairment of Assets) achieved a 100% compliance level by all companies in which it was applicable (3 companies in Egypt and 8 in Jordan), thereby emphasising the enormous impact of culture on disclosure practices in MENA stock exchanges. Although this standard was applicable to a limited number of companies in both jurisdictions, all of them fully complied with its

requirements, thereby supporting the proposition that as long as the requirements of a particular standard do not contradict with the dominant culture in a specific society, listed company management will be incentivised to fully comply with its requirements. Additionally, full compliance with the requirements of this standard may be attributed to the non-existence of any understanding or interpretation difficulties concerning those requirements. On the other hand, the EGX listed companies achieved the lowest levels of compliance with sub-index 16 (IAS 33: Earnings per Share), with an average compliance level of 31%. On the level of the ASE also, the average level of compliance with this standard's requirements was low (37%). Such low compliance levels are explained by the preference for secrecy and lack of awareness among different parties concerning the importance of compliance with all of the requirements of this standard for improving transparency. In respect of sub-index 10 (IAS 21:The Effects of Changes in Foreign Exchange Rates), the ASE-listed companies showed the lowest average level of compliance, with a gap in evidence between Egypt and Jordan (97% and 19% respectively). The low compliance level was mainly attributed to the impact of the inadequate qualification of accounting practitioners and the non-existence of an official Arabic translation of the IFRSs in Jordan.

4. The analysis of compliance levels with individual disclosure items (sub-section 6.2.3) revealed some similarities between the Egyptian and Jordanian management attitudes with respect to compliance with many of disclosure requirements. It was recognised that in most cases of Jordanian non-compliance, the shortage of competent qualified accountants was cited as the reason. However, in broad terms progress is evident in compliance levels with some IFRSs disclosure requirements that have been reported as not complied with in previous studies investigating the two stock exchanges on the individual country level (*e.g.,* Abd-Elsalam, 1999; Omar, 2007). This may be attributed to the improved awareness among managements of listed companies regarding the importance of compliance with these items (*i.e.,* compliance with these items has become embedded within the disclosure sub-cultural values), improved familiarity with respect to their proper application, and the improved monitoring of these items by the regulatory bodies in the two stock exchanges. One example is the disclosure of the capitalisation rate used to determine the amount of borrowing costs eligible for capitalisation (item 201) which achieved 98% and 83%

compliance by companies listed on the EGX and ASE respectively compared to 79% in Abd-Elsalam (1999) and 33% in Omar (2007).

The results of testing for significant statistical differences between the Egyptian and the Jordanian contexts (section 6.4), in connection with the first research hypothesis promulgated the existence of significant statistical differences between the Egyptian and the Jordanian contexts in the overall level of compliance with mandatory IFRSs disclosure requirements (dependent variable). In addition, the results showed that there are statistically significant differences between companies listed on the EGX and those listed on the ASE with respect to all test and control variables except government ownership ratio. Based on this finding the univariate and multivariate analyses were carried out on individual country level.

The univariate and multivariate analyses (sections 6.5, 6.6) to assess the association between levels of compliance with IFRSs disclosure requirements and corporate governance test variables (board leadership, board independence, board size, government ownership, management ownership, private ownership and public ownership) and control variables (company size, profitability, gearing, liquidity, type of business activity and type of audit firm) revealed the following:

1. On the level of the Egyptian context, the findings of the univariate and multivariate analyses implied that compliance behaviour with the overall mandatory IFRSs disclosure requirements by companies listed on the EGX do not follow any pattern in relation to any of the independent variables employed in this study. This may be due to the novelty of corporate governance and the lack of awareness about the importance and the advantages of complete *de facto* compliance with IFRSs disclosure requirements and corporate governance best practices in the Egyptian context. On the other hand, the non-existence of an association between compliance with mandatory IFRSs disclosure requirements by companies listed on the EGX and any of the corporate attributes employed as control variables following prior research that proved their influence on compliance behaviour by companies listed on the EGX (company size, profitability, gearing, liquidity, type of business activity and type of auditor), is to some extent a good sign that generally all companies listed on the EGX are now similar in their attitude towards compliance with many mandatory disclosure requirements (*i.e.,* they are now part of disclosure culture of all companies listed

on the EGX). Consequently, it can also be concluded that, non-compliance with some requirements, hence current gap between *de facto* and *de jure* compliance with overall IFRSs disclosure requirements is most likely influenced by the existence of some factors mainly related to the secretive culture that is dominant in the Egyptian context.

2. On the level of the Jordanian context, the univariate analysis revealed that public ownership has a significant negative relationship with the level of compliance with overall mandatory IFRSs disclosure requirements in the Jordanian context. Also, univariate analysis revealed that companies audited by big 4 audit firms comply better with IFRSs disclosure requirements than those audited by non-big 4 audit firms. These findings were confirmed by multivariate analysis which also revealed that company size has a significant positive association with compliance with mandatory IFRSs disclosure requirements in the Jordanian context. Regression analysis revealed that 24.5% of the variation in the total disclosure index (overall compliance with mandatory IFRSs disclosure requirements) in the Jordanian context is explained by the type of auditor, public ownership ratio and firm size.
3. Overall the findings of the univariate and multivariate analysis in both of scrutinised stock exchanges revealed that the impact of corporate governance best practice mechanisms is absent in both of scrutinised stock exchanges. Corporate governance codes for best practice were initiated in developed countries and only recently introduced in scrutinised MENA ones. Hence, its contribution towards enhancing capital market performance in such countries is subject to the extent to which the conditions for robust governance practice are consistent with the existing values and the needs of all parties involved in the financial reporting process. It is expected, therefore, to be some time before the impact of applying corporate governance can be measured in scrutinised contexts as this needs to develop, and favourable attitude and belief must be formed as well as efforts being made to develop the human resource capabilities that believe in and able to materially apply corporate governance requirements for best practice. Currently, there may be other factors that strongly influence attitudes to transparency in emerging MENA stock exchanges. These may not be easily quantifiable and testable using statistical models. This proposition is supported by the interviewee responses (section 7.4). Additionally, the efforts of stock market regulatory bodies are insufficient to close the gap

between *de jure* and *de facto* compliance in the two stock exchanges. Hence, it is expected that as national cultural values are developed to recognise the importance of compliance with IFRSs as is the case in developed countries where such standards originated, and as the qualification levels of the monitoring staff of the CMA and JSC and of accounting practitioners particularly in the Jordanian context improve, strictness of enforcement of mandatory disclosure requirements enhanced, so too will the levels of compliance with IFRSs disclosure requirements.

4. The results of this study support the existence of similarities between two emerging MENA stock exchanges (EGX and ASE) in terms of their reaction to the introduction of corporate governance mechanisms that are recommended by the OECD principles for corporate governance best practice. However, still both stock exchanges are not totally homogeneous; hence it can be argued that generalising the results of one developing country to others is not completely accurate.

Table 8.1 summarises the results of the univariate and multivariate analyses concerning the variables influencing levels of compliance with IFRSs disclosure requirements in each of the scrutinised contexts.

The interviews conducted with different parties affecting and being affected by financial disclosure practices in scrutinised stock exchanges supported the quantitative research findings and the applicability of the proposed theoretical foundation (see Chapter Seven). The interviewees pointed out to the negative impact of low non-compliance costs, low demand for more disclosures by investors, inadequate qualification of accounting practitioners and of compliance monitoring staff. They also highlighted the negative influence of management resistance to transparency and the irrelevance of some IFRSs requirements to the economic development stage of the scrutinised MENA emerging exchanges.

Table 8.1 Variables Influencing Levels of Compliance with Overall Mandatory IFRSs Disclosure

Requirements in Egypt and Jordan

Analysis	Egypt	Jordan
H2: BOD Independence (Neutral Association)		
Univariate	✓[1]	✓
Multivariate	✓	✓
H3:Board Leadership (Neutral Association)		
Univariate	✓	✓
Multivariate	✓	✓
H3:Board Size (Neutral Association)		
Univariate	✓	✓
Multivariate	✓	✓
H5a:Government Ownership (Neutral Association)		
Univariate	✓	✓
Multivariate	✓	✓
H5b:Managaement Ownership (Negative Association)		
Univariate	x[2]	x
Multivariate	x	x
H5c:Private Ownership (Neutral Association)		
Univariate	✓	✓
Multivariate	✓	✓
H5d:Public Ownership (Neutral Association)		
Univariate	✓	x
Multivariate	✓	x
Control Variables		
Firm Size (Sig.+)		
Univariate	x	x
Multivariate	x	✓
Profitability (Sig.+ or -)		
Univariate	x	x
Multivariate	x	x
Gearing (Sig.+ or -)		
Univariate	x	x
Multivariate	x	x
Liquidity (Sig.+ or -)		
Univariate	x	x
Multivariate	x	x
Type of Business (Sig. + or -)		
Univariate	x	x
Multivariate	x	x
Type of Auditor (Sig.+ if Big 4)		
Univariate	x	✓
Multivariate	x	✓

√ Research hypothesis is supported
X Research hypothesis is not supported

Finally, with respect to the applicability of the proposed theoretical framework to the scrutinised contexts, it can be assessed in relation to the following considerations:

- Firstly, whether the extent of *de facto* compliance with IFRSs disclosure requirements shows that the gap between *de facto* and *de jure* compliance is closed.
- Secondly, the interpretation of the findings of the analysis of the association between independent variables and levels of compliance with mandatory IFRSs disclosure requirements.
- Thirdly, the link between the notions of the proposed theoretical foundation and interview results.

The analysis of the 150 annual reports of companies listed on the EGX and the ASE to assess the extent of compliance with IFRSs disclosure requirements (Section 6.2) supported the notions of the institutional isomorphism theory, Gray's (1988) accounting sub-cultural model, agency theory, and cost-benefit analysis. In addition, the proposed theoretical foundation competently supported the interpretation of the findings of the statistical analyses of the association between levels of compliance with IFRSs disclosure requirements and corporate governance structures of companies listed on the EGX and the ASE. Moreover, the interviewee responses supported the notions of the proposed theoretical framework (see Section 7.6). The research findings are consistent with the institutional isomorphism theory as both MENA jurisdictions mandated the adoption of IFRSs under pressures from the international institutions to gain their legitimacy and respect without giving enough consideration to the importance of preparation of their markets by developing the national cultural values to perceive the importance of compliance with the IFRSs in the same way as it is perceived in developed countries where such standards were initially developed. Thus as long as all parties involved in the financial reporting process are not aware about the importance of transparency and *de facto* compliance with corporate governance and accounting international best practices and as public investors are not aware about the disclosures that must be made and they do not put any pressures on BOD or management to improve compliance with the IFRSs, it is impossible to close the gap between *de facto* and *de jure* compliance with IFRSs disclosure requirements in the scrutinised contexts. This is also consistent with Gray (1988) accounting sub-cultural model, as secretive culture of MENA societies is associated with strong uncertainty avoidance that results from the need to restrict information disclosure, so as to avoid conflict and competition and to preserve security. Secrecy is also associated with large power distance which results in the restriction of information to preserve power inequalities. On the other side, this lends support to the agency theory, as government, private and management stockholders are in a position to get access to all company information they need and as public investors do not demand more compliance with IFRSs disclosure requirements and do not put any pressures on BOD or management to improve compliance, hence monitoring costs will be low. This in turn will reduce management incentives to fully comply with IFRSs disclosure requirements. In addition, this result is consistent with the notions of cost-benefit analysis as weak enforcement of IFRSs disclosure requirements and weak sanctions if any cause non-compliance costs to be less than compliance costs for companies listed on the scrutinised MENA stock exchanges, thus direct management incentives toward non-compliance. All of this contributes to the problem of decoupling as companies listed on the scrutinised MENA stock exchanges state that they prepare their financial statements in accordance with the IFRSs, while none of them fully complies with those requirements.

8.3 Study Contribution

The contributions of this study can be summarised as follows:

1. The capital markets under scrutiny have been early mandatory adopters of IFRSs, implying that their companies have considerable experience with the use of IFRSs on a mandatory rather than on a voluntary basis. This is expected to add to the compliance literature since most previous IFRSs/IASs compliance studies scrutinised developed jurisdictions that apply IFRSs on a voluntary basis.
2. This study is one of the first, if not the first comparative study to investigate the influence of corporate governance structures on *de facto* compliance with IFRSs disclosure requirements between two leading MENA emerging capital markets that witnessed a change in the ownership structures of companies listed on their stock exchanges as a result of privatising government owned enterprises, and introduced corporate governance mechanisms that are based on the OECD corporate governance principles as a means to enhance transparency and disclosure by empowering boards to enable them to carry out effective monitoring of management behaviour.
3. This study provides recent evidence on the theoretical foundation of financial disclosure practices in the MENA region in addition to

being the first to employ the notions of the institutional isomorphism in explaining the influence of corporate governance structures on compliance levels in Egypt and Jordan.

4. The disclosure index used in this study to the best of the researcher's knowledge is the first to scrutinise compliance with IFRSs disclosure requirements within the scrutinised countries based on IFRSs disclosure requirements for the fiscal year beginning 1 January, 2007. Consequently, this study extends that of Al-Akra et al. (2010a) that investigates the influence of accounting disclosure regulation, governance reforms and ownership changes, resulting from privatisation, on the levels of compliance with mandatory disclosures under IFRSs in Jordan in 1996 and 2004 respectively, by using more recent data, recognising the amendments to the disclosure requirements in 2007 and comparing the results with those of another leading MENA stock exchange. Furthermore, this study to the best of the researcher's knowledge is the first to investigate the impact of board leadership on the levels of compliance with IFRSs disclosure requirements in Jordan and the first to investigate the association between corporate governance structures and the levels of compliance with IFRSs disclosure requirements in Egypt. The content of the disclosure index was refined to enable an objective comparison of compliance levels with IFRSs disclosure requirements between the group of companies listed on the EGX and those listed on the ASE. Furthermore, the disclosure index was divided into 20 sub-indices measuring compliance levels with disclosure requirements under each IFRS. Hence, this is expected to improve the objectivity of the comparison among the scrutinised countries as well as among companies within the same country. Consequently, this disclosure checklist represents advancement on the majority of disclosure checklists applied in other studies, which are organised by topic.
5. The use of both quantitative and qualitative research methods to triangulate the data, and a well developed theoretical foundation, presents a methodological extension to research in comparative accounting disclosure practices in emerging capital markets in general and in the MENA region in particular and helps to answer the question with respect to the possibility of generalising the findings of one developing country to others.
6. The results of the study have provided evidence on the applicability of theories originated in the developed context to the MENA emerging capital markets. This provides a better understanding not

only of mandatory disclosure practices in the MENA context but also of the factors that affect it. This encourages the use of the proposed theoretical framework in explaining disclosure practices in other developing contexts.

7. This study provides an overview of the perceptions of different parties involved in the financial reporting process in Egypt and Jordan regarding the barriers to full compliance with IFRSs and the impact of corporate governance structures on compliance behaviour of publicly listed companies.
8. Identifying the effect of different corporate governance variables on the extent of compliance with IFRSs will enhance knowledge about the level of awareness of the importance of *de facto* compliance with corporate governance best practice among different parties involved in the financial reporting process in the MENA region. Hence, this study provides timely findings to different stakeholders concerned with achieving *de facto* compliance with international best practices in the MENA region.

8.4 Implications of Research Findings

The results from this study provide evidence of *de jure* but not *de facto* compliance with IFRSs disclosure requirements by companies listed on the EGX and ASE. This was explained by the existence of barriers to compliance with IFRSs. These barriers are mainly related to a societal preference for secrecy, weak enforcement of IFRSs by capital market regulatory bodies, and low sanctions, if any. Furthermore, as indicated by interviewees, the inadequate qualification of the CMA and JSC monitoring staff stands as a major obstacle. It was also argued that for companies listed on the ASE, the shortage of qualified accountants is a principal problem.

Building on the above discussion, a number of political and theoretical implications can be formulated.

8.4.1 Policy Implications

There are implications of the research findings for the IASB, OECD, CMA, JSC and big 4 audit firms.

International Accounting Standard Board and the Organization for Economic Co-operation and Development

Almost all MENA countries mandated the adoption of IFRSs to gain legitimacy and respect from the international community. Most took this step without preparing the different parties involved in the financial reporting process to accept the importance of compliance with the requirements of those standards in the same way as they are accepted by their counterparts in developed countries where those standards originated. Thus, the IASB should give more attention to the issue of *de facto* compliance with IFRSs in developing countries. This can be achieved by allowing more developing countries to gain membership of the IASB and by issuing a formal translation of the IFRSs in Arabic, which will eliminate the possibility of mistranslation and misinterpretation.

The IASB should conduct workshops and training programmes to familiarise the IFRSs compliance monitoring staff at emerging stock exchanges (*e.g.*, MENA stock exchanges) with the IFRSs updates and their technical application. Likewise, it is also important to ensure that these staff accept the importance of compliance with such requirements in the same way as their counterparts in developed stock exchanges. It is crucial to develop a culture of compliance among those who are charged with enforcing IFRSs.

Furthermore, a committee from the IASB to check the quality of monitoring staff in different developing stock exchanges is necessary to create an element of competition and hence encourage a closing of the gap between *de jure* and *de facto* compliance with IFRSs requirements in such stock exchanges.

On the other hand, given the leading role of the OECD in spreading awareness and sponsoring the development of corporate governance reforms and codes that cope with the OECD corporate governance principles in many of the developing countries all over the world, including MENA countries, the OECD should reassess the applicability of its principles to such countries. This argument is supported by the findings of the international reports that reveal a *de jure* but not a *de facto* compliance with the requirements for good corporate governance best practice under the OECD principles. Furthermore, research evidence on the association between corporate governance mechanisms and compliance with IFRSs disclosure requirements in developing countries is not as strong as expected. Consequently, the OECD should think about the appropriate strategies that can foster the recognition of corporate governance mechanisms in practice. They should carry out more training programmes to capital market staff and members of the boards of directors and managers of listed companies to make sure that corporate governance best practices, are becoming part of their cultural values. They also should support a campaign to increase the awareness of the public regarding the importance of corporate governance and how best it can be achieved.

Stock Exchange Regulatory Bodies

The interviewees highlighted the lack of adequate qualification of IFRSs compliance monitoring staff in the CMA and JSC. In Jordan, this can be explained by the general shortage of qualified accounting practitioners which is the main barrier to quality financial reporting in the country, as stated by interviewees. However, in Egypt it may be explained by the low salaries paid to the CMA monitoring staff which renders such a position unattractive to qualified personnel. This implies the need to recruit qualified personnel in the CMA by improving the payment scheme, and to recruit qualified foreign personnel in the JSC which also requires the payment of higher salaries to attract them.

The CMA in Egypt and JSC in Jordan should issue a detailed official disclosure checklist in Arabic 1, which should be updated periodically to reflect changes in IFRSs requirements. Additionally, they should organise workshops for the CMA and JSC monitoring staff and accountants of listed companies to familiarise them with IFRSs updates and their proper application. They should also arrange workshops for managements of listed companies to ensure greater awareness of the importance of full compliance with each disclosure item even if items are perceived as too detailed or open to misuse by competitors. The importance of transparency must be instilled within all parties to the financial reporting process.

The CMA in Egypt and JSC in Jordan should also be more stringent in imposing sanctions on non- compliant companies. This is expected to help to close the gap between *de facto* and *de jure* compliance with IFRSs requirements. Simultaneously, the capital market regulators should monitor the performance of auditors by providing them with mandatory IFRSs requirements and other mandatory regulations periodically. They should also impose sanctions on audit firms which issue unqualified audit reports for companies which do not comply with mandatory IFRSs requirements.

The results showed limited impact of good corporate governance practices on compliance with IFRSs disclosure requirements in Egypt and in Jordan, although they were recognised. This reveals the existence of another gap between *de facto* and *de jure* compliance with corporate governance best practice. *De facto* compliance requires the creation of a cultural change which takes time as it involves an evolution of national values and behaviours. Training, education and awareness building about the importance and relevance of a governance culture among regulators, management of listed companies, and other stakeholders is essential to develop such a culture in the MENA region[1]

In Egypt the CMA has a disclosure checklist which is supposed to be followed by listed companies, but it is neither detailed nor updated on a regular basis.

The unexpected negative impact of the dominance of public ownership on levels of compliance with IFRSs disclosure requirements in Jordan raises the need to develop awareness among small investors about their rights and how to exercise these. Additionally, they should be aware of what information must be disclosed, and of their entitlement to pressure the BOD and management to comply with disclosure requirements and improve transparency. Hence, the ASE and the EGX should launch a media campaign to educate small investors.

Finally, the CMA and JSC should obligate listed companies to make their complete annual reports and details of their corporate governance structures available to the public in Arabic and in English. The enhancement of transparency and commitment is essential to develop the performance and reputation of MENA stock exchanges.

Big 4 Audit Firms

The majority of companies listed on the EGX and ASE are audited by affiliates of big 4 audit firms, and the issuance of unqualified audit reports for companies that do not fully comply with IFRSs raises the need to reconsider the quality of the audit work performed by these affiliates. Undoubtedly, the big 4 audit firms should give more attention to the qualification of auditors appointed in their affiliates in developing markets. Furthermore, they should monitor the quality and credibility of audit reports issued by these affiliates.

8.4.2 Theoretical Implications

The results of the quantitative and qualitative analyses supported the applicability of the notions of the proposed theoretical foundation (the institutional isomorphism, Gray's (1988) secrecy versus transparency accounting sub-cultural value, agency theory and cost-benefit analysis), all of which originated in the developed capital markets, to the emerging MENA stock exchanges examined in this study. This raises the need to

---

[1] In Egypt the CMA has a disclosure checklist which is supposed to be followed by listed companies, but it is neither detailed nor updated on a regular basis.

explore the applicability of the proposed theoretical foundation to other developing contexts. This is justified on the grounds that developing societies are characterised by preference for secrecy which is associated with strong uncertainty avoidance, collectivism and large power distance which results in restriction of information to preserve power inequalities. Consequently, recognition of the impact of secrecy is expected to help in interpreting mandatory disclosure practices within developing contexts. With respect to the agency theory, as in most of the developing countries, there is a lack of separation between ownership and control, major stockholders have access to all company information and naive investors do not put any pressure on BOD or management to improve disclosures, monitoring costs are low, so management will not be incentivised to fully comply with IFRSs disclosure requirements. Furthermore, as in most of the developing countries enforcement of regulations is not as effective as in developed countries, non-compliance costs are lower than compliance costs. This in turn adversely impacts compliance with IFRSs disclosure requirements. Finally, with respect to the institutional isomorphism, the decoupling problem is clear in many of developing countries. Although the first glance may show that such countries adopt all forms of institutional isomorphism, whereas formal structures and systems are harmonised with the international best practices, the existence of a gap between *de facto* and *de jure* compliance with mandatory disclosure requirements shows that the adopted formal structures and systems may be a window dressing to impress external communities such as the WB and the IMF, in order to gain legitimacy as well as their financial and political support. This raises the need to consider the influence of the cultural context within developing countries as *de facto* compliance should be seen as the outcome of the interaction between cultural context and institutional pressures.

8.5 Limitations

1. There was a difficulty in obtaining the annual reports and corporate governance information for all of non-financial companies listed on the EGX and ASE at the time of commencing this study (2008). The study intended to investigate the annual reports for the fiscal year ending 31 December, 2007, for the entire population of non-financial companies listed on scrutinised exchanges (a total of 311 companies -145 from Egypt and 166 from Jordan), but the unavailability of complete annual reports and/or corporate governance structure-related information for all listed companies at

the time of collecting the data for this study (the beginning of 2009), reduced the final sample to 150 companies. The difficulty of collecting research data is a common problem in developing countries (*e.g.,* Wallace, 1988; Abd-Elsalam, 1999; Hassan, 2006; Omar, 2007), and provided a major reason for not conducting a longitudinal study. However, this issue is relatively solved in Jordan since the second half of 2009, as the ASE began to provide the annual reports of publicly listed companies on its website. Annual reports for almost all companies listed on the ASE for the years 2009 and 2010 are available which saves time, effort and costs for carrying out future research.

2. The construction of the disclosure index and the assigning of scores incorporate some degree of researcher subjectivity. Additionally, the accuracy of scoring may be affected by the availability of annual reports in Arabic and the use of different Arabic vocabulary by Egyptian and Jordanian companies. However as indicated in sub-section 5.5.1, every possible effort was made to reduce subjectivity by following the procedures recommended by prior researchers. These included ascertaining the validity and reliability of the disclosure index and those of the disclosure scores as well as the researcher competency in Arabic.
3. The study investigated the association between levels of compliance with IFRSs disclosure requirements and corporate governance related variables in only two MENA stock exchanges. However, as indicated in Section 1.2 the choice of Egypt and Jordan is justified as leading MENA exchanges that although non-oil exporters as GCC member countries, they achieved extraordinary economic progress in 2007 and are working on developing their stock exchanges to be the main vehicle for economic development for their future generations. Furthermore, this choice is made in the light of time and cost considerations for carrying out this study.
4. The regression model developed failed to report any results on the level of the Egyptian context (*i.e.,* the compliance behaviour by companies listed on the EGX did not follow any pattern in relation to the variables under study), however it reported an adjusted R2 of 24.5% on the level of the Jordanian context. This implies that the 13 variables included in the model were not able to explain the variation in the levels of compliance with total disclosure index in the Egyptian context (compliance with the overall mandatory IFRSs disclosure requirements), however they explained 24.5% of

such variation in the Jordanian context. Thus, the unexplained variation may be attributable to factors that cannot be easily quantified and tested using statistical models. This raises the need to reconsider the development of a model with a higher explanatory power to capture the variation in overall compliance based on the interview findings, which revealed some other factors, mainly related to the cultural context and technical difficulties, as determinants of overall levels of compliance.

5. The interviews were conducted in Arabic and the transcripts subsequently translated into English. Translation may not give the exact meaning as some words in one language may not have equivalents in the other language. To reduce the potential subjectivity resulting from translation the researcher gave considerable time to the translation process to ensure an English version that conveys the exact meaning, and asked a linguistic specialist to review her work to ensure its validity.

8.6 Future Research

1. This study investigated compliance with mandatory IFRSs disclosure requirements using the annual reports in two leading MENA stock exchanges and hence, future research may investigate disclosures in quarterly and interim reports among a number of countries. This can help in ascertaining the possibility of generalising the findings of one developing country to others.
2. This study investigated the association between corporate governance structures and levels of compliance with IFRSs disclosure requirements for a single year. Future longitudinal research is needed to extend the current study to a longer period of time and to explore the progress in the explanatory power of corporate governance-related variables over a number of years.
3. This study investigated the association between corporate governance structures and levels of compliance with IFRSs disclosure requirements in two of the MENA region stock exchanges (the EGX and the ASE). Consequently, it will be interesting to replicate the study using a larger number of MENA stock exchanges to determine whether they are homogeneous. Additionally, it will be interesting to further investigate the extent to which the findings on the level of one country are statistically different from those related to other countries by introducing country as a dummy variable, and interacting this dummy with all

test and control variables. Such studies would contribute to the literature on comparative international accounting.

4. This study investigated the association between the extent of compliance with mandatory IFRSs disclosure requirements and corporate governance structures. Future research can investigate the association between levels of compliance with IFRSs measurement requirements and corporate governance structures to get a complete picture regarding the association between corporate governance structures and levels of compliance with all requirements under IFRSs. Additionally, an examination of the association between corporate governance structures and voluntary disclosure practices among MENA region emerging stock exchanges, would be valuable in order to put hands on the influence of corporate governance mechanisms on disclosure practices in the MENA context and whether such influence is the same among different MENA countries.
5. This study employed an unweighted disclosure index. The use of a weighted disclosure index to assess the importance of each item from the perspective of a specific user group (*e.g.*, foreign investors, international financial analysts), could be adopted in a future research, and the outcomes compared with the results of this study to ascertain the impact of the type of the disclosure index (weighted versus unweighted) on the research findings.
6. An investigation of the association between levels of compliance with IFRSs disclosure requirements by companies listed on different MENA stock exchanges and stock prices or dividends policy in those companies is also worthwhile to determine the economic consequences of compliance with mandatory disclosure requirements. Attracting more investors is expected to reduce the cost of capital for listed companies. Furthermore, using the disclosure index construction approach employed in this study will enable the relationship between the level of compliance with each IFRS and stock prices to be established.
7. An investigation of the association between levels of compliance with IFRSs by companies listed on emerging exchanges and the type of audit report would also be an interesting topic for a longitudinal research as it will enable the examination of the quality of audit work performed in emerging MENA exchanges. Furthermore, although the impact of the existence of an audit committee on the levels of compliance with IFRSs disclosure requirements has been examined by Al-Akra et al. (2010a) in

Jordan and by Alanezi and Albuloushi (2011) in Kuwait, investigating such issue among a number of developing countries will enrich emerging capital markets' comparative research as audit committee is one of the most important corporate governance mechanisms in monitoring internal control within business firms hence the existence of an audit committee is supposed to improve compliance practices.

8. An assessment of the levels of compliance with IFRSs and their association with corporate governance best practice after the recent 2011 revolutions in several MENA region countries, and a comparison of those findings with those relating to periods before these revolutions would also be a worthwhile topic for future research to scrutinise the progress in enforcement of laws and the developments in transparency practices, indicating the aspirations of the countries involved in respect of economic development.

APPENDIX A

EMPIRICAL FINANCIAL DISCLOSURE STUDIES

The following table summarises prior empirical research related to financial disclosure practices. Studies are classified into three groups; single developed capital market studies, single developing capital market studies and cross-national comparative capital market studies. For each study, it is indicated whether it scrutinises mandatory, voluntary or an aggregate disclosure, whether it applies a weighted or un-weighted disclosure index, the explanatory variables used if any and the main findings.

Table A.1 Empirical Financial Disclosure Studies

Study (year)	Country	Independent Variables	Findings
I. Single Developed Capital Market Studies			
Cerf (1961)	USA	Asset size Rate of return Number of shareholders Listing status	Companies listed on New York Stock Exchange disclose significantly more information than non-listed companies. Positive relationship between extent of disclosure and company size, profitability and number of shareholders. Asset size is the main explanatory variable of corporate financial disclosure
Singhvi & Desai (1971)	USA	Asset size Number of shareholders Listing status Audit firm (CPA firms) Rate of return Earnings margin	Positive relationship between the extent of financial disclosure and each of the identified company characteristics.
Buzby (1975)	USA	Firm size Listing status	Positive relationship between extent of financial disclosure and firm size and no association between financial disclosure and listing status.
Stanga (1976)	USA	Firm size Industry type	Aggregate disclosure is on average 45.32%. Only industry type is a significant explanatory variable.
Belkaoui & Kahl (1978)	Canada	Asset size Sales size Profitability Liquidity Capitalisation ratio	Financial disclosure is positively associated with company size and liquidity. There is a negative association between financial disclosure and both capitalisation rate and profitability
Firth (1979)	UK	Company size (sales turnover and capital employed); share listing and the auditor type.	Positive association between company size; listing status and the level of voluntary disclosure. Auditor type is insignificant.
Firth (1980)	UK	Company size	While there was no significant difference in the extent of disclosure between the new issues and their control group three years before raising capital, there was a significant difference between the two groups immediately after raising capital. Similar results were also reported for the rights issues made by smaller companies. As for the rights issues made by larger companies, it was found that there was no significant difference in the extent of disclosure between this group and its control, whether this was three years before or immediately after raising capital. Larger companies had less scope for disclosure improvement since they go to the

			market frequently and already have high levels of disclosure.
McNally et al. (1982)	New Zealand	Company size Rate of return Growth Auditing firm Industry groups.	The level of voluntary disclosure was very low. Only 50% of the 41 items included in the index were disclosed by 10 companies. Size was found to be the only significant variable. The remaining explanatory variables are insignificant. There is a considerable disagreement between disclosure practices and the importance perceived by users
Cooke (1989a)	Sweden	Quotation status; company size (total assets, sales and number of shareholders) Industry type and parent company relationship	Average of financial disclosure is 51.27%. Low level of disclosure for some areas in the balance sheet and income statement (e. g. leased property, provision for doubtful debts and cost of goods sold). High level of disclosure about acquiring and disposing of business. Consequently, disclosure is extensive in consolidated accounts. Only 7% of the companies disclose information about research and developments. Deferred taxes are rarely recognised. Inventory information is highly disclosed. 70% of companies disclose information about methods and rates of depreciation and 6% do not disclose any information about depreciation. 60% of disclosure is explained by the independent variables Only listing status and company size are significant
Cooke (1989b)	Sweden	Listing status Industry type Firm size Parent company relationship	On average, extent of voluntary disclosure is 36.67% Only listing status, firm size and industry type are significant.
Cooke (1991)	Japan	company size (total assets, number of shareholders, and turnover), listing status and industry type.	Company size, listing status and industry type, were positively associated with the level of voluntary disclosure.
Cooke (1992)	Japan	Company size (8 measures), listing status (domestic/international) and industry type	On average extent of financial disclosure is 55.8% 60% of disclosure variation explained by independent variables. Large companies, multi-listed companies and manufacturing companies disclose more information
Cooke (1993)	Japan (Tokyo Stock Exchange)	Listing status (listed/unlisted/multiply listed)	Multiply listed companies disclose more voluntary information than others)
Malone et al. (1993)	USA	Debt/equity ratio; number of shareholders; total assets; industry type; rate of return; earning margin; audit company; listing status; foreign operations; and proportion of outside directors	29% of disclosure variation explained by independent variables. There was a significant and positive relationship between the level of financial disclosure and listing status, debt/equity ratio and number of share holders. There is no relationship between financial disclosure and other company characteristics.

Wallace et al. (1994)	Spain	Structure related variables which included: company size (measured by total assets, and total sales), gearing (measured as debt\equity ratio); secondly, performance-related variables which included the liquidity ratio (measured as earnings return, and profit margin); finally market-related variables which included industry type, listing status, and audit type.	65% of variation in the level of compliance with mandatory disclosure requirements is explained by independent variables. On average, extent of compliance with disclosure requirements is 59.26%. Asset size and listing status are positively associated with mandatory disclosure. Liquidity is negatively Associated with the level of mandatory disclosure in Spain. No association is reported between disclosure and the remaining variables.
Hossain et al. (1995)	New Zealand	Firm size Foreign listing status Leverage Proportion of assets in place Audit firm type	On average extent of voluntary disclosure is 18% Voluntary disclosure is significantly associated with firm size, foreign listing status and leverage and not associated with the remaining variables
Raffournier (1995)	Switzerland	Company size (total assets, total sales), Leverage (Debt/assets), Profitability (net profit/ equity), Ownership structure, Internationality level, Auditor size, Percentage of fixed assets, and Industry type.	The extent of disclosure has been found significantly related to size, internationality level, percentage of fixed assets, size of auditing firms and, to a smaller extent, to industry type and profitability. Inversely, no significant relationship was found for leverage and ownership diffusion. When examined simultaneously, the only significant variables were size and internationality. High correlations between size and other variables suggest that size serves as a proxy for several influences. Size and internationality play a major role in the disclosure policy of firms, large and internationally diversified companies tending to disclose more information than small purely domestic enterprises. Company size measured as log of sales and level of internationality, were significant. Percentage of fixed assets and size of auditors were significantly associated with level of voluntary disclosure. Less significant association appeared with industry type and profitability. Leverage and the ownership structure were statistically insignificant.
Inchausti (1997)	Spain	Company size (total assets and sales); stock exchange cross listing; profitability, leverage, auditing firm, industry type and dividend policy.	43% of the differences in financial disclosure among sampled companies is explained by independent variables. There is a significant positive relationship between the level of financial disclosure and firm size, auditing company and the listing status. There is no relationship between financial disclosure and profitability, leverage, industry type and the dividend payouts Financial disclosure is significantly related to Spanish legislation.

Depoers (2000)	France	Company size (sales), Foreign activity, Ownership structure, Leverage (debt on total assets), Auditor size, Proprietary costs related to competition, Labour pressure	Independent variables explain 65% of the variation in the levels of voluntary disclosure. Managers disclose more information when a firm's size and foreign activity are important, but they hide information whose disclosure may compromise the firm's competitive advantage or increase labour pressure. No significant effect due to leverage has been observed. The influence of ownership structure and auditor size disappears in the multiple regressions.
Street & Gray (2002)	USA	Company size (measured as total assets, total sales, and market capitalization), profitability (as net income before tax/equity), industry type, country of domicile, size of home stock market, auditor size, type of auditing standards, and the way in which the auditors express their opinions.	There is a significant extent of non-compliance as the level of compliance with IAS was on average 74%. There is a significant relationship between the level of compliance of companies listed in the US, specifically companies in commerce and transportation, and companies audited by big audit firms.
Glaum &Street (2003)	Germany	Audit firm type Multiple listing Reference of using International Standards of Auditing (ISA) or US GAAS in the audit companies Firm size	Financial disclosure averages 83.7%. The average compliance level is significantly lower for companies that apply IAS as compared to companies applying US GAAP. Extent of financial disclosure is positively associated with all independent variables except firm size
Anderson & Daoud (2005)	Sweden	Role duality Existence of audit committee Number of shareholders Board composition The existence of compensation committee Firm size Multiple listing Management ownership The proportion of non-executive directors Audit firm size Diffuse ownership Board size The existence of nomination committee Board activity Industry type	There is a positive relationship between financial disclosure and role duality existence of audit committee, number of shareholders board composition, the existence of compensation committee, firm size and multiple listing however there is no association with other independent variables.

Arcay & Vazquez (2005)	Spain	Independent non-executive directors Audit committee Chairman of the board and chief executive officer being the same person Board participation in the capital of the company Stock option plans as directors' pay Board size. Level of ownership concentration. Firm size Dual listing Industry type	Corporate decisions regarding the provision of voluntary information are complex processes affected by a number of interrelated factors: the governance rules followed by the firm, corporate size, cross-listing status, and the ownership structure of the firm. The adoption of a number of good governance practices such as the appointment of independent directors, the formation of audit committees, participation of the board in the capital of the company, and establishment of stock option plans as a means of director remuneration exert a significant influence on corporate voluntary disclosure. Independent directors and audit committees strengthen the monitoring function of the board, so that firms become more responsive to stakeholders' demands for information. Directors' participation in the capital of the company and stock option plans contribute to the alignment of managers' and shareholders' interests as they help reduce management reluctance to disclose voluntary information. Neither the separation of the functions of the CEO and Chairman, nor compliance with the recommendation of the Olivencia Code (1998) regarding the size of the board is significantly associated with the provision of voluntary information.
Owusu-Ansah & Yeoh (2005)	New Zealand		On average extent of compliance with financial disclosure requirements is 92.61%. Univariate paired t-test reveals that the compliance level for post FRA period (1996-1997) is higher than in the pre FRA period (1992-1993). Multivariate analysis indicates that the enactment of the FRA was the reason for the improvement in the disclosure compliance of New Zealand companies. Moreover, sensitivity analysis shows that, after controlling the effects of other variables which are related to mandatory disclosure, the introduction of FRA was significant in improving the compliance level.
Yeoh (2005)	New Zealand		There is a high degree of corporate compliance with the financial reporting requirements. However, the compliance rate is higher with respect to the Statements of Standard Accounting Practices (SSAPs) than to both the Financial Reporting Standards (FRSs), and listing rules of the stock market. Extent of compliance with mandatory disclosure requirements ranges from 84.1% to a maximum level of 99.5%. The number of companies whose compliance rate was between 90% and 100% of statutory and regulatory disclosure requirements consistently increased over time from 84% in 1996 to 98% in 1998.

II. Single Developing Capital Market Studies			
Singhvi (1968)	India	Asset size, Rate of return, Earnings margin Type of management Number of shareholders	On average extent of financial disclosure is 35.60% There is a strong positive relationship between the quality of financial disclosure and asset size, rate cf return, earnings and type of management. No relationship identified between the quality of financial disclosure and size of audit firm.
Chow & Wong-Boren (1987)	Mexico	Company size (market value of equity plus the book value of debt), financial leverage (the book value of debt divided by size),and assets in place(dividing the book value of fixed assets net of depreciation, by total assets).	Multiple regression shows that the adjusted R2 for the weighted index was 14% and for the un-weighted index was 15%; The t-test for both indices indicated that company size is significantly associated with the level of voluntary disclosure in Mexico, and leverage and assets in place are insignificant regarding the level of voluntary disclosure. There are no differences in the results between the weighted and un-weighted disclosure index.
Wallace (1988)	Nigeria	Firm size Profitability Liquidity Management type Business type Country of the origin Of the multinationals.	Overall level of financial disclosure in Nigerian companies' annual reports is below 50% in each year (39.75% in 1982; 38.23% in 1983; 43.11% in 1984; 40.46% in 1985 and 37.55% in 1986) There are no significant differences between the results of weighted and un-weighted disclosure indices. Weak positive relationship between extent of financial disclosure and firm size and no relationship between financial disclosure and other identified company characteristics.
Tai et al. (1990)	Hong Kong	Firm size (shareholder fund), Business sector of the company and Type of audit firm	On average the level of compliance was 78% company size is significantly associated with mandatory disclosure. Smaller and larger companies have significantly less non-compliance than medium sized companies. There is no significant relationship between the business sector or audit companies and the compliance with mandatory disclosure requirements
Abayo et al. (1993)	Tanzania	If annual reports are available; If companies are profit seeking; If they fall under the NBAA (National Board of Accountants and Auditors); and iv. if they fell into four industrial groups - distribution, chemical, textiles, and metal goods Timeliness of their financial reports.	The quality of companies' annual reports in Tanzania is very low (the average of compliance with mandatory disclosure is 52.6%, and the average of the level of voluntary disclosure is 15.8%). There is a weak, positive relationship between voluntary disclosure and mandatory disclosure.

Ahmed & Nicholls (1994)	Bangladesh	Company size (total assets and total sales), Total debt, Multinational company influence, Professional qualifications of the principal accounting officer Size of audit firm	The level of compliance with mandatory requirements is on average 58.7%. The multiple regression analysis, Stepwise, explains 50% of disclosure variation among the sampled companies. The t-test results report that multinational companies and large audit firms have a significant, positive relationship with the level of compliance. Weaker significant positive association between level of financial disclosure and company size. Less effect on the level of compliance by professional qualification of the principal accounting officer is observed, and company size and debt appeared to have no effect on the level of compliance.
Hossain et al. (1994)	Malaysia	Company size (market capitalisation), Ownership structure (the number of shares held by the top 10 shareholders), Leverage (as ratio based on the book value, of long-term debt to owners' equity), Proportion of assets-in place (as ratio, based on book value, of fixed assets to total assets), Audit Company, Foreign listing status.	On average the extent of voluntary disclosure is 15.8% The results of the univariate analysis shows that there is a significant association between voluntary disclosure and company size, the big six audit firms and companies' ownership structure. A marginally positive association with leverage is found, while there is no significant relationship with assets-in-place. The multiple regression indicates that only 28% of the disclosure variation is explained by the independent variables. The t-test shows different results from the univariate analysis - company size and ownership structure were significantly associated with voluntary disclosure and the remaining variables were insignificant.
Wallace & Naser (1995)	Hong Kong	Asset size Scope of business operation Auditor type Profitability Liquidity Leverage Proportion of shares held by outsiders Market capitalisation	There is a positive relationship between compliance with mandatory disclosure and asset size, scope of business operation (i.e., industry type) and auditor type. There is a negative relationship between compliance with mandatory disclosure and profitability. However there is no association between compliance level and the remaining independent variables.
Al-Mulhem (1997)	Saudi Arabia	Company size (total assets and annual sales), Listing status, Industry type, Profitability ratios (rates of return and earning margin) Type of audit firm	The level of disclosure in corporate annual reports in Saudi Arabia varies considerably. The disclosure index means were found to range from the lowest being 38 % to the highest being76%. Results obtained from univariate and multivariate analyses showed that firm size and Listing status are significantly related to the extent of disclosure.

			Listing status, however, was found to contribute most to explaining the variability in the extent of disclosure. In contrast, profitability, industry type and type of audit firm are not significant explanatory factors. The results revealed that none of the sampled corporations complied fully with mandatory regulations and items perceived as important by different user groups. There is a significant, positive relationship between financial disclosure and company size, rate of return, and listing status, while there is no association with industry types and type of audit firm. Finally, none of the companies fully complied with the mandatory disclosure requirements and the important items for different users.
Patton & Zelenka (1997)	Czech Republic	Company size (as total assets), Performance (as return on equity), Risk factors (as percentage of intangible assets and leverage), Listing status, Number of employee, Audit firm type Industry type.	60% average level of companies' compliance with mandatory requirements was reported, and the logarithm regression explained only 25% of the variation in the level of companies' compliance. Univariate analyses generally support the existence of the hypothesized relationships between extent of disclosure in annual reports and firm size, profitability performance, financial risk, and monitoring variables. Multivariate regressions explain about 25% of the variance in the extent of disclosure in annual reports. Statistically significant variables in the multiple regressions include type of auditor, number of employees, stock exchange listing status, and rectum on equity performance.
Suwaidan (1997)	Jordan	Company size (total assets market capitalisation, sales/revenues, net income),number of Shareholders, institutional ownership ratio, government ownership, industry type, size of auditing firm, international contacts of auditing company, profitability (return on assets and return on equity), and frequency of external financing	The lowest level of voluntary disclosure (2.61%) is found in the market-based information group, while the balance sheet group shows the highest level (65.39%). In addition, there is a wide variation in disclosure for individual items within each type of information group. The actual level of voluntary disclosure in Jordanian corporate annual reports is low, with 61% of the items disclosed in less than half the annual reports. The results of univariate and multivariate analyses identified the size of the company, size of auditing firm, government ownership and the industry type to be significant variables in explaining variation in the level of disclosure. Among these variables, size was the most important variable in explaining variation in the disclosure of different types of information and within each industry. Finally, the study found that companies have significantly increased their level of voluntary disclosure around the time they raised equity capital in AFM.

Owusu-Ansah (1998b)	Zimbabwe	Company size (total assets, and market values of equity shares), quality of external audit, ownership structure, industry type, company listing age, multinational companies (MNC) affiliation, profitability (return on turnover and return on capital employed) and liquidity.	74.43% of compliance was identified. Robust regression explains 40% of the variation in the companies' compliance, and the t-test indicates that company age, profitability, multinational corporation affiliation, company size and ownership structure have a significant and positive association with the level of compliance, whereas the quality of external audit, industry type and liquidity are insignificant.
Abd-Elsalam (1999)	Egypt	Legal form Company size Share trading in the stock exchange Type of business activity Audit firm type Profit ratio Gearing Liquidity	Mandatory disclosure (three indices) and partial mandatory disclosure (each index) of Egyptian listed companies have increased significantly in 1995 compared to 1991, however no company shows 100% compliance with any index. The level of compliance with mandatory requirements by Egyptian listed companies in 1995 is (CML, 84% and IASs, 85%) which is considered high compared to companies in other developing countries. Compliance with mandatory disclosure requirements is found to be positively associated with legal form, company size and share trading in the stock exchange; however it is not associated with the remaining variables. Companies audited by one of the big audit firms offer the highest disclosure on items required by the IASs while large public sector companies which were actively traded in the national stock exchange provide the highest disclosure on items required by the Egyptian new disclosure regulation. Agency and capital need theories appear to be applicable to the findings regarding Egypt, but the applicability of signaling theory is not clear.
Haniffa (1999)	Malaysia	Seven corporate governance variables (cross-holdings of directorships, role duality, board composition, ratio of family members on the board, cross-holdings by Chairperson, position of Chairperson and significance of finance director sitting on the board). Size Industry type Listing age Foreign listing status Foreign activities Complexity of business Level of diversification Gearing / Profitability Type of auditors Assets in place	Profitability, top 10 shareholders and industry type are significant for both non-social voluntary disclosure and social reporting disclosure. In the case of the former, one additional variable found significant was diversification while for the latter, listing status and size. There is a significant association between levels of voluntary disclosure and Chair with cross-holdings and a non-executive Chair. Personal characteristics seem to have a significant influence only in social reporting and two variables, the ratio of bumiputra directors on boards and bumiputra finance directors, were found to be significant.

		Ownership structure.	
Ho & Wong (2001)	Hong Kong	Existence of audit committee Firm size Industry type Proportion of family members in the board Ratio of independent directors to total directors in the board Family ownership Profitability Assets in place Leverage	On average the extent of voluntary disclosure is 29% There is a positive relationship between the level of voluntary disclosure and the existence of audit committee, firm size and industry type. There is a negative relationship between level of voluntary disclosure and the proportion of family members on the board. There is no relationship between the level of financial disclosure and the remaining variables.
Al-Hajraf (2002)	Kuwait		78% of the total sample said it is important for the users to know more about the international accounting standards in general and disclosure standards in particular. 68% of the total sample said that it is important for banks' management to disclose more information according to the international accounting standards requirements and to those special requirements of the Central Bank of Kuwait and the Kuwait stock exchange market. 38% of the total sample agreed that the Kuwaiti financial market is advanced and can compete with the world's financial Markets. Disclosure level has improved toward more compliance with the IAS 30 requirements from 57% in 1994 to 64.3% in 2000.
Haniffa & Cooke (2002)	Malaysia	Proportion of non-executive directors Proportion of family members on the board Role duality Position of Chair person Cross directorship of board members Cultural characteristics Education-board of directors Education of financial controller Firm size Gearing Diversification Asset in place Ownership structure Profitability Industry type Type of auditor Listing age	On average the extent of voluntary disclosure is 31.3% Results based on the full regression model with thirty-one variables indicated that only two groups of variables, namely corporate governance and firm-specific characteristics, were associated with the extent of disclosure. The significance of the two corporate governance variables (i.e., family members sitting on board and non-executive Chairman) identified indicates the importance of these variables as determinants of voluntary disclosure. Specifically, the Chairperson as nonexecutive director is negatively associated with the extent of voluntary disclosure which contradicts with agency theory model. A cultural factor (race), measured as the proportion of Malay directors on the board, was found to be significant. The findings of no significant association between disclosure and any of the cultural variables in the full model supports the suggestion of culture-free theorists that, over time, societal values converge resulting from technological development.

		Foreign activities	
Naser et al. (2002)	Jordan	Firm size Audit firm status Gearing Profitability Liquidity Number of shareholders Industry type Ownership structure	On average the extent of voluntary disclosure is 63.51% There is a positive relationship between the extent of financial disclosure and firm size, audit firm status, gearing and profitability. There is a negative relationship between extent of disclosure and liquidity while there is no association with the remaining variables.
Al-Shiab (2003)	Jordan	Firm size Industry type Size of audit firm Profitability Capital structure	The findings of this study showed that the compliance with IASs was higher for the post mandatory action period (1998-2000) than the pre-mandatory action period (1995-1998). The level of disclosure is quite low over not only pre but also post the mandatory action for implementing the IAS suggesting that the government and the ASE systems regarding the financial reporting in Jordan are loose. Level of compliance with IASs ranges from 45 in 1995 to 56% in 2000. In the manufacturing sector, mining and building equipment companies were higher disclosing companies than others, except chemical companies
Abdelsalam & Weetman (2003)	Egypt	Size, Profitability, Type of business, Audit firm, Gearing, Legal form, Share trading, The presence of an IAS compliance note, The presence of a note of compliance with International Standards on Auditing (ISAs).	On average the level of compliance with IASs was 83% for Egyptian companies, which did not represent full compliance. A relatively high compliance with the familiar requirements represented in IAS(CA) (mean 0.94) but relatively lower compliance with the less familiar requirements represented in IAS(CMLA) (mean 0.73). The lowest average compliance was in IAS(NA) (mean 0.36) where unfamiliarity is compounded by the language factor. The multiple regression confirms the significance of the legal form variable. Actively traded companies scored significantly higher than the rarely traded companies. From both univariate and multivariate analyses, a conclusion can be drawn that both agency theory and capital need theory, which have frequently been used in explaining disclosure practices by companies, do not apply in the same strength where there are other factors which can interfere with these theories such as familiarity and a language barrier. Signaling theory is generally weak across all categories, which may reflect the relatively early stages of development of the capital market. Various regression models explained only 21–46% of changes in disclosure indices of Egyptian listed companies.

Eng & Mak (2003)	Singapore	Government ownership Proportion of outside directors Firm size Leverage Managerial ownership Block holder ownership (percentage of ordinary shares held by substantial shareholders, 5% or more) Industry type Profitability	On average the extent of voluntary disclosure is 21.75% There is a positive relationship between the extent of disclosure and governmental ownership, proportion of outside directors and firm size. There is a negative relationship between level of disclosure and managerial ownership and leverage while there is no association with the remaining independent variables.
Al-Razeen & Karbhari (2004)	Saudi Arabia		Saudi companies in general complied with mandatory requirements, on average by 88%, and that there was a low level of voluntary disclosure related to mandatory disclosure and voluntary disclosure, on average 32%. There is a significant, positive relationship between mandatory disclosure and voluntary more related to mandatory disclosure, and a weak relationship between voluntary disclosure and the other two indices.
Al-Htaybat (2005)	Jordan	size, age, profitability, industry type, ownership structure and auditor size	Jordanian manufacturing companies did not fully comply with mandatory disclosure requirements in 1997 and 2002. For 1997 a positive effect of the natural resources industry on the level of compliance was identified. Company profitability had a negative association, and none of the other variables contributed to explaining the variation in the level of companies' compliance in 1997. Financial disclosure theories (agency, signaling, Political costs and capital need theories) fail to explain disclosure practices in Jordan in 1997. For 2002 due to developments witnessed by ASE Company age appears to have a significant effect on the mandatory disclosure in 2002 in the normal score regression, alongside the food & clothing industry. These results were consistent with the theoretical predictions of agency, signaling, political and capital need theories. The average voluntary disclosure increased from 58% in 1997 to 61% in 2002. For 1997 company size, profitability, Natural resources and food & clothing industries are significantly ,positively associated with voluntary disclosure. None of the other company variables able to explain the variation in voluntary disclosure in 1997.

			For 2002 company size, government ownership, company profitability, foreign ownership and the food & clothing industry have some effect on the level of voluntary disclosure. company age, auditor size and other dummy variables did not affect the level of voluntary disclosure in the Jordanian manufacturing companies' annual reports in 2002. The overall level of printed financial disclosure was improved, from 87% in 1997 to 95% in 2002. The result of the Internet disclosure investigation shows that 55 (29%) out of 190 Jordanian companies listed on in August 2004 had active, accessible websites. A positive association between increasing financial disclosure in the printed companies' annual reports in 2002 and the level of Internet usage for financial disclosure in 2004. There is a significant and positive association between company size and the level of the Internet financial disclosure in 2004.
Akhtaruddin (2005)	Bangladesh	Firm size Profitability Listing age Industry group	The extent of compliance with disclosure requirements is positively associated with profitability and firm size (except sales), however it is not associated with listing age and industry group.
Aksu & Kosedag (2006)	Turkey	Firm size Profitability Market to book ratio Profitability Leverage	Financial disclosure is positively associated with firm size, profitability and market to book ratio and profitability however, results show no association between financial disclosure and leverage.
Barako et al. (2006)	Kenya	Presence of audit committee Percentage of stock owned by institutional shareholders The proportion of foreign ownership Firm size Leverage The proportion of non-executive directors on the board Board leadership structure Liquidity Profitability Type of external audit firm	There is a positive relationship between level of financial disclosure and the presence of audit committee, percentage of stock owned by institutional shareholders, the proportion of foreign ownership, firm size and leverage. There is a negative association between the level of financial disclosure and the proportion of non-executive directors in the board however there is no association with the remaining independent variables.

Ghazali & Weetman (2006)	Malaysia	Number of employees Profitability Proportion of family members on the board Proportion of shares held by executive directors Government ownership Proportion of independent non-executive directors on the board Presence of independent non-executive Chairman on the board Company competitiveness Industry competitiveness	On average the extent of voluntary disclosure is 31.4% There is a positive association between the level of voluntary disclosure and the number of employees and profitability of the firm. There is a negative association between level of disclosure and the proportion of family members on the board and proportion of shares held by executive directors. However, there is no association with the remaining variables.
Hassan (2006)	Egypt	Firm size Legal form Gearing Profitability Stock activity.	Individual measures of disclosure levels are negatively associated with estimated market beta. Disclosure is positively associated with firm value. Investors in Egypt pay much attention to income and dividends figures when making investment decisions. Disclosure level is negatively associated with market beta after controlling for other accounting measures of risk namely; asset size, profitability, gearing, growth, liquidity and dividend payout.
Naser et al. (2006)	Qatar	Firm size Dividends paid Gearing Ownership structure growth	Average corporate social disclosure is very low (33%). Companies that are expected to be large in size, maintaining growth and are highly leveraged are more likely to voluntary disclose social responsibility information.
Samaha (2006)	Egypt		There are large variations among listed companies in terms of the level of compliance with IASs. The overall level of compliance with IASs among listed companies is very low (50% with disclosure IASs and 56% with measurement IASs). Compliance level for actively traded companies is 64% for disclosure and 71% for measurement which reflect the poor performance of the Egyptian Stock Exchange.
Abdelsalam & Weetman (2007)	Egypt	Legal form Activity of share trading Audit firm IASs compliance note	Compliance with the established regulation improved between 1991–1992 and 1995–1996 because companies responded to the new economic policy of privatization, the increase in stock exchange activity, and the expanded ownership base.

			The disclosure of some of the items required by the new regulations (CML and IASs) that were voluntarily disclosed in 1991–1992 before the new accounting regulations were enacted (mean 73% and 76%, respectively) significantly increased in 1995–1996 (mean 84% and 84%, respectively). In 1995-1996 balance sheet disclosures and accompanying notes were improved to correct previous omissions during the central planning period.
Dahawy & Conover (2007)	Egypt		Low levels of compliance with IASs. Disclosure levels range from 52% to 76% with average level 62% which is attributed to secrecy. The lowest levels of compliance relate to consolidated financial statements (44%) and leasing (45%).
Omar (2007)	Jordan	Firm size, Leverage, Profitability, Number of shareholders, Listing status, Industry type, Assets-in-place, Ownership structure, Liquidity, Audit firm Size, Listing age	There is a significant increase in the level of aggregate disclosure (its average IS 69%) compared to previous studies in Jordan. The extent of mandatory and voluntary disclosures is 83% and 34% respectively. Disclosure level is high in financial statements of Jordanian companies (e. g. balance sheet and income statement) and general information in the annual reports, but low in the voluntary item groups such as market based and financial history information. Univariate analysis indicates that firm size, profitability, number of shareholders, listing status, industry type, audit firm size and listing age are significant variables in explaining the variation in the level of aggregate disclosure among Jordanian companies. Multivariate analysis reveals that these variables are significantly associated with the level of aggregate disclosure: firm size (sales), profitability (ROE), audit firm size, industry type and listing status. There is a significant increase in the level of aggregate and mandatory disclosure for Jordanian companies in 2003 compared to 1996. However, the level of voluntary disclosure is not significantly different in the two periods.
Al-Jifri (2008)	UAE	Sector type (banks, insurance, industrial, and service) Size (assets) Debt equity ratio profitability	Significant differences are found among sectors. Firm size, the debt equity ratio, and the profitability were found to have insignificant association with the level of disclosure.

III Cross-national Comparative Capital Market Studies			
Choi (1973)	11 countries; Australia Belgium Denmark France Germany Italy Japan The Netherlands Norway Sweden Switzerland (which tapped the Euro-currency bond market for financing prior to July 1971)	Entry into a broadly based capital market.	Entry into a broadly based capital market has a significant influence on disclosure behavior of borrowing enterprise-investors.
Barrett (1976)	US, UK, Japan, France, West German, Netherlands, and Sweden		US and UK companies are superior and France is the last in terms of extent of financial disclosure
Spero (1979)	France Sweden UK		Different weighting schemes are not as important as item selection because companies that view disclosure positively disclose many items and have high scores regardless of item weight. Using OLS regression, capital need theory is partially supported in scrutinised countries.
Meek et al. (1995)	US, UK and Continental Europe	company size (revenue), leverage (long-term debt to equity ratio), multinationality (ratio of sales from outside companies' home countries to total sales), profitability (ratio of return of sales), country/region, industry type, and listing status.	Independent variable explain 35% of voluntary disclosure variation. Company size, country/region, industry type and international listing status are the most significant explanatory variables, however other company characteristics appear insignificant.

Hussain (1996)	US Netherlands		Large Duch companies provide significantly more disclosure compared to their US counterparts. Disclosure demanded from large internationally oriented companies is different from that smaller more domestically oriented ones. Proposing the use of cultural analysis approach for the comparative study of financial reporting of different countries.
Zarzeski (1996)	France, Germany, Hong Kong, Japan, Norway, UK and USA		The average extent of financial disclosure is 73% in US, 68.7% in UK; 62.8% in France; 59.7% in Japan; 59.3% in Norway; 57.3% in Germany; 56.8% in Hong Kong
Craig & Diga (1998)	Singapore Malaysia Indonesia The Phillipines and Thailand	Firm size Industry group Country of origin Leverage International operations	In terms of disclosure requirements, Singapore has the highest level of disclosure requirements (393 items out of 530) while Indonesia has the lowest level of disclosure requirements (275 items out of 530). There is a positive association between the level of compliance and firm size, industry group and country of origin however there is no association with the remaining independent variables.
Tower et al. (1999)	Australia Thailand Singapore Malaysia Hong Kong The Phillipines	Country of reporting Length of time to report Firm size Leverage Profitability Industry type	There is a positive association between the level of compliance with IASs and country of reporting and a negative association with length of time to report, however, there is no association with other variables
Vlachos (2001)	Cyprus Greece	Company size Company age Company profitability Company liquidity Industry type Listing status Auditor type	The Cypriot and Greek corporate mandatory disclosure practices on the whole appear to be extensive. Cypriot public companies which are more profitable are classified as conglomerates or manufacturing or whose shares are listed on the main market of the Athens Stock Exchange tend to disclose significantly more extensive mandatory information in their 1996 annual reports. Comparative analysis reveals that although the influence of listing status and industry type on Cypriot and Greek mandatory disclosure practices is similar, the influence of company size is different. In contrast to Cyprus, company size has a negative influence on the extent of Greek corporate mandatory disclosure practices.

Camfferman & Cooke (2002)	UK Netherlands		Significant differences in disclosure between the two countries were found in 11 categories. The other two categories of disclosure items (three items on revaluation and two on deferred tax) were discovered to have no significant difference in disclosure between the UK and the Netherlands. British companies provide more comprehensive disclosures to comply with EU requirements than their Dutch counterparts with mean scores 58.74 and 54.32 for the UK and the Netherlands respectively.
Chau & Gray (2002)	Hong Kong And Singapore	Ownership structure, family ownership and control	For Hong Kong companies, the overall mean disclosure is 12.23% and the extent of disclosure varies from 9.77% for financial information to 18.49% for strategic information, with 10.49% disclosure for non-financial information. For Singapore companies, the overall mean disclosure is 13.83% and the extent of disclosure varies from 10.68% for financial information to 16.76% for non-financial information with 16% disclosure for strategic information. Level of voluntary disclosure with the exception of non-financial information, is approximately similar for companies in both countries. The results of the regression analysis explain the variation in the level of voluntary disclosure by 42% for HK and 72% for Singapore. The results suggest that there is a significant, positive relationship between wider ownership and the level of voluntary disclosure in both HK and Singapore companies, and there was a negative relationship between family ownership or control and the level of voluntary disclosure.
Archambault & Archambault (2003)	37 countries	Culture, National Political and economic systems, Corporate financial and operating system.	The average total disclosure was 75.69%, with a range from 16% to 94%.
Ali et al. (2004)	Bangladish Pakistan India	Firm size Profitability Multinational company Status Leverage Quality of external auditor	Level of compliance is 80% for the whole sample (81% for Pakistan, 79% for India and 78% for Bangladesh) The highest level of compliance was found for standards relating to depreciation, inventories and property, plant and equipment standards regarding leases and accounting borrowing costs had the lowest level of compliance. Compliance with disclosure requirements is positively associated with firm size, profitability, and multinational company status, however, it is not associated with leverage and quality of external auditor.

Al-Shammari et al. (2008)	Gulf Co-Operation Council (GCC) member states (Saudi Arabia, Qatar, Bahrain, UAE, Kuwait and Oman).	Country of origin Company size Internationality Ownership diffusion Company age Industry Leverage	The level of mandatory compliance (measurement and disclosure) with the 14 IASs, averaged over all companies and all years, was 0.75. The mean level of disclosure compliance was 0.69 and measurement compliance was 0.81. The level of compliance with IASs differs between the GCC member states. The highest average compliance level over all years sampled is found in the UAE (0.80). This is followed by Saudi Arabia (0.78), Kuwait (0.75), Oman (0.74), Bahrain (0.73), and Qatar (0.70). There is significant variation between countries and among companies levels of compliance based on size, leverage, internationality, and industry.

APPENDIX B

DISCLOSURE CHECKLIST

Table B.1 Disclosure Checklist

No	Item Reference	Disclosure Requirement
	IFRS 3	Business Combinations
		Disclosures for Business combinations effected during the period
1	IFRS 3.67(a)	The names and descriptions of the combining entities or businesses
2	IFRS 3.67(b)	The acquisition date
3	IFRS 3.67(c)	The percentage of voting equity instruments acquired
4	IFRS 3.67(d)	The cost of the combination
5	IFRS 3.67(d)	A description of the components of that cost
6	IFRS 3.70(a)	The revenue of the combined entity for the period
7	IFRS 3.70(b)	The profit or loss of the combined entity for the period
		Changes in the carrying amount of goodwill
	IFRS 3.75	The entity shall disclose a reconciliation of the carrying amount of goodwill at the beginning and end of the period, showing separately:
8	IFRS 3.75(a)	The gross amount at the beginning of the period
9	IFRS 3.75(a)	Accumulated impairment losses at the beginning of the period
10	IFRS 3.75(b)	Additional goodwill recognised during the period
11	IFRS 3.75(e)	Impairment losses recognised during the period
	Sub-index (1) Total	
	IAS 1	Presentation of Financial Statements
		Components of financial statements
12	IAS 1.8(a)	A balance sheet
13	IAS 1.8(b)	An income statement
14	IAS 1.8(c)	A statement of changes in equity
15	IAS 1.8(d)	A cash flow statement
16	IAS 1.8(e)	Notes, comprising a summary of significant accounting policies and other explanatory notes
		Fair presentation and compliance with IFRSs
17	IAS 1.14	The financial statements shall include an explicit and unreserved statement of compliance with IFRSs in the notes
		Going concern
	IAS 1.23	When the financial statements are not prepared on a going concern basis, the company shall disclose the following:

18	IAS 1.23	That fact
19	IAS 1.23	The basis on which the financial statements are prepared
20	IAS 1.23	The reason why the entity is not considered to be a going concern
		Comparative information
21	IAS 1.36	Comparative information shall be disclosed in respect of the previous period for all amounts reported in the financial statements
		Identification of the financial statements
22	IAS 1.44	The financial statements shall be identified clearly and distinguished from other information in the annual report
	IAS 1.46	The following information shall be displayed prominently:
23	IAS 1.46(a)	The name of the reporting entity
24	IAS 1.46(b)	Whether the financial statements cover the individual entity or a group accounts
25	IAS 1.46(c)	The balance sheet date or the period covered by the financial statements
26	IAS 1.46(d)	The presentation currency
27	IAS 1.46(e)	The level of rounding for amounts presented in the financial statements
		Balance sheet
		Current/non-current distinction
28	IAS 1.51	An entity shall present current and non-current assets, and current and non-current liabilities, as separate classifications on the face of the balance sheet except when a presentation is based on liquidity
28	IAS 1.51	If the presentation is based on liquidity, assets and liabilities shall be presented broadly in order of their liquidity (*either in increasing or decreasing order of liquidity*)
29	IAS 1.52	An entity shall disclose the amount expected to be recovered or settled after more than twelve months, for each asset and liability line item that combines amounts expected to be recovered or settled (a) no more than twelve months after the balance sheet date, and (b) more than twelve months after the balance sheet date
		Information to be presented on the face of the balance sheet:
30	IAS 1.68(a)	Property, plant and equipment
31	IAS 1.68(b)	Investment property
32	IAS 1.68(c)	Intangible assets
33	IAS 1.68(d)	Financial assets other than investments accounted for using the equity method; trade and other receivables; cash and cash equivalents
34	IAS 1.68(e)	Investments accounted for using the equity method
35	IAS 1.68(f)	Biological assets
36	IAS 1.68(g)	Inventories
37	IAS 1.68(h)	Trade and other receivables
38	IAS 1.68(i)	Cash and cash equivalents

39	IAS 1.68(j)	Trade and other payables
40	IAS 1.68(k)	Provisions
41	IAS 1.68(l)	Financial liabilities other than trade and other payables and provisions
42	IAS 1.68(o)	Minority interest (shareholding<5% according to compulsory disclosure requirements in investigated MENA Jurisdictions), presented with equity
43	IAS 1.68(p)	Issued capital attributable to equity holders of the parent
44	IAS 1.68(p)	Reserves attributable to equity holders of the parent
45	IAS 1.68A(a)	The total of assets classified as held for sale and assets included in disposal groups classified as held for sale
46	IAS 1.68A(b)	Liabilities included in disposal groups classified as held for sale
	IAS 1.74; IAS 1.75	Information to be disclosed either on the face of the balance sheet or in the notes
47	IAS 1.75	Items of property, plant and equipment are disaggregated into classes
	IAS 1.75	Receivables are disaggregated into:
48	IAS 1.75	Amounts receivable from trade customers
49	IAS 1.75	Receivables from related parties
50	IAS 1.75	Prepayments
51	IAS 1.75	Other amounts
	IAS 1.75	Inventories are sub-classified (in accordance with IAS 2, Inventories) into classifications such as:
52	IAS 1.75	Merchandise
53	IAS 1.75	Production supplies
54	IAS 1.75	Materials
55	IAS 1.75	Work in progress
56	IAS 1.75	Finished goods
	IAS 1.75	provisions are disaggregated into:
57	IAS 1.75	Provisions for employee benefits
58	IAS 1.75	Other items
	IAS 1.75	Contributed equity and reserves are disaggregated into various classes, such as:
59	IAS 1.75	Paid-in capital
60	IAS 1.75	Share premium
61	IAS 1.75	Reserves
	IAS 1.76(a)	The entity shall disclose the following, either on the face of the balance sheet or in the notes for each class of share capital:

62	IAS 1.76(a)	i) The number of shares authorised
63	IAS 1.76(a)	ii) The number of shares issued and fully paid
64	IAS 1.76(a)	ii) Issued but not fully paid
65	IAS 1.76(a)	iii) Par value per share, or that the shares have no par value
66	IAS 1.76(a)	iv) A reconciliation of the number of shares outstanding at the beginning and at the end of the period
67	IAS 1.76(a)	v) The rights, preferences and restrictions attaching to that class
	IAS 1.76(a)	Shares in the entity held by:
68	IAS 1.76(a)	vi) The entity itself
69	IAS 1.76(a)	vi) Subsidiaries
70	IAS 1.76(a)	vi) Associates
71	IAS 1.76(a	vii) Shares reserved for issue under options and contracts for the sale of shares; and
72	IAS 1.76(b)	A description of the nature of each reserve within equity
73	IAS 1.76(b)	A description of the purpose of each reserve within equity
		Income statement
		Information to be presented on the face of the income statement
74	1.81(a)	Revenue
75	1.81(b)	Finance costs;
76	1.81(c)	Share of profit or loss of associates accounted for using the equity method
77	1.81(c)	Share of profit or loss of joint ventures accounted for using the equity method
78	1.81(f)	Profit or loss
		Allocations of profit or loss for the period as follows:
79	1.82(a)	Profit or loss attributable to minority interest
80	1.82(b)	Profit or loss attributable to equity holders of the parent
		Information to be presented either on the face of the income statement or in the notes
81	IAS 1.93	If expenses are classified by function, the entity shall disclose additional information on the nature of expenses
82	IAS 1.95	The amount of dividends recognised as distributions to equity holders during the period (this information can also be disclosed on the face of the statement of changes in equity)
83	IAS 1.95	The related amount per share
		Statement of changes in equity
		Information to be presented on the face of the statement of changes in equity
84	IAS 1.96(a)	Profit or loss for the period
85	IAS 1.96(b)	Each item of income and expense for the period that is recognised directly in equity
86	IAS 1.96(b)	The total of these items
87	IAS 1.96(c)	Total income and expense for the period (calculated as the sum of (a) and (b)

88	IAS 1.96(c)	Total income and expense for the period (calculated as the sum of (a) and (b)), showing separately the total amounts attributable to equity holders of the parent and to minority interest
		Information to be presented either on the face of the statement of changes in equity or in the notes
89	IAS 1.97(a)	The amounts of transactions with equity holders acting in their capacity as equity holders
90	IAS 1.97(b)	The balance of retained earnings (i.e. accumulated profit or loss) at the beginning of the period
91	IAS 1.97(b)	The balance of retained earnings at the balance sheet date
92	IAS 1.97(b)	The changes during the period
		Notes
		The notes shall:
93	IAS 1.103(a)	Present information about the basis of preparation of the financial statements
94	IAS 1.104	Each item on the face of the balance sheet shall be cross-referenced to any related information in the notes
95	IAS 1.104	Each item on the face of the income statement shall be cross-referenced to any related information in the notes
96	IAS 1.104	Each item on the face of the statement of changes in equity shall be cross-referenced to any related information in the notes
97	IAS 1.104	Each item on the face of the cash flow statement shall be cross-referenced to any related information in the notes
		Disclosure of accounting policies
98	IAS 1.108(a)	The measurement basis (or bases) used in preparing the financial statements
99	IAS 1.108(b)	The other accounting policies used that are relevant to understanding of the financial statements
		Key sources of estimation uncertainty
100	IAS 1.116	Key assumptions concerning the future
101	IAS 1.116	Other key sources of estimation uncertainty at the balance sheet date that have a significant risk of causing a material adjustment to the carrying amounts of assets and liabilities within the next financial year
		For such assets and liabilities, the notes shall include details of:
102	IAS 1.116(a)	Their nature
103	IAS 1.116(b)	Their carrying amount as at the balance sheet date
		Capital
104	IAS 1.124B(a)	i) A description of what the entity manages as capital
105	IAS 1.124B(a)	ii) When an entity is subject to externally imposed capital requirements, the nature of those requirements
106	IAS 1.124B(a)	ii) How those requirements are incorporated into the management of capital
107	IAS 1.124B(a)	iii) How it is meeting its objectives for managing capital
108	IAS 1.124B(b)	Summary quantitative data about what it manages as capital
109	IAS 1.124B(c)	Any changes in 124B (a) and 124B (b) (see above) from the previous period
		Other disclosures
110	IAS 1.125(a) ; IAS 10.13	The amount of dividends proposed or declared before the financial statements were authorised for issue but not recognised as a distribution to equity holders during the period

111	IAS 1.125(a)	The related amount per share
		An entity shall disclose the following, if not disclosed elsewhere in information published with the financial statements:
112	IAS 1.126(a)	The domicile
113	IAS 1.126(a)	Legal form of the entity
114	IAS 1.126(a)	Its country of incorporation
115	IAS 1.126(b) IAS 24.12	A description of the nature of the entity's operations and its principal activities
116	IAS 1.126(c) IAS 24.12	The name of the parent entity
117	IAS 1.126(c)	The ultimate parent of the group
	Sub-index (2) Total	
	IAS 2	Inventories
118	IAS 2.36(a)	The accounting policies adopted in measuring inventories
119	IAS 2.36(b)	The total carrying amount of inventories
120	IAS 2.36(c)	The carrying amount of inventories carried at fair value less costs to sell
121	IAS 2.36(d)	The amount of inventories recognised as an expense during the period
122	IAS 2.36(e)	The amount of any write-down of inventories recognised as an expense in the period
123	IAS 2.36(h)	The carrying amount of inventories pledged as security for liabilities
	Sub-index (3) Total	
	IAS 7	Cash Flow Statements
		Classification of cash flows
124	IAS 7.10	Cash flows during the period are classified by operating, investing and financing activities
		Reporting cash flows from investing and financing activities
125	IAS 7.21	An entity shall report separately major classes of gross cash receipts and gross cash payments arising from investing and financing activities
		Foreign currency cash flows
126	IAS 7.28	The effect of exchange rate changes on cash and cash equivalents held or due in a foreign currency is presented separately from cash flows from operating, investing and financing activities
		Interest and dividends
127	IAS 7.31	Cash flows arising from interest and dividends received and paid shall each be disclosed separately
		Acquisitions and disposals of subsidiaries and other business units

128	IAS 7.39	The aggregate cash flows arising from acquisitions and from disposals of subsidiaries or other business units shall be presented separately
129	IAS 7.39	The aggregate cash flows arising from acquisitions and from disposals of subsidiaries or other business units shall be classified as investing activities
		An entity shall disclose, in aggregate, in respect of both acquisitions and disposals of subsidiaries or other business units during the period, each of the following:
130	IAS 7.40(a)	The total purchase or disposal consideration
131	IAS 7.40(b)	The portion of the purchase or disposal consideration discharged by means of cash and cash equivalents
132	IAS 7.40(c)	The amount of cash and cash equivalents in the subsidiary or business unit acquired or disposed of
133	IAS 7.40(d)	The amount of the assets and liabilities other than cash or cash equivalents in the subsidiary or business unit acquired or disposed of, summarised by each major category
		Components of cash and cash equivalents
134	IAS 7.45	An entity shall disclose the components of cash and cash equivalents
	Sub-index (4) Total	
	IAS 8	Accounting Policies, Changes in Accounting Estimates and Errors
		Disclosing changes in accounting policies
		When an initial application of a Standard or an Interpretation has an effect on the current period or any prior period, however it is impracticable to determine the amount of the adjustment, or might have an effect on future periods, an entity shall disclose:
135	IAS 8.28(a)	The title of the Standard or Interpretation
136	IAS 8.28(c)	The nature of the change in accounting policy
	IAS 8.28(f)	For the current period and each prior period presented, to the extent practicable, the amount of the adjustment:
137	IAS 8.28(f)	i) For each financial statement line item affected
138	IAS 8.28(f)	ii) For basic earnings per share
139	IAS 8.28(f)	ii) For diluted earnings per share
140	IAS 8.28(g)	The amount of the adjustment relating to periods before those presented
	IAS 8.29(c)	When a voluntary change in accounting policy has an effect on the current period or any prior period however it is impracticable to determine the amount of the adjustment, or might have an effect on future periods, an entity shall disclose for the current period and each prior period presented, to the extent practicable, the amount of the adjustment:
141	IAS 8.29(c)	i) For each financial statement line item affected
142	IAS 8.29(c)	ii) For basic earnings per share
143	IAS 8.29(c)	ii) For diluted earnings per share
144	IAS 8.29(d)	The amount of the adjustment relating to periods before those presented
		Disclosing the effect of a change in accounting estimate

145	IAS 8.39	The nature of a change in an accounting estimate that has an effect in the current period or which is expected to have an effect in future periods
146	IAS 8.39	The amount of a change in an accounting estimate that has an effect in the current period or which is expected to have an effect in future periods
147	IAS 8.40	If the amount of the effect in future periods is not disclosed because estimating it is impracticable, the entity shall disclose that fact
	Sub-index (5) Total	
	IAS 11	Construction Contracts
		An entity shall disclose each of the following for contracts in progress at the balance sheet date:
148	IAS 11.40(a)	The aggregate amount of costs incurred and
149	IAS 11.40(a)	Recognised profits (less recognised losses) to date
150	IAS 11.40(b)	The amount of advances received
151	IAS 11.40(c)	The amount of retentions
152	IAS 11.42(a)	The gross amount due from customers for contract work is presented as an asset
153	IAS 11.42(b)	The gross amount due to customers for contract work is presented as a liability
	Sub-index (6) Total	
	IAS 14	Segment Reporting
		Disclosures for primary reporting format
154	IAS 14.51	Segment revenue for each reportable segment
155	IAS 14.51	For each reportable segment, reporting separately segment revenue from sales to external customers and segment revenue from transactions with other segments
156	IAS 14.52	Segment result for each reportable segment
157	IAS 14.52	For each reportable segment, reporting separately segment result from continuing operations and segment result from discontinued operations
158	IAS 14.55	The total carrying amount of segment assets for each reportable segment
159	IAS 14.57	The total cost incurred during the period to acquire segment assets that are expected to be used during more than one period (property, plant, equipment, and intangible assets for each reportable segment)
160	IAS 14.58	The total amount of expense included in segment result for depreciation and amortisation of segment assets for the period for each reportable segment
	IAS 14.67	An entity shall present a reconciliation between the information disclosed for reportable segments and the aggregated information in the consolidated or individual financial statements, which includes a reconciliation of:
161	IAS 14.67	Segment revenue to entity revenue from external customers
	IAS 14.67	Segment result from continuing operations to:

162		i) A comparable measure of entity operating profit or loss from continuing operations
163	IAS 14.67	ii) Entity profit or loss from continuing operations
164	IAS 14.67	Segment result from discontinued operations to entity profit or loss from discontinued operations
165	IAS 14.67	Segment assets to entity assets
166	IAS 14.67	Segment liabilities to entity liabilities
167	IAS 14.81	The types of products and services included in each reported business segment
168	IAS 14.81	The composition of each reported geographical segment
	Sub-index (7) Total	
	IAS 16	Property, Plant and Equipment
		The financial statements shall disclose, for each class of property, plant and equipment:
169	IAS 16.73(a)	The measurement bases used for determining the gross carrying amount
170	IAS 16.73(b)	The depreciation methods used
171	IAS 16.73(c)	The useful lives or the depreciation rates used
172	IAS 16.73(c)	The gross carrying amount at the beginning and end of the period
173	IAS 16.73(c)	The accumulated depreciation (aggregated with accumulated impairment losses) at the beginning and end of the period
	IAS 16.73(e)	a reconciliation of the carrying amount at the beginning and end of the period showing:
174	IAS 16.73(e)	i) Additions
175	IAS 16.73(e)	ii) Assets classified as held for sale or included in a disposal group classified as held for sale
176	IAS 16.73(e)	iii) Acquisitions through business combinations
177	IAS 16.73(e)	iv) Increases or decreases resulting from revaluations
178	IAS 16.73(e) IAS 36.126 (c)	iv) Decreases resulting from impairment losses recognized directly in equity
179	IAS 16.73(e) IAS 36.126 (a)	v) Impairment losses recognised in profit or loss
180	IAS 16.73(e) IAS 36.126 (b)	vi) Impairment losses reversed in profit or loss in accordance with IAS 36
181	IAS 16.73(e)	vii) Depreciation
182	IAS 16.73(e)	viii) The net exchange differences arising on the translation of the financial statements from the functional currency into a different presentation currency
183	IAS 16.74(a)	The existence of restrictions on title, and property, plant and equipment pledged as security for liabilities
184	IAS 16.74(a)	Amounts of restrictions on title
185	IAS 16.74(b)	The amount of expenditures recognised in the carrying amount of an item of property, plant and equipment in the course of its construction

186	IAS 16.74(c)	The amount of contractual commitments for the acquisition of property, plant and equipment
		Assets carried at revalued amounts
187	IAS 16.77(a)	The effective date of the revaluation
188	IAS 16.77(b)	Whether an independent values was involved
189	IAS 16.77(c)	The methods and significant assumptions applied in estimating the items' fair values
190	IAS 16.77(e)	For each revalued class of property, plant and equipment, the carrying amount that would have been recognised had the assets been carried under the cost model
	Sub-index (8) Total	
	IAS 18	Revenue
191	IAS 18.35(a)	The accounting policies adopted for the recognition of revenue
	IAS 18.35(b)	The amount of revenues arising from:
192	IAS 18.35(b)	i) The sale of goods
193	IAS 18.35(b)	ii) The rendering of services
194	IAS 18.35(b)	iii) Interest
195	IAS 18.35(b)	v) Dividends
	Sub-index (9) Total	
	IAS 21	The Effects of Changes in Foreign Exchange Rates
196	IAS 21.52(a)	The amount of exchange differences recognised in profit or loss
197	IAS 21.52(b)	Net exchange differences classified in a separate component of equity
198	IAS 21.52(b)	A reconciliation of the amount of such exchange differences at the beginning and end of the period
	Sub-index (10) Total	
	IAS 23	Borrowing Costs
		Disclosures required where the benchmark treatment (expensing of borrowing costs) is adopted
199	IAS 23.9	The accounting policy adopted for borrowing costs
		Disclosures required where the allowed alternative treatment (capitalization of borrowing costs) is adopted
199	IAS 23.29(a)	The accounting policy adopted for borrowing costs
200	IAS 23.29(b)	The amount of borrowing costs capitalised during the period
201	IAS 23.29(c)	The capitalisation rate used to determine the amount of borrowing costs eligible for capitalisation
	Sub-index (11) Total	
	IAS 24	Related Party Disclosures
202	IAS 24.13	Disclosing the related party relationship when control exists, irrespective of whether there have been related party transactions
		Compensation of key management personnel
203	IAS 24.16	Disclosing key management personnel compensation in total

	IAS 24.16	An entity shall disclose key management personnel compensation for each of the following categories:
204	IAS 24.16(d)	Termination benefits
205	IAS 24.16(e)	Share-based payment
		Transactions between related parties
206	IAS 24.17	The nature of the related party relationship
207	IAS 24.17(a)	The amount of the transactions
208	IAS 24.17(b)	The amount of the outstanding balances
209	IAS 24.17(b)	i) Their terms and conditions, including whether they are secured
210	IAS 24.17(b)	i) The nature of the consideration to be provided in settlement
211	IAS 24.17(b)	ii) Details of any guarantees given or received
212	IAS 24.17(c)	Provisions for doubtful debts related to the amount of outstanding balances
	Sub-index (12) Total	
	IAS 27	Consolidated and Separate Financial Statements
		Minority interests
213	IAS 27.33	Minority interests shall be presented in the consolidated balance sheet within equity, separately from the parent shareholders' equity
214	IAS 27.33	Minority interests in the profit or loss of the group shall be separately disclosed
	Sub-index (13) Total	
	IAS 28	Investments in Associates
215	IAS 28.37(a)	Disclosing the fair value of investments in associates for which there are published price quotations
	IAS 28.37(b)	Summarised financial information of associates, including the aggregated amounts of:
216	IAS 28.37(b)	Assets
217	IAS 28.37(b)	Liabilities
218	IAS 28.37(b)	Revenues and
219	IAS 28.37(b)	Profit or loss
220	IAS 28.37(h)	h)The fact that an associate is not accounted for using the equity method
	IAS 28.37(i)	Summarised financial information of associates, either individually or in groups, that are not accounted for using the equity method, including the amounts of:
221	IAS 28.37(i)	Total assets
222	IAS 28.37(i)	Total liabilities
223	IAS 28.37(i)	Revenues and
224	IAS 28.37(i)	Profit or loss
225	IAS 28.40(a)	Investor share of the contingent liabilities of an associate incurred jointly with other investors
226	IAS 28.40(b)	Contingent liabilities that arise because the investor is severally liable for all or part of the liabilities of the associate

	Sub-index (14) Total	
	IAS 31	Interests in Joint Ventures
227	IAS 31.30,34	The venturer may combine its share of each of the assets, liabilities, income and expenses of the jointly controlled entity with the similar items, line by line, in its financial statements; <u>or</u>
227	IAS 31.30,34	The venturer may include separate line items for its share of the assets, liabilities, income and expenses of the jointly controlled entity in its financial statements
		Disclosures
228	IAS 31.54(a)	Any contingent liabilities that the venturer has incurred in relation to its interests in joint ventures
229	IAS 31.54(a)	Its share in each of the contingent liabilities that have been incurred jointly with other venturers
230	IAS 31.55(a)	Any capital commitments of the venturer in relation to its interests in joint ventures
231	31.55(a)	Venturer share in the capital commitments that have been incurred jointly with other venturers;
232	IAS 31.55(b)	Venturer share of the capital commitments of the joint ventures themselves
233	IAS 31.56	The proportion of ownership interest held in each of its jointly controlled entities
234	IAS 31.57	The method venturer uses to recognise its interests in jointly controlled entities
	Sub-index (15) Total	
	IAS 33	Earnings per Share
		Retrospective adjustments
235	IAS 33.64	If the number of ordinary or potential ordinary shares outstanding increases as a result of a capitalisation or bonus issue or share split, or decreases as a result of a reverse share split, the calculation of basic earnings per share for all periods presented shall be adjusted retrospectively
236	IAS 33.64	If the number of ordinary or potential ordinary shares outstanding increases as a result of a capitalisation or bonus issue or share split, or decreases as a result of a reverse share split, the calculation of diluted earnings per share for all periods presented shall be adjusted retrospectively
	IAS 33.68	An entity that reports a discontinued operation shall disclose:
237	IAS 33.68	The basic amounts per share for the discontinued operation either on the face of the income statement or in the notes
238	IAS 33.68	The diluted amounts per share for the discontinued operation either on the face of the income statement or in the notes
		Disclosures
239	IAS 33.70(a)	The amounts used as the numerators in calculating basic earnings per share;
240	IAS 33.70(a)	The amounts used as the numerators in calculating diluted earnings per share
241	IAS 33.70(b)	The weighted average number of ordinary shares used as the denominator in calculating basic earnings per share
242	IAS 33.70(b)	The weighted average number of ordinary shares used as the denominator in calculating diluted earnings per share
243	IAS 33.70(b)	A reconciliation of these denominators to each other
	Sub-index (16) Total	
	IAS 36	Impairment of Assets

244	IAS 36.126(a)	For each class of assets the line item(s) of the income statement in which those impairment losses are included
		Entities reporting segment information
245	IAS 36.129(a)	The amount of impairment losses recognised during the period
	Sub-index (17) Total	
	IAS 37	Provisions, Contingent Liabilities and Contingent Assets
		Information to be disclosed for each class of provision
246	IAS 37.84(a)	The carrying amount at the beginning
247	IAS 37.84(a)	The carrying amount at the end of the period
248	IAS 37.84(b)	Additional provisions made in the period
249	IAS 37.84(c)	Amounts used (i.e. incurred and charged against the provision) during the period
250	IAS 37.84(d)	Unused amounts reversed during the period
251	IAS 37.85(a)	A brief description of the nature of the obligation
252	IAS 37.85(a)	The expected timing of any resulting outflows of economic benefits
253	IAS 37.85(b)	An indication of the uncertainties about the amount or timing of those outflows
254	IAS 37.85(c)	The amount of any expected reimbursement, stating the amount of any asset that has been recognised for that expected reimbursement
		Contingent liabilities
255	IAS 37.86	A brief description of the nature of the contingent liability
256	IAS 37.86(b)	An indication of the uncertainties relating to the amount or timing of any outflow
		Contingent assets
257	IAS 37.89	A brief description of the nature of the contingent assets at the balance sheet date
	Sub-index (18) Total	
	IAS 38	Intangible Assets
		General disclosures
258	IAS 38.118(a)	Whether the useful lives are indefinite or finite
259	IAS 38.118(a)	The useful lives or the amortisation rates used for intangible assets with finite useful lives
260	IAS 38.118(b)	The amortisation methods used for intangible assets with finite useful lives
261	IAS 38.118(c)	The gross carrying amount at the beginning and end of the period
262	IAS 38.118(c)	Any accumulated amortisation (aggregated with accumulated impairment losses) at the beginning and end of the period
263	IAS 38.118(d)	The line item(s) of the income statement in which any amortisation of intangible assets is included
	IAS 38.118(e)	A reconciliation of the carrying amount at the beginning and end of the period showing:
264	IAS 38.118(e)	i) Additions;
265	IAS 38.118(e)	iii) Increases or decreases during the period resulting from revaluations
266	IAS 38.118(e)	iii) Increases or decreases from impairment losses recognised or reversed directly in equity (if any)

267	IAS 38.118(e)	vi) Any amortisation recognised during the period
		Research and development expenditure
268	IAS 38.126	The aggregate amount of research and development expenditure recognised as an expense during the period
	Sub-index (19) Total	
	IAS 40	Investment Property
269	IAS 40.75(a)	Whether the entity applies the fair value model or the cost model
270	IAS 40.75(d)	The methods applied in determining the fair value of investment property
271	IAS 40.75(d)	Significant assumptions applied in determining the fair value of investment property
	IAS 40.75(f)	The amounts recognised in profit or loss for:
272	IAS 40.75(f)	i) Rental income from investment property
273	IAS 40.75(f)	ii) Direct operating expenses (including repairs and maintenance) arising from investment property that generated rental income during the period
		If the entity measures investment property using the cost model because of the lack of a reliable fair value, an entity shall disclose:
274	IAS 40.78(a)	A description of the investment property
275	IAS 40.78(b)	An explanation of why fair value cannot be reliably determined
	Sub-index (20) Total	

APPENDIX C

NAMES AND SECTORS OF SCRUTINISED COMPANIES

Table C.1 Names and Sectors of Scrutinised Egyptian and Jordanian Listed Companies

Name of the Company	Industry
EGX	
Egyptian Electronics Technology Company	Manufacturing
Arab Ceramic Company	Manufacturing
Development and Engineering Consultants	Manufacturing
Egyptians Company for Housing Development Reconstruction	Non-manufacturing
Paints and Chemical Industries	Manufacturing
Oriental Weavers Carpet	Manufacturing
Orascom Hotel Holdings	Non-manufacturing
Egyptian Food Company	Manufacturing
International Company for Medical Investment	Manufacturing
Cairo Housing and Development Company	Non-manufacturing
Egyptian Media Production City	Non-manufacturing
Egyptian Iron and Steel Company	Manufacturing
Middle East Glass Manufacturing Company	Manufacturing
Amreyah Pharmaceutical Industries	Manufacturing
T3A Pharma Group	Manufacturing
Heliopolis Housing and Development Company	Non-manufacturing
International Agricultural Products	Manufacturing
Quena Paper Industry Company	Manufacturing
El Shams Hotels and Tourism	Non-manufacturing
Memphis Company for Pharmaceuticals and Chemical Industries	Manufacturing
T N Holdings for Investment	Manufacturing
El Ezz Aldekhela Steel	Manufacturing
National Investment and Reconstruction Company	Manufacturing
Palm Hills Developments	Non-manufacturing
Engineering Industries	Manufacturing
National Company for Housing for Professional Syndicates	Non-manufacturing
Misr Hotels Company	Manufacturing

Egyptian Real Estate Group	Manufacturing
Nile Clothing Company	Manufacturing
United Housing and Development	Non-manufacturing
Egyptian International Pharmaceutical Industries Company	Manufacturing
Alexandria Portland Cement Company	Manufacturing
South Cairo and Giza Flour Mills	Manufacturing
AJWA for Food Industries - Middle East	Manufacturing
Cairo Cotton Center	Manufacturing
Samad Misr (Egyfert)	Manufacturing
General Company for Research and Groundwater	Manufacturing
Alexandria for Real Estate Investments	Manufacturing
Medical Union Pharmaceuticals	Manufacturing
Al Ezz Steel Rebars	Manufacturing
Contact Car Trading Company	Non-manufacturing
Middle East Paper Company - Egypt	Manufacturing
National Company	Manufacturing
Orascom Hotels and Development	Non-manufacturing
Al Ahly Real Estate Development	Non-manufacturing
Egypt Gas Company	Manufacturing
El Nasr Transformers and Electrical Products Company	Manufacturing
Lecico Egypt	Manufacturing
Al Ezz Ceramics and Porcelain Company	Manufacturing
Kafr El Zayat Pesticides and Chemicals Company	Manufacturing
Abu Qir Fertilizers and Chemical Industries Company	Manufacturing
El Gezirah Hotels and Tourism Company	Non-manufacturing
Sinai Cement Company	Manufacturing
Delta Sugar Company	Manufacturing
Cairo Oil and Soap	Manufacturing
Misr Glass Manufacturing Company	Manufacturing
National Cement Company - Egypt	Manufacturing
El Badr Plastic	Manufacturing
National Glass and Crystal Company	Manufacturing
National Gas Company - Egypt	Manufacturing
Egyptian Fibers Company	Manufacturing
General Engineering Industries	Manufacturing
Egyptian Company for Mobile Services	Non-manufacturing
Egyptian Company for Tourim Resorts	Non-manufacturing
Ismailia Misr Poultry	Manufacturing
Aluminium Company of Egypt	Manufacturing
East Delta Flour Mills	Manufacturing
Electro Cable Egypt	Manufacturing

Misr Cement Company	Manufacturing
EI Wadi Export Company for Agricultural Products	Manufacturing
Egyptian Chemical Industries	Manufacturing
Orascom Telecom Holding	Non-manufacturing
Misr Mechanical Projects	Manufacturing
Amreyah Cement	Manufacturing
National Company for Maize Products	Manufacturing
ASE	
Universal Modern Industries Company	Manufacturing
Arab Company for Investment Projects	Manufacturing
Real Estate Development	Non-manufacturing
Amad Investment and Real Estate Development Company	Non-manufacturing
Union Land Development Corporation	Non-manufacturing
Comprehensive Multiple Projects Company	Manufacturing
Jordanian Duty Free Shops	Non-manufacturing
Unified Transport and Logistics Company	Non-manufacturing
Irbid District Electricity Company	Non-manufacturing
Jordanian Real Estate Company for Development	Non-manufacturing
Arab International Company for Education and Investment	Non-manufacturing
Jordan Telecom Group	Non-manufacturing
Jordan Ceramic Industries Company	Manufacturing
Al Faris National Company for Investment and Export	Manufacturing
Jordan Steel	Manufacturing
Arab Food and Medical Appliances	Manufacturing
Jordan Press and Publishing Company	Non-manufacturing
Jordan Paper and Cardboard Factories Company	Manufacturing
Jordan Sulpho Chemicals Company	Manufacturing
United Group Holdings - Jordan	Manufacturing
Jordan Express Tourist Transport	Non-manufacturing
Ittihad Schools	Non-manufacturing
Arab Potash Company	Manufacturing
Zarka Education and Investment Company	Non-manufacturing
Zara Investment (Holding) Company	Manufacturing
Jordan Magnesia Company	Manufacturing
Jordan International Trading Centre	Non-manufacturing

APPENDIX D

INVITATION LETTER

Dear Sir/Madam,

I am a PhD student at Aston Business School, Aston University, UK. My research study is entitled 'Corporate Governance and Compliance with IFRSs - MENA Evidence'. You are being invited to take part in this research study. Before you decide, it is important for you to understand why the research is being done and what it will involve. Please take time to read the following information carefully.

The main objective of my research is to investigate the extent of compliance with IFRSs disclosure requirements by companies listed on two of the best performing MENA stock exchanges; the Egyptian and Jordanian stock exchanges. In addition, this research aims to examine the influence of board characteristics and ownership structure on the levels of compliance with the IFRSs by companies listed on the stock exchanges of both jurisdictions. To achieve the above mentioned research objectives a disclosure index and interviews will be employed as research methods.

In general terms, the findings of this study are expected to be of interest to the national as well as the international community particularly stakeholders of the MENA region capital markets who are keen to know the strengths and weaknesses in disclosure practices among different MENA region capital markets. Furthermore, the findings of this study are not only of importance for current and potential investors but also are expected to provide regulators and policy-makers in each of the investigated capital markets with recent comprehensive evidence that is expected to enhance their knowledge about the position of their capital market among others within the region. This will help them to develop new approaches to reduce variation and strengthen enforcement mechanisms in order to improve financial disclosure practices within their markets and meet international best practices. With respect to the IASB the findings of this study are expected to provide an insight regarding the levels of de facto compliance with disclosure requirements of IFRSs by a range of emerging capital markets that follow IASB issued standards. Additionally, this study intends to explore the underlying theoretical rationale of corporate financial disclosure in the scrutinised MENA region capital markets.

I intend to conduct 40 interviews (20 in Egypt and 20 in Jordan). You have been chosen as one of the interviewees because of your position that relates to educating, practising, auditing, or enforcing the adoption of the IFRSs by companies listed on the stock exchange of your jurisdiction, or as a user of the annual reports of listed companies in making investment decisions. The interview questions are related to the barriers to de facto compliance (i.e., compliance in practice) with IFRSs disclosure requirements and the influence of corporate governance structures on the levels of compliance with the IFRSs by listed companies. The interview is expected to take approximately thirty minutes and you are free to withdraw at any time from the interview. Furthermore, if you prefer me to take notes instead of tape recording, I will do so and you will have the right to review these to make sure that they really reflect your points of view and that no words are missing. I would be grateful if you accept to participate.

You should know that the data collected will be treated confidentially and will be used only for research purposes. I guarantee anonymity. However, if you wish I could acknowledge your contribution in the thesis and in any related academic publications. Furthermore, if you wish I can send you an electronic copy of my thesis and of any other related publication. This will not be ready before the end of 2010. This research project has been approved by Aston University's Ethics Committee, and will be conducted in full in accordance with the principles laid down by it. If, however, you have any concerns about the way in which the interview will be conducted, you may contact the Secretary of the University Ethics Committee.

Many thanks in advance for your co-operation. I look forward to hearing from you. For any information, please do not hesitate to contact me.

Yours sincerely,
Marwa Hassaan
e-mail: hassanm3@aston.ac.uk

APPENDIX E

CONSENT FORM

INTERVIEWEE CONSENT FORM

Title of the Research Study: Corporate Governance and Compliance with International Financial Reporting Standards (IFRSs) - MENA Evidence.

Name of the Researcher: Marwa Hassaan

Tick

Box

---

1 I confirm that I have read and understand the information sheet for the above study. I have had the opportunity to consider the information, ask questions and have had these answered.

2 I understand that my participation is voluntary and that I am free to withdraw at any time without giving any reason, and without my legal rights being affected.

3 I agree to take part in the above study.

Name of Interviewee	Date	Signature
Name of Person taking consent (if different from researcher)	Date	Signature
Researcher	Date	Signature

APPENDIX F

TESTS OF NORMALITY ON INDIVIDUAL COUNTRY LEVEL

Table F.1 Tests of Normality

	country[1]	Kolmogorov-Smirnov[2]			Shapiro-Wilk		
		Statistic	Df	Sig.	Statistic	Df	Sig.
Board Independence	0	.102	75	.049	.977	75	.183
	1	.096	75	.085	.944	75	.002
Board Size Board	0	.173	75	.000	.894	75	.000
	1	.133	75	.002	.937	75	.001
Leadership Government	0	.343	75	.000	.636	75	.000
	1	.496	75	.000	.475	75	.000
Ownership Management	0	.298	75	.000	.693	75	.000
	1	.286	75	.000	.636	75	.000
Ownership Private	0	.409	75	.000	.551	75	.000
	1	.229	75	.000	.758	75	.000
Ownership	0	.233	75	.000	.742	75	.000
	1	.088	75	.200[3]	.946	75	.003
Public Ownership	0	.288	75	.000	.675	75	.000
	1	.145	75	.001	.897	75	.000
Total Assets ROA	0	.367	75	.000	.340	75	.000
	1	.319	75	.000	.452	75	.000
Debt to Equity	0	.158	75	.000	.865	75	.000
	1	.128	75	.004	.862	75	.000
Quick ratio	0	.180	75	.000	.873	75	.000
	1	.227	75	.000	.786	75	.000
Auditor Type	0	.205	75	.000	.864	75	.000
	1	.141	75	.001	.838	75	.000
Industry Type	0	.439	75	.000	.580	75	.000
	1	.378	75	.000	.629	75	.000
Total Score	0	.419	75	.000	.601	75	.000
	1	.350	75	.000	.636	75	.000
	0	.068	75	.200	.977	75	.200
	1	.105	75	.041	.960	75	.017

1 refers to Egypt, 2 refers to Jordan
Lilliefors Significance Correction
This is a lower pound of the true significance

APPENDIX G

PEARSON CORRELATIONS REPORTED WITH REGRESSION ANALYSIS USING NORMAL SCORES: EGYPT

Table G.1 Pearson Correlations Reported with Regression - Egypt

Pearson Correlation	Total score	Auditor	Industry	BOD lead	BOD Indp.	BOD Size	Gov. Own	Mngt. Own	Private Own	Public Own	Firm Size	Profit	Gear	Liquid
Total score	1.000													
Auditor	-.048	1.000												
Industry	.007	.062	1.000											
BOD lead	.071	.194	.046	1.000										
BOD indp	.032	-.039	.216	-.001	1.000									
BOD Size	.060	-.001	-.011	-.126	-.091	1.000								
Gov Own	.145	-.242	.065	-.107	.130	-.072	1.000							
Mngt Own	.017	.072	.033	.048	-.037	-.080	-.193	1.000						
Private Own	-.027	.010	-.099	-.049	-.090	.040	-.422	.624	1.000					
Public Own	-.079	.001	-.085	-.108	.074	-.004	.005	-.065	-.118	1.000				
Firm Size	.155	.310	.142	-.049	-.049	-.063	.182	.155	-.191	.097	1.000			
Profit.	-.053	-.080	-.014	-.002	.170	-.188	.176	-.264	-.130	-.130	-.008	1.000		
Gear	-.112	.102	-.166	.118	-.161	-.028	-.380	.122	.243	-.018	-.144	.018	1.000	
Liquid	.021	-.062	-.012	-.007	.129	.008	.182	-.279	-.109	-.005	-.190	.304	-.047	1.000

Sig.(1-tailed)													
Total score													
Auditor	.343												
Industry	.476	.297											
BOD lead	.272	.048	.347										
BOD indp	.391	.370	.031	.497									
BOD Size	.303	.497	.464	.140	.218								
Gov Own	.107	.018	.288	.180	.133	.269							
Mngt Own	.443	.270	.388	.340	.375	.247	.049						
Private Own	.410	.465	.200	.337	.222	.367	.000	.000					
Public Own	.249	.497	.233	.177	.265	.485	.484	.291	.157				
Firm Size	.092	.003	.113	.338	.337	.297	.059	.092	.050	.203			
Profit.	.326	.247	.451	.492	.073	.053	.066	.011	.132	.132	.473		
Gear	.170	.191	.077	.157	.084	.407	.000	.148	.018	.439	.109	.438	
Liquid	.430	.299	.460	.475	.135	.473	.059	.008	.176	.481	.051	.004	.344

APPENDIX H

COEFFECIENT ESTIMATES AND THEIR SIGNIFICANCE FOR STEPWISE REGRESSION EXCLUDED INDEPENDENT VARIABLES: JORDAN

Table H.1 Coeffecient Estimates and their Significance for Stepwise Regression Excluded Independent Variables- Jordan

Variable	Beta In	t	Sig.	Partial	Collinearity Statistics		
					Tolerance	VIF	Minimum
Type of Business Activity	.126	1.242	.219	.147	.983	1.018	.887
Board Leadership	-.105	-1.005	.318	-.119	.931	1.074	.888
Board Independence	-.001	-.011	.992	-.001	.752	1.330	.752
Board Size	.185	1.843	.070	.215	.977	1.024	.887
Government Ownership Ratio	.116	1.140	.258	.135	.984	1.016	.886
Management Ownership Ratio	.034	.327	.744	.039	.976	1.025	.882
Private Ownership Ratio	-.043	-.382	.704	-.046	.824	1.214	.751
Profitability	.074	.697	.488	.083	.908	1.101	.868
Gearing	.003	.024	.981	.003	.904	1.107	.847
Liquidity	.008	.079	.937	.009	.961	1.040	.878

APPENDIX I

COEFFECIENT ESTIMATES AND THEIR SIGNIFICANCE FOR STEPWISE REGRESSION EXCLUDED INDEPENDENT VARIABLES

Table I.1 Coeffecient Estimates and their Significance for Stepwise Regression Excluded Independent Variables

					Collinearity Statistics		
Variable	Beta In	t	Sig.	Correlation	Tolerance	VIF	Min.Tolerance
Country*type of Bus	.155	1.965	.051	.161	.854	1.170	.854
Country	.078	.748	.456	.062	.504	1.982	.504
Auditor	-.119	-1.059	.291	-.087	.433	2.311	.425
Type of Business	.092	1.245	.215	.102	.995	1.005	.966
BOD Leadership	.000	.006	.995	.001	.933	1.072	.933
Country*BOD Leadership	-.014	-.152	.880	-.013	.646	1.548	.646
BOD Size	.143	1.851	.066	.151	.896	1.117	.885
BOD Independence	.031	.380	.704	.031	.839	1.193	.815
Country*BOD Size	.140	1.494	.137	.123	.610	1.639	.610
Country*BOD Independence	.071	.845	.399	.070	.776	1.288	.776
Country*FirmSize	.115	1.221	.224	.101	.613	1.631	.599
Country*Profitability	.123	1.594	.113	.131	.905	1.105	.883
Country*Gearing	.086	.904	.368	.075	.595	1.681	.595
Country*Liquidity	.089	.932	.353	.077	.596	1.678	.596
Profitability	-.005	-.064	.949	-.005	.852	1.173	.852
Gearing	-.025	-.325	.746	-.027	.901	1.110	.875
Liquidity	.035	.468	.641	.039	.994	1.006	.964
Private Ownership	-.006	-.074	.941	-.006	.866	1.154	.866
Public Ownership	-.139	-1.826	.070	-.149	.917	1.091	.892
Country*Private Ownership	.051	.474	.636	.039	.480	2.081	.480
Country*Public Ownership	-.139	-1.468	.144	-.121	.604	1.656	.604
Government Ownership	.107	1.426	.156	.117	.965	1.036	.942
Management Ownership	-.003	-.033	.974	-.003	.953	1.050	.925
Country*Government Ownership	.118	1.496	.137	.123	.860	1.163	.860
Country*Management Ownership	.028	.324	.746	.027	.734	1.362	.734

APPENDIX J

INTERVIEW QUESTIONS (FIRST QUESTIONNAIRE)

Part One: Barriers to full compliance with IFRSs disclosure requirements

1. The results of the quantitative analysis revealed that none of the companies listed on the stock exchange of your jurisdiction makes full-compliance with total IFRSs disclosure requirements although they are mandatory. In your opinion what are the barriers to full compliance with IFRSs in your jurisdiction?

Part Two: Impact of corporate governance structures on the levels of compliance with IFRSs disclosure requirements

2. Do you think board independence affect the levels of compliance with IFRSs disclosure requirements by companies listed on the stock exchange of your jurisdiction? Why?
3. Do you think board leadership (*i.e.*, whether the CEO and the Chair positions are held by the same person or by two different persons) affects the levels of compliance with IFRSs disclosure requirements by companies listed on the stock exchange of your jurisdiction? Why?
4. Do you think dominance of government ownership in the companies listed on the stock exchange of your jurisdiction affects the levels of compliance with IFRSs disclosure requirements? Why?
5. Do you think dominance of management ownership in the companies listed on the stock exchange of your jurisdiction affects the levels of compliance with IFRSs disclosure requirements? Why?
6. Do you think dominance of private ownership in the companies listed on the stock exchange of your jurisdiction affects the levels of compliance with IFRSs disclosure requirements? Why?
7. Do you think dominance of public ownership in the companies listed on the stock exchange of your jurisdiction affects the levels of compliance with IFRSs disclosure requirements? Why?

APPENDIX K

INTERVIEW QUESTIONS (SECOND QUESTIONNAIRE)

Part One: Investor perceptions regarding the importance of compliance with IFRSs disclosure re- quirements

1. Do you think the companies listed on the stock exchange of your jurisdiction make all disclosures required to make rational investment decisions? Why?
2. Are you aware of the IFRSs?
3. What do you know about accounting disclosures that a listed company in your jurisdiction is obligated to make?

Part Two: Investor awareness of corporate governance and perceptions regarding the impact of corporate governance structures on disclosure behaviour of listed companies

4. Are you aware of corporate governance best practice?
5. What do you think about the possible impact of board independence (*i.e.*, appointing non-executive board members who are independent to the BOD of the company)?
6. In your opinion for better levels of compliance with IFRSs in your jurisdiction, is it better for the CEO and the Chair positions to be held by the same person or to be held by two different persons?
7. Do you think dominance of government ownership affects the levels of company compliance with mandatory disclosure requirements in your jurisdiction? Why?
8. Do you think dominance of management ownership affects the levels of company compliance with mandatory disclosure requirements in your jurisdiction? Why?
9. Do you think dominance of private ownership affects the levels of company compliance with mandatory disclosure requirements in your jurisdiction? Why?

10. Do you think dominance of public ownership affects the levels of company compliance with mandatory disclosure requirements in your jurisdiction? Why?

REFERENCES

Abayo, A. G., Adams, C. A., and Roberts, C. B. 1993. Measuring the Quality of Corporate Disclosure in Less Developed Countries: the Case of Tanzania. *Journal of International Accounting, Auditing and Taxation*, **2**(2), 145–158.

Abd-Elsalam, O. H. 1999. *The Introduction and Application of International Accounting Standards to Accounting Disclosure Regulations of a Capital Market in Developing Country: the Case of Egypt*. Ph.D. thesis, Herriot- Watt University, UK.

Abd-Elsalam, O. H., and Weetman, P. 2003. Introducing International Accounting Standards to an Emerging Capital Market: Relative Familiarity and Language Effect in Egypt. *Journal of International Accounting*, **12**, 63–84.

Abdelsalam, O., and El-Masry, A. 2008. The Impact of Board Independence and Ownership Structure on the Timeliness of Corporate Internet Reporting of Irish-listed Companies. *Managerial Finance*, **34**(12), 907–918.

Abdelsalam, O.H., and Street, D.L. 2006. An Examination of the Timeliness of Internet Reporting by London- listed Companies. *The Tenth International Association for Accounting Education and Research (IAAER) World Congress*, Nov. Turkey.

Abdelsalam, O.H., and Street, D.L. 2007. Corporate Governance and the Timeliness of Corporate Internet Reporting by UK Listed Companies. *Journal of International Accounting, Auditing and Taxation*, **16**, 111–130.

Abdelsalam, O.H., and Weetman, P. 2007. Measuring Accounting Disclosure in a Period of Complex Changes: The Case of Egypt. *Advances in International Accounting*, **20**, 75–104.

Abed, S., Al-Okdeh, S, and Nimer, K. 2011. The Inclusion of Forecasts in the Narrative Sections of Annual Reports and their Association with Firm Characteristics: The Case of Jordan. *International Business Research*, **4**(4), 264–271.

Abraham, S. 2008. *Essays in Corporate Disclosure Practices*. Ph.D. thesis, University of Exeter, UK.

Abu-Nassar, M., and Rutherford, B. 1996. External Users of Financial Reports in Less Developed Countries: The Case of Jordan. *British Accounting Review*, **28**, 73–87.

Adams, C., Hill, W.Y., and Roberts, C.B. 1998. Corporate Social Reporting Practices in Western Europe: Legitimation Corporate Behaviour. *British Accounting Review*, **30**, 1–21.

Adams, M., and Hossain, M. 1998. Managerial Discretion and Voluntary Disclosure: Evidence from the New Zealand Life Insurance Industry. *Journal of Accounting and Public Policy*, **17**, 245–281.

Ahmed, K., and Courtis, J. K. 1999. Association between Corporate Characteristics and Disclosure Levels in Annual Reports: A meta-analysis. *British Accounting Review*, **31**, 61–65.

Ahmed, K., and Nicholls, D. 1994. The Impact of Non-Financial Company Characteristics on Mandatory Disclosure Compliance in Developing Countries: The Case of Bangladesh. *The International Journal of Accounting*, **29**, 62–77.

Akhtaruddin, M. 2005. Corporate Mandatory Disclosure Practices in Bangladesh. *The International Journal of Accounting*, **40**, 399–422.

Aksu, M., and Kosedag, A. 2006. Transparency and Disclosure Scores and their Determinants in Istanbul Stock Exchange. *Corporate Governance*, **14**(4), 277–296.

Al-Akra, M., Ali, M., and Marashdeh, O. 2009. Development of Accounting Regulation in Jordan. *The International Journal of Accounting*, **44**, 163–186.

Al-Akra, M., Eddie, I., and Ali, M.J. 2010a. The Influence of the Introduction of Accounting Disclosure Regulation on Mandatory Disclosure Compliance: Evidence from Jordan. *The British Accounting Review*, **42**(3), 170–186.

Al-Akra, M., Eddie, I., and Ali, M.J. 2010b. The Association between Privatisation and Voluntary Disclosure: Evi- dence from Jordan. *Accounting and Business Research*, **40**(1), 55–74.

Al-Hajraf, N.F.M. 2002. *Disclosure in the Financial Statements of Banks: International Accounting Standard No. 30 and the Kuwaiti Banks*. Ph.D. thesis, University of Hull, UK.

Al-Htaybat, K. 2005. *Financial Disclosure Practices: Theoretical Foundation and an Empirical Investigation on Jordanian Printed and Internet Formats*. Ph.D. thesis, University of Southampton, UK.

Al-Jifri, K. 2008. Annual Report Disclosure in a Developing Country: The Case of the UAE. *Advances in Accounting Incorporating Advances in International Accounting*, **24**, 93–100.

Al-Mulhem, A.A. 1997. *An Empirical Investigation of the Level of Financial Disclosure by Saudi Arabia Corpora- tions*. Ph.D. thesis, University of Hull, UK.

Al-Najjar, B., and Taylor, P. 2008. The Relationship between Capital Structure and Ownership Structure: Evidence from Jordanian Panel Data. *Managerial Finance*, **34**(12), 919–933.

Al-Omari, A. 2010. The Institutional Framework of Financial Reporting in Jordan. *European Journal of Economics, Finance and Administrative Sciences*, 32–50.

Al-Razeen, A. 1999. *The Quality of Annual Financial Reporting of Saudi Corporations: Users' Perceptions and Companies Practices*. Ph.D. thesis, Cardiff University, UK.

Al-Razeen, A., and Karbhari, Y. 2004. Interaction between Compulsory and Voluntary Disclosure in Saudi Arabian Corporate Annual Reports. *Managerial Auditing Journal*, **19**(3), 351–360.

Al-Razeen, A., and Karbhari, Y. 2007. An Empirical Investigation into the Importance, Use and Technicality of Saudi Annual Corporate Information. *Advances in International Accounting*, **20**, 55–74.

Al-Shammari, B., Brown, P., and Tarca, A. 2008. An Investigation of Compliance with International Accounting Standards by Listed Companies in the Gulf Co-operation Council Member States. *The International Journal of Accounting*, **43**, 425–447.

Al-Shiab, M. 2003. *Financial Consequences of IAS Adoption: The Case of Jordan*. Ph.D. thesis, University of Newcastle Upon-Tyne, UK.

Alanezi, F., and Albuloushi, S. 2011. Does The Existence of Voluntary Audit Committees Really Affect IFRS- Required Disclosure? The Kuwaiti Evidence. *International Journal of Disclosure and Governance*, **8**(2), 148–173.

Ali, J., Ahmed, K., and Henry, D. 2006. Harmonization of Accounting Measurement Practices in South Asia. *Ad- vances in International Accounting*, **19**, 25–58.

Ali, M. J., Ahmed, K., and Henry, D. 2004. Disclosure Compliance With National Accounting Standards by Listed Companies in South Asia. *Accounting and Business Research*, **34**(3), 183–199.

Allen, D.E. 1983. *Finance: A Theoretical Introduction*. Oxford: Martin Robertson.

Alsaeed, K. 2005. The Association between Firm-Specific Characteristics and Disclosure: The Case of Saudi Arabia. *Journal of American Academy of Business*, **7**(1), 310–321.

Aly, D., Simon, J., and Hussainey, K. 2010. Determinants of Corporate Internet Reporting: Evidence from Egypt. *Managerial Auditing Journal*, **25**(2), 182–202.

Anderson, K.L., Deli, D.N., and Gillan, S.L. 2006. Boards of Directors, Audit Committees, and the Information Content of Earnings. *Working paper. Georgetown University.*

Anderson, M., and Daoud, M. 2005. *Corporate Governance Disclosure by Swedish Listed Corporations*. M.Phil. thesis, Jonkoping University, Sweden.

Arcay, M.R.B., and Vazquez, M.F.M. 2005. Corporate Characteristics, Governance Rules and the Extent of Voluntary Disclosure in Spain. *Advances in Accounting*, **21**, 299–331.

Archambault, J.J., and Archambault, M.E. 2003. A Multinational Test of Determinants of Corporate Disclosure. *The International Journal of Accounting*, **38**(2), 173–194.

Armstrong, S., Barth, E., Jagolinzer, A., and Riedl, E. 2009. Market Reaction to the Adoption of I.F.R.S in Eu- rope. *Working Paper*. Available: http://papers.ssrn.com/sol3/papers.cfm?abstract_id=903429. Accessed: 25/12/2009.

Asfour, B.J. 2004. From "Guidance to Sanctions" - The Role of Market Regulator Enforcing Disclosure. *Second Middle East and North Africa Forum on Corporate Governance Improving Transparency and Disclosure*, Jun. Beirut.

Atrill, P., and Mclaney, E. 2008. *Financial Accounting for Decision Makers*. 5 edn. Essex: Pearson Education Limited. Baker, M.J., and Foy, A. 2008. *Business and Management Research: How to Complete your Research Successfully*. 2 edn. Agryll: Westburn Publishers Ltd.

Ball, R., Robin, A., and Wu, J.S. 2003. Incentives Versus Standards: Properties of Accounting Income in Four East Asian Countries. *Journal of Accounting and Economics*, **36**, 235–270.

Barako, D.G., Hancock, P., and Izan, H.Y. 2006. Factors Influencing Voluntary Corporate Disclosure by Kenyan Companies. *Corporate Governance*, **14**(2), 107–125.

Barrett, M.E. 1976. Financial Reporting Practices: Disclosure and Comprehensiveness in an International Setting. *Journal of Accounting Research*, 10–26. Spring.

Barth, M.E., Landsman, W.R., and Lang, M.H. 2008. International Accounting Standards and Accounting Quality. *Journal of Accounting Research*, **46**(3), 467–498.

Baskerville, R.F. 2003. Hofstede Never Studies Culture. *Accounting, Organisations and Society*, **28**(1), 1–14. Basoglu, B., and Goma, A.

2002. *International Accounting Standards and Selected Middle East Stock Exchanges*. Available: http://www.luc.edu/oLqs/meea/volume4/ BasoqIu/20Revipsded. Accessed: 15/3/2010.

Baysinger, B., and Butler, H. 1985. Corporate Governance and Board of Directors: Performance Effects of Changes in Board Composition. *Journal of Law. Economics and Organization*, 101–124.

Beasley, M.S. 1996. An Empirical Analysis of the Relation between the Board of Directors' Composition and Finan- cial Statement Fraud. *The Accounting Review*, **71**(4), 443–465.

Beattie, V. 2005. Moving the financial accounting research front forward: the UK contribution. British Accounting Review. *Accounting Forum*, **37**(1), 85–114.

Beattie, V., McInnes, B., and Fearnley, S. 2004. A Methodology for Analysing and Evaluating Narratives in Annual Reports: A Comprehensive Descriptive Profile and Metrics for Disclosure Quality Attributes. *Accounting Forum*, **28**, 205–236.

Belkaoui, A., and Kahl, A. 1978. Corporate Financial Disclosure in Canada. *Research monograph of the Canadian Certified General Accountants Association*. Vancouver.

Ben Othman, H., and Zeghal, D. 2008. A Study of Corporate Governance Disclosure and its Country-level Determi- nations in the Emerging Markets. *Research in Accounting in Emerging Economies*, **8**, 125–155.

Ben Othman, H., and Zeghal, D. 2010. Investigating Transparency and Disclosure Determinants at Firm-Level in MENA Emerging Markets. *International Journal of Accounting, Auditing and Performance Evaluation*, **6**(4), 125–155.

Benston, G.J. 1976. Corporate Financial Disclosure In The UK And The USA. *Saxon House*. London.

Bhagat, S., and Black, B. 2000. The Non-correlation between Board Independence and Long Term Firm Performance. *Journal of Corporation Law*, **27**, 231–274.

Bhusan, R., and Lessard, D.R. 1992. Coping With International Accounting Diversity: Fund Managers Views On Disclosure. Reconciliation and Harmonisation. *Journal of International Financial Management and Accounting*, **4**(2), 149–163.

Biondi, Y., Giannoccolo, P., and Reberioux, A. 2009. Financial Disclosure and the Board: Is Independence of Directors Always Effecient? *Forum de La Regulation*, Oct. Paris.

Black, G. 2003. *Students' Guide to Accounting and Financial Reporting Standards*. 9 edn. Harlow: Financial Times Prentice Hall.

Boytsun, A., Deloof, M., and Matthyssens, P. 2011. Social Norms, Social Cohesion, and Corporate Governance. *Corporate Governance: An International Review*, **19**(1), 41–60.

Brickley, J. A., Coles, J.L., and Jarrell, G. 1997. Leadership Structure: Separating the CEO and the Chairman of the Board. *Journal of Corporate Finance*, 189–220.

Bromwich, M. 1992. Financial Reporting Information and Capital Markets. *Pitman Publishing.*

Brown, N., and Deegan, C. 1998. The Public Disclosure of Environmental Performance Information-A Dual Test for Media Agenda Setting Theory and Legitimacy Theory. *Accounting and Business Research*, **29**(1), 21–41.

Brown, P. 2011. International Accounting Standards: What are the Benefits? *Accounting and Business Research*, **41**(3), 269–285.

Brown, P., and Tarca, A. 2005. A Commentary on Issues Relating to the Enforcement of International Financial Reporting Standards in the EU. *European Accounting Review*, **14**(1), 181–212.

Brown, R.Jr. 2007. Corporate Governance, the Securities and Exchange Commission, and the Limits of Disclosure. *Catholic University Law Review*, **57**, 45–92.

Burrell, G., and Morgan, G. 1979. Sociological Paradigms and Organisational Analysis. *Heinemann*. London. Buzby, S.L. 1974. Selected Items of Information and Their Disclosure in Annual Reports. *The Accounting Review*, Jul, 423–435.

Buzby, S.L. 1975. Company Size, Listed Versus Unlisted Stocks, and the Extent of Financial Disclosure. *Journal of Accounting Research*, **13**(1), 16–37.

Byrd, J., and Hickman, K. 1992. Do Outside Directors Monitor Managers? Evidence from Tender Offer Bids. *Journal of Financial Economics*, **32**, 195–207.

Cadbury Committee Report. 1992. *Report of the Cadbury Committee on the Financial Aspects of Corporate Gover- nance*. Tech. rept. Cadbury Committee, Gee. London.

Camfferman, K., and Cooke, T.E. 2002. An Analysis of Disclosure in the Annual Reports of U.K. and Dutch Compa- nies. *Journal of International Accounting Research*, **1**, 3–30.

Carpenter, V.L., and Feroz, E.H. 2001. Institutional Theory and Accounting Rule Choice: an Analysis of Four US State Governments' Decisions to Adopt Generally Accepted Accounting Principles. *Accounting, Organizations and Society*, **26**(7/8), 565–96.

Carruthers, B.G. 1995. Accounting, Ambiguity and the New Institutionalism. *Accounting, Organizations and Society*, **20**(4), 313–328. CASE. 2001. *Fact Book*.

Cerf, R. A. 1961. *Corporate Reporting and Investment Decisions*. Berkley: University of California Press.

Chamisa, E. 2000. The Relevance and Observance of the IASC Standards in Developing Countries and the Particular Case of Zimbabwe. *The International Journal of Accounting*, **35**(2), 267–286.

Chand, P. 2005. Impetus to the Success of Harmonization: The Case of South Pacific Island Nations. *Critical Perspectives on Accounting*, **16**, 209–226.

Chand, P., and Patel, C. 2008. Convergence and Harmonization of Accounting Standards in the South Pacific Region. *Advances in Accounting, Incorporating Advances in International Accounting*, **24**, 83–92.

Chandler, R.A. 1992. The International Harmonization of Accounting. *International Journal of Accounting*, **27**, 222–233.

Chau, G.K., and Gray, S.J. 2002. Ownership Structure and Corporate Voluntary Disclosure in Hong Kong and Singa- pore. *The International Journal of Accounting*, **37**, 247–265.

Chen, C.J.P., and Jaggi, B. 2000. Association Between Independent Non-executive Directors, Family Control and Financial Disclosures in Hong Kong. *Journal of Accounting and Public Policy*, **19**(4), 285–310.

Cheng, E.C.M., and Courtenay, S.M. 2006. Board Composition, Regulatory Regime, and Voluntary Disclosure. *The International Journal of Accounting*, **41**, 262–289.

Choi, F. 1973. Financial Disclosure and Entry to the European Capital Market. *Journal of Accounting Research*, **11**(2), 159–175.

Choi, F.D.S., Frost, C.A., and Meek, G.K. 2002. *International Accounting*. 4 edn. Upper Saddle River: Prentice Hall.

Chow, C.W., and Wong-Boren, A. 1987. Voluntary Financial Disclosure by Mexican Corporation. *The Accounting Review*, **62**(3), 533–541.

CIA World Factbook Egypt. 2008. Available: http://www.bartleby.com/151/eg.html#Background. Accessed: 25/1/2010.

CIA World Factbook Jordan. 2008. Available: https://www.cia.gov/library/publications/the-world-factbook/geos/jo.html. Accessed: 15/2/2010.

CIPE. 2003. *Corporate Governance in Morroco, Egypt, Lebanon and Jordan- Countries of the MENA Region*. Middle East and North Africa Corporate Governance Workshop. The Center for International Private Enterprise.

CMA. 2003. *Economic Bulletin Stock Exchange*. Tech. rept. Capital Market Authority Information Center, Cairo. In Arabic.

Cochran, P.L., and Wartick, S.L. 1988. *Corporate Governance-A Review of the Literature, in International Corporate Governance: Text, Readings and Cases*. 1 edn. Singapore: Prentice-Hall.

Collis, J., and Hussey, R. 2003. *Business Research: A Practical Guide for Undergraduate and Postgraduate Students*. 2 edn. Basingstoke: Palgrave Macmillan.

Cooke, T. 1989a. Disclosure in the Corporate Annual Reports of Swedish Companies. *Accounting and Business Research*, **19**(74), 113–124.

—. 1991. An Assessment of Voluntary Disclosure in Annual Reports of Japanese Corporations. *International Journal of Accounting*, **26**(3), 174–189.

—. 1992. The Impact of Size, Stock Market Listing and Industry Type on Disclosure in the Annual Reports of Japanese Listed Corporations. *Accounting and Business Research*, **22**(87), 229–237.

Cooke, T., and Wallace, R. 1989. Global Surveys of Corporate Disclosure Practices and Audit Firms: A Review Essay. *Accounting and Business research*, 47–57. Winter.

Cooke, T.E. 1989b. Voluntary Corporate Disclosure by Swedish Companies. *Journal of International Financial Management and Accounting*, **1**(2), 171–195.

—. 1993. Disclosure in Japanese Corporate Annual Reports. *Journal of Busincss Finance and Accounting*, **20**(4), 521–535.

—. 1998. Regression Analysis in Accounting Disclosure Studies. *Journal of Accounting and Business Research*, **28**(3), 209–224. Summer.

Cooper, K., and Keim, G.D. 1983. The Economic Rationale for the Nature and Extent of Corporate Financial Disclo- sure Regulation: A Critical Assessment. *Journal of Accounting and Public Policy*, **2**, 189–205.

Cotter, J., Shivdasani, A., and Zenner, M. 1997. Do Independent Directors Enhance Target Shareholder Wealth During Tender Offers? *Journal of Financial Economics*, **43**, 195–218.

Craig, R., and Diga, J. 1998. Corporate Accounting Disclosure in ASEAN. *Journal of International Financial Management and Accounting*, **9**(3), 246–274.

Craswell, A.T., and Taylor, S.L. 1992. Disclosure of Reserves by Oil and Gas Companies: An Economic Analysis. *Journal of Business Finance and Accounting*, **19**(2), 295–308.

Creswell, J.W. 2003. *Research Design: Qualitative, Quantitative, and Mixed Methods Approaches*. Thousand Oak: Sage.

Crotty, M. 2007. *The Foundations of Social Research: Meaning and perspective in the research process*. London: Sage Publications Ltd.

Dahawy, K. 2007. Developing Nations and Corporate Governance. The Story of Egypt. *Working Paper.*

—. 2009. Company Characteristics and Disclosure Level: The Case of Egypt. *International Research Journal of Finance and Economics*, **34**, 194–208.

Dahawy, K., and Conover, T. 2007. Accounting Disclosure in Companies Listed on the Egyptian Stock Exchange. *Middle Eastern Finance and Economics*, **1**, 5–20.

Dahawy, K., and Samaha, K. 2010. An Investigation of the Views and Perceptions of External Users of Corporate Annual Reports in Emerging Economies: the Case of Egypt. *International Journal of Accounting and Finance*, **2**(3/4), 331–367.

Dahya, J., and Travlos, N.G. 2000. Does the One Man Show Pay? Theory and Evidence on the Dual CEO Revisited. *European Financial Management*, **6**, 85–98.

Dahya, J., Lonie, A.A., and Power, D.M. 1996. The Case for Separating the Roles of Chairman and CEO: An Analysis of Stock Market and Accounting Data. *Corporate Governance - An International Review*, **4**(1), 71–77.

Daily, C.M., Dalton, D.R., and Cannella, Jr.A. 2003. Corporate Governance: Decades of Dialogue and Data. *The Academy of Management Review*, **28**(3), 371–382.

Darrough, M.N. 1993. Disclosure Policy and Competition: Cournot vs. Bertrand. *The Accounting Review*, **68**(3), 534–561.

Daske, H., Hail, L., Leuz, C., and Verdi, R. 2008. Mandatory IFRS Reporting around the World: Early Evidence on the Economic Consequences. *Journal of Accounting*, **46**(Dec), 1058–1142.

Debreceny, R., Gray, G.L., and Rahman, A. 2002. The Detenninants of Internet Financial Reporting. *Journal of Accounting and Public Policy*, **21**(4/5), 371–394.

Del Guercio, D., Dann, L.Y., and Partch, M.M. 2003. Governance and Boards of Directors in Closed-end Investment Companies. *Journal of Financial Economics*, **69**(1), 111–152.

Demb, A., and Neubauer, F.F. 1992. *The Corporate Board: Confronting the Paradoxes*. Oxford: University Press.

Denis, Diane, and McConnell, John. 2003. International Corporate Governance. *Working paper. European Corporate Governance Institute.*

Denis, D.K. 2001. Twenty-five Years of Corporate Governance Research… and Counting. *Review of Financial Economics*, **10**, 191–212.

Depoers, F. 2000. A Cost-Benefit Study of Voluntary Disclosure: Some Empirical Evidence from French Listed Companies. *The European Accounting Review*, **9**(2), 245–263.

Desoky, A. 2009. Company Characteristics as Determinants of Internet Financial Reporting in Emerging Markets: The Case of Egypt. *Research in Accounting in Emerging Economies*, **9**, 31–71.

Dey, A. 2008. Corporate Governance and Agency Conflicts. *Journal of Accounting Research*, **46**(5), 1143–1181.

Diamond, D.W., and Verrecchia, R.E. 1991. Disclosure, Liquidity and the Cost of Capital. *The Journal of Finance*, **46**(4), 1325–1359.

DiMaggio, P.J., and Powell, W.W. 1983. Institutional Isomorphism and Collective Rationality in Organizational Fields. *American Sociological Review*, **48**(2), 147–160.

Donaldson, L., and Davis, J.H. 1991. Stewardship Theory or Agency Theory: CEO Governance and Shareholder Returns. *Australian Journal of Management*, **16**(1), 49–63.

Dumontier, P., and Raffournier, B. 1998. Why Firms Comply Voluntarily With IAS: An Empirical Analysis With Swiss Data. *Journal of International Financial Management and Accounting*, **9**(3), 216–245.

Easterby-Smith, Mark, Thorpe, Richard, and Lowe, Andy. 1993. *Management Research: An Introduction*. 4 edn. London: Sage Publications.

EIoD. 2006. *Egyptian Institute of Directors*. Available: http://www.cipe.org/programs/corp_gov/pdf/EIODCASEStudy.pdf. Accessed: 25/1/2010.

Eisenhardt, K. 1989. Making Fast Strategic Decisions in High-Velocity Environments. *Academy of Management Journal*, **32**(3), 543–576.

El-Gazzar, S.M., Finn, P.M., and Jacob, R. 1999. An Empirical Investigation of Multinational Firms' Compliance with International Accounting Standards. *The International Journal of Accounting*, **34**(2), 239–248.

Ellabbar, K. 2007. *Capital Market and Accounting Disclosure in Emerging Economies: The Case of Libya*. Ph.D. thesis, University of Salford, UK.

Elsayed, K. 2010. A Multi-theory Perspective of Board Leadership Structure: What Does the Egyptian Corporate Governance Context Tell Us? *British Journal of Management*, **21**(1), 80–99.

Elsayed, M., and Hoque, Z. 2010. Perceived International Environmental Factors and Corporate Voluntary Disclosure Practices: An Empirical Study. *The British Accounting Review*, **42**, 17–35.

Emenyonu, E.N.O. 1993. *International Accounting Harmonization in Developed Stock Market Countries: An Em- pirical Comparative Study of Measurement and Associated Disclosure Practices in France, Germany, Japan, United Kingdom and the United States of America*. Ph.D thesis, University of Glasgow, UK.

Eng, L.L., and Mak, Y.T. 2003. Corporate Governance and Voluntary Disclosure. *Journal of Accounting and Public Policy*, **22**(4), 325–345.

Ezat, A., and El-Masry, A. 2008. The Impact of Corporate Governance on the Timeliness of Corporate Internet Reporting by Egyptian Listed Companies. *Managerial Finance*, **34**(12), 848–867.

Fama, E.F., and Jensen, M.C. 1983. Separation of Ownership and Control. *Journal of Law and Economics*, **88**, 301–325.

Felo, A.J. 2009. Voluntary Disclosure Transparency, Board Independence and Expertise, and CEO Duality. *Working Paper*.

Fencher, H.H.E., and Kilgore, A. 1994. The Influence of Cultural Factors on Accounting Practice. *The International Journal of Accounting*, **29**, 265–277.

Field, A. 2005. *Discovering Statistics Using SPSS*. 2 edn. London: Sage Publications.

Fields, T.D., Lys, T.Z., and Vincent, L. 2001. Empirical Research on Accounting Choice. *Journal of Accounting and Economics*, **31**, 255–307.

Finkelstein, S., and D'Aveni, R.A. 1994. CEO Duality As A Double-edged Sword: How Boards of Directors Balance Entrenchment Avoidance and Unity of Command. *Academy of Management Journal*, **37**(5), 1079–1108.

Firth, M. 1979. The Impact of Size, Stock Market Listing, and Auditors on Voluntary Disclosure in Corporate Annual Reports. *Accounting and Business Research*, **9**(36), 273–280. Autumn.

—. 1980. Raising Finance and Firms' Corporate Reporting Policies. *Abacus*, **16**(2), 100–115.

Fofack, H. 2009. Poverty Reduction and Economic Mnagement Division. *Working Paper, The world Bank Institute*, Aug.

Forker, J. 1992. Corporate Governance and Disclosure Quality. *Accounting and Business Research*, **22**(86), 111–124. Foster. 1986. *Financial Statements Analysis*. New Jersey: Prentice Hall.

GAFI. 2007. *Egyptian Code of Corporate Governance*. Tech. rept. General Authority for Investment and Free Zones. Available:

http://www.ecgi.org/codes/documents/egyptiancodeofcorporategovernance_en.pdf. Accessed: 25/2/2010.

Gelb, D. 2000. Managerial Ownership and Accounting Disclosures: An Empirical Study. *Review of Quantitative Finance and Accounting*, **150**, 169–185.

Gernon, H., and Wallace, R.S.O. 1995. International Accounting Research: A review of its Ecology, Contending Theories and Methodologies. *Journal of Accounting Literature*, **14**, 54–106.

Ghazali, N.A.M. 2004. *Exploring Theoretical Explanations of Voluntary Disclosure by Quantitative and Qualitative Investigations: Evidence from Malaysia*. Ph.D. thesis, University of Strathclyde, UK.

Ghazali, N.A.M., and Weetman, P. 2006. Perpetuating Traditional Influences: Voluntary Disclosure in Malaysia Following the Economic Crisis. *Journal of International Accounting, Auditing and Taxation*, **15**, 226–248.

Ghosh, S. 2006. Do Board Characteristics Affect Corporate Performance? Firm-level Evidence for India. *Applied Economic Letters*, **13**(7), 435–443.

Gibbins, M., Richardson, A., and Waterhouse, J. 1990. The Management of Corporate Financial Disclosure: Oppor- tunism, Ritualism, Policies and Processes. *Journal of Accounting Research*, **28**(1), 121–143. Spring.

Gill, J., and Johnson, P. 1997. *Research Methods for Managers*. London: Paul Chapman Publishing.

Glaum, M., and Street, D.L. 2003. Compliance with the Disclosure Requirements of Germany's New Market: IAS versus US GAAP. *Journal of International Financial Management and Accounting*, **14**(1), 64–100.

Gray, R., Kouhy, R., and Lavers, S. 1995. Methodological Themes - Construction Research Database of Social and Environmental Reporting by UK Companies. *Accounting Auditing and Accountability Journal*, **8**(2), 78–101.

Gray, S.J. 1988. Towards a Theory of Cultural Influence on the Development of Accounting Systems Internationally. *Abacus*, **24**(1), 1–15.

Gray, S.J., and Roberts, C.B. 1998. *Voluntary Information Disclosure and the British Multinationals: Corporate Perceptions of Costs and Benefits*. New York: Prentice-Hall. International Pressures for Accounting Change.

Gray, S.J., and Vint, H.M. 1995. The Impact of Culture on Accounting Disclosures: Some International Evidence. *Asia-Pacific Journal of Accounting*, Dec, 33–43.

Gray, S.J., Campbell, L.G., and Shaw, J.C. 1984a. *A Comparative International Survey of Accounting Requirements and Practices in Financial Reporting in 30 Countries*. London: Macmillan.

Gul, F.A., and Leung, S. 2004. Board Leadership, Outside Directors Expertise and Voluntary Corporate Disclosures. *Journal of Accounting and Public Policy*, **23**, 351–379.

Haddad, E. 2005. *The Impact of Voluntary Disclosure Level on the Cost of Equity Capital in an Emerging Capital Market: The Case of Amman Stock Exchange*. Ph.D. thesis, University of East Anglia, UK.

Hail, L. 2002. The Impact of Voluntary Corporate Disclosures on the Ex-Ante Cost of Capital for Swiss Firms. *The European Accounting Review*, **11**(4), 741–773.

Hail, L., Leuz, C., and Wysocki, P. 2010. Global Accounting Convergence and the Potential Adoption of IFRS by the U.S. (Part I): Conceptual Underpinnings and Economic Analysis. *Accounting Horizons*, **24**(3), 355–394.

Haniffa, R.M. 1999. *Culture, Corporate Governance and Disclosure in Malaysian Corporations*. Ph.D. thesis, University of Exeter, UK.

Haniffa, R.M., and Cooke, T.E. 2002. Culture, Corporate Governance and Disclosure in Malaysian Corporations. *Abacus*, **38**(3), 317–349.

Hassaan, M. 2007. *Analytical Study of the Egyptian Accounting Standards in the Light of the Characteristics of Build, Operate and Transfer Contracts*. M.Phil. thesis, Mansoura Faculty of Commerce, Egypt.

HassabElnaby, H.R., and Mosebach, M. 2005. Culture's Consequences in Controlling Agency Costs: Egyptian Evi- dence. *Journal of International Accounting, Auditing and Taxation*, **14**(1), 19–32.

HassabElnaby, H.R., Epps, R.W., and Said, A.A. 2003. The Impact of Environmental Factors on Accounting Devel- opment: An Egyptian Longitudinal Study. *Critical Perspectives on Accounting*, **14**(3), 273–292.

Hassan, M.K. 2008. The Development of Accounting Regulations in Egypt: Legitimating the International Accounting Standards. *Managerial Auditing Journal*, **23**(5), 467–484.

Hassan, O.A.G. 2006. *The Economic Consequences of Increased Disclosure in the Egyptian Emerging Capital Mar- ket*. Ph.D. thesis, University of Abertay Dundee, UK.

Hassan, O.A.G., Giorgioni, G., and Romilly, P. 2009. The Extent of Financial Disclosure and its Determinants in an Emerging Capital

Market: the Case of Egypt. *International Journal of Accounting, Auditing and Performance Evaluation*, **3**(1), 41–67.

Healy, P.M., and Palepu, G. 2001. Information Asymmetry Corporate Disclosure, and the Capital Markets: A Review of the Empirical Disclosure Literature. *Journal of Accounting and Economics*, **31**, 405–440.

Hendriksen, E., and Van-Breda, M.F. 1992. *Accounting Theory*. 5 edn. Boston: Irwin Inc.

Ho, S.S.M., and Wong, K.S. 2001. A study of the Relationship between Corporate Governance Structures and the Extent of Voluntary Disclosure. *Journal of International Accounting, Auditing and Taxation*, **10**, 139–156.

Hofstede, G. 1980. *Culture's Consequences: International Differences in Work-Related Values*. Newbury Park, CA: Sage.

Hope, O.K. 2003. Disclosure Practices, Enforcement of Accounting Standards, and Analysts' Forecast Accuracy: An International Study. *Journal of Accounting Research*, **41**(2), 235–272.

Hopper, T., and Powell, A. 1985. Making Sense of Research in to the Organisational and Social Aspects of Manage- ment Accounting. *Journal of Management Studies*, **22**(5), 429–465.

Hossain, M., Tan, L.M., and Adams, M.C. 1994. Voluntary Disclosure in an Emerging Capital Market: Some Em- pirical Evidence from Companies Listed in the Kuala Lumpur Stock Exchange. *The International Journal of Accounting*, **29**, 334–351.

Hossain, M., Perera, M.H.B., and Rahman, A.R. 1995. Voluntary Financial Disclosure in the Annual Reports of New Zealand Companies. *Journal of International Financial Management and Accounting*, **6**(1), 69–85.

Hussain, M.E. 1996. A Comparative Study of Cultural Influences on Financial Reporting in the US and Netherlands. *International Journal of Accounting*, **31**(1), 95–120.

Hussey, J., and Hussey, R. 1997. *Business Research: A practical guide for Undergraduate and Postgraduate Students*. Basingstoke: Macmillan.

Huther, J. 1997. An Empirical Test of the Effect of Board Size on Firm Efficiency. *Economics Letters*, **54**, 259–264. IASB. 2008. *International Accounting Standards and SIC interpretations*. London: IASC.

IFC and Hawkamah. 2008. *A Corporate Governance Survey of Listed Companies and Banks Across the Middle East and North Africa*. Tech. rept. Available: http://www.ifc.org. Accessed 25/2/2010.

IMF. 2007 (Dec). *Arab Republic of Egypt: 2007 Artical IV Consultation-Staff Report; Staff Statment; Public Informa- tion Notice on the Executive Board Discussion; and Statment by the Executive Director for the Arab Republic of Egypt*. Tech. rept. 380. Internationl Monetary Fund.

Inchausti, B. 1997. The Influence of Company Characteristics and Accounting Regulation on Information Disclosed by Spanish Firms. *European Accounting Review*, **6**(1), 45–68.

Ismail, T.H., Shehata, N.F., and Dahawy, K. 2010. Firm Characteristics Determinants and Disclosure Level in Emerg- ing Market of Egypt' in Ismail, T. (2010). *Perspective in Accounting Practices: Corporate Disclosure, Perfor- mance, Governance and Risk Management*.

Jaggi, B., and Low, P. Y. 2000. Impact of Culture, Market Forces, and Legal System on Financial Disclosures. *The International Journal of Accounting*, **35**(4), 495–519.

Jamal, Karim et al. 2010. A Research-based Perspective on the SEC's Proposed Role-Roadmap for the Potential Role of Financial Statements Prepared in Accordance with International Financial Reporting Standards (IFRS) by U.S. Issuers. *Accounting Horizons*, **24**(1), 139–147.

Jensen, M. C., and Meckling, W. H. 1976. Theory of the firm: Managerial Behaviour, Agency Costs and Ownership Structure. *Journal of Financial Economics*, **3**, 305–360.

Jensen, M.C. 1993. The Modern Industrial Revolution, Exit, and the Failure of Internal Control Systems. *The Journal of Finance*, **48**, 831–880.

John, K., and Senbet, L.W. 1998. Corporate Governance and Board Effectiveness. *Journal of Banking and Finance*, **22**, 371–404.

Johnson, J.L., Daily, C.M., and Ellstrand, A.E. 1996. Board of Directors: A Review and Research Agenda. *Journal of Management*, 409–438.

Joshi, P.L., Bresmer, W.G., and Al-Ajmi, J. 2008. Perceptions of Accounting Professionals in the Adoption and Implementation of a Single Set of Global Accounting Standards: Evidence from Bahrain. *Advances in Accounting Incorporating Advances in International Accounting*, **24**, 41–48.

Kanaan, T., and Kardoosh, M. 2002 (Oct).*The Story of Economic Growth in Jordan: 1950-2000*. Available: http://cloud2.gdnet.org/cms.php?id=research_paper_abstract&research_paper_id=10466. Accessed: 12/3/2010.

Kapaya, G. 2000. International Accounting Standards and Accounting in Developing/Emerging Nations-How About Fresh Start? *Discussion Paper Series: Accounting and Finance*, Sep.

Kasznik, R., and Lev, B. 1995. To Warn or Not to Warn: Management Disclosures in the Face of an Earnings Surprise. *The Accounting Review*, **70**, 113–134.

Kelly, L. 1983. The Development of a Positive Theory of Corporate Management's Role in External Financial Re- porting. *Journal of Accounting Literature*, 111–150. Spring.

Kelton, A.S., and Yang, Y. 2008. The Impact of Corporate Governance on Internet Financial Reporting. *Journal of Accounting and Public Policy*, **27**(1), 62–87.

Khan, Md. H.U.Z. 2010. The Effect of Corporate Governance Elements on Corporate Social Responsibility (CSR) Reporting. Empirical Evidence from Private Commercial Banks of Bangladesh. *International Journal of Law and Management*, 82–109.

Klein, A. 2002. Audit Committee, Board of Director Characteristics, and Earnings Management. *Journal of Accounting and Economics*, **33**, 375–400.

Koh, T.N. 1994. Principles, Practice and Prospects of Corporate Governance: The Malaysian Legal Framework. *The Malaysian Accountant*, Oct, 23–30.

Kvale, S. 1996. *Interviews: An Introduction to Qualitative Research Interviewing*. Thousand Oaks: Sage Publications.

Lakhal, F. 2003. *Earning Voluntary Disclosures and Corporate Governance: Evidence from France*. Available: http://papers.ssrn.com/sol3/papers.cfm? abstract_id=500283.

Land, J., and Lang, M.H. 2002. Empirical evidence on the evolution of international earnings. *The Accounting Review*, **77**(suppl.), 115–133.

Landau, S., and Everitt, B.S. 2004. *A Handbook of Statistical Analysis Using SPSS*. Boca Raton: Chapman & Hall/CRC Press LLC.

Lang, M., and Lundholm, R. 1993. Cross-Sectional Determinants of Analyst Ratings of Corporate Disclosure. *Journal of Accounting Research*, **51**(1), 246–271. Autumn.

Larson, R.K. 1993. International Accounting Standards and Economic Growth: an Empirical Investigation of their Relationship in Africa. *Research in Third World Accounting*, **2**, 27–43.

Laskawy, P. 2009. *Generally Accepted Accounting Practices Under International Financial Reporting Standards*. West Sussex: John Wiley & Sons Ltd.

Lavers, S. 1993. *An Empirical Investigation of UK Social and Environmental Disclosure: A Political Economy Per- spective and Analysis*. M.Phil. thesis, University of Dundee, UK.

Leventis, S., and Weetman, P. 2004. Voluntary Disclosures in an Emerging Capital Market: Some Evidence from the Athens Stock Exchange. *Advances in International Accounting*, **17**, 227–250.

Levitt, A. 1998. The Importance of High Quality Accounting Standards. *Accounting Horizons*, **12**(1), 79–82.

Li, J., and Harrison, R. 2008. Corporate Governance and National Cluture: A Multi-contury Study. *Corporate Governance*, **8**(5), 607–621.

Licht, Amir. 2001. The Mother of All Path Dependencies Towards a cross Cultural Theory of Corporate Governance Systems. *Delaware Journal of Corporate Law*, **26**(1), 147–205. Available: http//:www.ssrn.com. Accessed: 25/3/2010.

Maassen, G. 2002. *An International Comparison of Corporate Governance Models- A Study on the Formal Indepen- dence and Convergence of One-tier and Two-tier Corporate Boards of Directors in the United States of America, the United Kingdom and the Netherlands*. 3 edn. PhD Series in General Management. Netherlands: Rotterdam School of Management.

Macdonald, N., and Beattie, A. 1993. The Corporate Governance Jigsaw. *Accounting and Business Research*, **23**(91A), 304–310.

Mallin, C.A. 2009. *Corporate Governance*. 3 edn. New York: Oxford University Press.

Malone, D., Fries, C., and Jones, T. 1993. An Empirical Investigation of the Extent of Corporate Financial Disclosure in the Oil and Gas Industry. *Journal of Accounting, Auditing and Finance*, **8**(3), 249–273.

Mangel, R., and Singh, H. 1993. Ownership Structure, Board Relationships and CEO Compensation in Large US Corporations. *Accounting and Business Research*, **23**(91A).

Marston, C., and Shrives, P. 1996. A Review of Empirical Research into Financial Disclosure. *IAAER International Accounting Research Conference*.

Marston, C.L., and Polei, A. 2004. Corporate Reporting on the Internet by German Companies. *International Journal of Accounting Information Systems*, **5**(3), 285–311.

Marston, C.L., and Shrives, P.J. 1991. The Use of Disclosure Indices in Accounting Research: A Review Article. *British Accounting Review*, **23**, 195–210.

Mavrommati, K. 2008. *A Contribution to the Study of Corporate Governance in the Context of the Greek Legal Order*. Ph.D. thesis, University of Warwick.

McColgan. 2004. *Corporate Governance in the UK Post-Cadbury*. Ph.D. thesis, University of Strathclyde, UK.

McKinnon, J., and Dalimunthe, L. 1993. Voluntary Disclosure of Segment Information by Australian Diversified Companies. *Accounting and Finance*, **33**(1), 33–50.

McNally, G., Eng, L., and Hasseldine, C. 1982. Corporate Financial Reporting in New Zealand: An Analysis of Users Preferences, Corporate Characteristics and Disclosure Practices for Discretionary Information. *Accounting and Business Research*, **13**(49), 11–20. Winter.

Meek, G. K., Roberts, C. B., and Gray, S. J. 1995. Factors Influencing Voluntary Annual Report Disclosures by U. S., UK. and Continental European Multinational Corporations. *Journal of International Business Studies*, **26**(3), 555–572.

Mensah, S. 2002 (Dec). Corporate Governance in Ghana: Issues and Challenges. In: *African Capital Markets Con- ference*.

Miles, M.B., and Huberman, A.M. 1994. *Qualitative Data Analysis*. 2 edn. Sage Publications. Ministry of Foreign Trade. 2002. Monthly Economic Digest. Aug. in Arabic.

Mir, M.Z., Chatterje, B., and Rahman, A.S. 2009. Culture and Corporate Voluntary Reporting. *Mangerial Auditing Journal*, **24**(7), 639–667.

MOEFT. 2000. Monthly Economic Digest. *Ministry of Economy and Foreign Trade*, Dec. in Arabic.

Momany, M.T., and Al-Shorman, S.A.D. 2006. Web-based Voluntary Financial Reporting of Jordanian Companies. *International Review of Business Research Papers*, **2**, 127–39.

Morris, R.D. 1987. Signalling, Agency Theory and Accounting Policy Choice. *Accounting and Business Research*, **18**(69), 47–56.

Mueller, G.G. 1967. *International accounting*. New York: Macmillan & Co.

Mueller, G.G., Gernon, H., and Meek, G.K. 1987. *Accounting: An International Perspective*. Illinois: Homewood.

Muslu, V. 2005. Effect of Board Independence on Incentive Compensation and Compensation Disclosure: Evidence from Europe. *Working Paper*. Available: http://www.ssrn.com. Accessed:23/9/2009.

Muth, M.M., and Donaldson, L. 1998. Stewardship Theory and Board Structure: a Contingency Approach. *Corporate Governance: an International Review*, **6**(1), 5–28.

Naser, K. 1998. Comprehensiveness of Disclosure of Non-Financial Companies Listed on the Amman Financial Market. *International Journal of Commerce and Management*, **8**(1), 88–119.

Naser, K., Al-Khatib, K., and Karbhari, Y. 2002. Empirical Evidence on the Depth of Corporate Information Disclosure in Developing Countries: The Case of Jordan. *International Journal of Commerce and Management*, **12**, 122–155.

Naser, K., Al-Hussaini, A., Al-Kwari, D., and Nuseibeh, R. 2006. Determinants of Extent of Corporate Social Dis- closure in Developing Countries: The Case of Qatar. *Advances in International Accounting*, **19**(1–23).

Neuman, W. L. 2006. *Social Research Methods: Qualitative and Quantitative Approaches*. 6 edn. Boston: Pearson International Edition.

Ngangan, K., Saudagaran, S.M., and Clarke, F.L. 2005. Cultural Influences on Indigenous Users' Perceptions of the Importance of Disclosure Items: Empirical Evidence from Papua New Guinea. *Advances in International Accounting*, **18**, 27–51.

Nobes, C. 2006. The Survival of International Differences under IFRSs: Towards a Research Agenda. *Accounting and Business Research*, **36**(3), 233–245.

Nobes, C.W. 1991. *Harmonization of Financial Reporting in Comparative International Accounting*. London: Prentice-Hall.

Nobes, C.W., and Parker, R.H. 2004. *Comparative International Accounting*. 8 edn. London: Prentice-Hall. Norusis. 1993. *SPSS for Windows: Base System User's Guide, Release 6.0*. SPSS Inc.

OECD. 2004. *OECD Principles of Corporate Governance, OECD Publications*. Paris: Organization for Economic Cooperation and Development.

Okcabol, F., and Tinker, T. 1993. Dismantling Financial Disclosure Regulations: Testing the Stigler-Benston Hypoth- esis. *Accounting, Auditing and Accountability Journal*, **6**(1), 10–38.

Oman, C.P. 2001. *Corporate Governance and National Development*. Paris: Development Centre Technical Papers, OECD.

Omar, B.F.A. 2007. *Exploring the Aggregate, Mandatory and Voluntary Financial Disclosure Behaviour Under a New Regulatory Environment: The Case of Jordan*. Ph.D. thesis, The University of Hull, UK.

Oppenheim, A.N. 1992. *Questionnaire Design, Interviewing and Attitude Measurement*. Pinter Publishers.

Owusu-Ansah, S. 1998a. *The Adequacy of Corporate Mandatory Disclosure Practices on Emerging Markets: A Case Study of the Zimbabwe Stock Exchange*. Ph.D. thesis, Middlesex University, UK.

Owusu-Ansah, S. 1998b. The impact of Corporate Attributes on the Extent of Mandatory Disclosure and Reporting by Listed Companies in Zimbabwe. *The International Journal of Accounting*, **33**(5), 605–631.

Owusu-Ansah, S., and Yeoh, J. 2005. The Effect of Legislation on Corporate Disclosure Practices. *Abacus*, **41**(1), 92–109.

Pallant, J. 2001. *SPSS Survival Manual: A Step by Step Guide to Data Analysis Using SPSS*. 1 edn. Buckingham: Open University Press.

Patton, J., and Zelenka, I. 1997. An Empirical Analysis of the Determinants of the Extent of Disclosure in Annual Reports of Joint Stock Companies in the Czech Republic. *The European Accounting Review*, **6**(4), 605–626.

Pearce, J.A., and Zahra, S.A. 1991. The Relative Power of CEO and Board of Directors: Associations With Corporate Performance. *Strategic Management Journal*, **12**(2).

Pearce, J.A., and Zahra, S.A. 1992. Board Composition from a Strategic Contingency Perspective. *Journal of Man- agement Studies*, **29**(4), 411–438.

Peasnell, K. 1993. Accounting in Developing Countries; the Search for Appropriate Technologies. *Research in Third World Accounting*, **2**, 1–16.

Perera, H. 1994. Culture and International Accounting: Some Thoughts on Research Issues and Prospects. *Advances in International Accounting*, **7**, 265–283.

Perera, M.H.B. 1989. Towards a Framework to Analyse the Impact of Culture Upon Accounting. *International Journal of Accounting, Education and Research*, **24**(1), 42–56.

Perera, M.H.B., and Mathews, M.R. 1990. The Cultural Relativity of Accounting and International Patterns of Social Accounting. *Advances in International Accounting*, **3**, 215–251.

Pettigrew, A., and McNulty, T. 1995. Power and Influence in and Around the Boardroom. *Human Relations*, **48**(8), 845–873.

Pratt, J., and Beaulieu, P. 1992. Organisational Culture in Public Accounting: Size, Technology, Rank and Functional Area. *Accounting, Organisation and Society*, **17**, 667–684.

Punch, K. F. 1998. *Introduction to Social Research - Quantitative & Qualitative Approaches*. London: Sage Publica- tions.

Qu, Wen, and Leung, Philomena. 2006. Cultural Impact on Chineese Corporate Disclosure- a Corporate Governance Perspective. *Mangerial Auditing Journal*, **21**(3), 241–264.

Raffournier, B. 1995. The Determinants of Voluntary Financial Disclosure by Swiss Listed Companies. *The European Accounting Review*, **4**(2), 261–280.

Rechner, P.L., and Dalton, D.R. 1991. CEO Duality and Organisational Performance: A Longitudinal Analysis. *Strategic Management Journal*, **12**, 155–160.

Robson, C. 1993. *Real World Research: a Resource for Social Scientists and Pracctitioner Researchers*. Oxford: Blackwell.

Rodrigues, L.L., and Craig, R. 2007. Assessing International Accounting Harmonization Using Hegelian Dialectic, Isomorphism and Foucault. *Critical Perspectives on Accounting*, **18**(6), 739–757.

ROSC. 2001. Report on the Observance of Standards and Codes (ROSC). Corporate Governance Country Assessment: Arab Republic of Egypt. *World Bank*, Sep.

— . 2002. Report on the Observance of Standards and Codes. Corporate Governance Country Assessment: Arab Republic of Egypt. *World Bank*, Aug.

—. 2004. Report on the Observance of Standards and Codes (ROSC). Corporate Governance Country Assessment: Arab Republic of Egypt. *World Bank*, Sep.

—. 2005. Report on the Observance of Standards and Codes (ROSC). Corporate Governance Country Assessment: Hashemite Kingdom of Jordan. *World Bank*, Feb.

—. 2009. Report on the Observance of Standards and Codes (ROSC). Corporate Governance Country Assessment: Arab Republic of Egypt. *World Bank*, Jun.

Ross, S.A. 1979. *Disclosure Regulation in the Financial Markets: Implications of Modern Finance Theory and Signalling Theory*. New York: McGraw Hill. in Edwards, F.R. (Ed.) Issues in Financial Regulation: Regulation of American Business and Industry.

Rubin, H., and Rubin, I. 1995. *Qualitative Interviewing: The Art of Hearing Data*. Thousand Oaks: Sage.

Samaha, K. 2006. *Compliance with International Accounting Standards: Some Empirical Evidence from the Cairo & Alexandria Sock Exchange*. Accounting, Management and Insurance Review, Cairo University Press.

—. 2010. Do Board Independence and Audit Committees Motivate Disclosure on Different Corporate Governance Information Categories in the Annual Reports in Developing Countries? *International Research Journal of Finance and Economics*, 206–225.

Samaha, K., and Dahawy, K. 2010. Factors Influencing Corporate Disclosure Transparency in the Active Share Trading Firms: An Explanatory Study. *Research in Accounting in Emerging Economies*, **10**, 87–118.

Samaha, K., and Dahawy, K. 2011. An Empirical Analysis of Corporate Governance Structures and Voluntary Cor- porate Disclosure in Volatile Capital Markets: The Egyptian Experience. *International Journal of Accounting, Auditing and Performance Evaluation*, **7**(1/2), 61–93.

Samaha, K., and Stapleton, P. 2008. Compliance with International Accounting Standards in a National Context: Some Empirical Evidence from the Cairo and Alexandria Stock Exchanges. *Afro-Asian Journal of Finance and Accounting*, **1**(1), 40–66.

Samaha, K., and Stapleton, P. 2009. Firm-specific Determinants of the Extent of Compliance with Internatonal Ac- counting Standards in the Corporate Annual Reports of Companies Listed on the Egyptian Stock Exchange: A Positive Accounting Approach. *Afro-Asian Journal of Finance and Accounting*, **1**(3), 266–294.

Sarantakos, S. 2005. *Social Research*. Basingsstoke: Palgrave Macmillan.

Saudagaran, S. M. 2004. *International accounting: A user perspective*. South-Western, Ohio: Thomson.

Saudagaran, S.M., and Meek, G.K. 1997. A review of Research on the Relationship Between International Capital Markets and Financial Reporting by Multinational Firms. *Journal of Accounting Literature*, **16**, 127–159.

Saunders, M., Lewis, P., and Thornhill, A. 2003. *Research Methods for Business Students*. London: Prentice Hall. Schadewitz, H.J., and Blevins, D.R. 1998. Major Determinants of Interim Disclosures in an Emerging Market. *American Business Review*, **16**(1), 41–55.

Schipper, K. 1981. Discussion of Voluntary Corporate Disclosure: the Case of Interim Reporting. *Journal of Account- ing Research*, **1**(Supplement), 85–88.

Scott, W. R. 1995. *Institutions and organizations*. London: Sage Publications.

—. 2003. *Financial Accounting Theory*. 3 edn. Toronto: Pearson Education Canada Inc.

Sekaran, U. 1992. *Research Methods for Business: A Skill-Building Approach*. New York: John Willey & Sons Inc. Seligman, J. 1983. The

Historical Need for a Mandatory Corporate Disclosure System. *Journal of Corporation Law*, **9**. Fall.

Shanikat, M., and Abbadi, S. 2011. Assessment of Corporate Governance in Jordan: An Empirical Study. *Australasian Accounting Business and Finance Journal*, **5**(3), 93–106.

Sharar, Z. 2007. *A Comparative Analysis of the Corporate Governance Legislative Frameworks in Australia and Jordan Measured Against the OECD Principles of Corporate Governance 2004 as an International Benchmark*. Ph.D. thesis, School of Law. Bond University, Australia.

Shleifer, A., and Vishny, R. 1997. A Survey of Corporate Governance. *Journal of Finance*, **52**(2), 737–783.

Singh, M., Mathur, I., and Gleason, K.C. 2004. Governance and Performance Implications of Diversification Strate- gies: Evidence from Large US Firms. *Financial Review*, **39**, 489–526.

Singhvi, S., and Desai, H. 1971. An Empirical Analysis of the Quality of Corporate Financial Disclosure. *The Accounting Review*, **46**(1), 129–138.

Singhvi, S.S. 1968. Characteristics and Implications of Inadequate Disclosure: A Case Study of India. *International Journal of Accounting*, **3**(2), 29–43.

Solomons, D. 1986. *Making Accounting Policy the Quest for Credibility in Financial Reporting*. New York: Oxford University Press.

Spero, L. L. 1979. *The Extent and Cases of Voluntary Disclosure of Financial Information in Three-European Capital Markets: An Explanatory Study*. Ph.D. thesis, Harvard University.

Stanga, K. 1976. Disclosure in Published Annual Reports. *Financial Management*, 42–52. Winter.

Stewart, R. 1991. Chaiman and Cief Executives: An Exploration of Their Relationship. *Journal of Management Studies*, **28**(5), 511–527.

Stiles, P., and Taylor, B. 2001. *Boards at Work- How Directors View their Roles and Responsibilities*. Oxford: Oxford University Press.

Street, D.L., and Bryant, S.M. 2000. Disclosure Level and Compliance with IASs: A Comparison of Companies with and without U.S. Listings and Filings. *The International Journal of Accounting*, **35**(3), 305–329.

Street, D.L., and Gray, S.J. 2002. Factors Influencing the Extent of Corporate Compliance with International Ac- counting Standards: Summary of a Research Monograph. *Journal of International Accounting, Auditing and Taxation*, **11**, 51–76.

Street, D.L., Gray, S.J., and Bryant, S.M. 1999. Acceptance and Observance of International Accounting Standards: An Empirical

Study of Companies Claiming to Comply with IASs. *The International Journal of Accounting*, **34**(1), 17–48.

Sutton, T.G. 1984. Lobbying of Accounting Standard-Setting Bodies in the U.K. and the U.S.A.: A Downsian Analysis. *Accounting, Organizations and Society*, **9**(1), 81–95.

Suwaidan, M.S. 1997. *Voluntary Disclosure of Accounting Information: the Case of Jordan*. Ph.D. thesis, University of Aberdeen, UK.

Tabachnick, B.G., and Fidell, L.S. 2001. *Using Multivariate Statistics*. 4 edn. Allyn and Bacon.

Tai, B., Au-Yeung, P.K., Kwok, M., and Lau, L. 1990. Non-compliance With Disclosure Requirements in Financial Statements: The Case of Hong Kong Companies. *The International Journal of Accounting*, **25**(2), 98–112.

Tower, G., Hancock, P., and Taplin, R.H. 1999. A Regional Study of Listed Companies' Compliance with International Accounting Standards. *Accounting Forum*, **23**(3), 293–305.

Trabelsi, S., and Labelle, R. 2006. Evidence that Corporate Websites is a Part of the Firm's Overall Disclosure Package. *Working Paper. Brock University. St Catherines.* Available: http://accounting.uwaterloo.ca/seminars/old_papers/TrabelsiLabelleWP-may2-2006.pdf. Accessed: 12/5/2010.

Treichler, C.M. 1995. Diversity of Board Members and Organizational Performance: An Integrative Perspective. *Corporate Governance: An International Review*, **3**(4), 189–200.

Tricker, Bob. 2009. *Corporate Governance: Principles, Policies and Practices*. New York: Oxford University Press.

Tricker, R. I. 1994. *International Corporate Governance: Text, Readings and Cases*. Singapore: Prentice-Hall.

Tricker, R.I. 1984. *Corporate Governance: Practice, Procedures and Powers in British Companies and their Boards of Directors*. Aldershot: Gower Publishing Company Ltd.

Tsamenyi, Mathew, Enninful-Adu, Elsie, and Onumah, Joseph. 2007. Disclosure and Corporate Governance in De- veloping Countries: Evidence from Ghana. *Mangerial Auditing Journal*, **22**(3), 319–334.

UNCTAD. 2007. *Review of the Implementation Status of Corporate Governance Disclosures: Case Study Egypt*. Tech. rept. Available: http://www.unctad.org/en/docs/c2isarcrp7_en.pdf. Accessed 25/2/2010.

Verrecchia, R. 1983. Discretionary Disclosure. *Journal of Accounting and Economics*, **5**, 179–194.

Verrecchia, R.E. 2001. Essays on Disclosure. *Journal of Accounting and Economics*, **32**, 97–180.

Violet, W.J. 1983. The Development of International Accounting Standards: An Anthropological Perspective. *Inter- national Journal of Accounting Education Research*, 1–12. Spring.

Vlachos, C. 2001. *An Empirical Investigation of the Financial Disclosure Practices of Cypriot and Greek Companies*. Ph.D. thesis, Middlesex University, UK.

Wallace, R., Naser, K., and Mora, A. 1994. The Relationship between the Comprehensiveness of Corporate Annual Reports and Firm Characteristics in Spain. *Accounting and Business Research*, **25**(97), 41–53.

Wallace, R.S.O. 1987. *Disclosure of Accounting Information in Developing Countries: A Case Study of Nigeria*. Ph.D. thesis, Exeter University, Exeter. UK.

—. 1988. Corporate Financial Reporting in Nigeria. *Accounting and Business Research*, **18**(72), 352–362.

Wallace, R.S.O., and Naser, K. 1995. Firm-Specific Determinants of the Comprehensiveness of Mandatory Disclosure in the Corporate Annual Reports of Firms Listed in the Stock Exchange of Hong Kong. *Journal of Accounting and Public Policy*, **14**, 311–368.

Walliman, N. 2006. *Social Research Methods*. London: Sage Publications Ltd.

Watson, A., Shrives, P., and Marston, C. 2002. Voluntary Disclosure of Accounting Ratios in The UK. *British Accounting Review*, **34**, 289–313.

Watts, R., and Zimmerman, J. 1978. Towards a Positive Theory of the Determination of Accounting Standards. *Accounting Review*, **63**(1), 112–134.

Weber, R.P. 1990. *Basic Content Analysis*. 2 edn. London: Sage Publications.

Weir, C., and Laing, D. 2001. Governance Structures, Director Independence and Corporate Performance in the UK. *European Business Review*, **13**, 86–94.

Wilmshurst, T.D., and Frost, G.R. 2000. Corporate Environmental Reporting- A Test of Legitimacy Theory. *Account- ing, Auditing and Accountability Journal*, **13**(1), 10–26.

Xiao, J.Z., Yang, H., and Chow, C.W. 2004. The Determinants and Characteristics of Voluntary Internet-Based Dis- closures by Listed Chinese Companies. *Journal of Accounting and Public Policy*, **23**, 191–225.

Yeoh, J. 2005. Compliance with Mandatory Disclosure Requirements by New Zealand Listed Companies. *Advances in International Accounting*, **18**, 245–262.

Zarzeski, M.T. 1996. Spontaneous Harmonization Effects of Culture and Market Forces on Accounting Disclosure Practices. *Accounting Horizons*, **10**(1), 18–37.

INDEX